ECONOMICS HANDBOOK SERIES

SEYMOUR E. HARRIS, Editor

UNITED STATES ECONOMIC POLICY
AND INTERNATIONAL RELATIONS

ECONOMICS HANDBOOK SERIES

SEYMOUR E. HARRIS, Editor

ADVISORY COMMITTEE: Edward H. Chamberlain, Gottfried Haberler, Alvin H. Hansen, Edward S. Mason, and John H. Williams. *All of Harvard University.*

United States Economic Policy
and International Relations

Raymond F. Mikesell

Professor of Economics
University of Virginia

FIRST EDITION

NEW YORK   TORONTO   LONDON
McGRAW-HILL BOOK COMPANY, INC.
1952

UNITED STATES ECONOMIC POLICY AND INTERNATIONAL RELATIONS

Library of Congress Catalog Card Number: 51–12630

This book is dedicated to
my mother and father

Preface

THIS BOOK represents an attempt to present both a brief survey and an analysis of the foreign economic policy of the United States. In particular the author has sought to indicate both the domestic economic interests and the political and security motives behind certain major developments in United States international economic policies since World War I. That this is too ambitious a task for one short volume the author is the first to admit. Consequently, he has selected for emphasis those aspects of his subject in which he has some special interest or experience or which he believes have not been adequately dealt with in other treatises on the subject.

Present writers in the field of current international economic problems are likely to be embarrassed both by their conclusions and by their selection of problems by the time they see their material in print. Economists who were writing on the "dollar shortage" or the "dollar gap" or on commodity surpluses a year or so ago have found that many of their problems have been either solved or greatly altered by the time their books or articles were published. One might take some consolation in the often-expressed idea that history repeats itself, but it rarely does so before most people have forgotten what the author has said. Although the first draft of this book was written in the pre-Korean era, the author has had an opportunity to give it something of a post-Korean flavor. Nevertheless, events have moved too rapidly since mid-1950 for an adequate appraisal of the policy developments in the defense period. But history does not move altogether in terms of crises and sharp breaks with the past, as one might suppose by reading newspaper headlines. America's foreign economic policies in the defense period, or even in an all-out war period which may lie ahead, will be molded in large measure from the materials of the past. It is with this in mind that the author hopes that an analysis of America's foreign economic policies in the immediate past will have relevance for those who will be reading somewhat different headlines in the future.

A debt of gratitude is due those who have read all or parts of the manuscript and have given the author the benefit of their comments. These include Antonin Basch, Henry J. Bittermann, William Adams Brown, Jr., Isaiah Frank, Ervin Hexner, Gardner Patterson, J. J. Polak, Alex Rosenson, Robert L. Sammons, and John Parke Young. Finally, the author wishes to acknowledge the invaluable services of Miss Ruth Ritchie, secretary of the University of Virginia Institute for Research in the Social Sciences, and of Mrs. Goode Love, Miss Anne Haden, and Miss Anne Fisher, of the Department of Economics of the University of Virginia, for their assistance in the preparation of the manuscript.

RAYMOND F. MIKESELL

CHARLOTTESVILLE, VA.
August, 1951

Contents

Editor's Introduction

FOR YEARS many teachers of economics and other professional economists have felt the need of a series of books on economic subjects which is not filled by the usual textbook or by the highly technical treatise.

This present series, published under the general title of The Economics Handbook Series, was planned with these needs in mind. Designed first of all for students, the volumes are useful in the ever-growing field of adult education and also are of interest to the informed general reader.

The volumes are not long—they give the essentials of the subject matter within the limits of a few hundred pages; they present a distillate of accepted theory and practice, without the detailed approach of the technical treatise. Each volume is a unit, standing on its own.

The authors are scholars, each writing on an economic subject of which he is an authority. In this series the author's first task was not to make important contributions to knowledge—although many of them do—but so to present his subject matter that his work as a scholar will carry its maximum influence outside as well as inside the classroom. The time has come to redress the balance between the energies spent on the creation of new ideas and on their dissemination. Economic ideas are unproductive if they do not spread beyond the world of scholars. Popularizers without technical competence, unqualified textbook writers, and sometimes even charlatans control too large a part of the market for economic ideas.

In the classroom The Economics Handbook Series will serve, it is hoped, as brief surveys in one-semester courses, as supplementary reading in introductory courses, and in other courses in which the subject is related.

In this book, Professor Raymond Mikesell deals with major issues of international economic policies: the balance of payments, assistance and loan policies, inclusive of the European Recovery Program, dollar shortage, tariff and other restrictive policies, the International Trade Organization, the International Monetary Fund and the International Bank, foreign exchange rates, and exchange controls. The reader will find in this book the major facets of the substantial issues in the area of international economic policies discussed and opposing positions weighed. Preliminary to the discussion of the significant problems of the last ten years, Professor Mikesell presents a brief historical survey.

Professor Mikesell has been on the faculties of the University of Washington and the University of Virginia and is now a Professor of Economics at the latter institution. His experience with government as an advisor to several governmental departments and agencies dealing with international economic policies has prepared him well for the writing of this book. Professor Mikesell has been much more than an outsider looking in. He has helped formulate policies and work out directives from above. In the Middle East, at Bretton Woods, and as a co-author of the Gray Report, Professor Mikesell not only contributed much to recent international economic policies, but he has learned a great deal about how policies are made, the relevance of accepted international trade theory, and particularly the conflict of interests that emerge in the formulation of plans.

The editor welcomes Professor Mikesell's volume to the Handbook Series, the seventh in the series.

SEYMOUR E. HARRIS

Introduction

THE FOREIGN economic policy of a nation is largely determined by two independent and sometimes contradictory forces, namely, its domestic economic interests and its international political objectives, including that of national defense. We may perhaps legitimately add a third force, humanitarianism or universal idealism, but it is very difficult to distinguish this factor from the other two in the formation of policy. Foreign economic policy is concerned with a large number of official actions and attitudes with respect to the manifold economic relations between nations, including those economic actions which are specifically undertaken in support of some political objective, *e.g.*, a foreign loan or grant to achieve some purely political purpose. Foreign economic policy rarely forms a consistent whole even in the most authoritarian states, since complete coordination of all its aspects in terms of the complexity of its motivating forces would be extremely difficult to achieve. Laws and regulations with respect to commercial dealings with other countries frequently cannot be revised in time to meet changing economic interests and political objectives. This is particularly true in the United States, where the executive and legislative branches of the government are separated. For example, prohibitive tariffs, burdensome customs procedures, and the "Buy America" act still remain on the statute books at a time when it is generally recognized that increased imports would contribute to the domestic economic interest of the United States. The Johnson Act prohibiting private loans to European governments which had defaulted on their war debts was still on the statute books long after this country was making large governmental grants and loans to the defaulting nations. To an even greater degree do we find clear conflicts between actions taken in the interest of some domestic economic objective and those taken in the interest of foreign political objectives. We shall be concerned with a number of such contradictions in the course of this study.

Foreign economic policy in the United States may be determined in a large number of ways: acts and resolutions of Congress, Presidential orders and executive agreements, statements and actions of the representatives of governmental agencies operating in the foreign economic

1

field, or even decisions of judicial bodies. More than a dozen agencies of the United States government including the Departments of State, Treasury, Commerce, Justice, Agriculture, and Defense, the Export-Import Bank, the Tariff Commission, the Federal Reserve Board, the Economic Cooperation Administration, the National Security Resources Board, and indeed the President and the White House Staff make decisions relating to our foreign economic policy, and these decisions are by no means fully coordinated. To a far lesser degree, however, are Congressional policies coordinated even with respect to legislation passed during the same Congressional term. This is perhaps inevitable in our system of government, where conflicting interests are decided not so much by how individual actions will fit into a logically consistent policy, but by the number of votes that can be mustered in the legislature for or against a particular measure as determined by the complex of political pressures which are exerted with respect to it. Because the policy-making machinery of our government is exceedingly complex, it is sometimes difficult to determine just how and why certain foreign economic policy decisions were arrived at or, in some cases, even to discover a consistent line of policy from a series of actions, since the actions may represent little more than an illogical compromise between conflicting policies.

It is the purpose of this book to trace through the major developments in America's foreign economic policy over the past three decades and to indicate the principal determinants of those policies. In considering these determinants, it is first of all obvious that the dominant factor in the development of our foreign economic policy is to be found in the changing international political environment. The political isolationism of the 1930's had its counterpart in the Johnson Act, in our foreign-trade policies, and in our uncooperative stand on exchange rates at the London Economic Conference in 1933. The shift to internationalism during World War II was a potent factor in America's taking the lead in the field of international economic cooperation after the war. The emergence of the cold war with Russia and the realization of the implications of a bipolar world have forced America to assume a new role. Slowly and perhaps a little reluctantly we are moving into a position of primary responsibility for the economic welfare of our half of the world. The Economic Cooperation Administration and Point Four programs are examples of how we are meeting this new responsibility, but the logic of international political developments may require us to go much further in identifying our own interests with those of the rest of the world. In meeting this challenge, this country will undoubtedly be forced to compromise many of its traditional economic interests and attitudes.

While our foreign economic policies have been enormously influenced by international events and objectives, they have also reflected to a considerable degree the evolving domestic economic policies and interests of this nation. The more liberal commercial policies of today are not simply a reflection of America's international political interests and responsibilities, but they also represent on the part of our national leaders and the majority of the public a different economic philosophy from that which prevailed in the 1920's. Similarly, our attitude toward alterations in the values of foreign currencies has changed from one of primary concern over maintaining our competitive advantage in world markets to one of primary concern with establishing the conditions for international equilibrium. On the other hand, American concern with the elimination of exchange and trade restrictions, bilateral agreements, and preferential arrangements is deeply rooted in the character of the American economy and our traditional business practices.

Part One of this book summarizes the major economic policies of the United States during the interwar period and discusses their impact on America's international economic and political relations. Much of this background is essential for an understanding of the development of America's foreign economic policies during and following World War II. The author has also attempted to show the relationship between America's international political interests and objectives and the development of those economic policies which affect the welfare of other nations.

Part Two is devoted to an analysis of America's post-World War II foreign economic policies and the basic domestic economic and foreign political factors responsible for their development. Chapters 7 and 8, which deal with America's domestic and foreign policies during and immediately following World War II, provide the link between the two postwar periods. During World War II there occurred far-reaching changes in the attitudes of government officials, Congressional representatives, and the majority of the American people toward such matters as domestic full employment, collective security for the maintenance of peace, international lending, and foreign assistance and cooperation to achieve both political and economic objectives. While most of America's objectives in the field of commercial and financial policy were firmly rooted in the structure of the American economy and in her traditional domestic economic interests, the postwar enthusiasm for realizing these objectives through international cooperation grew out of the marked change in her international political attitudes. International monetary policies, investment policies, commercial policies, and foreign-assistance policies are taken up in separate chapters, and the outstanding developments from the war period up to the time of writing are analyzed in terms of the domestic economic and foreign political factors out of which they emerged. While foreign-aid programs such as the Marshall Plan were developed largely in response to the need for implementing America's political objectives, we nevertheless find a number of elements in these programs which are directly related to domestic economic interests and attitudes.

The final chapter is devoted to a discussion of the future of American domestic and foreign economic policy, particularly as it concerns the problem of global defense. The disappointing political developments of the postwar years and the failure to realize certain of our basic commercial and financial policy objectives have necessitated a reappraisal of America's postwar economic policies. In such a reassessment we must keep in mind both the immediate objective of political security and the longer run objective of building a world in which the economic welfare of all peoples can be maximized. It is the firm conviction of the author that America's long-run economic and political interests lie in the development of the conditions for the mutual welfare of all peoples. In recent years, America's desire to cooperate with the nations of the non-Soviet world for the promotion of their economic welfare has been dominated by fear of a common enemy. We may hope, however, that when the threat of aggression fades into the background, nations may be drawn together and their economic policies coordinated, not out of fear, but out of a desire for the mobilization of the world's resources for the mutual economic welfare of all nations. The political barriers to the realization of a fairly high degree of economic integration of the national economies of the world are not insurmountable. Rules of fair trading determined in accordance with the principles of mutual commercial advantage are possible in a world of capitalist, socialist, and "mixed" economies. Mutually profitable international investment is also possible in a world of differing economic systems. We do not need to remake the world in our own image in order to save it. Rather, America in cooperation with all nations of good will must work out a system of international relations and rules of fair dealing which will be consistent with the internal economic and political structures of all countries and which will promote the economic well-being of all peoples.

Part One

American Economic Policies in the Interwar Period, 1919 to 1939

CHAPTER 1

America's Position in the World Economy

THE UNITED STATES emerged from World War I with an economy untouched by the ravages of war and producing large exportable surpluses of the commodities the rest of the world desperately needed to reconstruct their economies and keep their peoples from starving. Rarely, if ever, in the history of the world has a country risen so rapidly to a position of economic dominance as did the United States in the period from 1914 to 1919. The war had reduced European production to a low level, while American production had risen. Industrial production in the rest of the world recovered rapidly, so that by 1929 it was about 53 per cent above the level of 1922; American industrial production also increased by nearly the same percentage from the 1922 level.[1] Thus in the period from 1925 to 1929 it is estimated that United States industrial production was 46 per cent of the world's total, and in 1929, United States national income was equal to the combined incomes of 23 of the world's most important countries, including the United Kingdom, Germany, France, Japan, and Canada.[2]

The world's economic dependence upon the United States at the end of the war was reflected in the latter's huge merchandise export surplus of over $4 billion in 1919. Although there was an import surplus with the rest of the world of $440 million, America's merchandise surplus with Europe was nearly $4½ billion. This surplus was rapidly reduced in the postwar years, but Europe never regained her prewar position as a supplier of United States imports. Before 1870, the United States was in approximate balance with Europe on merchandise account, and our imports were largely in the form of manufactures. After 1870, our export surplus with Europe rose steadily, and during the first decade of the twentieth century it averaged around a half billion dollars. Following the war, America's export surplus with Europe on merchandise account averaged over a billion dollars annually from 1920 to 1930, and

[1] See *The United States in the World Economy,* Department of Commerce, 1943, p. 150.

[2] *Ibid.,* p. 28.

7

the percentage of United States total imports supplied by Europe averaged about 30 per cent as compared with over 50 per cent before 1914. This shift in the pattern of United States trade was largely the result of the increasing industrialization of this country. This process was hastened by the war which resulted not only in a 15 per cent expansion of United States industrial output but also in the establishment of a number of industries producing commodities for which we formerly depended upon European sources.

The war also hastened industrialization in other areas of the world outside of Europe such as Canada and other British Dominions, Japan, and certain of the Latin-American nations. The trend, which began in the latter part of the nineteenth century, of reduced dependence upon the older industrial countries of Europe for manufactured commodities continued all through the interwar period. The failure of Europe to adjust to the industrialization of the newer economic areas of the world, including the United States, is perhaps the most significant element in the disequilibrium which has characterized the periods following both world wars. The increasing trade surplus with Europe and the shift in the character of United States imports from manufactures to raw materials created no difficulties so long as the United States was a large debtor to Europe. But the emergence of the United States as a creditor nation at the end of World War I meant that the continuation of the surplus depended upon United States foreign investments and imports of gold and the existence of a European surplus on current account with third areas which was settled with gold and dollars. Thus when United States international investments practically dried up during the early 1930's, a world-payments crisis was precipitated.

Not only did the United States become the world's largest exporter in the 1920's, but she also became the most important market for semi-finished and raw materials. Thus in 1927–1928, it is estimated that this country's share in the consumption of nine principal raw materials and foodstuffs was 39 per cent of the total for the 15 most important trading nations.[3] Since several of these commodities were largely supplied by countries with whom the nations of Europe maintained export surpluses, America's export surplus with Europe depended in considerable measure upon the volume of these imports. The importance of United States imports is indicated by the fact that the United States took over 12 per cent of the world's merchandise exports in 1929, a percentage which was exceeded only by the United Kingdom.

[3] *Ibid.*, p. 29. The nine commodities are cotton, wheat, sugar, rubber, silk, copper, tin, tea, and coffee.

Another element in the dominant economic role of the United States after World War I was her position as a supplier of capital. In the decade following the war, the United States not only assumed the major burden of providing international reconstruction capital, but she also took over from Europe the role of supplying capital to underdeveloped areas. In 1914, America was a net debtor on international account to the extent of $3.7 billion, but by 1929 she was a net international creditor on private and governmental account by nearly $20 billion, or by more than $8 billion on private account alone.[4] (It will be recalled that most of the war debts were being serviced in 1929.) Although Britain's creditor position on private account exceeded that of the United States by a considerable margin, by the 1930's Britain's balance of payments had become adjusted to the position of a mature creditor nation.

The shift in America's creditor-debtor position following World War I had some important implications both for the United States and for the world generally. In the prewar period when America was rapidly expanding her frontiers and providing productive capital for the large volume of immigrants which entered her borders every year, the volume of domestic savings frequently fell short of the demand for capital. After the war, however, the greatly expanded productivity of this well-developed nation provided a surplus of saving over the domestic demand for investment funds. A balance of saving and investment consistent with a reasonably high level of employment was achieved by means of a surplus on current account which averaged around three-quarters of a billion dollars from 1922 to 1930. This surplus was sustained largely by means of foreign investments and the importation of gold. Thus in 1929 and 1930, net foreign investment was about 5 per cent and 7 per cent, respectively, of the total outlets for United States gross saving.

But the implications for the rest of the world of the rapid shift to a creditor status by the United States were much greater. The liquidation of European investments in the United States during the war reduced dollar earnings, while the sudden growth of dollar obligations on the part of these same countries added to their payments burden. The foreign investments of Britain, the Netherlands, and other Western European countries were built up over several generations, to a large extent in the form of direct investments, or in the form of portfolio investments, which directly contributed to the productive capacity of the borrowing country. Moreover, the borrowing countries were to a considerable degree the source of raw-material imports for the lending countries whose markets for raw materials were continually expanding. On

[4] Cleona Lewis, *America's Stake in International Investments*, The Brookings Institution, Washington, D.C., 1938, pp. 454–455.

the other hand, a large part of the lending undertaken by the United States in the immediate postwar period was for reconstruction and relief purposes to nations whose exports were competitive rather than complementary to those of the United States. Even the loans to the less developed countries of Latin America and elsewhere were frequently dissipated in higher consumption on the part of the public or were used for highways and public works, which contributed little to the improvement of the balance of payments of the borrower. In some cases, foreign dollar loans were floated by Latin-American countries to refund internal debts.[5] It was not simply the follies of the borrowers and of the lenders (who operated largely with other people's money) which were responsible for the defaults of the early 1930's. More fundamentally, it was the fact that the balance of payments of the United States was not adjusted to her pattern of international investment in the interwar period.

The above survey has indicated some of the reasons for America's strategic position in the world economy after the first world war. The events of history had thrust a relatively young nation into the role of the world's leading economic and political power. For over a hundred years, this country had been concerned almost exclusively with her own domestic problems and national ambitions (which occasionally ran into conflict with those of her next-door neighbors). After her independence was secure, America's chief concern in foreign affairs was to stay out of Europe's political entanglements and to keep them from spilling over into the Western Hemisphere, where her own position was unchallenged. After having played a decisive role in the successful termination of a European war which had threatened to get out of hand and endanger her security, the United States was eager to retire from the scene with a firm determination not to be drawn in again. The implications of America's position as a great power were not generally realized in the United States following World War I. Although this country came close to playing a leading political role—Senate ratification of membership in the League of Nations was lost only by one vote—few people were aware of America's economic responsibilities beyond that of providing emergency loans (to be repaid with interest) for reconstruction and for the prevention of starvation. This awareness did not develop until we were drawn into another and far more costly world war.

Before a sense of responsibility for international economic affairs could become a significant element in American foreign policy, the people of this country and its government had to reach several important convictions which could only grow out of hard experience. First, there had

5 *Ibid.*, p. 383.

to be an appreciation of the role of governmental action in economic affairs, both domestic and international. People had to become convinced of the responsibility of government for maintaining reasonably high levels of employment and income at home before they could have an appreciation of our economic responsibilities abroad. The former developed out of America's experience with the depression following 1929, but a realization of the relationship between governmental action in international economic affairs and domestic prosperity came somewhat later. As we shall see later on, an appreciation of the relationship between world economic stability and domestic prosperity did not develop in the United States to a significant degree until World War II.[6] The second prerequisite for international economic responsibility was the adoption of a policy of international political responsibility in place of the political isolationism of the interwar period. It was this shift in America's international political philosophy which led us to the third condition for international economic responsibility, namely, an awareness of the role of economic policy in the realization of international political and security objectives. This awareness led to the adoption of the Marshall Plan for Western Europe and the Point Four program for the underdeveloped areas, but its full implications may go far beyond the immediate problems of the cold war with Russia.

It will be the author's purpose in the next few chapters to examine the basic economic policies of the United States in the interwar period with a view to determining their effects on other countries in the light of the position of this country in the world economy. Except in a few instances, American economic policy was not dictated by international considerations. There was neither the political basis for such influence nor much general awareness of the repercussions of our foreign policies on the American economy. Balance-of-payments analysis and the complications of the transfer problem, though familiar to academic economists, had not penetrated the thinking of most government officials and congressmen of the Coolidge era. The idea of governmental responsibility for domestic economic conditions had not progressed beyond the employment of proper central-banking policies during the 1920's, and the significance of the supply of dollars for the world economy was not officially recognized by the Federal government for a quarter of a century after the dollar had become a key currency.

[6] A principal motivating force behind the United States sponsorship of the International Monetary Fund, the trade-agreements program, including the proposed International Trade Organization and the loan to Britain in 1946, was to achieve international economic conditions which were favorable to American prosperity.

CHAPTER 2

America's International Accounts

BEFORE TAKING up the discussion of America's international economic policies during the interwar period, we shall present a brief analysis of the American balance of payments in this period. Our purpose will not be to give a systematic account of the international transactions of the United States,[1] but rather to comment on certain aspects which will assist in the analysis of the policies which emerged in this period. Also the interwar experience should provide some help in analyzing the problems of the present and in indicating what policies ought to be followed in order to achieve a more balanced world economy.

The first three postwar years were characterized by a large export surplus on merchandise account, which was settled largely by governmental loans, governmental grants and personal remittances, and gold imports. The depression of 1920–1921 sharply reduced imports, but they recovered rapidly in 1922 and thereafter reached a peak in quantitative terms in 1929. It is commonplace to say that during the period from 1922 to 1929 United States international accounts were in a precarious state of balance. It is worth noting, however, that in 1922, 1926, and 1927 current payments, including net private remittances, plus net long-term capital outflow, exceeded current receipts.[2] Over the period from 1922 to 1929, the aggregate United States surplus on current account, including unilateral transfers, amounted to $5,737 million and net long-term capital outflow aggregated $4,678 million, or an average of $585 million per year. Gold production outside the United States averaged around $350 million per year, and since this is a normal export of large gold producers such as South Africa, it would be expected that the United

[1] The best account of United States international transactions in the interwar period is to be found in *The United States in the World Economy*, Department of Commerce, 1943. United States balance-of-payments data used in this chapter are largely taken from the revised figures found in *The Balance of International Payments of the United States, 1946–1948*, Department of Commerce, 1950, pp. 272–274.

[2] Until recently, the Department of Commerce included private remittances in the current account, but they are now classified as unilateral transfers along with governmental grants. Since a large part of these transfers during the interwar period represented immigrant remittances and institutional remittances of a more-or-less regular nature, they are included as a part of the current account in the analysis presented in this chapter.

States should import at least $100 million annually, or $800 to $1,000 million for the period. Thus if we add normal gold acquisitions to current payments, the current-account surplus was approximately offset by net long-term capital outflow. Considering the national income and the volume of savings in the United States, a net volume of foreign investment of $500 to $1,000 million annually for this period would not have been unreasonable.

The point to be made here is that there was nothing inherent in the structure of the United States balance of payments in the 1920's which would have made a sound balanced position impossible. True enough the war-debt settlements and the "hot-money" flights were disturbing factors, and some of the foreign investments in the United States securities market should have been curbed by countries which could ill afford to export capital to the United States. But these difficulties could have been corrected by appropriate governmental and central-banking policies.

Beginning with 1930, United States merchandise imports declined sharply from the level of $4,463 million in 1929 to a low of $1,343 million in 1932. By volume, this represented a decline of 40 per cent, which happened to be the percentage decline in United States real national income. Undoubtedly the Tariff Act of 1930 was also a factor making for reduced imports.[3] United States exports also fell sharply during this period from a level of $5,347 million in 1929 to $1,667 million in 1932. The decline in United States exports is definitely traceable to both the fall in national incomes in foreign countries and to a general increase in tariff and other restrictions abroad. Currency depreciations against the dollar and preferential tariff and trade restrictions against United States commodities tended to reduce the relative share of the United States in total world imports from 16.8 per cent in 1929 to an average of 12.8 per cent for the 1933 to 1938 period.[4]

United States merchandise imports recovered very slowly after 1932 and did not regain the 1929 volume until 1937, after which they dropped off quite sharply in the recession of 1938. In general, the variations in imports followed closely the change in real national income, except in the 1938 recession when the percentage decline in imports was about three times that of the percentage decline in real national income.[5]

[3] See H. J. Adler, "United States Import Demand during the Interwar Period," *American Economic Review*, June, 1945, pp. 418–430.

[4] *The United States in the World Economy*, pp. 55, 64.

[5] For the interwar period as a whole, the percentage change in real income and the percentage change in the volume of imports tended to be about the same. See Adler, *op. cit.*, p. 427.

Exports also rose slowly, reaching a peak with imports in 1937, but the volume of exports was substantially below the level of 1929. This is especially significant in view of the fact that foreign national incomes

Table 1. Indexes of the Quantity of United States Imports and Exports
(1936–1938 = 100)

Year	Imports	Exports
1929	116	136
1932	69	70
1937	114	108
1938	82	108

SOURCE: *Foreign Trade of the United States, 1936–1949*, Department of Commerce, 1951, pp. 6–9.

and physical production tended to fall somewhat less after 1929 and recover much more rapidly after 1932 than in the case of the United States.[6] The United States merchandise export surplus was much smaller up to 1938 than in the 1920's. Moreover, the over-all current balance was not only much smaller than in the 1920's, but in the years 1935 and 1936 the United States had a current-account deficit. In 1938 and 1939, there were large merchandise export and over-all current-account surpluses, reflecting the 1938 United States recession and the rearmament of foreign countries.[7] The average current-account surplus for the period from 1930 to 1938 was $295 million, and if we exclude the first and last years it was only $96 million per year.

We concluded that there was nothing inherent in world economic conditions in the 1920's which would have made a sound and continued balanced international position impossible. How did the structure of the world's trade and payments in the 1930's compare with that of the 1920's? In the first place, the current-account surplus of the United States during the 1930's was not of unmanageable proportions.[8] After 1932,

[6] See *The United States in the World Economy*, pp. 64, 184.

[7] Unilateral transfers included in current account.

[8] J. M. Keynes, in his article, "The Balance of Payments of the United States," *Economic Journal*, June, 1946, pp. 172–187, points out that the current-account surplus of the United States during the period from 1930 to 1938 was much less favorable than that of the United Kingdom at the time when the United Kingdom was building up its overseas investments and about the same as the British favorable balance in the period from 1923 to 1929.

the world's gold production outside the United States averaged over a billion dollars per year (valued at $35 per ounce), and it would be reasonable to expect the United States to absorb at least $250 million annually of the production of the large gold-exporting countries such as South Africa and Canada. During the period from 1930 to 1938, the United States merchandise surplus averaged $394 million, but if we leave out 1930 (while there was still a substantial volume of long-term capital outflow) and 1938 (which was greatly influenced by the sharp drop in United States imports due to the recession coupled with a large foreign demand caused by the rearmament program), we find an average merchandise surplus of only $184 million per year. A considerable portion of the merchandise surplus during the 1930's was offset by a continual deficit on other current-account transactions, which averaged about $100 million annually for the period from 1930 to 1938. During the period from 1922 to 1929 on the other hand, the United States was in approximate balance on account of other current transactions. The different behavior of this element in the balance of payments may be explained partly by the fact that interest payments on war debts and certain defaulted private debts were not being paid during a good part of the 1930's.

In considering the United States current account during the 1930's, we should also keep in mind the large silver purchases by the United States government under the Silver Purchase Act of 1934. The net purchases of silver during the period from 1933 to 1938 amounted to $936 million, and for the period from 1930 to 1938 net silver purchases averaged over $100 million annually. Since silver was a special (and we hope a nonrecurring) item in the United States balance of payments during this period, there is some justification for omitting it from the current account. If we omit silver, the average current-account surplus for the period from 1930 to 1938 becomes about $400 million, or if we exclude 1930 and 1938 the average current-account surplus without silver becomes $200 million.

The fact that the United States current-account surplus during the 1930's was not an unmanageable one and could probably have been handled by exporting a portion of the world's current gold production to the United States should not lead us to conclude too much regarding the structural conditions for equilibrium in this period. We must remember that many countries were maintaining severe restrictions on imports, and on United States imports in particular. We must also take into consideration the defaults on international obligations both private and public. Had service on these obligations been maintained, the United States current-account surplus would have been considerably larger or

United States exports would have been lower than they actually were. On the other hand, if service on private overseas investment had been maintained, the United States long-term capital account might have shown an outflow of capital rather than a heavy inflow representing net disinvestment abroad.

True equilibrium can exist only in the absence of trade and exchange controls imposed for balance-of-payments reasons. Just how much foreign consumers would have imported from this country during the 1930's if tariffs, quotas, and other barriers had been no more restrictive than in the latter part of the 1920's is difficult to judge. In 1929, the volume of United States commodity exports was about 50 per cent greater than the average volume of exports during the period from 1930 to 1938. National incomes and industrial production in foreign countries fell less than in the United States after 1929, and by 1934–1935 national income and industrial production abroad had regained the 1929 level and were substantially above that level during the next 4 years.[9] Had foreign countries maintained full employment during the period in the face of the United States depression, the degree of disequilibrium as measured by the potential demand for dollar goods and services over the amount of dollars currently supplied would have been even greater. We may conclude, therefore, that in spite of the appearance of near balance in the United States current-account position during the 1930's, given the state of the world's demand for United States goods and services, the level of United States national income and tariffs, and the debt service obligations inherited from the 1920's, the United States could not have been in equilibrium with the rest of the world without substantial capital exports.

Instead of capital exports during the 1930's, the United States received large amounts of capital from foreign investors, and Americans repatriated large amounts of capital which they had previously invested abroad. The high point in United States private foreign investment was reached in 1928, when net long-term capital invested abroad amounted to $1,261 million and net long-term capital outflow was $798 million.[10] In 1929, net United States long-term investments abroad fell to half the 1928 level, while net imports of capital from abroad remained fairly high, with the result that the total net capital outflow amounted to only $240 million. In 1930, there was a total net capital outflow of $221 million, but net long-term investments of Americans abroad declined to only $287

[9] See *The United States in the World Economy*, pp. 30, 44.

[10] In 1927, net long-term capital outflow was larger ($991 million) owing to a smaller movement of capital into the United States from abroad, but net United States private foreign investment was only $941 million.

million. Owing to uncertain business conditions in the United States, net long-term investments of foreigners in the United States amounted to only $66 million in 1930. It was not until 1931, however, that there was an actual net disinvestment of American long-term holdings abroad, and except during 1933 there was net disinvestment of foreign assets every year thereafter to the end of the decade. For the period from 1930 to 1938, total net capital inflow amounted to about $2.4 billion, of which approximately one-third represented net disinvestment of long-term foreign assets by Americans and the remainder represented net long-term investments by foreigners in this country.

During the period from 1930 to 1933, there were substantial net short-term capital exports, but following the stabilization of the dollar in January, 1934, there were large short-term capital inflows during the remainder of the period. The large short-term and long-term capital movements were of course reflected in the heavy gold imports beginning in 1934 and aggregating nearly $7 billion for the period from 1930 to 1938. It should be noted that this inward gold movement was far in excess of the aggregate current-account surplus of the United States, which was only $2.7 billion for the period. Even after allowing for net American disinvestment abroad, there remained about $3.5 billion of the gold inflow to be accounted for by long- and short-term foreign capital imports into the United States. This movement was engendered largely by political and security factors, and most of it could have been prevented by capital controls on the part of foreign governments, with little additional interference to current trade.[11]

In summary, we may say that there was a fundamental imbalance in the international accounts of the United States with the rest of the world during the 1930's. This imbalance was the result of the decline in United States income, the stoppage of the flow of American investment capital abroad, the inflow of "hot" money from Europe, and restrictive United States commercial policies, on the one hand, and the failure of foreign countries as a whole to adjust to the precipitous decline in the world's supply of dollars, on the other. A complete adjustment to the decrease in the supply of dollars would probably have required considerably more deflation in other countries, a step which they quite properly refused to take. There was also some overvaluation of currencies in this period, and the failure of the gold-bloc countries to devalue in 1933 relative to the dollar and the pound sterling was probably an additional factor contributing to disequilibrium. In addition, there was an element of structural disequilib-

[11] For an excellent analysis of United States capital imports during the 1930's, see Arthur I. Bloomfield, *Capital Imports and the American Balance of Payments, 1934–39*, University of Chicago Press, Chicago, 1950.

rium underlying the whole interwar period, particularly as regards the industrial countries of Europe.[12]

These sources of imbalance may have resolved themselves in time, however, given the existence of an adequate system of international payments and a more favorable political atmosphere. Nations may have had to balance their external accounts by means of tariffs and other forms of trade controls until structural adjustments could be made by foreign countries or until American prosperity was restored and American foreign investment was revived. These adjustments became difficult or impossible with the partial breakdown of the international payments system, which led to the growth of bilateralism in Central Europe and to some extent in Europe's trade with Latin America. This breakdown of the payments mechanism was caused in large measure by the heavy capital flights and also by the failure to reach a workable settlement of the problem of intergovernmental debts. Had proper capital controls been introduced along with a more reasonable settlement of the war-debt issue and if Continental countries had adopted more flexible exchange-rate systems along with the countries of the sterling area, the system of multilateral payments might have been preserved. As things actually developed, the monetary chaos provided fertile soil for the ideas of Dr. Schacht and his compatriots, who were motivated by the desire to rebuild the economic and military power of the German state.

Gold and Short-term Capital Movements

An important consequence of World War I was the shift in the financial center of the world from London to New York. Whereas before the war the bulk of the world's trade was financed from London and sterling was the most important currency for financing international transactions, following World War I the dollar became a strong rival of sterling as a "key" currency.[13] Foreign countries, therefore, tended to hold monetary reserves and working balances in the form of deposits and short-term assets in the United States. At the end of 1929, short-term liabilities to foreigners totaled about $3,030 million, of which $1,708 million represented deposits in American banks, while short-term American-owned assets in foreign countries totaled $1,708 million, of which only $210 million represented bank balances. There had been an inflow of short-term capital into the United States of $2,600 from July, 1922, to the

[12] For a good discussion of this problem, see *International Transactions of the United States during the War, 1940–45*, Department of Commerce, 1948, pp. 158–163.

[13] By "key currency" we generally mean a currency widely used in international transactions.

end of 1929, and an outflow of $900 million (largely in the form of short-term loans) over the same period.[14] Several factors were largely responsible for this influx of short-term capital. (1) There was the need for large banking balances on the part of foreigners for financing dollar trade, just as there was a need for large sterling balances for financing sterling trade. (2) There was a desire on the part of foreign central banks and private individuals to hold reserves and liquid funds in the form of dollars rather than gold or other gold currencies. In June, 1927, the Federal Reserve bank estimated that foreign central banks held $1 billion in reserves in the form of dollar exchange.[15] Central banks found it advantageous to hold reserves in the form of foreign balances which could readily be employed as working balances or serve as an earning asset when invested in securities. Finally, a considerable part of these short-term funds arose from the flotation of long-term loans in the United States securities market during this period.

Net gold movements into the United States over the period from 1922 to 1930 totaled $688 million, or about $76 million annually. This was not a large net inflow relative to the world's current gold production outside the United States. It was not large enough to balance the influx of short-term capital during the period. It is apparent, therefore, that long- and short-term United States lending financed both the current-account surplus and a large part of the long- and short-term capital assets in the United States acquired by foreigners from 1922 to 1930. In the period from 1931 to 1933, there was a net outflow of gold from the United States amounting to $338 million, but beginning with 1934 and thereafter to the end of the decade there occurred quite large gold imports. In the period from 1931 to 1938, there was a net inflow of gold amounting to $6.6 billion, and in 1939, an influx of over $3 billion. These inflows were far in excess of what might be considered normal inflows and were also in excess of the amounts needed for settling the world's current-account deficit with this country. These movements are to be accounted for largely by the liquidation of American long- and short-term assets abroad and the acquisition by foreigners of long- and short-term assets in the United States.

Short-term capital movements between countries during the interwar period tended to have more of an autonomous and erratic character rather than of a balancing one. The movements were often motivated by speculative and security influences and did not respond readily to changes in money rates in different countries. Moreover, for reasons which will be discussed in Chap. 3, these inward movements had only

14 *The United States in the World Economy*, pp. 112–113.
15 *Ibid.*, p. 115.

limited effects on American business activity and prices. The American dollar was not ideally suited as a major world currency, since the dependence of the United States on world trade was not great enough for changes in the balance of payments to exert much influence on domestic income and prices; nor was the United States propensity to invest abroad or to import stable enough to ensure a steady supply of dollars to the rest of the world. The pound sterling was a much better international currency from this standpoint. Not only was Britain heavily dependent upon imports, but her political and economic ties throughout the world provided a wide area for investments.[16]

Summary

The structure of the American balance of payments during the interwar period indicated a strong tendency toward a current-account surplus. This meant that given the existing pattern of world production, trade, and exchange rates, equilibrium could be achieved only under conditions of domestic prosperity and a substantial outflow of American capital. Although during a large part of the 1920's the current-account surplus was largely offset by long-term capital outflow and normal gold imports, after 1930 the essential conditions for equilibrium were not present in the American economy. In addition to the effects of depression and the decline in foreign investment, the supply of dollars was further reduced by America's international commercial and financial policies during the 1930's.

[16] For a discussion of the international payments mechanism after World War I, see W. A. Brown, Jr., *The International Gold Standard Reinterpreted, 1914–1934,* National Bureau of Economic Research, New York, 1940.

CHAPTER 3

United States Financial Policies

IN THIS chapter we shall be concerned with the international repercussions of United States monetary policies during the interwar period. With few exceptions, positive measures relating to the control of business activity in the pre-New Deal era were largely confined to those of the Federal Reserve system. Treasury policy was dominated by the desire to reduce the national debt, and although tax rates were reduced sharply from wartime levels, total interest-bearing debt was reduced from $25.6 billion in December, 1919, to a postwar low of $15.8 billion in December, 1930. In spite of the downturn in business activity, Treasury receipts were higher in 1930 than in any previous year since 1921, and the excess of receipts over expenditures in 1930 was $738 million, slightly larger than in 1929. A deficit of nearly a half billion dollars appeared in 1931, the first since 1919, and grew to $2.5 billion in 1932. So far as the international repercussions of the government's fiscal policy were concerned, the large Treasury surpluses helped to offset the effects of our export surpluses on national income, and hence upon the level of imports. While debt reduction was not undertaken as an antiinflationary measure, it could be justified in most years before 1930 in view of the inflationary tendencies in the American economy.[1]

Federal Reserve Policies

In the development of central-banking policies in the United States after World War I, the Federal Reserve authorities were faced with the problem of dealing with large gold inflows which involved a consideration of both domestic and international monetary objectives.[2] The basic domestic credit policy which emerged in the early 1920's was that the Federal Reserve banks should control credit so as to promote sound business conditions, *i.e.*, to meet the legitimate needs of industry, agriculture, and commerce for short-term working capital and to avoid fi-

[1] See S. E. Harris, *The National Debt and the New Economics*, McGraw-Hill, New York, 1947, pp. 265–267.

[2] For a discussion of United States gold policy in the 1920's see S. E. Harris, *Twenty Years of Federal Reserve Policy*, Harvard University Press, Cambridge, Mass., 1933, Vol. I, pp. 341–371.

nancing speculative booms. The large influx of gold which began in 1921 and continued until 1925 made it unnecessary for the Reserve authorities to concern themselves with the gold ratio, which remained substantially above the legal limits for Federal Reserve notes and deposits. The principle of "sound credit conditions" coincided with the desire on the part of the Reserve authorities not to employ the large gold inflows as a basis for an expansion of Reserve credit, although a large part of the gold inflow was allowed to increase member bank reserves. The desire to prevent the incoming gold from being used as a basis for a secondary expansion of member bank reserves was based on the belief that, after European currencies were stabilized, this gold would return to Europe. Just how this return movement was to take place was not clear, since short-term assets of foreigners increased only about $100 million from 1919 to the end of 1924, and there was a substantial reduction in the holdings of long-term United States assets by foreigners. It would appear that the gold was used chiefly as a means of settling the large United States current-account surplus during this period. From 1925 to the end of 1929, however, short-term dollar assets of foreigners did increase by about $2 billion.

In general, through the period from 1923 to 1928 the Reserve authorities expanded credit when business activity fell off and contracted credit when an inflationary situation was threatening. Although on certain occasions, notably in 1924 and 1927, the influx of gold was advanced by the Reserve authorities as a reason for expanding credit, Dr. Charles O. Hardy points out that the actions on these occasions would have been taken anyway on the grounds that the domestic situation demanded an easy-money policy.[3]

It is frequently said that America contributed to the breakdown of the gold standard through its failure to adhere to the rules of the gold-standard game, i.e., alternate credit expansion and contraction with the inflow and outflow of gold. It is argued that the Reserve authorities neutralized a large part of the gold inflow during the 1920's, particularly during the period from 1921 to 1924.[4] According to the classical doctrine, credit expansion and lower interest rates would tend to reverse an influx of gold via the effects on commodity prices and short-term capital movements. These effects would of course be reinforced by credit contraction and rising interest rates in the countries losing gold. While orthodox policy might require the central banks of countries which lost gold to

[3] C. O. Hardy, *Credit Policies of the Federal Reserve System*, The Brookings Institution, Washington, D.C., 1932, p. 107.

[4] See Ragnar Nurkse, *International Currency Experience*, League of Nations, Geneva, 1944, Chap. IV, for a discussion of neutralization of gold movements.

adopt restrictive measures, a central-banking policy based on the maintenance of sound domestic credit conditions was frequently inconsistent with the expansion of credit with an influx of gold, or a contraction of credit with an outflow of gold. The presence of large excess gold reserves at the time when Federal Reserve credit policies were being formulated made it possible to develop principles of credit control which ignored the gold-reserve ratio. Moreover, unlike the situation in most other countries, America's international position had not figured prominently in the development of credit policies, and this aspect had been largely ignored in the discussions leading up to the passage of the Federal Reserve Act of 1913. Except for a brief period in 1931 when the loss of gold threatened the legal-reserve ratio, Reserve policy was never primarily dictated by gold movements. This situation may be contrasted with that of Britain during the period from the stabilization of the pound sterling in 1925 to the departure from the gold standard in September, 1931, when the Bank of England's discount policy was in large part dictated by Britain's reserve position.

In considering the Federal Reserve System's gold policy, it should be pointed out that during the early 1920's no attempt was made to neutralize completely the effects of the gold inflows as was the case during the Treasury's gold sterilization program in 1936–1937. Dr. Hardy has pointed out that if the Reserve authorities had actually offset the effects of the gold movements on member bank reserves between 1921 and 1929, member bank reserves would have been $1,750 million (the level of 1921) instead of $2,374 million at the end of 1929.[5] Moreover, total bank deposits rose from $33 billion in June, 1921, to $51 billion at the end of 1929. While it is true that the incoming gold was not permitted to have its maximum effect upon the volume of credit, it is difficult to argue that a nation which is maintaining a fairly high degree of prosperity should be called upon deliberately to inflate its currency in order that gold imports should have the effects assigned to them by classical economics.

Even if our Reserve authorities had chosen to follow the rules of the gold-standard game, it is doubtful if their operations would have secured the adjustments in the international balance of payments envisaged by classical theory. The large gold inflows which occurred in the early 1920's could not be explained in terms of differences in prices and interest rates here and abroad. The trade surplus with Europe was due largely to the need for goods for reconstruction and restocking and could not be eliminated by small changes in relative prices. Capital flight also

[5] Hardy, *op. cit.*, pp. 187–188.

played a considerable part in the gold and capital movements during the entire interwar period. Moreover, the reluctance of commercial banks to incur a large indebtedness to the Reserve banks and their unwillingness or inability to employ excess reserves made available through open market operations of the Reserve banks would have placed a severe limit on the ability of the Reserve authorities to expand credit to the full amount of the increase in gold reserves.

There are other factors which hindered the operation of the so-called "automatic correctives" of the balance of payments which are allegedly set into motion by gold movements. The growth of trade barriers, domestic price- and income-stabilization policies, and the decline of competition in internationally traded commodities tend to interfere with the responsiveness of the balance of payments to movements of gold and short-term balances among countries. These tendencies were already developing in the 1920's. Finally, international short-term capital movements came to be influenced more and more by security and speculative influences rather than by movements in interest rates in the interwar period.

Federal Reserve policy in 1928 and 1929 was in large measure influenced by a desire to stem the speculative movement in the security and real-estate markets. The Federal Reserve Bank of New York's discount rate was raised from 5 to 6 per cent in August, 1929, after general business conditions had turned downward. The net result appeared to be that the credit contraction was not great enough to stem the tide of speculation until it had run its course in October, 1929, but was probably severe enough to contribute to the decline in business activity which began in the summer of 1929. After the fall in the securities market, credit conditions were gradually eased, Reserve bank rates were reduced and Reserve bank security holdings increased. This policy was continued until October, 1931, when large gold outflows brought about by the devaluation of the pound sterling in the preceding month caused the reserve ratio of the Reserve banks to fall to a dangerously low level. The Federal Reserve Bank of New York raised its discount rate from $1\frac{1}{2}$ to $3\frac{1}{2}$ per cent in October, 1931, and the buying rate for bills was raised from $1\frac{1}{4}$ to $3\frac{1}{8}$ per cent. Following the passage of the Glass-Steagall Act of February, 1932, which authorized the use of government securities as collateral for Federal Reserve notes, the Reserve banks increased their government security holdings from $740 million at the end of February, 1932, to $1,891 million by the end of July, 1932. The large increase in the demand for gold and gold certificates in February, 1933, again reduced the reserve ratio to a low point, causing the Federal Reserve Board to suspend the reserve requirements of the Federal Reserve banks for 30 days. Money rates rose sharply, and the Federal Reserve Bank of New York discount rate was raised from 2½ to 3½ per cent.

After the bank holiday in March, 1933, discount rates were reduced and open-market purchases expanded. The large inflow of gold following the stabilization of the dollar in January, 1934, expanded excess reserves of member banks until they had reached a level of about $3 billion in the latter part of 1935. The principal concern of the Reserve Board during this period was to regain a measure of control over the banking-credit structure in the event that a dangerous inflationary situation should develop. So long as banks had huge excess reserves, the rediscount rate was of little significance and the Reserve banks did not have sufficient government securities at their disposal to mop up the excess reserves even if they could have done so without creating difficulties for the Treasury. Two devices were employed to deal with this situation. The Banking Act of 1935 gave to the Reserve Board power to increase reserve requirements up to 100 per cent of the existing legal requirements of the member banks. While not desiring to reverse the existing easy-money policy, the Reserve authorities exercised their new power by doubling reserve requirements. This action was supplemented by the Treasury's gold sterilization policy in 1937. The Treasury Department undertook in December, 1936, to prevent incoming gold from further increasing the excess reserves of the banking system by purchasing incoming gold with funds derived from the sale of Treasury bills in place of the usual method of purchase by drafts on its accounts at the Federal Reserve banks created by the deposit of gold certificates. Through these actions, excess reserves were reduced to less than a billion dollars in May, 1937. In the latter part of 1937, the Treasury Department terminated its gold sterilization program and member bank excess reserves climbed rapidly to a level of more than $5 billion by September, 1939. This rise was due almost entirely to the importation of gold. The rate of gold inflow was probably not influenced to any significant degree by either the reserve and credit policies of the Reserve Board or the gold sterilization policy of the Treasury. The influence of the Treasury's gold-buying and exchange-rate policies on gold movements after March, 1933, will be taken up in the next section.

Treasury Financial Policies after 1932

Whereas before 1933 monetary management in the United States was in the hands of the Federal Reserve System, after March, 1933, the locus of monetary authority shifted to the Treasury. This situation, which the author believes will prove to be a more or less permanent one, was the result of several factors. (1) The large gold inflows which took place beginning in 1934 rendered the banking system more or less independent of the Reserve banks, and borrowing from the Reserve banks declined to negligible amounts. Total Reserve credit outstanding, including government securities held by the Reserve banks, remained quite stable at around $2.5 billion through the remainder of the decade, and excess reserves remained high throughout the period. (2) Congress provided the Treasury Department with a number of very powerful monetary weapons which for the most part were never used since they were not needed for the maintenance of easy-money conditions. More significantly, the attack on the depression was one involving the use of fiscal and administrative control measures, with the role of Reserve credit policy being confined to a relatively passive one. (3) It may be said that the idea of monetary policy operating independently of political control by the administration was definitely abandoned in the New Deal period. This is a logical consequence of the development of governmental responsibility for economic conditions, since monetary policy cannot operate independently of fiscal and other governmental policies directed toward broad objectives for the economy as a whole.

In this section on Treasury financial policy, we shall be concerned largely with gold, silver, and exchange-rate policy rather than with fiscal policy, since it is in the former fields that United States financial policy more directly affected the interests of other countries. Fiscal developments were of course highly significant in determining the level of United States income and prices and hence the level of imports. But a study of governmental receipts and expenditures in relation to income, private investment, and employment during the period following 1932 fails to reveal any consistent fiscal policy. To quote Dr. Gerhard Colm on this point: [6]

> For example, at least until the recession of 1937–38, Government deficits were more the unintentional results of policies designed to give relief to farmers, home owners, business, and unemployed workers, than the conscious aim of a recovery policy through deficit spending. . . . Only when the recession occurred in the fall of 1937 was a comprehensive recovery program formulated and discussed by a top Government committee on monetary and fiscal policy. This program, which was, broadly speaking, in line with Keynes' recommendations for a national investment policy, never became a reality because of Congressional disapproval.

One can say, in general, that the fiscal program adopted by the government was inadequate to provide a reasonably high level of employ-

[6] *The New Economics,* edited by S. E. Harris, Knopf, New York, 1947, p. 451.

ment and income throughout the 1930's. Had high levels of employment been maintained, it is reasonable to assume that United States imports would have been 40 to 50 per cent higher by volume in the 1930's
than they actually were.[7] If, in addition, the level of foreign investment
attained during the 1920's had been maintained, the world's supply of
dollars would have been even larger. Undoubtedly the economic history
of the world, and possibly its political history, would have been very
different if the supply of dollars in the 1930's had been 50 to 75 per cent
higher than it actually was.[8]

The Gold-buying Program of 1933

Unlike the case of most countries which have in the past abandoned
the gold standard and depreciated their currencies because of adverse
payments balances and the depletion of monetary reserves, the United
States took this step as a means of raising internal commodity prices
from their depressed levels. The gold stock was over $4 billion at the
time of the bank holiday, a level which exceeded that of 1928–1929, and
neither the external nor the internal drain had reached alarming proportions. In fact, both the internal and the external drains were due in
considerable measure to the lack of confidence in the banking system,
and after the banks were reopened there is every evidence that the dollar
could have been maintained at parity without excessive gold outflows;
in fact, the net movement of gold would probably have been inward.[9]
Nor can it be said that devaluation was required to protect the reserves
of either the Federal Reserve banks or the member banks. The nationalization of gold had eliminated the internal drain, and gold stocks were
abundant to handle almost any conceivable external drain. Member
bank excess reserves were $366 million at the end of April, 1933, and the
Reserve banks held excess reserves of $1.3 billion on the same date. More-

[7] For an excellent discussion of the United States propensity to import, see C. P.
Kindleberger, *The Dollar Shortage*, Wiley, New York, 1950, Chap. 3.

[8] Allowing for a secular increase of real national income of 3 per cent per year after
1929, average real national income during the period from 1930 to 1938 should have
been about 45 per cent higher than it actually was. Most calculations of the United
States propensity to import indicate an income elasticity of demand for imports during
the interwar period of about unity. (See J. H. Adler, "United States Import Demand
during the Inter-war Period," *American Economic Review*, June, 1945, pp. 418–427.)
Hence a level of imports 40 to 50 per cent higher during the 1930's under conditions of
full employment would seem reasonable.

[9] For discussions of the dollar devaluation in 1933, see S. E. Harris, *Exchange Depreciation*, Harvard University Press, Cambridge, Mass., 1936; and G. G. Johnson, *The
Treasury and Monetary Policy, 1933–1938*, Harvard University Press, Cambridge, Mass.,
1939.

over the Agricultural Adjustment Act (AAA) of May, 1933, gave the President authority to permit the Reserve banks to purchase up to $3 billion worth of United States government obligations, the Reserve banks to be relieved of any penalty for any resulting deficiency of reserves.[10]

The deliberate depreciation of the dollar was undertaken as a part of a program for raising domestic commodity prices. There is little evidence of any desire on the part of the administration to stimulate employment by encouraging a favorable balance of trade through competitive depreciation or other so-called "beggar-my-neighbor" practices. The exact process by which a lowering of the gold value of the dollar was expected to achieve a rise in prices is the subject of considerable debate. The administration was considerably influenced by the theories of Professors Warren and Pearson who held that "by reducing the weight of the gold dollar, any desired price level can be established." [11] The fallacy of this theory, based on the historical relationship between changes in gold output and the volume of production, has been abundantly demonstrated and need not concern us here. A more valid purpose of devaluation was to prevent depressed prices in terms of gold currencies abroad from interfering with domestic programs such as the AAA for raising commodity prices. The President evidently had this purpose in mind in his radio address of October 22, 1933, when he discussed the nature of the gold-purchase program.[12]

> Finally, I repeat what I have said on many occasions, that ever since last March the definite policy of the government has been to restore commodity price levels. . . .
>
> Because of conditions in this country and because of events beyond our control in other parts of the world, it becomes increasingly important to develop and apply further measures which may be necessary from time to time to control the gold value of our own dollar at home.
>
> Our dollar is now altogether too greatly influenced by the accidents of international trade, by the internal policies of other nations and by political disturbance in other continents.
>
> Therefore the United States must take firmly in its own hands the control of the gold value of our dollar. This is necessary in order to prevent dollar disturbances from swinging us away from our ultimate goal, namely, the continued recovery of our commodity prices.

In order to depreciate the gold value of the dollar, the Treasury began buying gold on October 25, 1933, at an initial price of $31.36 and gradually raised this price in the following weeks until it was stabilized on

[10] The Secretary of the Treasury was also authorized to issue up to $3 billion in United States notes.

[11] See G. F. Warren and F. A. Pearson, *Prices*, Wiley, New York, 1933, p. 370.

[12] Frederick A. Bradford, *Money and Banking*, Longmans, New York, 1939, pp. 83–84.

January 31, 1934, at $35 per ounce as the new gold parity of the dollar established under the authority of the Gold Reserve Act of January, 1934. In spite of the uncertainty of the future value of the dollar, substantial amounts of gold were purchased during this period in order to drive up the dollar price of gold, an indication that the dollar was being deliberately undervalued.[13]

There was no valid reason for believing that prices in the United States would rise in proportion to the increase in the price of gold. From March, 1933, to December, 1934, United States wholesale prices rose 27.7 per cent, while the price of gold had risen by 59 per cent. The average value of farm products, however, was 38.5 per cent higher in 1934 than in 1932 and 66.2 per cent higher in 1935 over 1932. Although the bulk of the rise in prices can be explained in terms of the purely domestic programs such as the AAA, the National Recovery Act (NRA), deficit financing of public works and relief, and the efforts to restore confidence in the monetary and banking system, the question remains as to how much of the rise is attributable to the devaluation of the dollar. No quantitative answer to this question can be given, but the general conclusion of economists who have investigated this problem is that exchange depreciation played a significant role in raising the prices of export commodities, particularly farm commodities.[14] Both the value and quantity of United States exports rose in 1934 over 1933, and although imports also rose in value and quantity, the merchandise surplus rose by about a quarter of a billion dollars. As might be expected, however, the rise in exports was greatest in the case of those commodities whose prices had risen least. Thus between 1933 and 1934 the export price of cotton rose by 34 per cent, but the quantity exported actually declined by 30 per cent, while the prices of automotive exports remained constant but the number of automobiles and trucks exported increased 120 per cent.[15] Import prices also rose in 1934 and 1935, reflecting the increase in business activity in the world generally and the depreciation of other currencies in addition to the dollar. Import prices rose somewhat less than export prices in the period from 1932 to 1939. The failure of import prices to rise by the amount of the devaluation in terms of gold is to be found in the depreciation in terms of gold of a number of other currencies during this period, and perhaps also in the fact that the supply functions of United States imports were fairly ine-

[13] From Oct. 25, 1933, to Jan. 31, 1934, the Treasury and the Reconstruction Finance Corporation purchased $187.8 million worth of gold. Johnson, *op. cit.*, p. 24.

[14] See, for example, Harris, *Exchange Depreciation*, pp. 333, 348–349; see also N. L. Silverstein, "Effects of the American Devaluation on Prices and Export Trade," *American Economic Review*, June, 1937, p. 293.

[15] *Summary of United States World Trade 1934*, Department of Commerce, p. 4.

lastic.[16] For example, the world prices of a number of important raw materials tend to be made in the dollar market.

There are, in general, two ways in which the devaluation assisted in the rise of United States commodity prices. First, the lower prices of United States commodities in terms of foreign currencies tended to increase the demand for United States exports. Of course to the extent that United States export prices in terms of dollars rose, this competitive advantage was nullified. Some significance can also be attached to the direct effects of higher dollar prices of foreign commodities on prices in American markets. Undoubtedly the devaluations which had taken place abroad during the period from 1931 to 1933 had brought pressure on American prices, directly and indirectly. This may have been true even though the United States balance of payments was not directly affected, since American firms were able in many instances to meet the price competition of depreciated currencies.[17] Still another effect of the American devaluation was to force other countries to depreciate their currencies in order to meet the competition of American exporters. Although this action wiped out the price advantage of United States exports over foreign-produced commodities, the net effect was to permit a general reflation of world commodity prices.

Table 2. United States Export and Import Unit-value Indexes and Wholesale-price Indexes, 1932–1935

(1936–1938 = 100)

Year	Export prices *	Import prices *	Wholesale prices †
1933	80	77	80
1934	94	88	91
1935	96	90	98

* *Foreign Trade of the United States, 1936–1949*, Department of Commerce, 1951, pp. 6–9.
† Bureau of Labor Statistics.

We now turn to the highly controversial question of the repercussions of the American devaluation on other countries. If the only justification

[16] That is to say, foreign sellers, rather than reduce sales to the United States, maintained their dollar prices by lowering prices in terms of their own currencies.

[17] See A. Hansen, "Fundamental Disequilibrium," in *Foreign Economic Policy for the United States,* edited by S. E. Harris, Harvard University Press, Cambridge, Mass., 1948, pp. 379–380.

for a devaluation is the existence of a "fundamental disequilibrium" and if by this we mean the existence of a deficit in a country's current international accounts not offset by long-term capital imports, the United States was most certainly not in fundamental disequilibrium in 1933–1934. If, on the other hand, devaluation is justifiable on grounds that falling foreign prices (either due to devaluation or otherwise) have brought deflationary pressure on domestic prices and thereby contributed to domestic unemployment, there is some justification for the American action.[18] There can be little doubt but that the American devaluation brought pressure on other countries both by increasing the United States export surplus and by forcing down prices, particularly in the gold-bloc countries.[19] The United States could not justify the devaluation from the viewpoint of its international relations unless the adverse competitive effects on other countries was offset by a larger United States demand for imports associated with the expansion of United States income, which may result from larger exports and higher prices. If the key to the restoration of world prosperity was the recovery of the American economy, it might be argued that other countries could well afford to pay the price of an adverse-payments balance and deflationary pressure on their prices in order that American national income, imports, and perhaps capital exports should expand. This argument may have more force today than it did in the 1930's when compensatory fiscal policies, exchange controls, and other devices were not so widely employed by other countries as they are at present. Thus it might be argued that other countries are now better able to protect themselves against deflationary pressures originating in the United States. Nevertheless, the United States devaluation did contribute to the loss of gold, deflation, and the eventual abandonment of the gold standard by the gold-bloc countries. The author seriously doubts whether or not the added boost which the American devaluation gave to United States prosperity was worth the price paid by the other countries. Certainly, the same or much better results could have been achieved by a more vigorous and consistent policy of deficit financing in the United States. If after full employment had been achieved, a United States balance-of-payments deficit existed, appropriate adjustments in the value of the dollar could have been made. In view of

[18] For a discussion of these two points of view, see A. Hansen, "Fundamental Disequilibrium," and G. Haberler, "Currency Depreciation and the International Monetary Fund," in *Foreign Economic Policy for the United States*, edited by S. E. Harris, pp. 379–396.

[19] French prices fell from 87 in 1932 (1913 = 100) to 69 in 1935. Similar price declines occurred in Belgium and Switzerland.

the competitive strength of American exports, however, it is hard to believe that such a course would have been necessary.

The Gold Reserve Act of 1934 authorized the President to fix the gold value of the dollar at a level between 50 and 60 per cent of its then statutory weight, with authority to change the weight from time to time between these limits. The fact that the weight of the gold dollar was fixed at 59.06 per cent of its former level gave the President the power to devalue by another 9 per cent, a power which was retained until June 30, 1945. This was undoubtedly a powerful weapon in the hands of the administration, a weapon which could be used to threaten other countries when they sought to nullify the effects of the American devaluation by a further devaluation of their own. As late as 1943, the Secretary of the Treasury argued strongly for the retention of this power: [20]

> This power was given to the President in the midst of a deep depression, unquestionably prolonged and intensified by the general depreciation of other currencies which destroyed the markets for American products abroad and brought ruinously low prices. The revaluation of the dollar was an unavoidable step in the restoration of foreign and domestic markets for the industrial and agricultural products of the American people.
>
> This power given to the President to determine within limits the gold content of the dollar could not safely be terminated until a satisfactory means was available for assuming the stabilization of the appropriate exchange relation among currencies and avoiding competitive currency depreciations. The President recommended and the Congress enacted extensions of this power in 1937 and again in 1939 and 1941.
>
> We are all agreed that no one can benefit from a competitive race in the depreciation of currencies. If such a development is to be avoided, we must frankly face the danger of competitive currency depreciation in the post-war period. It is not possible at this time to foresee the patterns of post-war monetary developments. But this we do know: That if we are to avoid competitive depreciation of currency after the war, it would be helpful to be armed with this power as a warning that we shall not permit the international economic position of this country to be undermined by competitive currency depreciation.

It should be pointed out that, while in 1933 and 1934 the relative value of the dollar was thought of as a matter for unilateral decision on the part of the United States with sole reference to the welfare of the domestic economy, by 1943 the country had come to think of currency values as a matter for international agreement. Plans for the Bretton Woods Conference were already well under way by April, 1943.

[20] Statement of Secretary Morgenthau before the Senate Committee on Banking and Currency, Apr. 16, 1943.

The United States Exchange Stabilization Fund

Two billion dollars of the devaluation profit was earmarked by the Gold Reserve Act of 1934 for a fund to stabilize the external value of the dollar. It is the general consensus of students of the Stabilization Fund [21] that the administration and Congress had only the vaguest notion of what could be done with a fund of this size, and in fact only a small portion of it was ever actively used (until $1.8 billion was set aside in 1945 to be used for making the United States subscription to the International Monetary Fund).

There are three generally recognized uses for an international stabilization fund: (1) It can be used to support the gold value of a currency and offset speculative and other pressures. Since the United States was on an international gold standard, had ample gold reserves, and tended to have gold inflows rather than outflows, the fund was obviously not needed to support the dollar. (2) A stabilization fund could be used to support the value of other currencies in terms of the dollar. This operation, however, requires dollars, and the United States Fund originally consisted entirely of gold. This was remedied however in April, 1934, when $200 million of the Fund's gold was converted into dollar deposits by issuing gold certificates to the Federal Reserve Bank of New York.[22] But supporting foreign currencies involves risks unless one purchases only gold or gold-guaranteed currencies and converts them immediately into gold. The Fund was unwilling to take the risk of supporting inconvertible currencies without a gold guarantee or even of holding gold currencies for any period of time. Hence its stabilization operations were limited to gold arbitrage and technical cooperation with other countries under a gold guarantee. (3) A stabilization fund may be used to neutralize the effects of gold movements on the domestic credit structure. But in the case of a country with a strong currency, this objective requires a fund with domestic currency assets and not simply gold. The influx of gold during the period from 1934 to 1938 was too large for the Federal Reserve authorities to offset, even with their expanded power over member bank reserve requirements. The stabilization Fund would have had to borrow the dollars in the money market in order to pay for the incoming gold in a manner which would not add to the reserves of the banking system. Actually, the gold sterilization

---

[21] For discussion of the United States Exchange Stabilization Fund, see Johnson, *op. cit.*, Chap. 4; and A. I. Bloomfield, "Operations of the American Exchange Stabilization Fund," *Review of Economic Statistics,* May, 1944, pp. 69–87.

[22] See Bloomfield, *op. cit.*, p. 70.

program was handled by the Treasury Department directly, and the existence of the gold stabilization fund made no real contribution to this operation.

The United States Exchange Stabilization Fund did not stabilize the foreign-currency value of the dollar in any substantial manner. It did render technical assistance in cooperation with other countries under the Tripartite Agreement, which will be discussed later on. In essence, it performed the function of an efficient gold arbitrager in a period when inconvertible currencies and shaky gold currencies made private gold arbitrage too risky to maintain foreign-exchange rates within narrow limits set by the normal gold shipping points. Later on, the United States Exchange Stabilization Fund actually acquired foreign currencies for the purpose of holding them over a period of time. But these were not stabilization operations; they were loans.

The Silver-buying Program

The United States silver-buying program of the 1930's provides one of the most irrational chapters in American financial history. The 1929 depression brought to life many ghosts of the past, not the least of which was the free coinage of silver. As Dr. G. G. Johnson has pointed out,[23] the silver movement of the 1930's cannot be explained simply in terms of a wicked plot on the part of a handful of silver-state Senators, any more than the Bryan free-silver movement which enveloped the debtor class and the "reflationists" all over the country can be explained solely in terms of the silver-mining interests. Sentiment against the gold standard as the instrument of deflation was strong, and the monetization of silver was somehow considered as a means of reducing the influence of gold. The public was tired of deflation and was willing to support any and all of the devices which were believed to make for reflation. Congress was willing to vote for all these devices in 1933 and 1934—the monetization of silver, devaluation, departure from the gold standard, the issue of greenbacks by the Treasury, and the purchase of government obligations by the Federal Reserve banks to the extent of $3 billion without regard to the maintenance of reserve requirements. The President was given the power under the Thomas inflation amendment of May, 1933, to begin unlimited coinage of gold and silver at a ratio to be determined by administrative decision. Although the President did not put the country on a bimetallic standard, there was a real danger that Congress would enact mandatory legislation. The Silver Purchase

[23] Johnson, *op. cit.*, p. 161.

Act of 1934 was a compromise agreed to by the administration to avoid the establishment of a bimetallic standard. It required the President to purchase silver at home and abroad until the monetary silver stock was equal to one-third of the total gold stock. Although at the time the Act was passed, the Treasury in order to meet this goal would have had to purchase about 1.3 billion ounces of silver, the continual inflow of gold prevented any substantial progress toward the required ratio, and by the end of 1939 the required ratio was more distant than when the program began.

The fallacies of the silver-purchase program as a reflationary device are familiar to all students of monetary affairs. Of the various devices which were employed by the government in the 1930's, the silver program was probably the least effective from a domestic standpoint and the most harmful to certain other countries, in fact the very countries which the program was supposed to assist. The silver purchases with silver certificates added to the already excessive banking reserves, and the high domestic support prices caused domestic silver production to triple between 1933 and 1937. It might be argued that this increased employment, but the social value of the product of the least efficient WPA project was certainly greater than the hoard of silver accumulated by the Treasury. A large part of the Treasury's acquisitions came from abroad, with the result that from 1934 to 1939 United States silver imports aggregated over a billion dollars.[24] For example, in 1935 net silver imports amounted to $396 million, a situation which made possible an over-all current deficit of $156 million in that year, the first current-account deficit since long before World War I. It might be thought that the silver-purchase program performed a valuable service in adding to the world's supply of dollars, but this conclusion must be severely qualified.[25] In so far as the foreign silver purchases provided a market for the newly mined output of Mexico and other silver-producing countries, current dollar receipts of foreigners were expanded. (This was partially offset by the fact that Americans were heavy investors in Mexican silver mines.) But a large part of the silver came from accumulated hoards or currency circulations in China and other silver-using countries, where the effect was to drain off monetary reserves and cause severe deflation. The rise in the world price of silver from 25 cents an ounce in 1932 to a high of 81 cents in April, 1935, had the effect of greatly appreciating the currencies of silver-standard countries such as China, thereby handicapping their exports. Moreover, the sale of silver for dollars did not

[24] *The United States in the World Economy,* Department of Commerce, 1943, p. 86. Silver exports during this period were negligible.

[25] *Ibid.,* p. 86.

for the most part represent current receipts available for imports but rather "the conversion of one type of capital asset into another." [26] Ironically, one of the effects of the silver-purchase program was to force the one major country remaining on the silver standard to abandon silver for a paper-currency system.

During World War II, a portion of the United States silver stock was put to good use by loaning it to domestic industries and lend-leasing it for industrial and coinage purposes to other countries. All lend-lease silver is to be returned to the Treasury in accordance with special lend-lease agreements. At the time of writing, the Treasury is not buying any foreign-produced silver but is continuing to purchase all domestically mined silver at a price of 91 cents per ounce, which until recently was 10 to 20 cents above the world market price.[27]

Conclusion

From the foregoing outline of United States financial policies during the interwar period, it will be seen that these policies were dictated almost exclusively by what were believed to be America's domestic economic interests without regard to either the longer run economic impact of possible adverse repercussions on the economies of other countries or the impact of these repercussions upon America's political and security interests. While it was concluded that America's gold policy during the 1920's was justifiable both from a national and an international point of view, the same could not be said of the gold and silver policies of the 1930's. As will be seen in Chap. 5, the forced depreciation of the dollar was undertaken in the face of strong objections on the part of a large number of other countries and involved a refusal on the part of this country to enter into international cooperation for currency stabilization. Moreover, the devaluation policy could not be justified as a condition for American economic recovery. After 1935, America became interested in currency stabilization largely as a means of maintaining the competitive position of American exports. Cooperation in this field was, however, limited to technical assistance through the operations of the Exchange Stabilization Fund under the Tripartite Agreement.

The greatest damage to both the national and international interests of the United States resulted from the failure of her monetary and fiscal

[26] *Ibid.*

[27] During the fiscal year 1948, the Treasury Department purchased nearly 35 million ounces of domestically mined silver. *Annual Report of the Secretary of the Treasury for the Fiscal Year Ended June 30, 1948,* p. 143. In January, 1951, the free market price of silver rose to about 90 cents per ounce.

policies to prevent the depression of the early 1930's and to restore full prosperity during the middle and late 1930's. The conclusion which emerges most emphatically from a survey of the international economic developments of the interwar period is the fundamental importance of maintaining domestic economic conditions conducive to a stable and ample flow of dollars in our transactions from the rest of the world.[28]

[28] This sentence is a paraphrase of a statement in the Foreword (by Wayne C. Taylor, Under Secretary of Commerce), in *The United States in the World Economy*, p. v.

CHAPTER 4

War Debts and Foreign Investment Policy

THE CONTRAST between America's international policy after the first and after the second world wars is nowhere more clearly illustrated than in the field of intergovernmental debt settlements. After America's entry into the war in April, 1917, it became obvious that the maximum prosecution of the war required supplementing the resources of our Allies for the purchase of supplies in this country. The Allies were in no position to haggle as to the terms of this assistance, and the rates of interest charged were related to the cost of United States government borrowing from its own citizens, the rates varying from 3 per cent in April, 1917, to 5 per cent in May, 1918. By the end of 1918, the United States government had loaned $7.7 billion, and postwar lending for relief and reconstruction purposes continued until May, 1922. By the end of 1922, $9.4 billion in government loans to foreign countries were outstanding, of which the share of the United Kingdom was $4.1 billion, France $2.9 billion, Italy $1.6 billion, and the remainder divided among Belgium, Cuba, Czechoslovakia, Greece, Rumania, Russia, and Yugoslavia.[1] The American public and Congress assumed that these debts would be paid in full, and this attitude was reflected in the provisions of the Act of February 9, 1922, which established the World War Foreign Debt Commission. This Act empowered the Commission to negotiate with the foreign debtors for funding the debt, but the Commission was severely limited in the terms which it could accept. The rate of interest must not be less than $4\frac{1}{4}$ per cent, the maturity of the obligations no longer than 25 years; there was to be no cancellation of principal and no transfer of allied obligations for reparations due from enemy countries.[2] There was in this Act no recognition of the principle of capacity to pay and no hint of the complexities of the transfer problem.

[1] Cleona Lewis, *America's Stake in International Investments*, The Brookings Institution, Washington, D.C., 1938, p. 362.

[2] See Moulton and Pasvolsky, *World War Debt Settlements*, Macmillan, New York, 1929, pp. 111–112.

The American public and most of the United States officials saw little distinction between internal and external debts. Debt repayment was a matter of the honor and integrity of the borrower. Moreover, the prevailing public sentiment of the 1920's was that the war was not one in which the United States had an equal stake with its European allies but rather a conflict of European origin into which we had been (perhaps unfortunately) drawn in order to help those countries which were the victims of German aggression. The least that the Allied powers could do to show their appreciation for the sacrifices of the American people in their behalf was to repay the money America had loaned them. In contrast with the American attitude, Europe took the view that the war was a common fight against an attempt by Germany to achieve worldwide dominion and that the Allies had borne the brunt of a fight in which America was an equal benefactor. Since America did not claim reparations from Germany, Europeans largely accepted the idea that a large share of the payments which they expected to receive from Germany would be paid to the United States for discharging the debt. There was, however, an early recognition, particularly in Britain, of the danger of saddling upon Germany, reparations which exceeded her capacity to pay.[3] As difficulties developed in the collection of reparations from Germany, Europeans took the position that the indebtedness to America should be scaled down accordingly. The United States government, however, steadfastly maintained the position that there was no relation between reparations and the war debts and refused to negotiate on this basis.

The history of the debt settlements began with the negotiations with Britain in the latter part of 1922 and continued on with other debtors until 1926. In the course of these discussions, there developed a gradual recognition of the principle of ability to pay on the part of the American government. Although the terms of the British settlement called for full repayment of principal, the interest rate was reduced from the minimum established by Congress in February, 1922, to an average of 3.3 per cent and the maturity extended to 62 years. Settlements with Finland, Hungary, Poland, Lithuania, Latvia, Estonia, Czechoslovakia, and Rumania followed more or less the pattern of the British settlement. A substantial departure from the British terms came with the Belgian settlement in August, 1925, in which the average interest to be paid was reduced to 1.8 per cent.[4] But official recognition of the principle of capacity to repay was not given until the French settlement in Septem-

---

[3] In this connection J. M. Keynes, *The Economic Consequences of the Peace,* Harcourt, Brace, New York, 1920, had an enormous influence on British thought.

[4] Moulton and Pasvolsky, *op. cit.,* pp. 117–118.

ber, 1925, which provided for rates which averaged 1.6 per cent for the payment period of 62 years.[5] On October 1, 1925, the following statement was made by the American Commission: "We believe it is fully recognized by the Commission that the only basis of negotiation fair to both peoples is the principle of the capacity of France to pay." [6]

Further expression to this principle was given in the Italian debt settlement of November, 1925, which provided for average interest payments of only four-tenths of 1 per cent. These settlements required Congressional approval since they went beyond the terms of reference of the Commission as established by the Act of 1922. Secretary of the Treasury Mellon's justification of the Italian debt settlement before the House Ways and Means Committee in January, 1926, is worth noting in this connection.[7]

> Europe is our largest customer. Unless the finances of Europe can be restored, her currency placed on a sound basis, and her people able to earn and to spend, this country will not be able to dispose of its surplus products of food, materials, and goods. . . . America with its excess of capital seeking profitable investment, must aid by making private loans to Europe for productive purposes. Only from these private loans during the past year have the countries abroad been able to pay for our wheat and cotton. It is these loans which make our exports possible. . . .
>
> But the settlements are made in the real interests of those American producers who must have a foreign market able to pay. The American producer needs these debt settlements. The entire foreign debt is not worth as much to the American people in dollars and cents as a prosperous Europe as a customer.

These are familiar arguments which have been frequently employed in the present postwar period not to justify generous maturity and interest terms for war debts (which were largely avoided in World War II through the mechanism of lend-lease) but rather to justify large grants for relief and rehabilitation and loans for reconstruction and currency stabilization at low rates of interest. It is interesting to note that it was the commercial interest of American exporters rather than the general economic and political interest of the United States in the economic welfare of foreign countries that was stressed most heavily by Secretary Mellon. Although it may be admitted that the American government was aware of the problem of the capacity of individual countries to make foreign payments, there was little recognition of the relationship of the American balance of payments to the capacity of the world as a whole to make dollar payments. Capacity to pay was based on the total balance

[5] *Ibid.*, p. 94.   [7] *Ibid.*, pp. 399–401.
[6] *Ibid.*, p. 119.

of payments of the debtor and not upon the capacity of the individual debtor or of the world as a whole to pay dollars. The settlements which were considered to be generous and fair by the American government involved a sizable portion of the world's current dollar income from American imports of commodities and services. Total principal and interest to be paid by 13 war debtors aggregated over $22 billion, nearly $10 billion of which was to be paid in the first 30 years, beginning with 1926. This represented an annual rate of about a third of a billion dollars per year.[8] For the first five years, payments required under the settlements aggregated about $1.1 billion, and the vast bulk of these payments was in fact made.[9] Beginning with the Hoover moratorium in 1931, most debtors defaulted in whole or in part upon their obligations to the United States government, and although token payments continued to be made until 1933, thereafter only Finland among the European debtors continued to meet the debt payments. No formal settlement of these obligations has ever been made, and they still stand on books of the Treasury. At the beginning of 1945, European countries owed on account of World War I debts $14.7 billion, of which $11.4 billion represented unpaid principal.

Private Loans and Investments

Payments on the war debts throughout the 1920's were made possible in considerable measure by private loans to Germany which enabled her to meet her reparation obligations to the Allies. In the period from 1924 to 1929, short- and long-term dollar loans to Germany amounted to nearly a billion dollars.[10] Large loans were also made to Italy, Poland, Belgium, France, Norway, Sweden, Austria, and other European countries during the 1920's. Private dollar loans to all countries during the period from 1920 to 1929 aggregated about $7.6 billion, of which $7.3 billion were outstanding at the end of 1929.[11] Over the period from 1919 to 1930, total private capital outflow in the form of subscriptions to new foreign issues and direct investments abroad amounted to $11.4 bil-

[8] See Moulton and Pasvolsky, *op. cit.*, p. 103.

[9] Receipts from United States government settlements from 1926 through 1930 totaled $1,147 million, largely representing payments of interest and principal on the war debts. (See *The United States in the World Economy*, Department of Commerce, 1943, Appendix B, Table I.) Total receipts from government settlements amounted to approximately $3.7 billion between 1919 and 1939, representing chiefly collections by the United States on loans to foreign governments made between 1917 and 1920. (*Ibid.*, p. 84.)

[10] Lewis, *op. cit.*, pp. 393, 620.

[11] *Ibid.*, pp. 369, 393–394.

lion, or a gross long-term capital outflow of nearly a billion dollars annually. To this amount must be added a net increase of a billion dollars in American short-term assets abroad over the period. By far the largest part of the long-term capital outflow took the form of American purchases of new foreign security issues, direct investments amounting to only $3.3 billion of the total. Considerably more than half the securities sold to Americans were obligations of foreign governments. This is in sharp contrast to the situation in post-World War II when private portfolio investment in foreign securities (excluding those of the International Bank for Reconstruction and Development) has been negligible. Many of the private loans to Europe in the early 1920's were for reconstruction, restocking, and currency-stabilization purposes. Thus they were not tied to some new capital development project which was expected to earn directly or indirectly the foreign exchange necessary to service the loan. Even the loans made to the underdeveloped countries of Latin America and elsewhere frequently did not meet the tests of sound international lending in the sense that they were expended in a manner which would provide the means of repayment through the effects on the balance of payments of the borrowing country. The story of the follies of the lenders and borrowers in this period is well known.[12] Even in the most favorable international climate, a large number of defaults would have occurred, just as a large amount of defaults occurred within the United States even during the more prosperous years. More significant are the causes of the wholesale defaults on both good and bad loans which occurred after 1929.

The first factor to be considered is the erratic pattern of United States capital outflow during the interwar period. Table 3 shows the trend of United States foreign lending and direct investments after governmental lending had virtually ceased in 1923 to 1932 when foreign investment became a negligible factor in the United States balance of payments. It may be noted that direct investment was more closely correlated with United States national income, reaching a peak in 1929, while new foreign loans followed a somewhat more erratic pattern dictated by the vicissitudes of the American securities market. In 1929, new foreign loans declined to 40 per cent of their 1928 level but recovered sharply in 1930. It would appear that the low value of foreign loans in 1929 was due in large measure to the greater attractiveness of American securities in that year, and also to the crash in the securities market in October, 1929, which seriously hampered the flotation of both foreign and domestic issues. Direct investments declined relatively less than

[12] See *ibid.*, Chap. XVIII.

loans until the deep depression year of 1932, a year in which gross private domestic investment had fallen to less than a billion dollars and net new domestic investment was a negative figure. Direct foreign investments failed to recover with the recovery of gross private domestic investment in 1935 (to the 1931 level) largely because of the growth of payments and other restrictions abroad.

*Table 3. New United States Foreign Loans and Direct Investment, 1923–1932 **

(In millions of dollars)

Year	New loans	Direct investments †	Total
1923	$ 317	$148	$ 465
1924	823	182	905
1925	824	268	1,092
1926	921	351	1,272
1927	1,114	351	1,465
1928	1,019	558	1,577
1929	415	602	1,017
1930	775	294	1,069
1931	190	222	412
1932	51	16	67

* *The United States in the World Economy*, Department of Commerce, 1943, Appendix B, Table II.   After 1922, United States foreign lending was almost exclusively private lending.
† Figures for new direct investments are net, *i.e.*, they represent the excess of new investments over liquidation of old investments.

Certain tentative conclusions may be drawn from the foreign-investment experience of the interwar period. First, direct foreign investment appears to be related to gross private domestic investment and to the political and economic environment for such investments abroad. Private portfolio investment however is subject to an additional variable, namely, the receptivity of the American securities market to foreign issues. Interest and amortization obligations on foreign loans tend in the short run to decline relatively little with a decline in capital outflow, thereby setting up a severe strain on the balance of payments. Earnings on direct investments tend to decline with a fall in prices and business activity, and repatriation of capital is ordinarily a small fraction of the total amounts invested. These factors raise the question as to whether private foreign investment through bond issues is compatible with the maintenance of a sufficiently steady flow of investment to assure balance-of-payments equilibrium. Intergovernmental loans also involve a fixed obligation, but this medium presents greater possibilities for the planning of loans and for flexibility in repayment.

One of the important lessons to be learned from our lending experience in the 1920's is that not only must consideration be given to the over-all balance of payments of the borrowing country, but also account must be taken of balance of payments of the large creditor country or countries vis-à-vis the rest of the world. When the bulk of the foreign lending is concentrated in a large country like the United States, changes in net capital flows must be accompanied by appropriate shifts in the current account if international equilibrium is to be maintained. Unfortunately there is no dependable mechanism for adjusting the world's demand for dollar goods to a decrease in United States foreign lending. In fact, the decline in private foreign investment is likely to come at a time when United States imports are also declining. Foreign countries are understandably unwilling to undertake deflationary measures to reduce their demand for United States imports without the use of direct trade and exchange controls. Price adjustments through currency depreciation may not operate fast enough in the short run to restore the balance. In order for a given export surplus for the lending country to be maintained, there must be an increasing rate of gross investment to compensate for interest, dividend, and amortization payments as well as for maintaining the original rate of capital outflow. The avoidance of disequilibrium from foreign investment may therefore require an ever-increasing outflow of capital from the creditor countries until the marginal propensity to import in such countries rises to the point where they are able to accept an import surplus and live off the returns from their foreign investments. England's position in the 1930's is the classic example of a mature creditor nation, but the time required for the United States to arrive at such a position may involve several generations. United States foreign-investment experience during the interwar period gave little assurance of a steadily rising level of gross private foreign investment, even if the special obstacles to such a flow had not occurred. We shall take up the solution to this problem in a later chapter.

The Defaults

The wave of defaults on both governmental and private loans after 1931 together with the restrictions on the transfer of earnings and capital repatriation of direct investments virtually terminated private foreign investment for the rest of the decade. By 1933, some $3 billion in foreign dollar bonds were in default, or 37 per cent of the total issues outstanding, and by 1938 this percentage had increased to about 40.[13] The reaction of the United States government to these defaults provided a sad chapter in the history of United States foreign relations. The first serious mistake lay in the refusal of the government to accede to the requests of the debtor nations to discuss the war-debt problem. The Hoover moratorium of 1931 was in the nature of a *force majeure* and was no substitute for international discussions of the entire problem of intergovernmental debts. Had the war debts been scaled down at this time, the way might have been opened for international cooperation in dealing with the entire debt problem, public and private. Instead, this country steadfastly refused to permit a discussion of the debt question at the London Economic Conference of 1933. The second mistake was the passage of the Johnson Act of 1934, which prohibited both private and public loans to the governments of nations in default to the United States. Although the Johnson Act probably did not represent a significant deterrent to foreign lending at the time of its passage, its psychological effects were certainly damaging to our future foreign economic and political relations. The following quotation from the Senate Judiciary Committee's Report on the Johnson Bill indicates the attitude of the American Congress in 1934: [14]

> Sums of money to the amount of billions of dollars are now due to the American people upon the bonds and obligations of foreign governments, including political subdivisions thereof and municipalities which have defaulted not only in interest payments but which hold meager hope of payment of any considerable part of the principal.
>
> These foreign bonds and obligations, of course, in some instances were issued and were sold in good faith, while in some instances the testimony has demonstrated that they were issued by the borrower merely to obtain money, with little expectation of redemption, and were sold by the American financiers to make outrageously high profits, and both had reasonable cause to believe that the American public purchasing such bonds or other obligations would be the ultimate sufferer. The bill was introduced, after the revelations concerning the sale of bonds and other obligations of foreign governments by American financiers and bankers, to prevent a recurrence of the practices which were shown by the investigation to be little less than a fraud upon the American people. The bill seeks, therefore, to make it unlawful to loan money to, or to purchase or sell the bonds or other obligations of, any foreign government, including any political subdivision thereof,

---

[13] See *Bulletin* 110, Institute of International Finance of New York University, May 13, 1940.

[14] See Report of Senate Judiciary Committee on the Johnson Bill, Senate Report 20, 73d Congress, 1st Session, Apr. 6, 1933.

while such foreign government, or political subdivision thereof, is in default in the payment of its obligations to our people or to our Government. It is a brief penal statute, protective in character. The investigation referred to, regarding foreign securities, not only justifies the enactment of this bill, but demands it in behalf of the American public. Moreover, much that has occurred since that investigation, and subsequently to the introduction originally of the bill, in the matter of the obligations due to the United States Government from certain foreign governments, emphasizes not only the justice of the measure, but its necessity. It would be unjust to permit the further sale of securities of a defaulting government, the sale of whose securities heretofore in this country have brought distressing loss upon our people, or the further offering for sale of the bonds and obligations of a foreign country able indeed to pay its obligations to our own Government but repudiating its solemn agreements.

The Johnson Act was purported to be a measure for the protection of the American investor against loans to poor credit risks engendered by greedy American bankers.[15] It was in fact an expression of angry resentment on the part of isolationist-minded American congressmen who had little sympathy for the problems of foreign countries and no appreciation of America's responsibility in world economic and political affairs. Fifteen years later we are trying to undo the damage done by this Act by seeking ways to encourage private lending to these same countries who were not frightened into paying a penny on their World War I debts by the Johnson Act.

If the sponsors of the Johnson Act had really wanted to protect American investors, they might have sought to provide for some regulation of investment bankers in floating foreign securities. Some protection was in fact offered by the Securities and Exchange Act. But our securities regulations do not deal with the soundness of loans and investments, still less the balance-of-payments prospects of the borrowing country. There may, however, be a field for government guidance and protection of American foreign investments, a subject which will be discussed in a later chapter.

Private Investment Experience, 1920–1940

In spite of the large volume of defaults on dollar loans and interferences with transfer payments on American investments abroad, the over-all experience of the American foreign investor was not unfavorable. The Department of Commerce has estimated that over the period

[15] *Ibid.*

from 1920 to 1940 Americans received about $8.8 billion more in amortization payments and earnings from foreign investments (excluding war debts) than was put in.[16] What Americans "put in" included (1) $6,456 million as the estimated value of outstanding investments at the end of 1919; (2) $3,609 million net additional portfolio investments over the period; and (3) $3,554 net additional direct foreign investments. What Americans got out up to the end of 1940 was composed of (1) $4,950 in income from foreign dollar bonds and other portfolio investments; (2) $4,391 million in income from direct investments; and (3) $10,065 million representing the outstanding value of United States foreign investments at the end of 1940, with foreign dollar bonds taken at their market values. Exclusive of losses on income account, there was a net capital loss to American investors of $3,554 million to the end of 1940. All in all, however, the total amount received or still outstanding after deducting the net capital loss was about 65 per cent greater than the amount put in over the period. While admitting that a reasonably conservative investor could have done much better by investing in domestic assets over the 21-year period, the over-all record is not so bad as is popularly assumed.

Taking the direct investments by themselves over the interwar period, the yield to the American investor in foreign enterprise was quite favorable. The value of United States direct investments at the end of 1919 was $3.9 billion and at the end of 1940, $7.3 billion, while net income from these investments over the period was $7.3 billion after deducting for losses. Although net direct investment was almost negligible after 1932, and there was some disinvestment, receipts from this source had recovered to $440 million by 1938 as compared with $474 million and $467 million in the boom years of 1928 and 1929, respectively.

The American investors' position was not severely impaired by World War II, since by 1940 three-fourths of United States foreign investments were in the Western Hemisphere or in areas not severely affected by the war. Receipts from both direct and portfolio investments held up surprisingly well during the war period. Receipts of income from American direct investments in foreign countries averaged 5.1 per cent on their equity value during the period from 1940 to 1945, while income from dollar bonds averaged 3.5 per cent on their par value.[17] By the end of 1949, United States direct investments abroad totaled $12.5 billion as compared with $7.3 billion at the end of 1940, while private investment

[16] "Private United States Direct Investments Abroad," *Survey of Current Business,* Department of Commerce, November, 1949, p. 20.

[17] *International Transactions of the United States during the War, 1940–1945,* Department of Commerce, 1948, p. 68.

in foreign securities was $3.8 billion at the end of 1949 as compared with $2.7 billion at the end of 1940.[18]

Conclusion [19]

One of the tragic consequences of the American depression and breakdown of the international currency system in the early 1930's was the precipitous decline in United States private investments abroad. This decline was caused by a complex of economic, political, and psychological factors, most of which can be traced to the American depression of 1929. As was pointed out in Chap. 2, given the structure of international trade and indebtedness which characterized the interwar period, a substantial volume of American foreign investment was one of the essential conditions for world equilibrium. In addition, however, world economic progress and the correction of the structural maladjustments left over from World War I required a steady flow of international capital. Since America was responsible for a large part of the world's savings and tended to have a surplus of savings over the demand for capital on the part of domestic investors, the United States was the logical source for meeting the world's capital needs.

America's withdrawal from the position of international investor, together with the defaults on both private and public foreign investments, had serious international political repercussions. The large foreign investments of the 1920's undoubtedly stimulated the interest of the government in world affairs, a stimulus which was largely lacking in the 1930's. But the defaults engendered animosities and bitterness which were perhaps even more damaging to international cooperation. The attitude of the American government toward international debts and investments was, however, in large measure a reflection of its general international political policy during the 1930's. A government which adopts a policy of political isolationism is unlikely to recognize any responsibility for its economic policies beyond the borders of its own country.

[18] "Private United States Direct Investments Abroad," *Survey of Current Business,* November, 1949, p. 20; see also *Business News Reports,* Department of Commerce, June 29, 1950.

[19] Since this chapter was written, there has appeared a short but excellent account by Dr. Herbert Feis of United States government policy with regard to private foreign investments in the period from 1919 to 1932: *The Diplomacy of the Dollar,* Johns Hopkins Press, Baltimore, 1950.

CHAPTER 5

International Financial Cooperation

IN THIS chapter we shall be concerned with the major developments in the field of international financial cooperation during the interwar period. Since United States monetary policy during the 1920's was dominated largely by the Federal Reserve System, international financial cooperation was chiefly a matter of cooperation between the Reserve system and foreign central banks. With the advent of the New Deal, the balance of power in the monetary field shifted to the Treasury Department, and that agency has remained dominant in the international monetary field to the present time.

Central-banking Cooperation

Although United States monetary policies were determined almost exclusively with reference to domestic business conditions, there were several important instances of international monetary cooperation in the 1920's. The United States as the only major country on the gold standard in the immediate postwar period was anxious to see the world return to gold as rapidly as possible. One form of central-banking cooperation was represented by actions on the part of the Federal Reserve System which sought to reduce the inflow of gold. In 1924, the Federal Reserve authorities adopted a policy of monetary ease ostensibly as a means of helping Britain to return to the gold standard in 1925.[1] Again in 1927, the Reserve authorities after consultation with the heads of the central banks of England, France, and Germany decided upon a policy of easy credit conditions in the United States in order to reduce pressure on European currencies which had recently been stabilized.[2] It is quite unlikely, however, that these actions would have been undertaken had there been strong inflationary pressures in the United States requiring opposite policies.

[1] Dr. Goldenweiser believes that this policy did in fact assist Britain in returning to gold but he is also of the opinion that it was a mistake to expand domestic credit at this time. See E. A. Goldenweiser, *Monetary Management,* McGraw-Hill, New York, 1949, pp. 50–53.

[2] *Ibid.,* p. 51.

Although the United States government did not formally participate in the international financial conferences at Brussels (1920) and Genoa (1921), the Reserve authorities cooperated with foreign central banks by exchanging information with them and by providing direct financial assistance from time to time. In order to assist European countries in stabilizing their currencies at new gold parities, the Federal Reserve Bank of New York in cooperation with other Reserve banks made stabilization loans and credits available to several European nations. For example, in 1925 the Federal Reserve Bank of New York agreed to sell gold against sterling up to $200 million at any time within two years.[3] This credit was never drawn upon. Also in 1925, secured loans for stabilization purposes were made to Poland and Czechoslovakia, followed by similar arrangements with Bulgaria, Italy, and Rumania. In addition to direct loans and credits, the Reserve banks occasionally bought and held foreign currencies as a means of preventing gold movements from the countries whose currencies were supported. For example, in the fall of 1930 over $30 million in sterling was held for this purpose.[4]

The loans, credits, and foreign-currency purchases made during this period were true stabilization operations undertaken by our central-banking system in cooperation with the central banks of other countries. The United States Treasury played little part in these developments. These and other cooperative activities among the central banks of the major powers were in part an outgrowth of the Genoa Economic Conference of 1922. This Conference, attended by European monetary authorities, favored the establishment of the gold-exchange standard and a rapid stabilization of rates on the basis of free exchange markets. Most countries did not seek to stabilize their rates by means of exchange controls in the early 1920's, but rather permitted them to fluctuate until they could be stabilized on the basis of new gold parities.

Conditions in the early 1920's were in sharp contrast with those following World War II when free exchange markets were almost non-existent outside the United States and nations maintained the same parities which had existed before the war by means of rigid controls. Although so-called stabilization loans have been made by the International Monetary Fund and by the Treasury, they have not been employed for the most part for true stabilization purposes. Rather they have been made to enable countries to meet balance-of-payments deficits which show little promise of being reversed within a reasonable period of time

---

[3] C. O. Hardy, *Credit Policies of the Federal Reserve System,* The Brookings Institution, Washington, D.C., 1932, pp. 100–101.

[4] *Ibid.,* p. 102.

in the future. In its purest form, the ideal stabilization loan is one which the borrower does not expect to have to use.

The London Monetary and Economic Conference

Although the United States was invited to participate in the Brussels International Financial Conference of 1920 and the Genoa Economic and Financial Conference of 1922, the government refrained from doing so on the grounds that it did not want to be drawn into a discussion of the crucial issue of war debts and that pressure might be brought on this country to provide additional financial assistance.[5] These conferences failed to deal in any concrete way with the financial problems of Europe and were largely devoted to the passing of resolutions with regard to sound internal financial practices and the desirability of returning to the gold standard as quickly as possible. Prominent Americans played a leading role in the Dawes Reparations Conference of 1924 and again at the reparations conference in Paris in 1929 under the direction of Owen D. Young. The United States, however, was not a party to either the Dawes or the Young plans for the payment of German reparations, choosing to handle the German indebtedness to the United States on a bilateral basis. Likewise, the United States government was not associated with the Bank for International Settlements set up under the Young Plan, although stock in this institution was acquired by private American banks and Americans have been prominent in its management.

The growing difficulties in meeting Germany's payments under the Young Plan and the dependence of the Allied powers on reparations for meeting their war-debt obligations to the United States led President Hoover to suggest a 1-year moratorium on all intergovernmental debts in June, 1931. In response to an appeal by the Advisory Council of the Young Plan for a decision on the intergovernmental debt situation, a conference was called in Lausanne in which the United States was asked to participate.[6] The United States, however, was still opposed to any discussion which linked the war debt and the reparations problems together, but this government did agree to participate in a financial conference to consider "methods to stabilize world commodity prices." [7] The issue was decided by calling a conference at Lausanne to consider the reparations problem (without the United States) and another con-

[5] See Dean E. Traynor, *International Monetary and Financial Conferences in the Interwar Period*, Catholic University Press, Washington, D.C., 1949, pp. 49, 70.

[6] *Ibid.*, pp. 91–92.

[7] Department of State, Press Release, June 4, 1932; see also Traynor, *op. cit.*, p. 92.

ference to deal with other economic and financial questions at a later date. The Lausanne Conference quite expectedly failed to solve the reparations problem, but it did make preparations for the London Monetary and Economic Conference which was to follow. The author will not attempt a comprehensive discussion of the work of the London Economic Conference held in the summer of 1933.[8] Rather we shall be concerned with certain important American policies revealed during this Conference.

The decision to convoke the London Economic Conference on June 12, 1933, was made in April, 1933, in the course of a series of bilateral consultations to which President Roosevelt had invited important foreign officials, including the prime ministers of Britain, France, and Canada.[9] The dominant economic interest of the United States government at this time lay in monetary measures for raising prices. The dollar had been divorced from its fixed relationship to gold and, on April 20, 1933, the Thomas inflation amendment, giving broad monetary powers to the President, was introduced in Congress. The President did not want to enter into any international agreements which would limit his powers to employ monetary measures for increasing prices. The primary purpose of the forthcoming conference from the American point of view is revealed in the following portion of the joint Roosevelt-MacDonald statement made public at the time of the Washington consultations: [10]

> The necessity for an increase in the general level of commodity prices was recognized as primary and fundamental. To this end simultaneous action needs to be taken both in the economic and in the monetary field. Commercial policies have to be set to a new orientation. There should be constructive effort to moderate the network of restrictions of all sorts by which commerce is at present hampered, such as excessive tariffs, quotas, exchange restrictions, etc. Central banks should by concerted action provide an adequate expansion of credit and every means should be used to get the credit thus created into circulation. Enterprise must be stimulated by creating conditions favorable to business recovery, and governments can contribute by the development of appropriate programs of capital expenditure. . . .
>
> The ultimate re-establishment of equilibrium in the international exchange should also be contemplated. We must, when circumstances permit, re-establish an international monetary standard which will operate successfully without depressing prices and avoid the repetition of the mistakes which have produced such disastrous results in the past. In this connection, the ques-

[8] For a discussion of the London Economic Conference, see Traynor, *op. cit.*, Chap. IV; see also Leo Pasvolsky, *Current Monetary Issues*, The Brookings Institution, Washington, D.C., 1933, Chaps. IV, V, and the Appendix.

[9] For a discussion of these consultations, see Pasvolsky, *op. cit.*, pp. 55–60.

[10] *Ibid.*, p. 57.

tion of silver, which is of such importance in trade with the Orient, was discussed, and proposals were tentatively suggested for the improvement of its status.

Although currency stabilization was to be a subject of the Conference, it was clear the United States government was not ready to reestablish a fixed gold parity for the dollar. What appeared not to have been clear, however, was whether or not the President would agree to a temporary truce on exchange rates or to any form of international consultation with respect to exchange rates which would in any way limit unilateral action by the United States in the exchange field. It was this uncertainty regarding the President's attitude which brought about the fiasco in which the President repudiated the position of his own representatives.[11] Just exactly what the United States government expected in the way of concrete accomplishments of the Conference is difficult to determine. It did want an international agreement for raising the price of silver. This agreement was achieved largely because this country was willing to bear the cost of such an operation. In fact, the international silver agreement turned out to be the only concrete accomplishment of the Conference. It is also evident that the United States wanted to see other countries adopt the same monetary and credit expansionist and deficit financing policies which the New Deal itself was embarking upon. The American delegation thus proposed a program of continuing consultation for the achievement of parallel monetary and fiscal policies among nations.[12] Secretary Hull had a personal interest in the reduction of tariffs and other trade barriers, but since the submission of his reciprocal tariff program to the Congress had been delayed until the following year, the American delegation had nothing concrete to offer. Hull, who was a sincere believer in economic cooperation through trade negotiations, expressed his own views regarding the foreign economic policy of the New Deal administration in the following quotation from his *Memoirs:* [13]

There were some signs of approaching trouble in the fact that the new agencies, National Recovery Administration and Agricultural Adjustment

[11] The unfortunate outcome of the London Conference was due in part to the action of the President in sending Raymond Moley to the Conference as his personal emissary. Moley operated largely without consulting Secretary of State Hull, who was chief of the American delegation. Moley was largely responsible for the acceptance by the American delegation of the joint declaration on monetary policy which was rejected by President Roosevelt in his message to the Conference of July 3, 1933. See Cordell Hull, *The Memoirs of Cordell Hull,* Macmillan, New York, 1948, Vol. I, pp. 260*ff*.

[12] See "Draft Resolution on Credit and Prices," proposed by the United States delegation, Pasvolsky, *op. cit.*, Appendix C.

[13] Hull, *op. cit.*, p. 248.

Administration, were coming into being with their new remedies for recovery. Basically they believed in cutting the United States off from the rest of the economic world, which they regarded as of little importance. They wanted to concentrate on lifting prices and restoring business in this country by purely domestic measures. As prices rose they felt the need for import embargoes and higher tariffs to keep out imports from abroad which would interfere with the increasing price scale.

In sharp contrast to the American position, the gold-bloc countries of France, Belgium, the Netherlands and Switzerland sought an agreement for the return to the gold standard at fixed parities, together with some machinery for cooperation among central banks and treasuries for dealing with speculative movements in the foreign-exchange markets. Moreover, these countries rejected the monetary and fiscal measures advocated by the American delegation as unsound financial practices. The British represented a somewhat compromising position which favored easy credit conditions but not deficit spending. On the issue of exchange-rate stabilization, the British believed that, while a return to fixed gold parities by countries not on the gold standard should be delayed until there had been a reflation of commodity prices, they nevertheless advocated a temporary truce on further exchange rate adjustments during the period of the Conference, and the establishment of machinery for the prevention of violent and unpredictable exchange rate fluctuations. It was along the lines of the British position on the gold standard and exchange rates that a draft declaration was prepared by the Conference and to which the American delegation under the influence of Raymond Moley agreed.[14] This declaration implied an agreement to limit, at least temporarily, fluctuations in the foreign-exchange value of the dollar. When this text was submitted to President Roosevelt on June 30, 1933, it was rejected for reasons stated in his message to the Conference on July 3.[15] The President stated that he could not agree to even a temporary fixing of the dollar exchange rate until the more fundamental problems of commodity prices and economic prosperity had been solved. He urged the Conference to concentrate on curing the more fundamental economic ills, which are more important than the exchange ratios of the world's currencies.

Following President Roosevelt's message many of the delegations urged immediate adjournment, since they were convinced that without some agreement on exchange stability little or nothing could be accomplished. Only through the vigorous efforts of Secretary Hull was the move for immediate disbandment defeated, and the Conference dragged

14 For the text of this agreement, see Pasvolsky, *op. cit.*, pp. 81–82.
15 For text of President's message, see *ibid.*, pp. 83–84.

on until it adjourned on July 27, 1933. Except for the agreement on silver,[16] the accomplishments of the Conference were limited to the adoption of reports by the various subcommittees covering monetary standards, commercial policy, central-banking cooperation, foreign-exchange practices, and a number of other economic matters.

It has frequently been said that the London Conference was held a year too soon, since by the middle of 1934 the interest of the United States had shifted from one of favoring a fluctuating rate for the dollar to one of exchange stability. On the other hand, 1933 was a critical year in the history of world affairs, and a conference in 1934 might have been too late to achieve significant results. Hitler had not yet completely solidified his position in Germany and still less so his economic and political position in Central Europe. Undoubtedly the failure of economic cooperation among the Western democratic powers in 1933 worked to Germany's advantage and helped to pave the way for World War II. We may seriously question, however, whether the limited international cooperation which this country would have been prepared to undertake even in 1934 would have had much effect upon the current deterioration of international economic relations and still less upon the political forces leading the world toward war.

The Tripartite Agreement

The most important instance of United States international financial cooperation in the 1930's was the Tripartite Agreement with France and Britain, later joined by Belgium, the Netherlands, and Switzerland.

[16] The resolutions on silver recommended an "agreement be sought between the chief silver-producing countries and countries which are the largest holders or users of silver with a view to mitigating fluctuations in the price of silver," that all nations should "refrain from new legislative measures which would involve further debasement of their silver coinage below a fineness of $800/1000$," and that silver coins should be substituted for notes of smaller denominations. (Pasvolsky, *op. cit.*, Appendix E.) These resolutions fell far short of the United States Senate resolution of May 8, 1933, urging the American delegates to the Congress to "work unceasingly for an international agreement to remonetize silver on a basis of a definite fixed ratio of not to exceed 16 fine ounces of silver to one fine ounce of gold." (G. G. Johnson, *The Treasury and Monetary Policy, 1933–1938*, Harvard University Press, Cambridge, Mass., 1939, p. 171.) Under the leadership of the American delegate, Senator Pittman, a supplementary agreement was announced on July 22, 1933, which included China, India, and Spain as users of silver, and Australia, Canada, Mexico, Peru, and the United States as producers. The users of silver agreed not to dispose of silver, and the five producers agreed to absorb 35 million ounces annually for 4 years. However, the United States, which produced only 24.7 million ounces of silver in 1932, as against 103 million ounces for the other four producing countries, agreed to purchase 24.4 million ounces as against 11.6 million ounces for the other four countries. (Johnson, *op. cit.*, p. 172.)

Although it would be a mistake to overemphasize the concrete accomplishments of the Agreement, which were largely in the field of technical cooperation, this Agreement was in a sense a forerunner of the international monetary institutions and agreements developed during and after World War II. Although the Tripartite Agreement bore little resemblance to the International Monetary Fund, the limited experience which it provided in the foreign-exchange field had educational value for both the executive and legislative branches of the United States government and laid the foundation for the more ambitious plans which began to be formulated as early as 1941.

During the first two and a half years of its existence, the United States Exchange Stabilization Fund's activities were largely confined to providing technical support to the gold-bloc currencies.[17] With the departure of the gold-bloc currencies from a fixed relationship to gold in September, 1936, it became almost impossible for the United States Fund to operate by supporting these currencies and quickly converting them into gold, without serious danger of loss. A similar problem was faced by Britain and the former gold-bloc countries—France, the Netherlands, Switzerland, and Belgium—all but the latter of which had established stabilization funds of their own. The problem which they all had in common was how to stabilize the exchange rates over short periods of time, since in the absence of fixed gold parities private gold-arbitrage operations could not be counted on to maintain rates within a narrow range. This problem was dealt with by an agreement on the part of the members of the Tripartite Pact to sell each other gold in exchange for the seller's own currency at a price to be guaranteed for 24 hours. Thus each member could stabilize the price of each of the other members' currencies in his own market and convert into gold any excess holdings of these currencies at the end of the 24-hour period at the guaranteed prices quoted by the countries whose currencies were tendered. Such cooperation in stabilizing exchange rates for short periods did not involve a genuine mutual support of the currencies of members.[18] Countries did not take risks in supporting currencies since they were purchased under a gold guarantee. Nevertheless, the technical cooperation was valuable since it made possible the maintenance of exchange rates within a narrow range of the announced gold-support price of each country.

[17] The Treasury Department was reluctant to support sterling because of the danger of loss. However in the spring of 1935, some purchases of sterling were made in periods when the pound was quite weak. See A. I. Bloomfield, "The American Exchange Stabilization Fund," *Review of Economic Statistics,* May, 1944, p. 73.

[18] See Bloomfield, *op. cit.,* p. 77.

Each member of the Pact took the initiative in fixing the gold value of his own currency for each 24-hour period, so that there was no mutual determination of exchange rates.[19] Although provision was made for consultation among members, no member was committed to any level of its exchange rate. In the official announcement by Secretary Morgenthau, it was stated that "the Government of the United States must, of course, in its policy towards international monetary relations take into full account the requirements of internal prosperity, as corresponding considerations will be taken into account by the Governments of France and Great Britain. . . ." [20] The announcement, however, recognized that countries have a mutual interest in exchange-rate stability.

The shift in United States policy on the exchange-rate issue from its position at the London Economic Conference of 1933 is clear. It desired exchange stability but appreciated the necessity of exchange-rate adjustments for itself and for other countries when dictated by economic necessity. It favored consultation on exchange-rate matters and hoped to avoid competitive exchange-rate practices. In fact the Treasury threatened to use the power of the executive further to depreciate the dollar as a means of combatting exchange-rate depreciation, and on one occasion this threat was made against a further depreciation of the pound sterling.[21] Had the war not intervened, it is possible that the Tripartite Pact may have developed into a more comprehensive agreement for international monetary cooperation.

Following the outbreak of war in September, 1939, exchange controls were established by all members of the Tripartite Agreement except the United States, and the operations of the stabilization funds in free markets came to an end. Since that time the operations of the American Stabilization Fund have been of an entirely different character. It has been used by the Treasury for various operations such as purchases and sales of gold for dollars and the purchase of foreign exchange, *e.g.* Swiss francs, needed by the government during the war, which could be more conveniently handled by the Fund. Apart from these service functions, the Treasury Department, beginning in 1940, has entered into a number of stabilization agreements with other countries whereby the Stabilization Fund would purchase up to specified amounts of foreign currencies in exchange for dollars. Some of these agreements

[19] The gold value of the United States dollar did not change during the period of the operation of the Tripartite Agreement, although the President was authorized to depreciate the dollar by another 9 per cent from the 1932 parity. The Belgian gold price, however, was fixed by law at a given level.

[20] See Johnson, *op. cit.,* pp. 115–116.

[21] See Bloomfield, *op. cit.,* p. 77.

have called for 100 per cent gold collateral, while others merely require a definite commitment on the part of the foreign country to repurchase with dollars the foreign exchange held by the Fund. Although these agreements did not commit either country to maintain a given exchange rate, provision was made in each of them for consultation on matters affecting exchange rates. Stabilization agreements were entered into with the governments of China, Brazil, Ecuador, Iceland, and Mexico. Special assistance was also rendered by the Fund to Cuba and Liberia. Unlike the arrangements under the Tripartite Pact, the Stabilization Fund does not operate directly in the foreign-exchange market to support foreign currencies. Although technically it sells dollars for foreign exchange tendered by the government of the foreign country, the transaction is in reality a loan on which interest is paid. The foreign currency is carried on the books of the Stabilization Fund as an asset under the heading "due from foreign banks." [22] It was this type of arrangement which became the basis for the proposals for an international stabilization fund which were developed in the Treasury Department in 1942 and which eventually were incorporated into the Bretton Woods Agreements. The postwar operations of the United States Exchange Stabilization Fund and its role in American foreign policy will be taken up in a later chapter.[23]

Conclusion

In this chapter we have reviewed the important instances of United States international financial cooperation in the interwar period and the American attitude toward such cooperation. It is worth noting that the cooperative efforts of the Federal Reserve banks in assisting European countries to stabilize their currencies during the 1920's represented a more substantial contribution than did the actions of the Treasury Department in this field during the 1930's. The monetary radicalism which pervaded the United States in the depression period made international monetary cooperation impossible at the time of the London Economic Conference, and in its almost exclusive concern with in-

[22] Statements of the assets and liabilities of the Exchange Stabilization Fund are published annually in the *Annual Report of the Secretary of the Treasury*.

[23] The first financial aid to China took the form of a stabilization agreement whereby the Treasury undertook to purchase $50 million worth of Chinese yuan in July, 1937. By 1938, $48 million worth of yuan had been purchased, but the entire amount was repurchased by October, 1942. This loan was fully collateralized by gold. In April, 1941, another agreement was entered into whereby the Treasury agreed to purchase $50 million worth of yuan without collateral. This amount was repurchased in April, 1943. (*United States Relations with China*, Department of State, August, 1949, p. 31.)

ternal economic problems the American government exhibited little interest in the economic welfare of the rest of the world. The American government was, however, in favor of vigorous national monetary and fiscal action on the part of all countries in order to achieve a worldwide rise in prices and business activity. The United States was correct in arguing that this was the most important step to be taken, as against the somewhat deflationist position of the gold-bloc countries which held that currency stabilization was the key to the solution of the world's ills. On the other hand, the stabilization of the dollar would not have interfered with American prosperity and would have given other countries an opportunity to establish the parities of their own currencies at levels which were consistent with equilibrium in their balances of payments.

Following the stabilization of the dollar in 1934, the United States sought to promote international currency stability. While the operations of the United States Exchange Stabilization Fund under the Tripartite Agreement involved little more than technical assistance in maintaining short-term rate stability, this experience helped to pave the way for the developments which led to the establishment of the International Monetary Fund.

CHAPTER 6

United States Commercial Policy

IN THIS chapter we shall be concerned with the development of those policies of the United States government which directly affected this country's foreign trade in goods and services during the interwar period. These policies include tariffs, agricultural policies, shipping policies, and cartel policies. Our purpose is not to provide a comprehensive review of United States commercial policy, but rather to present a broad outline of its development as a background for the emerging policies of the present era. As we shall see in later chapters, present American commercial policies and programs do not present a consistent pattern. While they have been influenced by the foreign economic and political conditions and requirements of the present, they are closely linked with the past. For the most part, the commercial policies of the interwar period were developed to meet the needs and interests of the American economy and of the special interests powerful enough to make their demands felt. These policies were a reflection of the prevailing political isolationism, and economic isolationism gave way to internationalism only to the extent that America was convinced that her own economic interests could be better served in the latter direction. Thus, for example, the reversal of America's high-tariff policy came with the realization that exports could be expanded by a reduction in duties on a reciprocal basis and not because of any general appreciation of the relationship of the American balance of payments to the health of the world economy. Although this country is presently negotiating reductions in its tariffs on the basis of the reciprocity provisions of the 1934 law, the administration's motive for tariff reduction lies perhaps less in the desire to gain concessions from foreign countries (since these concessions are frequently nullified by quantitative restrictions necessitated by balance-of-payments disequilibrium) than in the desire to employ a legal means of reducing our own tariffs in order to accomplish broad international-policy objectives. In addition, the operation of the most-favored-nation principle in our reciprocal tariff agreements makes possible an expansion of trade among other countries.

Tariffs

Protective customs duties in America date from our first tariff act of 1789, the preamble of which justified its existence "for the support of the government, for the discharge of the debts of the United States, and the encouragement and protection of manufactures." The arguments for protection so frequently heard today from the underdeveloped countries were never better stated than by Alexander Hamilton in his *Report on Manufactures* in 1791. But powerful vested interests in protection did not develop until after the Napoleonic wars. The controversy between the proponents of high and of low tariffs which began in the 1820's and continued for the next 100 years was of a quite different character than that of today. It concerned whether or not one group of Americans should be taxed for the benefit of giving encouragement and protection to those American industries producing in competition with imported commodities. So long as America's trade represented a small proportion of the world's total, there was no question of the effects of a limitation of United States imports upon her exports. The tariff issue concerned the pattern of the American economy and the distribution of its income. It was not until after World War I that American tariff policy became an important factor in the determination of the world's supply of dollars and hence the demand for her exports. But by that time, the tariff was no longer a sectional issue since it provided protection for both industry and agriculture and few voices were raised in the interest of the consumer. The national argument for tariff was no longer the infant industry one of Hamilton nor the sectional one of the industrial North after the Civil War, but the protection of the American standard of living. During the 1920's, the protectionists not only were successful in promoting the highest duties in our history but had won the support of business, agriculture, labor, and indeed of the Democratic party itself. Only the economists held out against protectionism, but their voices went unheeded until deep depression had set in.

It is not surprising that Woodrow Wilson, who was perhaps America's most outstanding internationalist, was in favor of tariff reduction. One of his first acts as President was to call a special session of Congress in 1913 to consider tariff reduction, the result of which was the passage of the Underwood-Simmons Act of 1913. Had not Wilson's principles of political internationalism been defeated at the polls in 1920, the Underwood Tariff, which in itself represented only a first step in tariff reduction, might have been followed by a movement toward liberal trade policies in the postwar period. The Democratic platform of 1920 contained the following statement on the tariff issue: [1] "We reaffirm the traditional policy of the Democratic Party in favor of a tariff for revenue only and we confirm the policy of basing the tariff revisions upon the intelligent research of a non-partisan commission, rather than upon the demands of selfish interests temporarily held in abeyance."

The Emergency Tariff Act of May, 1921, and the Fordney-McCumber Tariff of the following year were distinguished by the imposition of high duties on agricultural products as well as by duties on the products of a number of industries which feared postwar competition from abroad. The farmers were deluded into thinking that their postwar plight could be remedied by shutting out foreign competition. By 1928, the traditionally low-tariff Democratic party had greatly modified its stand on the tariff issue. While the Democratic platform of that year condemned logrolling, "monopolistic and extortionate" tariff rates, and favored the "restoration of the Wilson conception of a fact-finding Tariff Commission, quasi-judicial and free from Executive domination," it expressed the view that the "actual difference between the cost of production at home and abroad, with adequate safeguard for the wage of the American laborer, must be the extreme measure of every tariff rate." It also affirmed that protective tariffs were necessary for the maintenance of legitimate business and a high standard of wages for American labor.[2]

Few actions of the United States have been more detrimental to the foreign relations of this country than the Hawley-Smoot Tariff of 1930. The President and Congress were well aware of the reactions of foreign countries to the rates imposed by this bill, since communications of protest from 24 nations were received and published while the bill was being debated in the Senate.[3] The bill was an example of pure logrolling. It made no sense whatsoever from a national point of view. Almost none of the rates could be justified in terms of the infant-industries argument or on grounds of national security. Many of the items on which tariffs were imposed or the rates raised were not in direct competition with any American product. For example, the following communication was received from British India: "Please protest vigorously against States proposition of increase in duty on cashews because 1000 per cent increase unjustified whilst United States not producing cashews otherwise cashew industry in British India will be destroyed." [4] Nor could President Hoover

---

[1] Quoted by Asher Isaacs, in *International Trade,* Irwin, Chicago, 1948, p. 225.
[2] *Ibid.,* p. 229.
[3] *Tariff Act of 1929,* Hearings before a Subcommittee of the Committee on Finance, United States Senate, 71st Congress, 1st Session, on H.R. 2667.
[4] Quoted by Isaacs, *op. cit.,* p. 231.

have been in any doubt regarding the attitude of the vast majority of reputable economists regarding the Hawley-Smoot Bill. Over a thousand American economists signed a communication to President Hoover asking him to veto the bill and stating fully their reasons for opposing it. This communication, excerpts from which are reproduced in the Appendix to this chapter, was not just a recital of the principles of laissez-faire economics. It discussed the effects on consumers and exporters, the likelihood of retaliation from abroad, the effects of a general rise in barriers on world trade, and the ability of foreigners to service governmental and private debts, and pointed to "the bitterness which a policy of higher tariffs would inevitably inject into our international relations."

A number of countries quickly retaliated against the new American duties by raising rates on products of American exporters, and in many cases these rates were discriminatory in their application.[5] "The Hawley-Smoot Tariff in the United States was the signal for an outburst of tariff-making activity in other countries, partly at least by way of reprisals. Extensive increases were made almost immediately by Canada, Cuba, Mexico, France, Italy, Spain. During 1931, general tariff increases were announced by India, Peru, Argentina, Brazil, China, Italy, and Lithuania."[6] More serious than the reprisals, however, was the contribution of the 1930 tariff to the breakdown of the world's system of international payments. Statistical studies of the relationship between United States imports and national income show a sharp decline in imports for any given level of income after 1930.[7] Although there were undoubtedly other factors responsible for this shift in the United States income demand for imports, it would be difficult to argue that the high tariffs did not play a significant role.

Perhaps most important of all were the repercussions of the Hawley-Smoot Tariff on the general international economic and political relations of this country. It was viewed abroad as an unjust and unfriendly act of a powerful creditor country and became a symbol of American isolationism and uncooperativeness. Despite the change in the administration's tariff policy after 1933, the memory of this action has hampered the efforts of the government in reaching international agreements for the general reduction of trade barriers. Foreign countries are reluctant to plan their economic destinies in a manner which will make them de-

[5] See Joseph M. Jones, Jr., *Tariff Retaliation: Repercussions of the Hawley-Smoot Bill,* University of Pennsylvania Press, Philadelphia, 1934.

[6] Quoted by Isaacs, *op. cit.,* pp. 234–235, from the *League of Nations World Economic Survey,* 1932–1933. Dr. Isaacs suggests that the British imperial preference system of 1932 may have been in part inspired by the Hawley-Smoot Tariff.

[7] See *Survey of Current Business,* November, 1944, pp. 12–13.

pendent upon a large supply of dollars for fear that the advent of a depression or a new administration will be accompanied by a return to the tariff policies of 1930. Foreign exporters hesitate to build up markets in the United States for fear that they will be destroyed by new tariff barriers. Finally, one needs only to read the propaganda of the Fascists of the 1930's and the Communists of the present era to see how important a political weapon the 1930 tariff has been to the enemies of democracy.

In the Presidential campaign of 1932, the Republican party reaffirmed its belief in high protective tariffs while the Democratic party condemned the Hawley-Smoot Act, "the prohibitive rates of which have resulted in retaliatory action by more than forty countries, created international economic hostilities, destroyed international trade, driven our factories into foreign countries, robbed the American farmer of his foreign markets, and increased the cost of production." [8] The Democrats advocated in its place "a competitive tariff for revenue, with a fact-finding commission free from Executive interference, reciprocal tariff agreements with other nations, and an international economic conference designed to restore international trade and facilitate exchange." [9]

The Roosevelt administration was thus committed to both reciprocal tariff agreements and to participation in an international conference on trade and payments. The London Economic Conference of June, 1933, was dominated by the foreign-exchange issue, and nothing was accomplished in the field of trade barriers. Likewise, the monetary issues caused domestic legislation in the tariff field to be put aside in 1933, and Hearings on the Reciprocal Trade Agreement Amendent to the Tariff Act of 1930 did not begin until March, 1934. This bill did not become law until June 12, 1934. The major provisions of the Reciprocal Trade Agreements Act, which gave the President the power to reduce existing rates up to 50 per cent of the existing level by Executive Agreement, were not without precedent in American tariff history. The principle of tariff bargaining was authorized in a limited form in the McKinley Tariff Act of 1890 and again under the Dingley Act of 1897. The Fordney-McCumber Act of 1922 provided for administrative flexibility to the extent of 50 per cent of the rates upward or downward, and 37 rate changes were actually made in the period from 1922 to 1930, only 5 of which were in the downward direction.[10] Finally, the principle of "unconditional most favored nation treatment" embodied in the 1934 Act was well established, since by 1934 the United States had entered into 47 agreements with other countries pledging unconditional (MFN) treat-

8 Quoted by Isaacs, op. cit., p. 245.   10 Ibid., pp. 226–227.
9 Ibid.

ment.[11] What the Reciprocal Tariff Act represented was a combination of a number of established principles into one Act designed specifically to permit reciprocal tariff bargaining and backed by an administration with a will actively to promote such a program.

The ruling policy represented by the 1934 Act was that exports could be expanded by getting foreign duties reduced and that in order to obtain a reduction in foreign duties the United States would have to make some "concessions" on her own duties. Hence the tariff bargaining became something of a game in which we sought to obtain as many concessions as possible and give as few as possible in return. Since any concession made to one country was granted to the imports of that commodity from all others, an effort was made to limit concessions to the "chief supplier" of an imported commodity so as to preserve our bargaining power. This tended to limit the number of tariff reductions where more than one country was an important supplier of the commodity. Sometimes the problem was dealt with by means of a reclassification of the imported commodity which would permit the concession to apply to the particular grade or variation of the product produced by the country with whom negotiations were carried on. Frequently, only a small concession was made on the imported commodity so that further concessions could be made in bargaining with other suppliers. The truth of the matter was that it was primarily the concessions which we gave that expanded our exports, since in a world short of dollars exports depended in large measure upon the dollars which this country made available. This is much more obvious today, since nearly all countries retain restrictions on dollar imports and there is greater recognition of the desirability of reducing tariffs regardless of what concessions may be obtained in return. The most desirable policy from both the domestic and the international points of view would be to supplement reciprocal tariff reductions with unilateral reductions.

From the date of the passage of the bill to January 1, 1940, agreements were reached with 21 countries, accounting for 60 per cent of United States trade. Concessions were granted on 1,012 tariff rates, and we had received concessions on 1,600 tariff rates. There is no satisfactory method of measuring the effective reduction in import duties because of the continuing shift in the composition of trade. The ad valorem rate on dutiable imports into the United States declined from an average of around 50 per cent in the period June, 1930, to June, 1934, to about 37 per cent in 1939. It is impossible to tell just what effect the reciprocal-trade-agreements program had upon United States exports and still less

11 *Ibid.*, p. 256.

upon the trade balance.[12] Imports from agreement countries increased 21.6 per cent by value from 1934–1935 to 1938–1939 as compared with only 12.5 per cent for imports from other countries. United States exports to trade-agreement countries increased 62.8 per cent over the same period as compared with an increase of only 31.7 per cent to other countries.[13] These over-all results may overstate the significance of the tariff cuts since there may have been other more important factors which influenced the relative change in the sources of imports and the destination of exports. Although there is fairly conclusive evidence that imports and exports of particular commodities were affected by tariff cuts here and abroad, the total balance of payments of the United States was influenced by a number of complex factors unrelated to the level of duties.

The typical bilateral tariff agreement contains a number of provisions in addition to those pertaining to the schedules of tariffs on which concessions were made. These provisions deal with customs formalities, discriminatory treatment of foreign products and business enterprises, quotas, exchange controls, and other commercial policy matters. The principal purpose of including these provisions in the tariff agreements is to prevent countries from nullifying the tariff concessions through other types of controls. Some of these provisions have been included in our commercial treaties for many years. For example, the principle of national treatment, the unconditional most-favored-nation principle, and the general principle of nondiscrimination against American products and business enterprise have been traditional American commercial policies. Most of these commercial policies affecting trade were embodied in the American proposals for an International Trade Organization and later were, with certain modifications, embodied in the Havana Charter of the International Trade Organization and in the General Agreement on Tariffs and Trade.

In concluding this section on American tariff policy in the interwar period, it should be pointed out that the reciprocal tariff program of the 1930's by no means represented a conversion to the principles of free trade. The major emphasis was on the expansion of United States exports while limiting concessions on United States tariff rates in so far as possible to items which did not compete with domestic products.[14] In certain cases, tariff quotas were employed to limit the volume of imports

[12] For an analysis of this question, see Grace Beckett, *The Reciprocal Trade Agreements Program*, Columbia University Press, New York, 1941, Chap. VI.

[13] Report of Senate Committee on Finance, on House Joint Resolution 407, Mar. 8, 1940, Senate Report 1297, 76th Congress, 3d Session.

[14] See Margaret S. Gordon, *Barriers to World Trade*, Macmillan, New York, 1941, p. 396.

which were permitted to come in under the lower rates.[15] Moreover, the 1930 tariff rates were so high that even the full 50 per cent reduction permitted under the law still provided a large measure of protection for many commodities. Strong opposition to the trade agreements program and the necessity of renewing the Act every 3 years led the administration to follow a cautious policy in the reduction of tariffs on commodities where a domestic industry would be seriously affected. At the Congressional hearings on the bills for renewal of the Act, the administration leaders sought to justify the existence of the Act by demonstrating that the United States had gained as much or more in exports as it had "conceded" in permitting larger imports. No doubt the political necessity of this type of justification influenced those government officials responsible for conducting the negotiations. One thing is clear, however: the 1934 Act represented a significant turning point in American tariff history. A perusal of the Congressional debates on the renewal of the Act in recent years reveals that the principle of reciprocal tariff agreements has been accepted by both political parties, although there is still considerable difference as to its application.[16] We must now look forward to a more advanced step in our tariff policy, namely, that of encouraging imports for their own sake and as a means of promoting a better balance of world trade.

Other Interferences with Trade

Although the tariff has been the principal instrument of American protection, other measures have been employed directly or indirectly to achieve the same result. When a country adopts protection as a national policy, those responsible for administering its import regulations become conditioned to look upon imports as something less than desirable and, at the very least, feel no particular compunction to facilitate them. American customs officials probably have a better record on this score than those of most countries, but there is considerable evidence that cumbersome customs formalities, uncertainties, and delays (particularly in valuation) have provided a serious barrier to imports.[17] In addition to the regular tariff duties imposed by Congress, there have been a number of

[15] Tariff quotas were employed with respect to several agricultural products in the United States–Canadian trade agreements of 1935 and 1938. A tariff quota on petroleum was included in the agreement with Venezuela in 1939.

[16] The postwar developments in the reciprocal-trade-agreements program will be taken up in a later chapter.

[17] See Percy Bidwell, The Invisible Tariff, Council on Foreign Relations, New York, 1939, Chap. II.

laws which seek to protect American producers against "unfair" competition on the part of foreign sellers. Legislation requiring the imposition of countervailing duties on foreign goods, the production or sale of which has been subsidized, has existed since 1890. The Anti-Dumping Act of 1921 authorizes the Treasury Department to impose special antidumping duties whenever the exporters' sales price is less than the foreign market value. Except in the case of imports from Germany (where countervailing duties were applied against all imports of German origin in 1939), countervailing and antidumping duties have been employed in a relatively small number of cases.[18]

Buying foreign commodities in competition with American products has frequently been regarded as unpatriotic, and during the 1930's the "Buy American" campaign had widespread support in Federal, state, and local governments as well as the business community generally. A Federal Act of March, 1933, requires the American government to buy American products in preference to foreign goods, and many states have enacted laws requiring state purchasing agencies to purchase commodities within state borders whenever possible.[19] American customs regulations require marks of origin to be stamped on imported articles, and the legislative history of our customs laws clearly reveals that Congress intended the marks-of-origin requirements to discourage imports on the theory that American consumers prefer to buy American products.[20]

Another serious barrier to imports is involved in laws providing for control of the importation of animals and animal products for the purpose of preventing the spread of animal diseases. The Tariff Act of 1930 requires the complete exclusion of livestock and of fresh or frozen meat products from any country in which the Secretary of Agriculture finds that foot-and-mouth disease exists. The passage of this Act excluded the importation of fresh meat from most of South America, including Argentina, all of Africa, and most of Europe and Asia. Since the Department of Agriculture already had ample authority to exclude meat for sanitary reasons coming from any country or part of a country where the disease existed, "there can be no other explanation of the new legislation except that Congress designed it to afford economic protection to the American livestock industry." [21] The motive of protectionism has also been found

18 In April, 1939, only 13 findings of dumping were in effect and about 10 cases of countervailing duties. See Bidwell, *op. cit.,* pp. 95, 101.

19 By administrative order, United States government agencies may purchase foreign goods where comparable United States commodities are more than 25 per cent higher in price.

20 Bidwell, *op. cit.,* pp. 69*ff.*

21 *Ibid.,* p. 213.

in the administration of American laws with respect to the importation of foreign plants.[22]

Although opposition to the use of quotas for protectionist purposes is an important element in American commercial policy, this country has used quotas on a number of occasions, particularly in the field of agricultural imports. Quotas were applied to imports of petroleum, alcoholic beverages, lumber and timber products for a brief period under the National Recovery Act codes, and the original Agricultural Adjustment Act provided for quotas on potatoes and Cuban tobacco. Sugar quotas were imposed under the Jones-Costigan Act of May, 1934, while the Philippine Independence Act of March, 1934, provided for quotas on cordage from the Philippines.

The policy of maintaining American farm prices at or near parity resulted in the maintenance of domestic prices which have at times been higher than world prices. Unless imports from abroad were limited, such imports would under these circumstances increase the burden of the Department of Agriculture in supporting domestic prices at parity levels. Thus, for example, quotas were imposed on imports of wheat and wheat flour in 1941 when it became profitable at prevailing domestic prices to import Canadian wheat even after payment of the tariff.[23] The maintenance of artificial prices in the domestic market also interfered with exports when American prices of agricultural exports were above world prices. In spite of the existence of laws to counteract dumping by foreigners in American markets, the United States government began subsidizing wheat and wheat-flour exports in 1938 and cotton exports the following year.[24]

We shall consider America's postwar agricultural policies in relation to foreign trade in a later chapter. Meanwhile, it is worth pointing out that this is one area in which America's foreign economic policy has not discarded the cloak of economic isolationism which it inherited from the interwar period.

Aids to American Business Operating Abroad

The period from the Spanish-American War at the end of the nineteenth century to the inauguration of President Roosevelt's Good Neighbor Policy can properly be characterized as the era of American economic imperialism. American diplomacy vigorously protected the commercial

[22] *Ibid.*, pp. 239*ff.*

[23] See M. S. Gordon, "International Aspects of American Agricultural Policy," *American Economic Review,* September, 1946, p. 600.

[24] *Ibid.*, p. 602.

and investment interests of Americans abroad even to the point of supporting friendly governments against revolutionists by the use of American military forces and collecting American debts by the institution of customs receiverships.[25] The American government actively supported the establishment of American enterprise abroad through its insistence upon the Open Door Policy in China, Latin America, and in colonies and mandated territories of other nations. The State Department was especially active in helping American oil interests in securing concessions in Colombia, Iraq, and the Dutch East Indies.[26] In the case of mineral rights, the United States government was undoubtedly motivated by the desire of seeing foreign oil reserves in American hands, since during the early 1920's it was believed that indigenous American oil reserves would be exhausted within a few years. This interest subsided considerably with the discovery of the East Texas oil field and the development of a domestic petroleum surplus during the 1930's.

The American attitude toward the rights of her citizens in foreign countries is indicated by the statement of President Coolidge that "the person and property of a citizen are a part of the general domain of the nation, even when abroad." America's imperialistic actions in the 1920's, particularly as regards her weaker neighbors to the south, have resulted in deep-seated enmities from which we are only now beginning to recover. There is of course nothing improper in a policy which seeks to protect American citizens against expropriation without adequate compensation, confiscatory taxation, or discriminatory action of various kinds. The difficulty lies in the methods by which the United States government seeks to enforce these principles. The protection of American firms operating in other sovereign states must be secured through treaties which set up standards of fair treatment for foreign enterprises and not by the exercise or threat of force. The indifference of the American government toward foreign loans and investments during the 1930's was nearly as harmful to our international relations as the imperialistic policies of the first two decades of this century. Active promotion of American private and governmental investments abroad and the protection of those interests are essential to America's economic and political welfare.

Along with diplomatic protection and encouragement of American enterprise abroad went an expansion of government services rendered

[25] See B. H. Williams, *Economic Foreign Policy of the United States*, McGraw-Hill, New York, 1929, Chaps. VIII–IX. American forces have been sent to Nicaragua, Haiti, the Dominican Republic, and Cuba in protection of American interests.

[26] See *American Petroleum Interests in Foreign Countries*, Hearings before Special Committee Investigating Petroleum Resources, United States Senate, 79th Congress, 1st Session, June 27 and 28, 1945; see also Raymond F. Mikesell and Hollis B. Chenery, *Arabian Oil*, University of North Carolina Press, Chapel Hill, N.C., 1949, pp. 2–13.

largely by the Department of Commerce through its representatives at home and abroad.[27] The Department's Bureau of Foreign and Domestic Commerce prepares trade lists coverings potential commercial contacts and trade leads in foreign countries, surveys of markets and business conditions in foreign countries, and assists American business people in various ways through regional offices at home and consular offices abroad. Although information helpful to importers is provided, the major effort has been in the export-promotion field. Even at the present time when it is the official policy of the Department of Commerce to encourage imports, the author has been told by Department of Commerce field representatives that they would not dare actively to promote imports in competition with American goods in the same way that they promote exports, for fear of arousing the wrath of the business community.

The Export-Import Bank

A special form of governmental assistance to American traders was provided in 1934 by the creation by executive order of the Export-Import Bank of Washington.[28] During the early years of its existence, the operations of the Bank were largely confined to providing credits to exporters. These credits took three forms: (1) short-term credits (90 days) for financing the exportation of agricultural commodities, principally tobacco and cotton; (2) intermediate credits to exporters of industrial equipment; and (3) loans to Americans holding blocked foreign currencies. Operations were on a limited scale, and during the first three years of its existence authorizations totaled only $113 million, only a part of which was disbursed.[29] Only a few loans by the Bank have been made to

[27] Until 1939, commercial attachés in American foreign missions were employed by and reported to the Department of Commerce. They are now a part of the State Department's Foreign Service.

[28] The first Export-Import Bank was created in February, 1934, to finance trade with Russia. The Bank was created under the authority of the National Industrial Recovery Act of June 16, 1933, and the Reconstruction Finance Corporation Act of January 22, 1932. In March, 1934, a second Export-Import Bank was created to finance trade with other countries. No loans for the financing of Russo-American trade were made because of the dispute over the debt settlement, and the second Bank was merged with the first Bank. On January 31, 1935, the Export-Import Bank was specifically authorized by Congress and its existence extended to June 16, 1937. See Eleanor L. Dulles, "The Export-Import Bank of Washington," *Department of State Bulletin,* Dec. 3, 1944; see also Gardner Patterson, "The Export-Import Bank," *Quarterly Journal of Economics,* November, 1943, pp. 65–90.

[29] When Congress extended the life of the Bank for an additional 2 years in 1939, it limited its total obligations to $100 million. Later in 1940, the limit on total obligations was raised to $700 million.

finance imports, although loans have been made to assist in the development of foreign exports in which the United States has had a special interest. Although a few development loans were made in the 1930's, during and following the war the major emphasis of the Bank has been in this field. We shall review these operations in a later chapter.

Antitrust and Cartel Policy

Although American industrial development has been characterized by a concentration of economic power and a large element of monopolistic control, the policy of the United States government with respect to both privately sponsored and governmental monopolies in the industrial field is unique among the major trading countries of the world. Whereas most governments have in the past few decades encouraged or actively sponsored associations for the control of prices, output, and conditions of sale, the United States has, except possibly for the brief period of the National Industrial Recovery Act (1933 to 1935), maintained a policy of keeping industry as competitive as possible. While the judicial construction of the Sherman Antitrust Act has prevented action to make markets competitive in the economic sense, i.e., the breaking up of large industrial units controlling a sufficient proportion of total output to dominate the market, the government has to a large degree been successful in outlawing open agreements governing prices and output among sellers. In addition to outlawing restrictive agreements, the government has been successful in prosecuting a number of so-called unfair competitive practices which have been employed for purposes of securing monopolistic control of an industry. Thus "the rule of reason" of the courts has tolerated bigness, provided that large firms do not employ cutthroat or unreasonable measures designed to eliminate competition.

The policies of foreign governments with respect to business combinations present a sharp contrast to those of the United States. While in England the common law dealt severely with restraints of trade, the trend of legislation and court decisions since the latter part of the nineteenth century has been in the direction of weakening rather than implementing the common law in regard to restraints of trade.[30] During the 1920's, British industry with the encouragement of government turned more and more to "self-government." Until 1932, however, the British consumer was afforded a large measure of protection by the policy of free trade, except where the free movement of goods was threatened by international cartel agreements. With the introduction of tariffs on a

[30] See Fainsod and Gordon, *Government and the American Economy*, Norton, New York, 1941, pp. 558–561.

wide scale and the loss of markets engendered by the depression, the British government began actively to foster cartelization, including minimum prices and output control. Compulsory cartelization occurred in coal mining, iron and steel, shipbuilding, textile, and other industries,[31] while voluntary coordination through trade associations occurred in most of the other industries. The reasoning behind the British Government's policy was that competition is wasteful, involves duplication and inefficiency, while cartelization will permit "rationalization" through amalgamations and concentration of output in the most efficient plants. Naturally this appealed to businessmen in a period of declining demand since profits could be sustained through the avoidance of competition for dwindling markets. The Labor party, on the other hand, saw in price and output control a means of maintaining wages as a step toward governmental control and eventual socialization of industry. Moreover, socialist ideology is full of condemnation of competition as being wasteful and inefficient. Free competition has few friends in the country which produced Adam Smith and David Ricardo!

On the European continent there was not even the common-law tradition of Britain and America against business combinations. Nor have the teachings of the British classical school been so widely accepted by Continental economists. There was of course a strong laissez-faire movement in France following the French Revolution, but this had largely broken down by the end of the nineteenth century, and cartelization became widespread in the interwar period. After 1935, the French government actively promoted and participated in cartels which governed prices and output in a large number of industries.[32]

But it was in Germany that the cartel had its greatest development and employment as an instrument of national policy. Cartelization provided a means whereby the government could quickly mobilize industry in time of war, and participation in international cartels provided an opportunity for realizing certain international economic objectives necessary for the aggrandizement of the German state. This association between cartels and German political policy has been the most important motivating force behind America's present anticartel policy.[33]

Whereas today America's policy toward international cartels is to seek to eliminate them by international agreement (and in the case of Ger-

---

[31] *Ibid.*, pp. 560–561.

[32] *Ibid.*, pp. 561–563.

[33] Serious doubts have been expressed regarding the degree to which American company participation in German cartels weakened the military potential of the United States and provided Germany with information of military value. See C. R. Whittlesey, *National Interest and International Cartels*, Macmillan, New York, 1946.

many to weaken them by virtue of our military authority),[34] following
World War I, American policy was to permit American firms to emulate
European cartels as a means of equalizing bargaining power. Shortly
after the Federal Trade Commission was established (the Commissioners
took office in March, 1915), a study of the trade practices of foreign
countries was inaugurated and a two-volume report was presented to
Congress on June 30, 1916, entitled "Cooperation in American Export
Trade." [35] This Report, which became the basis for the Webb-Pomerene
Act of 1918, recommended that American exporters be permitted to
cooperate so as to be able to compete on more equal terms with foreign
competitors. The Report pointed to the development of international
combination abroad with monopolistic and monopsonistic powers and
advanced the position that while Congress sought to promote competition
at home it did not intend to prevent "the use in export trade of methods
of organization which do not operate to the prejudice of the American
public, which are lawful in the countries where the trade is to be carried on, and which are necessary if greater equality of opportunity is
to be afforded Americans in meeting foreign competition." [36] The Webb-
Pomerene Act of 1918 stated that the Sherman Act was not to apply to
associations "entered into for the sole purpose of engaging in export
trade . . . provided such association, agreement, or act is not in restraint
of trade within the United States, and is not in restraint of the export
trade within the United States, and is not in restraint of the export trade
of any domestic competitor of such association. . . ." [37]

This Act, which had the endorsement of the Wilson administration as
well as that of the leading American business organizations, is an example
of the lack of economic leadership and sense of international responsibility which characterized American international relations during the interwar period. In spite of America's own antitrust policy and antidumping
laws, she saw nothing wrong in licensing combinations of her own exporters to engage in practices abroad which were antithetical to her own
domestic policies. Although American export associations were not specifically permitted to participate in international cartels, a number of
associations have become members of international groups engaged in

[34] Recently, the cartel issue has been an important obstacle in the negotiations on the
Schuman plan for the pooling of Western European coal and steel output. The United
States has supported the French against Western Germany in favoring anticartel pro-
visions in the proposal. "Pool's Fate Hinges on Ruhr Cartels," *The New York Times,*
Feb. 5, 1951.

[35] See *Export Prices and Export Cartels,* Monograph 6, Temporary National Economic
Committee, 1941, pp. 113–118.

[36] *Ibid.,* p. 117.

[37] *Ibid.,* p. 120.

dividing up markets and fixing prices.[38] In 1939 there were 179 international cartels, and 109 of these included United States firms in their membership.[39] It was not until 1939 that the Department of Justice began to take action against American participation in international cartels. Suits against cartels in petroleum, synthetic rubber, plastics, explosives, aircraft accessories, optical instruments, and a number of other fields were instituted largely because the Department of Justice believed that these combinations were interfering with America's defense effort.

Most of the discussions of the merits and demerits of the Webb-Pomerene law have been concerned with the determination of whether or not the activities of the export association have raised prices to domestic consumers or restrained trade in the domestic markets.[40] Although there is evidence that consumers in the domestic market have been adversely affected by the actions of certain export associations, the over-all result is difficult to measure. Export associations on the average accounted for about 7 per cent of United States exports during the interwar period, and only 44 associations were operating in 1940. Irrespective of their efforts on domestic trade, the author believes that serious considerations ought to be given to the following conclusions of some members of the American Economic Association's Committee on the Webb-Pomerene Report: [41]

> We, therefore, recommend the repeal of the Webb-Pomerene Law on the general grounds that present American foreign policy calls for the removal of restraints in international trade rather than their elaboration in the form of defensive combinations in restraint of American export trade. The removal of such combinations should go along with the reduction of import duties as an earnest demonstration of the sincerity of American proposals with regard to freeing international trade. But, in addition, necessity for restraint of competition among importers is not proven. Finally, when repealed the act would remove a means of restraining trade within this country.

•

Maritime Policy

There can be little doubt that the relative comparative advantage of United States shipping is weak, both as a builder and operator of

[38] See "The Webb-Pomerene Law—A Consensus Report," *American Economic Review,* December, 1947, p. 852.

[39] Isaacs, *op. cit.,* p. 702.

[40] See *Export Prices and Export Cartels,* Monograph 6, Temporary National Economic Committee, 1941, pp. 91–93.

[41] "The Webb-Pomerene Law—A Consensus Report," *American Economic Review,* December, 1947, p. 863. Other members of the Committee took the position that the Webb-Pomerene law might be retained but amended so as to avoid certain undesirable

ships, and that from an economic standpoint we ought to depend upon the shipping services of other countries. Wages in the United States maritime industry are high relative to those abroad, without the offsetting advantages of greater comparative efficiency. The reasons advanced for the American policy of maintaining a substantial merchant marine through governmental subvention are clearly stated in the preamble of the Merchant Marine Act of 1920: "That it is necessary for the national defense and for the proper growth of its foreign and domestic commerce that the United States shall have a merchant marine . . . to carry the greater portion of its commerce and serve as a naval or military auxiliary in time of war or national emergency. . . ."

The national-defense argument is understandable for a country which expects either to remain neutral in a war or is making its defense preparations on a unilateral basis. This argument has little validity, however, for a nation which organizes its defense in cooperation with a number of closely allied powers. The second argument which relates a large merchant marine to the proper growth of foreign commerce has traditionally been important in American foreign policy. For example, in 1903 President Theodore Roosevelt, an ardent champion of a strong merchant marine, stated that: "It is as absurd for the United States to depend upon foreign ships to distribute its products as it would be for a department store to depend upon wagons of a competing house to deliver its goods." [42] Mr. Roosevelt might have argued with equal cogency that every manufacturer ought to operate his own railroad!

The government has implemented its merchant-marine policy by the exclusion of foreign ships from coastwise shipping, including that between the United States and its territories, and by a variety of subventions. Governmental subsidization of American shipping was, however, exceedingly niggardly and its merchant-marine policy poorly implemented until the passage of the Merchant Marine Act of 1936. An Act of 1920 resulted in sales of government ships built during the war at low cost to American shippers; the Merchant Marine Act of 1928 provided loan funds at low interest rates; and mail subsidies had been paid to shipowners since the passage of the Ocean Mail Act of 1891. The Act of 1936 provided for substantial construction and operating subsidies on a considerably larger scale than before.[43] Moreover, the new Maritime Commission in 1940

---

practices such as quota restrictions on supplies offered to the association for export marketing, p. 860).

[42] Isaacs, *op. cit.*, p. 713.

[43] Mail subsidies under the Act of 1928 amounted to $104 million as of June 30, 1934. See Ralph C. Dewey, "The Merchant Marine Act of 1936," *American Economic Review*, June, 1937, p. 241. Between July 1, 1937, and Oct. 31, 1939, $15 million in operating subsidies and $36 million in construction subsidies were paid out.

announced a goal of 500 new ships to be built by 1950. This goal was of course stepped up rapidly during the war, and by the end of the war the United States had a merchant fleet of 50 million tons, five times the size of the prewar fleet.

During the interwar period the bulk of American exports and imports and tourists were carried on foreign ships. By 1939, less than 25 per cent of United States exports and imports were carried in American vessels and more than 80 per cent of the fare payments of American overseas travelers in the years of high tourist traffic were paid to foreign ship-owners.[44] The United States net shipping account showed an average annual deficit of $76 million over the period from 1922 to 1939. Although this deficit was not large in the aggregate, payments to certain countries such as Britain represented an important source of dollar income. During and immediately following World War II, the United States had a large surplus on transportation account, but by 1950 this account began to show a small deficit as a result of the rebuilding of foreign shipping. Whether or not shipping will again provide a significant source of dollars for other countries will depend upon America's future maritime policy.

Conclusion

Until the world-wide depression of the 1930's, the tariff issue in the United States was largely a matter of conflicting interests between groups desiring protection for their domestic markets and groups desiring cheaper imports. The Reciprocal Tariff Act of 1934 recognized the relationship between United States import duties and foreign barriers to American exports. Not until after World War II and the widespread recognition of the dollar shortage was there a full realization of the relationship between the volume of dollars made available through United States imports and total exports. This realization has not yet resulted in a change in America's tariff law, but it has been reflected in administration policies. In spite of some liberalization in United States tariff policy after 1933, America's commercial policies during the interwar period were highly protectionist and there was little recognition of the over-all economic advantages to the United States of free trade or of the relationship of United States commercial policies to the economic welfare and political stability of the rest of the world.

[44] *The United States in the World Economy*, p. 73.

Appendix

Excerpts from the Statement Signed by 1,028 American Economists on the Hawley-Smoot Tariff Bill, May 5, 1930 [45]

We are convinced that increased restrictive duties would be a mistake. They would operate, in general, to increase the prices which domestic consumers would have to pay. By raising prices they would encourage concerns with higher costs to undertake production, thus compelling the consumer to subsidize waste and inefficiency in industry.

At the same time they would force him to pay higher rates of profit to established firms which enjoyed lower production costs. A higher level of duties, such as is contemplated by the Smoot-Hawley bill, would therefore raise the cost of living and injure the great majority of our citizens.

. . . .

There are already many evidences that such action would inevitably provoke other countries to pay us back in kind by levying retaliatory duties against our goods. There are few more ironical spectacles than that of the American Government as it seeks, on the one hand, to promote exports through the activity of the Bureau of Foreign and Domestic Commerce, while, on the other hand, by increasing tariffs it makes exportation even more difficult.

. . . .

Many of our citizens have invested their money in foreign enterprises. The Department of Commerce has estimated that such investments, entirely aside from the war debts, amount to between $12,555,000,000 and $14,555,000,000 on January 1, 1929. These investors, too, would suffer if restrictive duties were to be increased, since such action would make it still more difficult for their foreign debtors to pay them the interest due them.

. . . .

Finally, we would urge our government to consider the bitterness which a policy of higher tariffs would inevitably inject into our international relations. The United States was ably represented at the world economic conference which was held under the auspices of the League of Nations in 1927. This conference adopted a resolution announcing that "the time has come to put an end to the increase in tariffs and to move in the opposite direction."

. . . .

The originators and first signers were Profs. Paul Douglas, Irving Fisher, Frank Graham, E. M. Patterson, Henry R. Seager, Frank W. Taussig, and Clair Wilcox. The subsequent signatures came from 46 states and 179 colleges.

[45] *The New York Times,* May 5, 1930.

Part Two

American International Economic Policies after 1939

CHAPTER 7

America's International Economic Policies to the End of World War II

FROM NEUTRALITY TO LEND-LEASE

THE PERIOD from 1933 to 1937 has been described[1] by James P. Warburg as the era of "New Deal Nationalism." It was a period in which the American government accepted the responsibility for the economic welfare of its people (as opposed to the essentially laissez-faire policy of the Republican administration before 1932), but accepted little responsibility in world affairs except in matters immediately related to domestic objectives. While today it is all too clear that the momentous events of this period—the rearmament of Germany, the fascist revolt in Spain, the invasion of Ethiopia, and the China "incident"—were steps which led to a world war in which we must inevitably have become involved, these events merely hardened our determination to insulate America politically and economically from foreign wars.

The Neutrality acts of 1935 and 1937 clearly expressed the intention of the United States to keep out of the next war, the clouds of which were already discernible on the international horizon. As a nation we were convinced that the Western Hemisphere could be insulated from another world war. While deploring the aggressive policies of Germany and Japan, we believed that we could avoid being drawn into war if our ships and our citizens were kept out of the war zones. Moreover, the investigations of the Nye Committee had convinced many Americans that the munition makers were in considerable measure responsible for the generation of past wars.[2] The Neutrality Act of 1937, therefore, required the President to declare an embargo upon the exportation of arms, ammunition, and implements of war whenever there exists a state of war between two nations or a civil conflict within a foreign country. The 1937 Act also prohibited American vessels from transporting any articles whatsoever

[1] James P. Warburg, *Foreign Policy Begins at Home*, Harcourt, Brace, New York, 1944, p. 103.

[2] Report of the Special Committee on Investigation of the Munitions Industry, Senate Report 944, 74th Congress, 1st Session, Parts 1–7.

to nations at war and to place all exports to belligerent nations excepting the American republics on a cash-and-carry basis.[3] While this façade of neutrality was maintained until the repeal of the Neutrality Act of 1939 in 1941, the folly of this position was well recognized by President Roosevelt at least by October, 1937, when he made his famous "Quarantine Speech." In this address, the President said, "the peace-loving nations must make a concerted effort in opposition to those violations of treaties and those ignorings of human instinct which today are creating a state of international anarchy and instability from which there is no escape through mere isolation or neutrality." [4] While the country was not yet ready to accept the logic of the President's views, the administration proceeded to take such steps as it believed to be politically feasible to help the victims of aggressors. For example, in July, 1937, shortly after the Japanese attack on China, the United States Treasury entered into a stabilization agreement with the Bank of China calling for a loan of $50 million. Further assistance to China was afforded in December, 1938, when the Export-Import Bank authorized credits amounting to $25 million for the exportation of American industrial and agricultural products to China.

Beginning in 1938, the United States began to receive substantial orders for aircraft and munitions necessary for the rearmament of Europe. Foreign purchasing missions representing friendly powers were given assistance by United States govenmental officials,[5] while in the summer of 1938 Secretary of State Hull called for a "moral embargo" on the export of planes to Japan. The administration had determined that the United States should become an "arsenal of democracy" in the event of a war initiated by aggressor states, but this policy was severely hampered by the Neutrality Act of May, 1937, which prohibited exports of arms and munitions to belligerent countries, even on a "cash-and-carry" basis. Consequently in the spring of 1939, Secretary of State Hull asked Congress to repeal those sections of the 1937 Act which dealt with the arms embargo.[6] The failure of Congress to act on this legislation by the time of the outbreak of war in Europe in September, 1939, caused the President to convene an extraordinary session of Congress on September 21, 1939, to revise the existing neutrality legislation. The Neutrality Act which

[3] Public Resolution 27, 75th Congress, in *Documents on American Foreign Relations*, World Peace Foundation, Boston, 1939, Vol. I, pp. 525*ff*.

[4] Quoted by Warburg, *op. cit.*, pp. 121–122.

[5] See Edward R. Stettinius, Jr., *Lend-Lease, Weapon for Victory*, Macmillan, New York, 1944, Chap. 2.

[6] *Documents on American Foreign Relations*, Vol. I, pp. 536*ff*.

became law on November 4, 1939, repealed the arms embargo but retained the cash-and-carry provisions of the earlier law.[7]

The end of the "phony" war and the overrunning of France and the Low Countries in May, 1940, greatly speeded up America's own defense program and led the administration to a program of all-out aid short of war to the Western European allies. In September, 1940, arrangements were made for the transfer of 50 overage destroyers to Britain in exchange for the right to lease air and naval bases on British territories in the Westen Hemisphere. This exchange, according to the opinion of Attorney General Jackson of August 27, 1940,[8] did not require Congressional authorization so that the issue of financial assistance to a belligerent country was not brought before the Congress at this time. British dollar resources were, however, being drawn down rapidly, and by the end of 1940 it was apparent that supplies could not be sent to Britain much longer on a cash basis. Britain began the war with gold and dollar assets of nearly $4.5 billion, but by the end of 1940 this figure had fallen to less than $2.2 billion, of which only $651 million represented gold and dollar balances.[9] In his fireside radio address of December 29, 1940, the President stated that the support of Britain was vital to our own national security. "We must be the great arsenal of democracy. For us this is an emergency as serious as war itself. We must apply ourselves to our task with the same resolution, the same sense of urgency, the same spirit of patriotism and sacrifice as we would show were we at war." [10] This statement was followed a few days later by the President's Annual Message to Congress of January 6, 1941, in which he asked Congress "for authority and funds sufficient to manufacture additional munitions and war supplies of many kinds, to be turned over to those nations which are now in actual war with aggressor nations." [11] This was followed by the introduction of a bill (House Resolution 1776) which on March 11, 1941, became "The Lend-Lease Act," [12] and on March 27, 1941, Congress appropriated $7 billion for its implementation.[13] The operation of the Lend-Lease Act will be taken up in a later section.

Certain additional departures from the prewar neutrality policy of the United States are worth noting. Axis submarines and planes were greatly

[7] Public Resolution 54, 76th Congress, 2d Session, in *Documents on American Foreign Relations*, Vol. IV, pp. 656*ff*.

[8] For the text of this opinion, see *Department of State Bulletin* III, September, 1940, p. 201.

[9] *Federal Reserve Bulletin*, February, 1941, p. 99.

[10] For text, see *Documents on American Foreign Relations*, Vol. III, pp. 17–26.

[11] *Documents on American Foreign Relations*, Vol. III, p. 30.

[12] Public Law 11, 77th Congress.

[13] Public Law 23, 77th Congress.

hampering the delivery of American supplies to Britain and to the Middle East. On April 10, 1941, the President issued a proclamation permitting American ships to carry cargoes to Red Sea ports. This action led to the sinking of the American ship, the *Robin Moor*, in the South Atlantic while en route to South Africa. Although American ships were still barred by the Neutrality Act of 1939 from delivering cargoes to Britain, American naval vessels patrolled the sea lanes as a measure of protection to British shipping. In the course of such patrols the United States destroyer *Greer* was attacked by a German submarine on September 4, 1941, and the following month the U.S.S. *Reuben James* was sunk by a German submarine while convoying ships in the North Atlantic. While these activities on the part of the administration drew fire from the isolationist congressmen, a repeal of the most restrictive sections of the Neutrality Act of 1939 was not asked for until October 9, 1941, when the President transmitted to Congress a message recommending the repeal of Sec. 6 of the Act relating to the arming of American vessels.[14]

The Defense Program

While American expenditures for national defense increased each year from a level of $531 million in fiscal 1934 to $1,657 million in fiscal 1940, America's defense effort on a really significant scale did not commence until the end of the "phony" war in the spring of 1940. In his message on national defense on May 16, 1940, the President called for substantial additions to existing military programs; larger additional requests by the President followed on May 31 and July 10 of that year. Congress responded by appropriating $3,416 million for the Navy and $8,483 million for the War Department for fiscal 1941. Actual expenditures for military activities in fiscal 1941 amounted to $6,301 million, or about 6 per cent of gross national product for this period.[15]

In order to expedite America's own defense program and the production of war supplies for friendly belligerents, a number of measures were taken during 1940 and 1941 which involved the control of the domestic economy. The National Defense Act of June 28, 1940,[16] and the Selective

[14] Public Law 479, 77th Congress, in *Documents on American Foreign Relations*, Vol. IV, p. 112.

[15] Statistics on war expenditures, *Annual Report of the Secretary of the Treasury, 1945*, p. 441. Statistics on military appropriations, Bureau of the Budget. Statistics on gross national product, *National Income*, supplement to *Survey of Current Business*, July, 1947.

[16] Public Law 671, 76th Congress, in *Documents on American Foreign Relations*, Vol. II, pp. 802*ff*.

Service Act of September 16, 1940,[17] empowered the government to require priorities from private firms over all other orders and to compel acceptance of government orders. In December 21, 1940, the President created the Office of Production Management under William Knudsen, which was charged with determining priorities, expediting production for defense, and coordinating the procurement and other activities of the agencies of the government concerned with defense production. An Act of May 31, 1941,[18] authorized the government to establish mandatory priorities on all orders of foreign governments receiving lend-lease aid and permitted the control and allocation of supplies and materials in short supply needed for defense or essential civilian production. Authority for the control of exports of materials vital to the defense effort was provided by Congress on July 2, 1940.[19] Control over the licensing of exports was vested in the Economic Defense Board, created July 30, 1941, and headed by Vice President Wallace. Its name was later changed to the Board of Economic Warfare (BEW), the activities of which will be discussed later on.

The defense program together with the expanded foreign purchases had an enormous impact on national income, employment, and prices. National income rose from $79.9 billion (annual rate) in the second quarter of 1940 to $101.2 billion in the corresponding quarter of 1941.[20] Nonagricultural employment rose 8 per cent between May, 1940, and May, 1941.[21] Prices of 28 basic commodities rose 26 per cent, and the general wholesale price index rose 8 per cent over the same period. By the end of 1941 the prices of the 28 basic commodities had risen 35 per cent over the level of December, 1940, while the general wholesale price index had risen by 17 per cent. Although Congress did not authorize government price controls until the passage of the Emergency Price Control Act of January 30, 1942, the President created the Office of Price Administration and Civilian Supply (OPACS) under Leon Henderson

[17] Public Law 783, 76th Congress, in *Documents on American Foreign Relations*, Vol. III, pp. 672*ff*.

[18] Public Law 29, 77th Congress, in *Documents on American Foreign Relations*, Vol. III, pp. 748*ff*. Control over priorities and allocations which was for a time administered by OPM, was transferred on Aug. 28, 1941, to the Supply Priorities and Allocations Board headed by Vice President Wallace. On Jan. 16, 1942, this function was vested in the War Production Board, of which Donald Nelson was the first chairman.

[19] Public Law 703, 76th Congress, in *Documents on American Foreign Relations*, Vol. II, pp. 796–797.

[20] *National Income*, supplement to *Survey of Current Business*, July, 1947, p. 48.

[21] Seymour Harris, *The Economics of American Defense*, Norton, New York, 1941, p. 14.

on April 11, 1941.[22] This agency sought to limit price increases by making recommendations to military procurement officers, by informal controls achieved through voluntary cooperation of industry, and in a few cases by the issuance of formal price ceilings. Until the passage of the Price Control Act, however, the price-control authorities had to depend for compliance upon the withholding of government orders and public opinion.

The Wartime Economy

The governmental defense agencies, which had struggled with great difficulty with the problems of economic mobilization without adequate legislative authority and with indifferent public support, had at least laid the groundwork for full-scale national mobilization for war. Nevertheless, the greater part of the economy was untouched by the war, and in the autumn of 1941 the automobile companies were busy finding new ways to decorate their 1942 models with chrome, a strategic material. The magnitude of the job of converting the economy to a total war basis staggered the imagination. In his message to Congress on January 6, 1942, the President called for 60,000 planes, 45,000 tanks, 20,000 antiaircraft guns, and 8 million tons of shipping for 1942, and substantially higher targets were to be set for 1943.[23] In his budget message of January 7, 1942, the President estimated total Federal expenditures for the fiscal year 1943 of $62 billion, of which $53 billion represented war activities. "The estimates," stated the President, "reflect our determination to devote at least one-half of our national production to the war effort." [24] Actual expenditures for war activities were $72.1 billion in fiscal 1943, $87 billion in the fiscal year 1944, and $90 billion in fiscal 1945.[25]

In the calendar years 1943 and 1944, war expenditures represented 43.9 and 43.4 per cent, respectively, of gross national product.[26] The expansion of production for war, however, was achieved through an increase in total output rather than through a cut in consumption, since the real value of consumer expenditures actually rose between 1941 and 1944.[27] Gross

[22] Previous to the establishment of the OPACS, similar functions were performed by the Price Stabilization Division of the National Defense Advisory Commission.

[23] *Documents on American Foreign Relations,* Vol. IV, pp. 45ff.

[24] The President's Budget Message, Jan. 7, 1942, Bureau of the Budget.

[25] *Annual Report of the Secretary of the Treasury, 1945,* p. 441.

[26] Seymour E. Harris, *Inflation and the American Economy,* McGraw-Hill, New York, 1945, p. 94.

[27] Consumer expenditures rose by 30 per cent between 1941 and 1944, while the cost of living rose by about 20 per cent. For a discussion of this problem, see Harris, *Inflation and the American Economy,* pp. 97–101.

national product in current dollars rose from $90.4 billion in 1939 to $125.3 billion in 1941 and $210.6 billion in 1944.[28] The increase in the gross product in real terms between 1939 and 1944 has been estimated to be 70 to 90 per cent.[29] In contrast to the American experience, the British had to finance their war effort by a substantial reduction in consumption.[30] Moreover, according to a report of the lend-lease administration,[31] war expenditures by Britain in 1943 and 1944 represented a somewhat higher percentage of British gross national product than in the case of the United States.

Considering the rapidity and the magnitude of America's war mobilization, this country was quite successful in limiting price increases during the war period. The wholesale price index increased about 14 per cent between December, 1941, and V-J Day, while the cost-of-living index rose about 17 per cent over the same period. This record is all the more remarkable when we consider that only 38 per cent of the war expenditures was financed by taxation in 1943 and 45 per cent in 1944.[32] Although rationing played a part in limiting demand for gasoline and a number of food items, the bulk of the consumers' goods were unrationed. Price control was successful in holding the prices of a large number of commodities at levels below equilibrium levels.[33] The excessive demand which was permitted by the monetary and fiscal authorities was channeled into savings, which reached exceptionally high levels during the war period.[34] The large volume of savings was due in part to the Treasury's savings-bond campaign, but people were also led to save by the unavailability of commodities and a willingness to defer expenditures until after the war. Thus it was possible to permit an expansion of money incomes as an incentive to greater productivity and a fuller use of human and material resources, with a substantial part of the excessive purchasing power so created being kept off the market for goods.

As a result of the high volume of wartime savings induced by the inability to purchase goods and by the patriotic appeal of the Treasury, the end of the war found the economy with a large volume of suppressed inflation and a public eager to redeem the wartime promises of new

[28] National Income, supplement to Survey of Current Business, July, 1947, p. 19.

[29] Harris, Inflation and the American Economy, p. 99.

[30] Ibid., pp. 104–105.

[31] Twentieth Report to Congress on Lend-Lease Operations for the Period Ended June 30, 1945, p. 41.

[32] Harris, Inflation and the American Economy, p. 242.

[33] For a discussion of this problem, see S. K. Galbraith, "The Disequilibrium System," American Economic Review, June, 1947, pp. 287–302.

[34] During 1944, personal saving amounted to 24 per cent of personal disposable income as compared with 11 per cent in 1941.

houses, automobiles, and durable equipment of all kinds. The magnitude of the monetary inflation is difficult to measure, but it is worth noting that personal holdings of liquid assets rose from $55.2 billion in December, 1941, to $147.2 billion in December, 1945, of which $91.9 billion represented currency and bank deposits.[35] The gradual removal of rationing and price controls resulted in a rise of 18 per cent in the wholesale price index within a year after V-J Day, a rise which was larger than that which had occurred from December, 1941, to September, 1945. This rise occurred in spite of a decline in war expenditures from $90 billion in fiscal 1945 to $48.5 billion in fiscal 1946. By September, 1947, the wholesale price index had risen an additional 27 per cent over the preceding 12 months, while the Federal budget showed a surplus of receipts over expenditures.[36]

In addition to the governmental activities mentioned in the preceding paragraphs, the war-production program was implemented by a number of other control activities including those of the War Manpower Commission in controlling the employment of human resources, the War Labor Board in dealing with wage disputes and administering wage controls,[37] the BEW in administering export and import controls, the Reconstruction Finance Corporation (RFC) in subsidizing the production of strategic materials, and the Federal Reserve Board in controlling consumer credit. These activities have been described in detail elsewhere,[38] and we shall limit the remainder of our discussion of wartime economic policies to those which have a direct bearing on the international relations of the United States.

Lend-Lease

Although Congress had appropriated $7 billion for lend-lease transfer shortly after the Lend-Lease Act was passed on March 11, 1941, only $780 million worth of lend-lease goods was actually exported during 1941.[39] By December 7, 1941, more than $5.5 billion worth of lend-lease contracts had been let for aircraft, munitions, ships, and other

---

[35] "Estimated Liquid Asset Holdings of Individuals and Business," *Federal Reserve Bulletin,* September, 1947, pp. 1103–1104.

[36] The United States government had a cash surplus of $7.3 billion in fiscal 1947.

[37] The Stabilization Act of October, 1942, authorized the stabilization of wages at the level of Sept. 15, 1942.

[38] See, for example, Seymour E. Harris, *The Economics of America at War,* Norton, New York, 1943; and *Price and Related Controls in the United States,* McGraw-Hill, New York, 1945.

[39] *International Transactions of the United States during the War,* Department of Commerce, 1948, p. 15.

supplies.[40] These orders were an important factor in expanding the productive facilities of the United States prior to our entry into the war. Perhaps the most important direct assistance rendered by lend-lease in the first few months of its operation was in the form of food and other civilian supplies to Britain. Thus from the beginning, lend-lease aid encompassed all the supplies necessary for fighting a total war and not simply arms and munitions. Of the $9,632 million in lend-lease aid made available in the first two years, munitions accounted for 55 per cent, industrial materials and equipment 27 per cent, and food and other agricultural products 18 per cent.[41]

Before a country was eligible to receive lend-lease aid, the President had to declare that the defense of such country was vital to the defense of the United States. The conditions for eligibility were interpreted quite broadly, and by March, 1943, 43 nations, including a number of Latin-American and Eastern Hemisphere countries which were not at war with the Axis countries, were certified as eligible for lend-lease assistance. Eventually 38 countries actually received lend-lease assistance, including 19 American Republics and such Eastern Hemisphere countries as Saudi Arabia and Turkey, whose territory or armed forces were not involved in actual fighting. This concept of global defense and economic aid to countries whose territory or productive capacity was strategic in the defense effort has been carried over into the postwar period. As we shall also see, lend-lease aid and other wartime measures were important elements of the inter-American policy of the United States.

In addition to immediate aid to Britain and to her fighting forces in the Middle East during 1941, lend-lease assistance was extended to China in May, 1941. This was a continuation of United States aid to China which had begun on a small scale as early as 1937 shortly after the China incident, and included $120 million in loans from the Export-Import Bank over the two years prior to the passage of the Lend-Lease Act. Shortly after she was attacked by Germany in June, 1941, aid was extended to Russia, which since the Nazi-Soviet Pact of August, 1939, had not been able to obtain licenses to export some $9 million worth of goods accumulated by the Amtorg Trading Company.

After the United States entered the war, lend-lease appropriations and expenditures were practically on a par with those for America's own military operations. This was a total war in which all available resources were to be employed in the manner most suited to bring about a common objective, the defeat of the Axis. Resources and not money were the

[40] Stettinius, *op. cit.*, Chap. 9.

[41] *Eighth Quarterly Report to Congress on Lend-Lease Operations for the Period Ended March 11, 1943*, p. 7.

scarce factors. Coordination of production and distribution of resources were achieved through the creation of a number of Combined Boards whose members included representatives of the United States and Great Britain and, on certain occasions, Canadian representatives. What Britain and other countries received in the way of munitions under lend-lease and what was reserved for America's own use or distribution elsewhere were determined in consultation with the Munitions Assignment Board under the Combined Chiefs of Staff. Similarly, the Combined Raw Materials Board, the Combined Shipping Board, the Combined Production and Resources Board, and the Combined Food Board coordinated operations in their assigned fields. Since all shipping and most commodities under the control of the Allies were scarce, the Combined Boards coordinated governmental export and import controls over supplies going to all parts of the world free from domination by the enemy. Joint United States–United Kingdom agencies such as the North African Economic Board and the Middle East Supply Center had control over trade in particular areas of the world.

Not all American exports were transferred under lend-lease. What Britain and other countries paid cash for and what they received in the form of aid depended upon their ability to pay. Thus if British gold and dollar reserves were rising beyond a reasonable level, she might be required to pay dollars for a larger portion of what she received. Cash sales might be made through ordinary commercial channels (which were of course subject to United States export controls and foreign import controls), or in other cases procurement was made through the lend-lease authorities, but on a cash-reimbursable basis. In addition to cash payments for some United States exports, countries receiving lend-lease aid reciprocated in kind. Thus under the reciprocal-aid agreement with Britain, the British agreed to provide the following types of assistance to the United States as reciprocal aid: (1) military equipment, munitions, and military and naval stores; (2) supplies and facilities for American armed forces in the United Kingdom; (3) supplies, materials, and services needed for the construction of military projects in the United Kingdom and Colonial Empire, except for wages and salaries of United States citizens.[42] Similar arrangements were made with a number of other countries, and reverse lend-lease to the value of $7,346 million was received from 11 countries and their dependencies to V-J Day. This compares with a total of about $48 billion in lend-lease aid which was granted up to September 2, 1945.

[42] "United Kingdom Reciprocal Aid Agreement," *Eighth Quarterly Report to Congress on Lend-Lease Operations for the Period Ended March 11, 1943,* Appendix VII.

Tables 4 and 5 show lend-lease aid by countries up to September 30, 1946, and a breakdown of lend-lease aid by major categories. It should

Table 4. Lend-lease Aid, by Countries,
Mar. 11, 1941, to Sept. 30, 1946

(In millions of dollars)

British Empire	$31,392
U.S.S.R.	11,298
France and possessions	3,234
China	1,565
Brazil	332
Netherlands and possessions	249
Belgium	159
Greece	76
Norway	53
Other countries	243
Not charged by country	2,091
Total	$50,692

SOURCE: *Twenty-third Report to Congress on Lend-Lease Operations for the Period Ended September 30, 1946,* p. 27.

Table 5. Lend-lease Aid, by Category,
Mar. 11, 1941, to Sept. 30, 1946

(In millions of dollars)

Military equipment, ammunition, aircraft and parts, etc.	$20,629
Water craft	4,057
Motor vehicles and parts	2,547
Petroleum products	2,731
Industrial equipment and commodities	8,361
Food	5,829
Other agricultural commodities	853
Services	3,594
Lend-lease not charged to foreign governments	2,091
Total	$50,692

SOURCE: *Twenty-third Report to Congress on Lend-Lease Operations for the Period Ended September 30, 1946,* pp. 29–30.

be noted that about 85 per cent of all lend-lease aid went to the British Empire and Russia, and the bulk of the remainder went to France, China, the Netherlands, Belgium, Greece, Norway, and Brazil. Brazil was the only Latin-American country which received a substantial amount of lend-lease aid, largely out of recognition for her services in connection with the antisubmarine patrol. Most of the nonmilitary items received by the Latin-American countries were paid for in cash since these countries had plenty of dollars. Lend-lease procurement provided a means of obtaining essential civilian commodities which might not otherwise have been available. Canada received no straight lend-lease from this country, although she paid cash for commodities procured under lend-lease. Also, in accordance with the Hyde Park Declaration of April 26, 1941,[43] Britain obtained materials under lend-lease in the United States, which were then forwarded to Canada for manufacture into finished commodities to be sent to Britain. Not only did Canada not accept lend-lease aid from the United States, but in 1943 she inaugurated a $1 billion mutual-aid program of her own, similar to the United States lend-lease program.

The manner of repayment for lend-lease supplies depended upon the nature of the commodities and services lend-leased, the use to which they were put, and the financial circumstances of the receiving country. In the case of munitions and ordnance actually consumed before V-J Day, repayment was not expected. In the case of civilian supplies and equipment, payment was required either immediately or after delivery where the recipient could afford to make payment. Thus the French agreed to pay 100 per cent cash for civilian supplies delivered to French West and North Africa. In some cases, payment was made in local currencies, which were available to the United States for troop pay and other expenditures in these areas. Over $45 million worth of local currencies was received for lend-lease shipments to the Middle East and elsewhere, most of which has been used by the United States government.[44]

Permanent industrial installations of value to the civilian economy were to be paid for either immediately or after the war, depending upon the financial circumstances of the recipient. Final settlements for lend-lease deliveries will be discussed in the next section. Some 335 million ounces of silver for coinage and industrial purposes was lend-leased to Saudi Arabia, India, and other countries during the war. This silver, taken from Treasury stocks, must be returned ounce for ounce after the war, under the terms of special agreements with the Treasury Department.[45] The fact that an adequate supply of silver riyals for the nomadic

[43] Joint Statement of President Roosevelt and Prime Minister of Canada Mackenzie King, Hyde Park, N.Y., Apr. 20, 1941, in *Documents on American Foreign Relations*, Vol. III, pp. 161*ff*.

[44] For a statement of dollar and local currency receipts by the lend-lease administration, see *Twenty-sixth Report to Congress on Lend-Lease Operations for the Period Ended September 15, 1948*.

[45] *Annual Report of the Secretary of the Treasury, 1945*, p. 97.

tribes of Arabia was considered to be vital to the defense of the United States indicates the comprehensive character of global war.[46]

Post-V-J Day Lend-Lease and Settlements

On September 6, 1945, President Truman announced that he had instructed the Foreign Economic Administration (FEA) [47] to advise all foreign governments that lend-lease deliveries would cease on V-J Day, September 2, 1945.[48] Except for China, which continued to receive straight lend-lease for assistance in connection with the disarmament and evacuation of the Japanese forces in China, both military and civilian deliveries on a grant basis practically ceased. On V-J Day, however, there were uncompleted contracts for nonmunitions and finished goods in this country not yet transferred to lend-lease countries, amounting to about $2 billion and another $1 to $1½ billion of lend-lease supplies in stock piles abroad. Termination of these contracts would have worked a hardship on the foreign countries which had depended upon lend-lease supplies for the maintenance of their economies and, in some cases, upon American suppliers as well. It was therefore decided to permit deliveries of so-called "pipe-line" goods and services, i.e., lend-lease supplies and services under contract or agricultural commodities under allocation, under agreements with the recipient countries to pay for them either immediately upon delivery or on time. From V-J Day to September 30, 1947, $2.3 billion worth of lend-lease goods was delivered, including $778 million worth to China.[49] Over $1 billion of the pipe-line lend-lease represented agricultural and industrial commodities, and about $350 million represented ship transfers. Settlements for pipe-line supplies were included in the final settlements with the lend-lease recipients after the war.

The first over-all settlement of lend-lease and reciprocal aid was made with Britain on December 6, 1945.[50] This agreement, which provided for

[46] For a discussion of American aid to Saudi Arabia, see Raymond F. Mikesell, "Monetary Problems of Saudi Arabia," *Middle East Journal*, April, 1947, pp. 169–179.

[47] The Office of Lend-Lease Administration was transferred to the Foreign Economic Administration on Sept. 25, 1943. The FEA also took over the Office of Foreign Relief and Rehabilitation Operations, the Office of Economic Warfare, and the Office of Foreign Economic Coordination on the same date.

[48] *Documents on American Foreign Relations*, Vol. VIII, p. 126.

[49] *Twenty-sixth Report to Congress on Lend-Lease Operations for the Period Ended September 15, 1948.*

[50] *Anglo-American Financial and Commercial Agreements*, Department of State, December, 1945; see also "Memorandum Pursuant to Joint U.S.–U.K. Statement on Settlement for Lend-Lease, Reciprocal Aid, Surplus War Property and Claims," *Twenty-second Report to Congress on Lend-Lease Operations for the Period Ended December 31, 1945.*

the payment to the United States of $650 million in 50 annual install-
ments beginning December 31, 1951, at 2 per cent interest,[51] included
a settlement for lend-lease and reciprocal aid, for the acquisition by
Britain of surplus property and installations built by the United States
in the United Kingdom and for various other claims arising out of the
war. In arriving at this settlement, Britain was not obligated to pay for
military and civilian goods actually consumed during the war. Civilian
goods received after V-J Day and equipment and installations which were
of value to the peacetime economy were included.

The agreements with Britain announced on December 6, 1945, involved
far more than the settlement of war claims. They included an agreement on commercial policy which took the form of an agreement in
principle on the American "Proposals for Consideration by an International Conference on Trade and Employment," [52] which later became
the basis for the proposals for an International Trade Organization
drafted at the Havana Conference in the spring of 1948. This commercial agreement was a further development of the commercial-policy provisions to be found in the Atlantic Charter of August 12, 1941,[53] and in
Art. VII of the Master Lend-Lease Agreement with Britain and a number of other countries.[54] The provisions of Art. VII are worth quoting in
full because they indicate that the United States government was thinking in terms of international collaboration over a wide range of economic
problems as early as February, 1942, when this Agreement was signed.

ARTICLE VII

In the final determination of the benefits to be provided to the United
States of America by the Government of the United Kingdom, in return for
aid furnished under the Act of Congress of March 11, 1941, the terms and
conditions thereof shall be such as not to burden commerce between the two

[51] The terms of payment were the same as those provided under the Anglo-American
Financial Agreement in which the United States extended a credit to Britain of $3¾
billion. This agreement will be discussed in Chap. 11.

[52] Proposals for the Expansion of World Trade and Employment, Department of
State, November, 1945.

[53] The Atlantic Charter stated that the United Kingdom and the United States "desire
to bring about the fullest collaboration between all nations in the economic field with
the object of securing, for all, improved labor standards, economic advancement and
social security."

[54] For a text of the British Master Lend-Lease Agreement, see Eighteenth Report to
Congress on Lend-Lease Operations for the Period Ended December 31, 1944, Appendix
II. Similar agreements were signed with Belgium, China, Czechoslovakia, Ethiopia,
Greece, Iraq, Liberia, the Netherlands, Norway, Poland, the U.S.S.R., and Yugoslavia.
Australia and New Zealand also accepted the principles of the Master Agreements.

countries, but to promote mutually advantageous economic relations between them and the betterment of world-wide economic relations. To that end, they shall include provision for agreed action by the United States of America and the United Kingdom, open to participation by all other countries of like mind, directed to the expansion, by appropriate international and domestic measures, of production, employment, and the exchange and consumption of goods, which are the material foundations of the liberty and welfare of all peoples; to the elimination of all forms of discriminatory treatment in international commerce, and to the reduction of tariffs and other trade barriers; and, in general, to the attainment of all the economic objectives set forth in the Joint Declaration made on August 12, 1941, by the President of the United States of America and the Prime Minister of the United Kingdom.

At an early convenient date, conversations shall be begun between the two Governments with a view to determining, in the light of governing economic conditions, the best means of attaining the above-stated objectives by their own agreed action and of seeking the agreed action of other like-minded Governments.

Throughout the war years, the executive branch of the United States government (and other governments as well) worked on draft agreements in the trade and foreign-exchange fields for implementing the principles stated above. We shall discuss the development of these agreements, including the special financial agreement with Britain concluded at the time of the lend-lease settlement, in a later chapter.

The final settlement with the Provisional Government of France in May, 1946, was similar in many respects to that with Britain. Lend-lease aid to France amounted to some $3,235 million plus $130 million worth of civilian goods supplied by the military forces after the Normandy landings.[55] France had supplied about $868 million in reverse lend-lease and had paid $232 million in cash for lend-lease supplies. In the final settlement, France assumed $50 million in claims on the United States and agreed to pay $420 million subject to adjustment for certain pipe-line transfers not yet fully accounted for. Interest on the debt was fixed at 2 per cent, with payments to run over 30 years, the first payments being due in July, 1947. In addition to the lend-lease settlement, France agreed to pay $300 million for Army and Navy surplus property in France and French overseas territories, on the same terms as provided for in the lend-lease settlement. Just as in the case of Britain, the final settlement

[55] This represented the United States' share of so-called Plan A goods furnished jointly with Britain and Canada. Although it was originally agreed that Plan A supplies would be paid for, they were treated as lend-lease supplies in the final settlement. See *Twenty-third Report to Congress on Lend-Lease Operations for the Period Ended September 30, 1946*, pp. 8–11 and Appendix IV.

with France was accompanied by additional financial assistance in the form of a loan from the Export-Import Bank of $650 million.[56]

Lend-lease settlements were also made with India, Australia, New Zealand, Belgium, and Turkey in 1946, and by 1950 agreements with most of the important lend-lease recipients had been reached except the U.S.S.R., China, Greece, and Mexico. The Indian and American accounts were balanced off except for $160 million worth of lend-lease silver. Australia and New Zealand agreed to pay for certain surplus items which had been transferred to them by the United States military forces. In the case of Belgium, reverse lend-lease was actually larger than United States lend-lease aid, but this account was balanced off, except that Belgium agreed to pay for $18 million worth of surplus property. Turkey paid $4.5 million in cash for the residual value of lend-lease equipment of postwar civilian utility in Turkey.[57]

The lend-lease settlements of World War II may be contrasted with the war-debt settlements of World War I, which were reviewed in Chap. 4. Instead of saddling foreign governments with a large indebtedness for munitions and other supplies consumed in a common war, the lend-lease settlements wrote off all supplies delivered under straight lend-lease during the war, with the exception of equipment which had residual value to the postwar civilian economies of the recipients. The latter, together with post-V-J Day deliveries and surplus-property transfers (desired by the foreign countries), were provided on generous credit terms. All settlements were reviewed by the National Advisory Council on International Monetary and Financial Problems in the light of both the proper interests of the United States and the welfare and interests, including ability to pay, of the debtor countries.[58]

We may nevertheless question the wisdom of terminating straight lend-lease immediately after V-J Day and of requiring payment for items on which the Allied countries were counting to maintain their economies in the immediate future.[59] Britain and other nations allied with the United States in the war had greatly reduced their production of goods for export and for home consumption in order to maximize production for the war effort. They were able to do this because of the arrangement

[56] In March, 1949, the French lend-lease and surplus-property obligation was set at $653.3 million.

[57] Twenty-third Report to Congress on Lend-Lease Operations for the Period Ended September 30, 1946, pp. 11–16.

[58] Report of the Activities of the National Advisory Council on International Monetary and Financial Problems to March 31, 1947, pp. 6–7.

[59] In a recent interview with Arthur Krock, President Truman admitted that the termination of lend-lease in September, 1945, was a mistake. The New York Times, Feb. 15, 1950, p. 1.

whereby essential civilian needs would be met by lend-lease. But these nations could not reconvert their industries or restore their export markets the day after the war ended. It is difficult to see how the responsibility of the United States for meeting the essential civilian needs of her partners in a common war could end immediately with the termination of hostilities. Three years later this responsibility was realized, but only after valuable time had been lost and several billion dollars in debt burden was added to the future balance of payments of the European nations. But it was the specter of communism rather than a full realization of the postwar responsibilities of the United States which provided the principal motive for the European Recovery Program (ERP).

Surplus-property Disposal

As of June 30, 1949, government-owned property in foreign areas having an original cost of $10,444 million had been declared surplus. The disposal of the foreign surplus property was the responsibility of the Office of Foreign Liquidation Commissioner (OFLC) in the Department of State, and by June 30, 1949, all the declared surplus had been sold or otherwise disposed of, including transfers to the United Nations Relief and Rehabilitation Administration, donations, abandonments, etc. The bulk of this property represented items such as food, textiles, drugs, industrial products, motor vehicles, railroad and construction equipment, machinery, aircraft, and maritime property which was greatly needed by foreign countries.[60] As of June 30, 1949, sales (mostly to foreign governments and other noncitizens) of property with an original cost of $10,440 million had realized $1,892 million.[61] Moreover, most of the sales to foreign governments were made on credit with terms varying from 2 years (in the case of Uruguay) up to 35 years, (France) and 55 years (United Kingdom). Most agreements provided for 30-year terms, with interest at 2⅜ per cent.[62] As of December 31, 1949, $1,096 million in credits had been extended by the Foreign Liquidation Commissioner on the sale of foreign surplus property.[63]

In some cases the OFLC accepted local-currency payments for surplus property, the proceeds of which could be used for specified purposes

[60] Report to Congress on Foreign Surplus Disposal, July, 1946, Office of the Foreign Liquidation Commissioner, Department of State, Appendix II.

[61] Report to Congress on Foreign Surplus Disposal, July, 1949, p. 8.

[62] The British and French agreements called for the payment of interest at 2 per cent. See Report to Congress on Foreign Surplus Disposal, July, 1946, Appendix I.

[63] National Advisory Council on International Monetary and Financial Problems, Semiannual Report to the President and to the Congress, for the Period October 1, 1949 to March 31, 1950, p. 57.

within the foreign country. Some of these funds have been used to acquire real estate for American embassies, and some were made available
for educational purposes under the terms of the Fulbright Act.[64] This
Act provides that up to $20 million of the proceeds of the sale of surplus
property in each country may be used to finance scholarships for the
education and research of American students in the foreign countries or
of foreign students in the United States. Special agreements for the implementation of this Act have been made with a number of countries to
whom surplus-property sales have been made.

The War Assets Administration, which is charged with the disposal
of domestic surplus property owned by the government, has also extended credits to foreign governments in connection with domestic surplus-property sales. As of February, 1949, credit agreements totaling $117
million had been entered into with foreign governments for the sale of
such property, of which about $20 million had been actually granted.[65]
The United States Maritime Commission is also authorized to extend
credits to other countries in connection with the sale of war-built vessels.
As of December 31, 1949, the Maritime Commission had extended foreign credits amounting to $229 million in connection with ship sales,
$198 million of which represented credits to European countries.

Although the pipe-line lend-lease and surplus-property credits of various
kinds may properly be included as a part of postwar foreign assistance,
they are so closely related to the lend-lease settlements as to warrant a
brief discussion of them at this point. In the case of a number of countries, foreign surplus-property disposal was in fact included in the over-
all lend-lease settlements.

War and Postwar Relief

There was early recognition of the responsibility of the United States
in meeting the needs for relief and rehabilitation of liberated areas, and
formal studies with respect to the problem were initiated in the State Department in September, 1941. Provision was made for military relief programs to commence immediately on the heels of the fighting forces.
Meeting minimum civilian needs for the prevention of disease and unrest is of course necessary for military as well as humanitarian reasons.[66]

[64] Public Law 584, 79th Congress, 2d Session.

[65] *National Advisory Council on International Monetary and Financial Problems,
Semiannual Report to the President and to the Congress, for the Period October 1, 1948
to March 31, 1949,* p. 25.

[66] Provision of relief for occupied areas is also required by the Hague Convention of
1907.

The executive branch of the government, however, was anxious to have the provision and administration of relief in occupied areas turned over to civilian authorities as soon as military conditions permitted. Hence the President established the Office of Foreign Relief and Rehabilitation Operations (OFRRO) in the Department of State shortly after the North African invasion in November, 1942, and on December 2, 1942, Governor Herbert E. Lehman was appointed director of the organization.[67] The function of OFRRO was much broader than that of direct handouts and the establishment of "soup kitchens." A large part of the civilian supplies was sold through special relief stores under a relief-rationing program or through regular commercial channels. In addition, OFRRO instituted programs for the rehabilitation of agriculture and the local production and distribution of essential civilian supplies. OFRRO also dealt with the problem of war refugees in the occupied areas.

From the beginning it was expected that the work of OFRRO would be eventually taken over by a United Nations organization. On June 10, 1943, the Department of State submitted to the governments of the United and Associated Nations a draft agreement for a United Nations Relief and Rehabilitation Administration (UNRRA). This draft, with certain amendments, was signed on November 9, 1943, by 44 nations, and plans for the operation of UNRRA were formulated immediately thereafter under the directorship of Herbert Lehman. The scope of UNRRA's activities in the liberated areas included the provision of supplies of essential consumers' goods and services; the caring for displaced persons; rehabilitation supplies and services such as seeds, fertilizers, raw materials, and technical services to enable a recipient country to produce and transport relief supplies; and the rehabilitation of public utilities and services so far as they could be repaired or restored to meet immediate needs.[68] It was not the function of UNRRA to undertake programs of long-term reconstruction of industry, utilities, public buildings, and agriculture. Admittedly, the line between long-run reconstruction and rehabilitation for the production of relief needs and services was in many cases a difficult one to draw. Congress emphasized its desire that this distinction should be carefully adhered to,[69] since it was at that time desirous of dealing with long-term reconstruction on a loan basis.

[67] On Sept. 25, 1945, OFRRO was transferred to the FEA in the executive office of the President.

[68] See Resolutions on Policy of the First Session of the Council of UNRRA, held at Atlantic City, N.J., Nov. 10–Dec. 1, 1943, in *Documents on American Foreign Relations*, Vol. VI, pp. 257–294.

[69] See Report of Senate Committee on Foreign Relations, to Accompany House Joint Resolution 192, Feb. 14, 1944, Senate Report 688, 78th Congress, 2d Session, in *Documents on American Foreign Relations*, Vol. VI, pp. 296ff.

America's policies with respect to foreign relief in World War II differed from those of World War I in two important respects. First of all, in World War I the United States was opposed to international control of relief operations conducted and financed by this country and rejected all Allied proposals for joint relief.[70] The reason given for this opposition was the fear that American relief would be used for political purposes and that this country would be drawn into European disputes. In spite of his attitude toward the League of Nations, President Woodrow Wilson[71] supported this policy, as did Herbert Hoover who administered our European relief program. The second difference lies in the financing of the relief program. The United States required payment in dollars for the bulk of the relief shipments to Europe during and after World War I, and where cash payment could not be made, credits were advanced to the recipient countries. The United States advanced $194 million to liberated and enemy countries during the Armistice period for the purchase of relief supplies, but 94 per cent of these loans were defaulted. In contrast with this record, World War II relief was extended on the basis of the principle of capacity to pay, and no postwar indebtedness resulted from American relief operations.

Contributions to UNRRA were asked from member nations whose home territories had not been occupied by the enemy in amounts equivalent to 1 per cent of their national incomes. Subsequently, additional contributions were called for on the same basis. Not less than 10 per cent of the contributions were to be made in currency freely expendable in areas outside the contributing country. As of July 31, 1944, about $3.7 billion had been subscribed, the three largest contributors being the United States, $2.7 billion; the United Kingdom, $625 million; and Canada, $139 million. The contribution of the United States represented 73 per cent of the funds received by UNRRA. Recipient countries which were judged by the Council as not being in a position to pay for relief supplies in suitable foreign exchange were asked to make available the local-currency proceeds from the sale of the supplies, a large part of which was handled through ordinary commercial channels. The local-currency proceeds were used by UNRRA for meeting local expenses in connection with the administration of the program and for other operations within the country, including the care and movement of displaced persons.

The contribution of the United States to foreign relief involved much

[70] See Winifred N. Hadsel, "U.S. Relief for Europe in World War I," *Foreign Policy Reports* (Foreign Policy Association), Vol. XIX, No. 1, Mar. 15, 1943.

[71] Wilson always used the term "associated" power for the United States rather than including this country among the Allied powers.

more than the appropriation of funds. Scarce food supplies and other essential civilian commodities in short supply in this country were transferred to UNRRA or otherwise allocated for export. In February, 1946, President Truman inaugurated a program for the conservation of food, particularly wheat products, in this country. This program included limitations on the use of grains for the production of alcoholic beverages and an increase in the wheat-flour extraction rate to 80 per cent.[72]

UNRRA's relief operations were terminated in 1947. Although urgent relief needs remained in certain countries of Western Europe and in China, the growing political tension between the United States and the Soviet Union made it difficult to conduct relief operations on an international basis. There was considerable evidence of the political use of UNRRA relief supplies in Soviet-dominated areas. On February 27, 1947, the President asked the Congress to appropriate $350 million for post-UNRRA relief assistance to the liberated countries,[73] this assistance to be rendered directly by the United States rather than through an international organization. On May 31, 1947, Congress passed a Joint Resolution to provide such relief assistance, with up to $40 million of the $350 million eventually appropriated to be allocated to the International Children's Emergency Fund of the United Nations.[74] The Foreign Relief Program was administered by the Department of State, and relief programs were instituted for Austria, China, Greece, Italy, and Trieste.[75] Under the terms of the Act, assistance was limited to food, medical supplies, materials for clothing, fuel, fertilizer, insecticides, and seeds.

Scarcely 6 months had passed after the inauguration of the Foreign Relief Program when President Truman on September 30, 1947, asked Congress for additional aid for France, Italy, and Austria.[76] This program together with the ERP program and other foreign assistance will be considered under the heading of postwar reconstruction. It is difficult to determine, however, just where relief assistance ends and assistance in meeting chronic balance-of-payments deficits and reconstruction needs begins. It is perhaps reasonable to say that assistance which is provided more than two or three years after the cessation of hostilities is no longer in the category of relief but something else. At any rate we stopped calling

---

[72] See Statement by President Truman on the World Food Crisis, Feb. 6, 1946, in *Documents on American Foreign Relations,* Vol. VIII, pp. 381–383.

[73] *Documents on American Foreign Relations,* Vol. IX, pp. 129–130.

[74] Public Law 84, 80th Congress, 1st Session, in *Documents on American Foreign Relations,* Vol. IX, pp. 130–134.

[75] See *Second Report to Congress on the United States Foreign Relief Program,* Department of State, April, 1948.

[76] Special aid to Greece had already been provided for in the Greek-Turkish aid bill of May 22, 1947.

foreign assistance "relief" after 1947, except perhaps for China which was still engaged in "civil" war.

INTERNATIONAL TRADE AND PAYMENTS DURING WORLD WAR II

A study of America's international transactions during World War II reveals that the foreign political policies of the United States were the dominating factors in our foreign trade. United States merchandise exports rose from $4.4 billion in 1939 to a wartime peak of $21.4 billion in 1944, while imports increased from $2.4 billion to $5.6 billion over the same period.[77] Whereas in 1939 and 1940 America's export surplus was largely paid for by the liquidation of foreign gold and dollar assets, beginning with 1941 and on an increasing scale thereafter, this surplus was met by lend-lease, relief, military civilian supply shipments, and other unilateral transfers. In 1944, unilateral transfers (largely lend-lease) amounted to more than $14.5 billion, and for the period from 1943 to 1944 cash imports exceeded exports sold for cash or credit by $2.1 billion.[78] Government credits were a significant factor in financing United States exports in 1941, principally as a result of an RFC loan of $425 million to Britain in July of that year.[79] After 1941, government loans and credits were not an important element in financing our export surplus until 1945, when they rose to nearly a billion dollars.

While exports rose to record levels during the war and the value of imports more than doubled, imports were not so high as might have been expected in relation to national income.[80] This relative decline in imports was due to the shortages of commodities and shipping and enemy occupation of supplier countries. Although imports rose after the war, they did not regain their prewar position in relation to national income until 1950.

Government Control of Trade

Governmental control over trade which began in the defense period and eventually encompassed practically all the external trade of the

[77] Figures include both recorded and unrecorded exports and imports. Unrecorded figures include certain government transactions and other items not recorded by the Bureau of the Census. See *International Transactions of the United States during the War*, p. 15.

[78] *Ibid.*, p. 14.

[79] This loan was secured by British assets in the United States. $350 million of the loan was utilized in 1941. *Ibid.*, p. 95.

[80] *Ibid.*, pp. 36–38; see also *Survey of Current Business*, November, 1944, p. 12, and February, 1949, pp. 28–30.

United States took two general forms. There was first of all the control over exports and imports of private firms through licensing, priorities, and allocations, export and import price controls, prohibitions against exports to certain areas and individuals, the allocation of shipping, and controls over the use of funds and other assets owned by foreign nationals. The second general form involved direct import and export transactions by agencies of the United States government. Even where private firms engaged in foreign trade, a good part of the sales were made to foreign purchasing missions rather than through normal commercial channels, a situation which continued into the postwar period.

Although some control over exports was exercised under the Neutrality Act and the "moral embargo" instituted by the Secretary of State to discourage armament exports to aggressor nations, an organized system of export control was established by the President on July 2, 1940. Acting under the authority of Sec. 6 of "An Act to Expedite the Strengthening of National Defense," [81] there was appointed on this date an Administrator of Export Control to direct the issuing of export licenses by the Department of State for an initial list covering some 40 commodities. This list was rapidly expanded so that by the end of 1941 virtually all commodity exports except those to Canada were subject to control.[82] At first, the purpose of the controls was to conserve commodities and materials and equipment in short supply for the defense effort and to prevent their getting into the hands of the Axis countries. As America's participation in the war increased, these export controls became a part of the international system for the allocation of supplies in accordance with the principle of essentiality of need. The determination of criteria for the priority of orders and the issuance of export licenses and shipping priorities involved a complex of competing foreign-policy objectives. For example, the problem of what commodities and in what quantities should be shipped to Latin America involved a balancing of the need for a volume of exports to these countries which would assure friendly and cooperative relations with them, against alternative uses of commodities and shipping space in meeting the needs of the American economy and the economies of our allies in other parts of the world. The basic policy which was announced by Under Secretary of State Welles to the Inter-American Financial and Economic Advisory Committee, December 5, 1941, was as follows: [83]

[81] Public 703, 76th Congress, in *Documents on American Foreign Relations*, Vol. III, pp. 796ff.

[82] Control over the licensing of exports was transferred to the Economic Defense Board on Sept. 15, 1941 (later renamed the Board of Economic Warfare). Still later in September, 1943, the functions of the BEW were transferred to the FEA.

[83] *Documents on American Foreign Relations*, Vol. IV, pp. 386–387.

. . . to make every effort consistent with the defense program, to maintain
a flow to the other American Republics of materials to satisfy the minimum
essential import requirements of your countries. This policy is being interpreted by all of the appropriate agencies of the United States as calling for
recognition of and provision for the essential needs of the other American
Republics equal to the treatment accorded to United States civilian needs.

The principle of "parity" in meeting essential civilian needs is capable
of several interpretations and is in any case difficult to apply in practice.
Obviously, it did not mean equality of living standards, since this would
involve a substantial rise in the living standards of many areas as well
as a severe readjustment in those with high standards. It may mean, for
example, equality of sacrifice, but here again a number of difficulties arise.
Where certain areas are already on a subsistence level as regards basic
foodstuffs, a 10 per cent cut across the board would not be feasible. Moreover, in certain areas, there may be alternative foods in plentiful indigenous supply which because of the difficulties of transportation could not
be readily moved to other areas.[84]

For areas other than Latin America and Canada, no attempt was made
to apply the principle of parity. An effort was made to meet minimum
essential requirements of civilian goods even at the expense of the
American economy, both during the war and in the reconstruction period. It is worth noting that, in the case of the American Republics,
United States imports of commodities and services exceeded exports for
every year during the period from 1941 to 1945. In 1943 and 1944, the
United States surplus of imports of goods and services from these countries was $435 million and $347 million, respectively.[85]

In addition to the controls over private exports involved in the system
of export licensing and shipping priorities, certain other controls were
introduced in the defense period. One of these involved the blocking of
the American assets of countries occupied by the Axis for the purpose
of preventing their use to the advantage of the Axis governments and to
conserve them for eventual return to their owners. The control of foreign
funds by the Treasury Department was inaugurated by executive order
on April 10, 1940.[86] Dollar balances and other assets of occupied areas
located in the United States were frozen and were made available only
under license by the Treasury Department. Control of these assets was

---

[84] For a discussion of the "parity" principle, see Harris, *Inflation and the American
Economy*, pp. 138–141.

[85] *International Transactions of the United States during the War*, p. 132.

[86] *Documents on American Foreign Relations*, Vol. II, pp. 543*ff*.; and Vol. III, pp.
537*ff*. On June 14, 1941, the freezing control was extended to all countries on the continent of Europe and their nationals.

significant not only to prevent the funds from being used for exports from the United States to the benefit of the Axis countries, but also to prevent their being used to pay for commodities purchased by the Axis from neutrals. Although direct shipments to Axis countries were fairly well under control by 1941, indirect assistance to Axis countries was possible through exports to firms in Latin America which acted as their agents. In order to deal with this situation, the President issued on July 17, 1941, a Proclamation Authorizing a Proclaimed List of Certain Blocked Nationals.[87] The purpose of this list, which by 1942 contained over 8,000 names, was to prevent the exportation to certain persons of any commodity covered by the Export Control Act of July 2, 1940, and to treat these persons as if they were nationals of the Axis powers in the application of the order of June 14, 1941, freezing the funds of the governments and nationals of all countries on the continent of Europe.

Even more important than government control over private exports in determining the pattern of United States exports were the merchandise transactions of the government itself. Of the $63 billion worth of goods made available to other countries over the period from 1940 to 1945, about two-thirds was transferred directly by government agencies. Lend-lease transfers amounted to $39.5 billion through the end of 1945, while civilian supplies made available by the military forces and the United States contribution to UNRRA amounted to $1,445 million to the end of 1945.[88] Finally, about $600 million worth of foodstuffs and other commodities were sold by government corporations (largely by the Commodity Credit Corporation) and an additional $775 million worth of military supplies and equipment were sold by the armed forces and the OFLC over the same period.

Control over imports during the war was achieved largely through priorities on shipping and by means of direct government purchase. Most of the imports of strategic commodities and essential commodities in world short supply were handled by means of direct government acquisition, or their supply was controlled through allocation at the source. Nevertheless, the import-licensing system was helpful in implementing the allocations of the Combined Raw Materials Board and the Combined Food Board so far as private importers were concerned. So far as commodities in plentiful supply, such as tropical fruits, were concerned, the greatest need for import control was the necessity of conserving shipping. Shipping controls which were administered by the War Production Board were the most effective type of import control during the war.[89]

[87] *Documents on American Foreign Relations*, Vol. IV, pp. 752ff.

[88] *Ibid.*, pp. 19–27.

[89] Seymour Harris, *Price and Related Controls in the United States*, McGraw-Hill, New York, 1945, pp. 300–302.

For the period from 1940 to 1945, direct government purchases accounted for two-fifths of the $27 billion worth of goods made available to us by other countries. Of the $11.7 billion worth of goods acquired by the government from foreign countries, however, only $4,757 million represented nonmilitary purchases, most of which was resold to private industry. Of the remainder, $2,400 million was purchased by the armed forces, largely for their own use abroad, and $4,270 million represented reverse lend-lease, the bulk of which was also consumed abroad by our armed forces.[90] As early as 1939, the Procurement Division of the Treasury, under the authority of the Strategic Materials Act of June 7, 1939,[91] began acquiring strategic materials for stock-piling from foreign sources. In the same year, the Commodity Credit Corporation bartered 600,000 bales of American cotton for an equal value of rubber from British Malaya.[92] The growing threat of war in the Far East led to an expansion of the stock-piling program, and in 1941 government procurement abroad totaled $422 million or 12 per cent of total imports.[93]

The practice of governmental purchase of foreign commodities was employed for several reasons: (1) The necessity of building stock piles of strategic materials and of assuring adequate supplies for the economy as a whole could not be left to individual firms. (2) It was easier to arrange for shipping priorities and the allocation of scarce materials for war industries and essential civilian uses by centralized procurement. (3) Centralized procurement enabled the government to secure better terms than would have been possible in the case of purchase by competing private firms. In this way it was possible to keep down the cost of war production to the government and of essential civilian output by the public. In this connection, the government frequently subsidized imports of essential raw materials as a means of reducing the cost of the finished product to the government and of dampening inflationary pressures by

[90] *International Transactions of the United States during the War*, pp. 19–20.

[91] Public 117, 76th Congress, in *Documents on American Foreign Relations*, Vol. I, pp. 513*ff*. $100 million was appropriated to be used for stock-piling over a 4-year period.

[92] The principle of bartering of surplus agricultural commodities against foreign commodities for stock-piling purposes has many adherents in both the Congress and the executive branch of the government. It should be noted that this practice represents an important departure from the general trade policy of the United States, and one which may assume considerable importance in the future unless a determined effort is made in the executive branch to oppose it.

[93] *International Transactions of the United States during the War*, pp. 27–28. The bulk of the governmental purchases of commercial goods for importation into the United States was handled by subsidiaries of the RFC—the Rubber Reserve Corporation, the Metals Reserve Corporation, the United States Commercial Corporation, and the Defense Supplies Corporation—and the Commodity Credit Corporation, which purchased or bartered agricultural commodities.

keeping down the cost of essential civilian goods. (4) Government-procurement agencies sought to stimulate foreign production of strategic materials by advance payments and development programs in certain fields. For example, the Rubber Reserve Corporation in collaboration with the Brazilian government financed and provided technical services for the development of raw-rubber production in the Amazon Valley.

A fifth use of governmental procurement involved the preclusive buying operations of the United States Commercial Corporation, which frequently operated in cooperation with the United Kingdom Commercial Corporation. Large-scale purchases were made in Sweden, Spain, Portugal, Turkey, and other neutral countries, often at exorbitant prices and in quantities beyond the needs of the United States, in order to prevent their acquisition by the Axis. These operations frequently had the effect of stimulating increased production in the neutral countries, however.

Export and Import Price Controls

One of the functions of the Office of Price Administration (OPA) during the war was to control the prices of commodities entering into the foreign trade of the United States. In the case of exports to countries which were recipients of lend-lease grants, export price control was necessary to minimize the war expenditures of the United States, whether the commodities were procured under lend-lease or from the dollar resources of the importing countries.[94] But such control was also desirable in the case of Latin-American countries and others which had plenty of dollars. Although exports were under direct control, these controls were never perfect and the existence of price incentives to divert commodities from the domestic market or from other foreign markets to high-price markets abroad tended to weaken the direct controls over the distribution of commodities. The objective therefore was to set export price ceilings at levels which would neither unduly encourage or discourage exports to any particular area, so that the distribution between markets would be determined by the allocation and priorities system. But the control of export prices was closely related to our foreign-policy objectives, particularly as regards our relations with the American Republics. The Resolutions adopted at the Meeting of Ministers of Foreign Affairs of the American Republics in January, 1942, provided not only for the adoption of export policies which would secure a fair distribution of essential commodities in accordance with needs, but also that each nation would take steps to

[94] This was true to the extent that any shortage of dollar purchasing power of countries like Great Britain would need to be made up by larger lend-lease aid.

prevent the charging of excessive export prices for shipments to other American Republics.[95] Thus the control of export prices was necessary for implementing the policy of inter-American cooperation in prosecuting the war and in the furtherance of the Good Neighbor policy generally.[96] One difficulty with export-price regulations was that many countries did not have adequate control over import prices so that, owing to the limitations on exports, foreign consumers were charged exorbitant prices by importers and other middlemen.

Import-price controls were also established, although many of the regulations dealt only with the resale price in the United States and did not deal directly with the price paid by the importer. By limiting mark-ups on the resale of imported commodities, import-price control reduced pressures on direct controls over imports established through import licensing, shipping priorities, and allocations established by the Combined Boards. In some cases, pressure was brought on foreign sellers to limit price increases.[97] As was mentioned earlier, control over import prices of a number of commodities was achieved through government purchase. In the case of certain commodities such as coffee, cocoa, and petroleum, subsidies were paid in order to keep down prices to American consumers. A portion of the cost of freight and war risk insurance was also absorbed by the government as a means of subsidizing imports.[98]

SUMMARY AND CONCLUSION

World War II completely revolutionized America's domestic and foreign economic policies. The shift from political isolationism to international cooperation for defense was accompanied by a change in America's attitude toward international economic cooperation not only for reasons of security but also for the promotion of the mutual economic welfare of the world.

America's economic mobilization for war grew out of the realization that the outcome of the war in Europe was of paramount concern to the security and welfare of this country. Pearl Harbor found the United

[95] See Resolution III, Final Act and Resolution of the Third Meeting of the Ministers of Foreign Affairs of the American Republics, in *Documents on American Foreign Relations*, Vol. IV, pp. 308–310.

[96] On Apr. 26, 1942, the OPA announced its Maximum Export Price Regulation. For a discussion of the regulation, see Harris, *Price and Related Controls in the United States*, Chap. XV.

[97] *Ibid.*, Chap. XVI.

[98] See S. E. Harris, "Subsidies and Inflation," *American Economic Review*, September, 1943; see also R. F. Mikesell and C. E. Galbreath, "Subsidies and Price Control," *American Economic Review*, September, 1942.

States woefully unprepared in many ways, but this country was far better prepared than it was in 1917. The abandonment of the principles of the Neutrality Act and the decision to provide lend-lease aid to Britain and her Allies was accompanied by a substantial measure of military, industrial, civilian, and governmental preparedness which would most certainly not have been achieved before December 7, 1941, had America continued along the path of isolationism.

Faced with the necessity of mobilizing the resources of a large part of the world for the maximum prosecution of the war, the United States in cooperation with other nations developed techniques of resource distribution based on the principles of need rather than ability to pay. These techniques involved not only large grants to foreign countries but also a high degree of internal and external economic control. Some of these arrangements were carried over into the period of reconstruction and more recently into the programs of joint defense against aggression by the Soviet Union.

While the United States accepted the responsibility for the rehabilitation of the world to a far greater extent following World War II than was the case following World War I, there was nevertheless a substantial underestimation of the magnitude of the problem and of its significance for the future security of the country. In particular, the world was not able to make the adjustment from lend-lease to peacetime trade immediately after V-J Day. This point will be more fully developed in later chapters.

CHAPTER 8

Major Problems and Policies at the End of World War II

The Postwar Economy

JUST AS was the case at the end of World War I, America emerged from World War II as a tower of economic strength and abundance in a world of economic disorganization and want. There were, however, important differences between the two periods. The first was a matter of degree, since the relative importance of the American economy to that of the rest of the world and the disruption of economic life abroad were far greater after World War II. The second difference lies in the larger realization of the American people and their government as to both their position and their responsibilities to the rest of the world in the postwar period. Elaborate plans had been drawn up and organizations created before V-J Day to deal with the problems of the postwar. A third difference lies in the domestic stabilization policies of the government and the determination to avoid the extremes of inflation and deflation which characterized post-World War I. While moderate price inflation continued in the United States until the middle of 1948, the transition to peacetime production at high levels of employment was accomplished in a remarkably short period of time, and the American economy has been able to provide a vast amount of economic assistance to the rest of the world while enjoying a rising standard of living for her own people.

The magnitude of America's economic demobilization is indicated by the fact that, while in 1944 Federal government purchases of goods and services for war purposes amounted to $89 billion out of a gross national product (GNP) of $211 billion (or about 44 per cent), by 1946 government purchases totaled $21 billion out of a GNP of $204 billion (or about 10 per cent).[1] Many millions of men and vast quantities of resources had to be shifted to peacetime production, including the production of new facilities. This shift was accomplished with only a little over 2 million persons unemployed in 1946 and 1947 and only a moderate drop in real GNP, which could be accounted for partly by the reduction of overtime

[1] *National Income,* supplement to *Survey of Current Business,* July, 1947, p. 19.

and a decline of over 4 million persons in the total labor force (including the armed services) from 1945 to 1946.[2] Real GNP declined about 14 per cent from the level of 1944 and about 11 per cent from the level of 1945, but was 52 per cent higher in 1946 than in 1939.[3] The Federal Reserve index of industrial production fell from 235 (1935–1939 = 100) in 1944 to 170 in 1946 but rose again to 187 in 1947 and 192 in 1948. Gross private investment which had fallen to a level of only $4.6 billion in 1943 rose rapidly after the war to $26.5 billion in 1946 and in 1948 amounted to $40.8 billion, accounting for nearly 16 per cent of GNP in the latter year.

Contrary to the expectations of many economists, the chief problem of the transition period was not one of unemployment caused by a shortage in consumer and investment demand and the technical and organizational problems of industrial readjustment, but of a surplus of demand for both consumers' goods and productive resources, including labor. The major reason for the surplus was that the output of consumption goods at current prices was not sufficient to equal the high level of consumer demand out of current income backed up by a sizable backlog of liquid savings. Because of the unavailability of consumers' goods during the war and the pressure for savings-bond purchases, net saving as a percentage of disposable income reached 23.5 per cent in 1944 but fell rapidly after the war to 7.4 per cent in 1946 and 5.1 per cent in 1947. Although government (Federal, state, and local) cash receipts exceeded payments to the public by a small amount ($1.3 billion) in 1946 and by $6.7 billion in 1947, the governmental surplus was offset in the Nation's Economic Budget by an excess of business expenditures over receipts of $11.3 billion in 1946 and $10.7 billion in 1947.[4] In addition, net foreign investment amounted to $4.8 billion in 1946 and $8.9 billion in 1947.

The success of wartime controls in limiting the rise in wholesale prices from December, 1941, to V-J Day to less than 13 per cent recommended a continuation of the controls through the transition period. There were shortages of many durable goods such as automobiles and some nondurable goods such as fats and oils. In the first few months after the war, controls were fairly well maintained but ceilings were adjusted where necessary to stimulate output or relieve hardship. In the 9 months following V-J Day, wholesale prices rose about 7 per cent, but with the

[2] The decline in the total labor force was due to the return of women workers to domestic duties, enrollment in educational institutions, etc.

[3] Based on data from *The Economic Report of the President*, Jan. 8, 1947, p. 41.

[4] See *The Economic Report of the President*, January, 1948, and January, 1949, for tables on the Nation's Economic Budget.

temporary termination of price controls at the end of June, 1946, whole-sale prices rose by 25 per cent in the next six months of that year.

Following the war, there was a popular reaction against controls of all kinds, and when the Emergency Price Control Act which expired on June 30, 1946, came up for renewal, Congress passed a bill with amend-ments designed to remove ceilings on major food products and to re-quire adjustments in price ceilings to take account of advances in manu-facturing costs since 1941. President Truman vetoed this bill on the grounds that it was completely inadequate, and a compromise bill was passed in the latter part of July, 1946. Although this Act was better than no control, it could not prevent the rapid rise which took place once the line had been broken. Price ceilings were removed on a large number of commodities in the winter of 1946–1947 and the remainder in the spring of 1947, all food subsidies were abolished by April, 1947, and in-stallment credit controls administered by the Federal Reserve Bank came to an end in November, 1947. Rent controls were, however, retained. By December, 1947, wholesale prices were 46 per cent above the level of June, 1946, and this rise continued until August, 1948, when wholesale prices were 50 per cent above the level of June, 1946, or 81 per cent above the level of December, 1941.

A good part of the rise in prices in the United States during the period from 1945 to 1948 can be traced, not to the failure to apply selective controls, but to the failure to employ appropriate general antiinflationary devices which would limit consumer expenditures to the flow of available goods and services without price rises. This was largely a matter of mone-tary and fiscal policy. Although modest increases in interest rates over wartime levels were permitted, the administration decided against a policy of high interest rates and stringent credit conditions as a means of combating inflation. Several reasons have been advanced against such a policy. First, high interest rates would substantially increase the interest burden of the public debt, and efforts to reduce bank reserves in order to curb bank loans and investments would cause banks to sell govern-ment securities in large volume, thereby interfering with the debt-financ-ing operations of the Treasury. A large number of bankers were also against any action which would drive down the market value of govern-ment securities on the grounds that banking assets would be impaired.[5] So long as the Federal Reserve authorities were committed to support the government bond market, they were limited in their ability to control the expansion of bank loans and nongovernmental investments since banks

[5] Commercial banks held over $90 billion worth of government securities at the end of November, 1945, and held not less than $60 billion until 1951. *Federal Reserve Bulletin*, July, 1951, p. 831.

could always obtain funds by selling government securities to the Reserve authorities.[6]

The principal deflationary pressure in 1947 and 1948 was the existence of the government's cash surplus. It would have been highly desirable for this surplus to have been larger, but the administration wanted to accomplish this result by maintaining higher tax rates, while economy-minded congressmen believed it should be achieved through reduced spending. The international and defense responsibilities of the government which accounted for better than three-quarters of the budget prevented a decline in expenditures much below $40 billion. Although both income and corporate taxes were reduced during this period, the administration sought to raise revenue through higher corporate taxes,[7] but Congress was opposed to such legislation.

The Balance of Payments

While price inflation undoubtedly weakened the American economy, contributing to frequent wage disputes, misdirected production, and severe hardship on certain economic classes, the impact was especially severe on foreign countries. Unlike the situation under normal international economic conditions when a rise in United States prices with no change in exchange rates should improve the balance-of-payments position of other countries by expanding United States imports and reducing the competitive advantage of American commodities in foreign markets, the postwar price rise had the effect of worsening the position of foreign countries. Exports to the United States were limited by shortages of supply while there was an urgent need for United States products, exportable surpluses of which were not available elsewhere in the world. Since it became necessary for the United States to supplement the dollar resources of the countries of Western Europe and elsewhere, the additional cost resulting from higher export prices had to be borne in considerable measure by the American taxpayer.

United States merchandise exports fell rapidly in the second half of 1945 to an annual rate of $9.7 billion as compared with an annual rate

[6] For a discussion of Federal Reserve policies, see *Reply of the Chairman of the Board of Governors of the Federal Reserve System to the Questionnaire of the Joint Congressional Committee on the Economic Report*, November, 1948, Federal Reserve Board, Washington, D.C.; see also Monetary, Credit and Fiscal Policies, Report of the Subcommittee on Monetary, Credit and Fiscal Policies (Douglas Committee) of the Joint Committee on the Economic Report, Senate Document 129, 81st Congress, 2d Session, Jan. 23, 1950.

[7] See *The Economic Report of the President,* January, 1948, p. 48, and January, 1949, p. 10.

of $14.7 billion during the first half of 1945 and a wartime peak of nearly $17 billion in 1944.[8] In 1946, merchandise exports rose to $11.9 billion and reached a postwar peak of $16.1 billion in 1947, followed by a decline in 1948 to $13.4 billion and in 1949 to $12.3 billion. The character of United States exports after V-J Day changed substantially, however, since in 1944 about half of United States exports were for war purposes while, except for shipments to China, exports of war materials were practically eliminated after the close of hostilities. The destination of United States exports also changed substantially. Exports to Europe outside of Britain expanded rapidly after the liberation, while exports to the United Kingdom declined. Exports to Latin America, which averaged substantially less than $1 billion during the war, rose to $2.2 billion in 1946 and $3.9 billion in 1947. It should be remembered of course that a part of the increase in the value of civilian goods exports reflected the rapid rise in United States export prices.

With the release of shipping for peacetime traffic and the restoration of production in the liberated areas, imports of civilian goods also increased rapidly after the war. Recorded imports which were less than $4 billion in 1944 rose to $4.9 billion in 1946 and $5.7 billion in 1947. Although the huge wartime excess of exports over imports, which was largely sustained by wartime lend-lease, was appreciably narrowed after the war, a large excess was carried over into the postwar period. The huge export surplus of goods and services in 1946 ($7.8 billion), 1947 ($11.5 billion), and 1948 ($6.7 billion) was financed from four principal sources, namely, public and private grants, the liquidation of gold and dollar assets, loans and credits by the United States and international institutions, and United States private investments (see Table 6). Perhaps less than 25 or 30 per cent of this surplus was financed by normal means. (Under normal financing we would include private investments and International Bank loans; [9] some part, say 25 per cent, of the liquidation of gold and dollar assets; and a portion of the United States government loans and credits which might fall under the category of sound productive investments rather than emergency balance-of-payments loans.) Liquidation of gold and dollar assets which amounted to $1.9 billion in 1946 and $4.5 billion in 1947 fell off sharply in 1948 to $780 million. Latin-

[8] All balance-of-payments figures are taken from the *Survey of Current Business*. Figures for merchandise exports and imports include both recorded and unrecorded items unless otherwise specified.

[9] As will be pointed out in a later chapter, some of the important International Bank loans in the early period of the Bank's operations had more of the character of emergency balance-of-payments loans than loans to finance sound projects which directly contributed to the foreign-exchange earning capacity of the borrowing countries.

*Table 6. United States Exports of Goods and Services and Means of Financing, 1946–1950 **

(In millions of dollars)

Item	1946	1947	1948	1949	1950
Exports of goods and services.........	$14,741	$19,796	$17,092	$15,956	$14,351
Means of financing					
Foreign sources:					
United States imports of goods and services.....................	6,963	8,289	10,356	9,715	12,142
Liquidation of gold and dollar assets	1,932	4,462	780	2	−3,628
Dollar disbursements (net) by:					
International Monetary Fund.......	....	462	203	99	−20
International Bank...............	....	300	176	38	37
United States government:					
Grants and other unilateral transfers (net).........................	2,288	1,947	4,161	5,304	4,133
Long- and short-term loans (net)....	2,689	3,895	907	643	159
United States private sources:					
Remittances (net)................	679	665	652	515	439
Long- and short-term capital excluding purchases of obligations issued or guaranteed by the International Bank (net)....................	369	756	869*	616	1,089
Errors and omissions..............	−179	−980	−1,012	−976	

* Excluding $7 million of long-term and $1 million short-term notes guaranteed by the International Bank.

SOURCE: *Survey of Current Business*, June, 1950, and March, 1951.

American countries had built up large balances during the war as a result of their inability to obtain United States exports. Inflationary conditions plus the existence of a large deferred demand for consumers' and investment goods of all kinds led to a rapid liquidation of these balances as United States exports became available. European countries also drew heavily on their gold and dollar balances during 1946 and 1947 in order to pay for the large surplus of dollar imports over exports not otherwise financed.

Foreign gold and short-term dollar holdings amounted to $19.7 billion in June, 1945, as compared with $15.0 [10] billion at the end of 1938. This

[10] *First Semi-annual Report to Congress of the Export-Import Bank of Washington,* 1946, p. 41.

amount was, however, grossly inadequate to meet the minimum needs of the countries whose economies were seriously affected by the war. Not

Table 7. Estimated Foreign Gold and Short-term Dollar Balances
(In billions of dollars)

	June 30		
	1949	1948	1945
ERP countries and dependencies............	$ 7.5	$ 7.3	$10.5
Other European countries..................	0.7	1.0	1.0
Asia and Oceania.........................	2.1	2.0	2.0
Latin America............................	2.8	2.9	3.6
All other countries.......................	1.5	1.4	2.6
Total *...............................	$14.6	$14.6	$19.7

* Exclusive of international organizations and gold holdings of the U.S.S.R.
Source: *National Advisory Council on International Monetary and Financial Problems, Semiannual Report to the President and to the Congress, April 1 to September 30, 1949*, p. 9.

only were these assets not distributed in accordance with the urgency of the needs of the foreign countries, but the rise in prices necessitated larger working balances for all countries. Moreover, it would have been exceedingly dangerous for any country to permit its international reserves to fall to zero, since a sudden worsening of its position might result in widespread privation with attendant political breakdown before outside assistance could be obtained. Thus in spite of the very large demands for United States exports and fairly sizable gold and dollar assets still remaining in the hands of foreign countries, liquidation of gold and dollar assets declined sharply in 1948 and 1949 over the levels of 1946 and 1947. Undoubtedly this liquidation would have been higher without Economic Cooperation Administration (ECA) aid, but it was not the policy of the United States to ask foreign countries to disgorge every last dollar before rendering them assistance.

A considerable portion of the United States export surplus during 1946 and 1947 was met by United States relief-type assistance made available through United Nations Relief and Rehabilitation Administration and our military-occupation authorities, lend-lease pipe-line and surplus-property credits, and large balance-of-payments loans such as the $3¾ billion loan to Britain and the Export-Import Bank loan to France. These loans will be discussed in detail later on, but it should be pointed out that prior to the development of the European Recovery Program, foreign assistance was rendered largely on an *ad hoc* basis without an appreciation of either the magnitude or duration of the foreign reconstruction problem. It was expected by the wartime planners that the emergency relief needs would be handled by UNRRA, the financing of long-term reconstruction and development projects would be provided by the International Bank and private investment, and credits for currency-stabilization purposes would be the province of the International Monetary Fund. We shall see how these expectations were disappointed.

Private foreign investment, which had about disappeared during the 1930's, recovered rapidly after the war, with gross outflow amounting to $794 million in 1946, $1,268 million in 1947, and $1,599 million in 1948.[11] These investments were largely direct investments, three-fourths of which were in the petroleum industry, principally in South America and the Middle and Far East.

Export and Import Controls

Control over exports was retained after the war and the administration of the controls shifted from the wartime Foreign Economic Administration to the Department of Commerce. The purposes of peacetime export licensing controls were as follows: (1) to prevent damage to the domestic economy through excessive exports of industrial and agricultural commodities in short supply in the United States during the postwar transition period; (2) to provide a means of allocating scarce commodities where most needed for recovery abroad; (3) to assist production in foreign countries of materials urgently needed by the United States; and (4) to prevent certain countries from obtaining equipment and materials which would endanger the security of the United States.[12] All four of these objectives involve foreign-policy considerations. How much wheat and steel and lumber we shipped to a foreign country in 1946 and 1947 when these items were short in the United States was determined by our interest in assisting the economy of that country even at the expense of our own economy. On the other hand, steel sent to Venezuela or Arabia made possible larger supplies of petroleum for the United States. Export controls have been closely related to our aid programs since it is not only necessary to provide financing for needed exports to foreign countries,

[11] *The Balance of International Payments of the United States, 1946–1948,* Department of Commerce, 1950, p. 132.

[12] *Export Control and Allocation Powers, Sixth Quarterly Report,* Department of Commerce, January, 1949, p. 5.

but they must have priorities for getting the goods. As of March 1, 1948, shipments of all commodities to Europe were brought under export control. This action was in part intended to prevent the uneconomical use of European purchasing power and to direct exports of scarce commodities in a manner which would contribute the most to European recovery.[13] Thus membership in the ERP was a distinct advantage not only by reason of the financial assistance provided but also for obtaining priority for United States exports. The decision to control exports to all Europe and neighboring regions also provided an opportunity for the careful screening of exports to Eastern Europe. While it was an important objective of the ERP program to encourage East-West trade in Europe, ERP countries have been asked to adopt export-control policies parallel with those of the United States in trading with Eastern Europe.

During 1949 the world-supply situation for most commodities improved to the point where commodity surpluses as opposed to shortages were becoming the major problem. Consequently, export controls were removed or relaxed on a large number of items having little or no military importance. Most of the controls which were maintained were employed primarily for security reasons, *i.e.,* preventing commodities of military significance from being shipped directly or indirectly to Soviet-dominated areas.[14] Since the outbreak of war in Korea in the summer of 1950, United States export controls have been renewed on a number of commodities, including cotton, nonferrous metals, and certain electrical equipment. With growing commodity shortages and the adoption of national and international commodity-control arrangements, United States export controls are again serving the same purposes which they served during the war and immediate postwar periods.

The Second Decontrol Act of 1947 which authorized the extension of our wartime export controls also empowered the administration to control imports of fats and oils, rice and rice products, and nitrogenous fertilizer materials. The principal purpose of these controls was to enable the United States to cooperate effectively in the international distribution of these materials, the plans for which were drawn up by the International Emergency Food Council. Although the International Emergency Food Committee discontinued the international allocation of fats and oils in February, 1949, as a result of the improved supply position of these

[13] *Export and Allocation Powers, Third Quarterly Report,* Department of Commerce, Apr. 30, 1948, pp. 14–15. Export controls have been maintained under the Second Decontrol Act of July 15, 1947.

[14] For a discussion of postwar export controls, see Gardner Patterson, *Survey of United States International Finance, 1949,* International Finance Section, Princeton University, Princeton, N.J., 1950, pp. 169–172.

commodities, the United States maintained severe restrictions on imports of fats and oils (including a virtual embargo of butter) during 1949 solely for the purpose of protecting domestic producers. Protective import quotas on sugar, wheat, cotton, and other agricultural commodities have also been maintained in the postwar period.

Direct export and import controls have apparently become a more or less permanent part of the machinery for realizing America's foreign policy and national-security objectives. Aside from their use as a protective device, United States import controls help to make more effective arrangements for the international allocation of commodities in scarce supply. Export controls enable friendly countries to obtain essential supplies in accordance with the urgency of their needs at prices more or less in line with those prevailing in United States markets. They also enable the United States to limit exports in short supply to unfriendly countries in favor of other countries and to shut off exports of military significance to certain countries entirely. This is a powerful weapon of economic warfare, and although its use represents a contradiction of certain principles of our general foreign-trade policy, it is only one of a number of ways in which these principles have had to give way to the political necessities of the cold war.

International Implications of United States Full-employment Policy

The national and international problems which America faced at the close of World War II were far greater than this country or any other country had ever faced before. But fortunately there developed during the war period a far greater realization on the part of the majority of Americans, in and out of public office, of the responsibilities of their government for dealing adequately with these problems at home and abroad. On the domestic side, there was general agreement that the government must take steps to assist in the reconversion of the economy to peacetime operations, although there was considerable difference of opinion as to how long certain wartime controls such as price and allocation controls should be maintained. There was also a widespread view that the government was responsible for securing economic conditions which would permit high levels of productive employment, fair prices for the farmer, and which would avoid a recurrence of widespread business failures.

Because of the world-wide recognition of the importance of high and stable levels of income and employment in the United States for international trade, United States income and employment policies have considerable international as well as domestic significance. In fact, this country is committed in several international agreements to promote high-income and employment policies. America's basic policy in this field is stated [15] in the Employment Act of 1946, which

> declares that it is the continuing policy and responsibility of the Federal Government to use all practicable means consistent with its needs and obligations and other essential considerations of national policy . . . to coordinate and utilize all its plans, functions and resources for the purpose of creating and maintaining, in a manner calculated to foster and promote free competitive enterprise and the general welfare, conditions under which there will be afforded useful employment opportunities, including self-employment, for those able, willing, and seeking to work, and to promote maximum employment, production, and purchasing power.

Although this Act involved a weaker commitment on full employment and less specific means for carrying it out than in the case of the original bill,[16] the Act of 1946 nevertheless recognized as a matter of public policy the responsibility of the government for promoting "maximum employment, production, and purchasing power." [17]

The establishment of regular machinery in both branches of the government for carrying out an announced policy of high levels of income and employment was a significant landmark in the progress of national responsibility for economic welfare. It substituted a continuing responsibility and an orderly machinery for implementing a national policy for the haphazard national emergency and antidepression measures of the 1930's. Moreover, the definite assumption of governmental responsibility for national economic welfare provided the basic conditions for

[15] Public Law 304, 79th Congress, 2d Session.

[16] The original full-employment bill of 1945 (S. 380, 79th Congress, 1st Session) would have established in more specific terms a governmental policy of continuing full employment with any short-fall being made up through additional Federal investment and expenditure. This bill further provided that the President shall transmit to Congress at the beginning of each year a national production and employment budget designed to achieve a level of national income consistent with full employment for the economy. This bill had the support of the administration and of a large section of the public, but was not enacted.

[17] The Employment Act of 1946 established a Council of Economic Advisers in the Executive Office of the President, whose duty it was to advise the President as to the economic pulse of the nation and assist him in the preparation of an Annual Economic Report to the Congress. The purpose of the Economic Report is to analyze current developments in the American economy and to "recommend naitonal economy policy to promote employment, production and purchasing power under free competitive enterprise." A Joint Committee on the Economic Report consisting of members of both Houses of Congress was established to study matters relating to the Economic Report and to make recommendations to Congress with respect to those made by the President in the Economic Report.

the assumption of greater responsibility in international affairs. Thus when the United States joined the United Nations it formally recognized that not only were all the dealings of the American government and its citizens with other nations to be the subject of international consultation and friendly negotiation where conflicting policies or special problems arose, but even the operations of the domestic economy were a matter of international concern where they affected the welfare of other nations. Article 55 of the United Nations Charter declares:

> With a view to the creation of conditions of stability and well-being which are necessary for peaceful and friendly relations among nations based on respect for the principle of equal rights and self-determination of peoples, the United Nations shall promote:
> (a) Higher standards of living, *full employment* [18] and conditions of economic and social progress and development;
> (b) Solutions of international economic social, health, and related problems; and international cultural and educational cooperations; and
> (c) Universal respect, and observance of, human rights, and fundamental freedoms for all without distinction as to race, sex, language, or religion.
> Article 56: All Members pledge themselves to take joint and separate action in cooperation with the Organization for the achievement of the purposes set forth in Article 55.

While the above obligation is subject to a variety of interpretations, it is clear that the United States in joining the United Nations in 1945 recognized its international responsibility for maintaining high levels of domestic income and employment and for promoting the conditions for economic progress the world over.

Foreign Economic Policies at the End of World War II

Perhaps the most significant legacy of World War II was the renunciation of political isolationism even by many Americans who had been its champions before Pearl Harbor. During the course of the war, both the administration and the majority of Congress endorsed the principle of collective security.[19] Thus long before the end of the war the Ameri-

---

[18] Italics inserted.

[19] In his annual message to Congress on Jan. 11, 1944, the President announced his objective of collective security, not simply physical security but "economic security, social security, moral security—a family of nations." (*Documents on American Foreign Relations,* World Peace Foundation, Boston, 1939, Vol. VI, pp. 19–20.)

The principle of collective security was endorsed by Congress with the passage of the Fulbright Resolution by the House on Sept. 21, 1943 (the Senate concurring):

"That the Congress hereby expresses itself as favoring the creation of appropriate international machinery with power adequate to establish and to maintain a just and

can government and the vast majority of its people were resolved to participate actively in international affairs for the preservation of peace, through the use of collective force if necessary. But along with a realization of America's political responsibilities, there developed policies relating to her economic and social responsibilities. The formulation of postwar programs and policies in the international economic field had been carried on in the executive branch of the government throughout the war period. We shall survey the development of some of these programs and policies in the chapters to come. But programs and policies can only be translated into action by the enactment of appropriate legislation by Congress, which in turn reflects the sentiment of the majority of the American people. Hence in this discussion of where the United States had arrived in its thinking about the problems presented to it by the end of the war, we shall consider briefly the reports of the House Special Committee on Post-war Economic Policy and Planning (Colmer Committee) which was established in January, 1944. The Colmer Committee held hearings and made recommendations (many of which were enacted into law) on a wide range of postwar problems, including the settlement of terminated war contracts, surplus-property disposal, industrial demobilization and reconversion, transitional unemployment, public works, monetary and fiscal problems, agriculture, and foreign trade and shipping.[20] We are principally interested in the committee's report of May 8, 1945, entitled *The Post-war Foreign Economic Policy of the United States*,[21] since it provides perhaps the most representative statement of America's postwar economic policy on the eve of the termination of the war. Since the committee's conclusions and recommendations were developed in close cooperation with members of the executive branch, the general policies stated in its report were for the most part in harmony with those of the administration.

The general purpose of America's postwar foreign economic policy was stated by the Colmer Committee as follows: [22]

> The foreign economic policies recommended in this report are intended both to establish the economic foundations for a durable peace and to assist in providing high and expanding levels of income at home and abroad. In

---

lasting peace, among the nations of the world, and as favoring participation by the United States therein through its constitutional processes." (*Documents on American Foreign Relations*, Vol. VI, p. 315.)

[20] See Fourth Report of the Special Committee on Post-war Economic Policy and Planning, Sept. 8, 1944, House Report 1855, 78th Congress, 2d Session.

[21] House Report 541, 79th Congress, 1st Session.

[22] The Post-war Foreign Economic Policy of the United States, House Report 541, 79th Congress, 1st Session, p. 1.

developing a program with these aims in view, the committee has also been constantly aware of the importance of preserving the principles of individual freedom and private initiative which has contributed so much to our welfare in the past.

The basic assumption underlying United States foreign economic policy was that there exists a close relationship between a high level of world income and a high level of international trade conducted on a multilateral basis under private enterprise and that both are essential to a durable peace. In the development of economic measures for the realization of this threefold objective, attention was focused more on the general principles of commercial and investment policy than on the immediate problems of restoring foreign productive capacity and of the far-reaching adjustments in the structure of world trade which were necessary to overcome the deep-rooted maladjustments brought about by the cumulative effects of two world wars. Thus the policy outlined by the committee's report provided an admirable set of criteria to be followed by this country in a world which had already achieved a fair degree of equilibrium, but it was scarcely a prescription for arriving at this happy state of affairs.

The committee's report recognized the importance of a high level of United States income and employment as an essential requirement for an expanding world trade. It also recognized that, if United States exports were to be maintained at or near the wartime level, imports would need to increase several times their prewar level or foreign investments would need to be made on an unprecedented scale. In order to achieve a balanced expansion of trade, the committee recommended action in four principal fields: (1) foreign loans and investments, (2) international monetary policy, (3) commercial policy, and (4) shipping and shipbuilding.

1. The committee recommended a policy of encouraging a high level of private foreign investment supplemented by investment through public institutions such as the Export-Import Bank and the International Bank. It made a strong case for the benefits of foreign lending, both to the domestic economy and to world economic and political stability. It recognized the need for a stable level of foreign investment if the supply of dollars available for making interest and amortization payments was to be maintained, but attributed the cessation of investment in the 1930's to a loss of confidence brought about by the world depression.

If stable economic conditions can be restored . . . there is no reason to believe that productive foreign investment will be any more capricious and uncertain than domestic investment. Our foreign investment program, like almost all other foreign economic programs, thus depends for its success upon the maintenance of income and employment throughout the world. With a stable level of income, there is every reason to believe that private foreign investment can be resumed on a steady and reliable basis.

As to the problem of repayment, the committee's report pointed out the similarity between foreign and domestic investments. "In the absence of political or economic disturbances, there is no reason for supposing that in 20 or 30 years our savers will wish to hold a smaller proportion of their wealth in foreign assets than they wish to hold in that form in the immediate post-war period. From a national point of view, foreign investments are therefore quite as permanent as domestic investments." The report suggested that after 20 or 30 years of outpourings of American capital, the international capital position of the United States will become similar to that of Britain before the war, and our balance-of-payments position will have gradually adjusted itself to one which would permit this country to absorb an excess of imports representing the income from our foreign investments.

2. The recommendation of the Colmer Committee's report on international monetary policy closely paralleled the position of the American delegates at the Bretton Woods Conference in 1944, the development of which we shall consider in detail in a later chapter. Competitive currency depreciation, exchange controls, exchange discounts, and multiple-currency practices were all condemned as undesirable interferences with world trade and the free flow of foreign investment. The report recommended the establishment of equilibrium rates of exchange shortly after the war, with rate changes to be made only when absolutely necessary, through an international organization established for this purpose. To help countries maintain exchange rates in the face of temporary discrepancies in their foreign payments and receipts, there should be established a reserve of international currencies on which each country might draw in time of need. It is worth noting that here, as was also the case with the American authors of the preliminary drafts of the agreement for the establishment of the International Monetary Fund, the emphasis was on stabilizing exchange rates and the elimination of competitive currency depreciation. Except as a wartime measure, exchange controls and their counterparts, quota and licensing controls, were viewed largely in terms of unfair commercial practices or protective devices to be abolished by mutual agreement. The full nature of the problem of removing wartime trade and exchange controls in the postwar period in terms of both the international economic environment and of the serious policy conflicts between countries was not foreseen by our postwar policy makers.

3. In the field of commercial policy the House Committee's Report on Post War Foreign Economic Policy dealt with tariffs, quotas and other direct trade restrictions, commodity-price-stabilization agreements, and international cartels. The report, while justifying the protectionist policy of the United States during the nineteenth century as an aid to our industrialization, deplored the world-wide growth of protectionism in the 1930's and suggested that American industry could gradually adjust itself to lower tariffs in the future. The report therefore recommended a renewal of the Reciprocal Trade Agreements Act which was to expire in June, 1945, and an expansion of the President's power to reduce tariffs on a reciprocal basis. As a means of eliminating other objectionable trade controls such as import quotas and export subsidies, the report recommended the calling of an international conference whose aim would be to achieve a general agreement on trade barriers and to arrange for a permanent organization to implement a broad program in this field after the war.

4. The committee's recommendations on shipping reaffirmed the prewar policy of maintaining a large United States merchant marine for reasons of national security and called for operating and construction subsidies to the extent needed for merchant vessels "the operation of which is considered essential in the interest of national security." The committee recognized, however, that many countries depended upon the sale of shipping services as a source of dollars. The report therefore stated, "For shipping not considered essential for national security, the comparative cost of rendering transportation service should be the determining factor. No subsidies should be provided to such shipping." Unfortunately, the committee failed to recognize the possibility of applying the principles of collective security to shipping. The comprehensive nature of the requirements of modern warfare provide an argument for self-sufficiency in the production of a large proportion of its essentials, unless nations allied for their common defense, *e.g.*, the Atlantic Treaty nations, agree in advance upon a program of pooling all their scarce resources in time of war. Only in this way can the security interest be prevented from grossly interfering with the maximization of the gains from international specialization.

The policies outlined above, which in general reflected the views of both branches of the government and of the American public, represented a major advance over America's prewar international economic policies and reflected a desire on the part of the United States to play a leading role in international political and economic affairs in the postwar period. Long before the end of the war, plans had been developed, largely initiated by the United States, for a number of specialized international organizations and commissions dealing with almost every conceivable international economic and social problem and interest: foreign exchange, foreign investment, shipping, aviation, communications, agriculture, labor, health, refugees, and general economic welfare and full employment. Only a few of these organizations can be dealt with in this volume, however.

In the development of the implementation of America's postwar foreign economic policies, we shall see that the principal weakness lay in the preconceptions regarding the postwar economic and political environment on which they were based. There was first of all an underestimation of the magnitude and duration of the problems of postwar reconstruction, particularly as regards Europe but also as regards the world economy generally. Secondly, the political course of events, especially as regards America's relations with Russia, was not foreseen. The inability of the United Nations to deal with the fundamental political conflicts has made it necessary to orient American foreign economic policy in large measure in the direction of achieving political rather than broad economic and humanitarian objectives. Sometimes these objectives have coincided, but frequently they have been in conflict. Thus, for example, our trade and investment policy with Eastern Europe has had to be one of restricting trade and economic development in that area for reasons of national security.

Another weakness of our foreign economic policy lies in the failure to resolve conflicts between our general policy and certain other deep-rooted American policies. For example, our foreign agricultural program which provides for export subsidies and import quota controls is sharply at variance with our general international economic policy. Finally, our policies have frequently come into conflict with the interests and policies of other countries. Countries which have adopted a policy of socialization and governmental control of industry are unable to accept American trade and foreign-exchange policies. Many countries have for one reason or another not instituted domestic fiscal and monetary policies which would make it possible for them to remove controls on foreign trade. Underdeveloped countries seeking to industrialize have insisted on their right to employ protective measures for this purpose, just as the United States fostered its own industrialization in the nineteenth century through tariff protection. America has been accused of seeking to remake the world in its own image and of trying to force upon the rest of the world those policies best designed to provide its own welfare. We shall consider this thesis as we survey the postwar development of this policy.

The remaining chapters of this book will be devoted to a discussion of America's postwar policies in the following fields: (1) international monetary policy, (2) foreign investment, (3) commercial policy, (4) extraordinary foreign assistance, and (5) the economic policies relating to the defense of the free world. In setting the stage for the discussion to follow, we must keep in mind the motivating forces of American foreign policy. The general foreign economic policies discussed earlier in this chapter are firmly rooted in American economic tradition and practice and point to the creation of a world in which American private enterprise would feel itself at home everywhere in the world. This policy reflects a growing responsibility on the part of the American government for the economic welfare of its own people and of the world economy generally. But, by and large, the programs initially conceived for the implementation of this policy were those appropriate for a predominantly free world economy in which a substantial measure of economic and political stability had already been achieved. American policy and action in the years following V-J Day have had to be adapted to a far different set of circumstances than were preconceived at the time our basic policy lines were determined.

CHAPTER 9

International Monetary Policy: Exchange Rates and Gold Policy

WE SHALL divide our discussion of America's postwar international monetary policy into the following major subjects: (1) exchange-rate stabilization, (2) gold policy, (3) stabilization credits, (4) exchange controls, (5) the sterling area, and (6) intra-European payments arrangements. The first two of these closely related subjects will be dealt with in this chapter, while the remainder will be taken up in Chaps. 10 and 11, together with a summary of these chapters at the end of Chap. 11.

Although much of our postwar international monetary policy centers around the International Monetary Fund, the Fund is by no means the sole instrument through which American policy is expressed in this field.[1] We must consider the Anglo-American financial agreement, the United States Exchange Stabilization Fund, and the highly significant developments in the foreign-exchange field in the countries of Western Europe, with which the Economic Cooperation Administration has been intimately concerned. Moreover, the policies of the Monetary Fund, an international institution, are by no means identical with those of the United States even though they have been largely supported by the American government. Most of the policies and activities of the Fund represent a compromise of the positions of its members. This is not simply a matter of voting strength, since few issues in the Fund are ever brought to a formal vote. The United States with over 30 per cent of the voting strength in the Fund could corral a majority of the votes on most issues, but it would be an empty victory in most cases. Except as a safeguard

---

[1] The Bretton Woods Act of 1945 established the National Advisory Council on International Monetary and Financial Problems, "to coordinate the policies and operations of the representatives of the United States on the Fund and the Bank and of all agencies of the Government which make or participate in making foreign loans or which engage in foreign financial, exchange or monetary transactions. . . ." The Council consists of the Secretary of the Treasury, as Chairman, the Secretary of State, the Secretary of Commerce, the Chairman of the Board of Governors of the Federal Reserve System, the Chairman of the Board of Directors of the Export-Import Bank of Washington and, during the period of the Economic Cooperation Administration, the Administrator for Economic Cooperation.

against a misuse of the Fund's resources, America's preponderance of voting strength in the Fund is of little value in achieving our foreign-policy objectives. No policy of the Fund is likely to be successful in the face of a strong minority opposition. The Fund has no power over its members except that of persuasion and the withholding of its largess, and these powers have shown themselves to be exceedingly weak in the case of serious conflicts involving the fundamental national interests of its members.

For reasons cited above, our approach to American international economic policy will not be in terms of the development of institutions as such, but rather we shall seek to trace each major aspect of that policy as it has expressed itself in international conferences and organizations and in concrete measures for its implementation. Unfortunately, the deliberations of the executive directors of the Monetary Fund and of recent bilateral negotiations with other countries on monetary matters are confidential and cannot be revealed. But we do know the basic policies of the United States and of other countries, most of the factual circumstances surrounding the negotiations, and the decisions arrived at by the negotiations. The rest we can only conjecture, but the main lines of policy development and its rationale will be clear.

EXCHANGE-RATE STABILIZATION

In Chap. 5 we saw how after the stabilization of the dollar in January, 1934, and the creation of an Exchange Stabilization Fund, the United States embarked upon a cautious program of promoting the stability of international currencies. Once the policy of manipulating the gold value of the dollar as a means of raising domestic prices was abandoned, the United States sought to further its commercial interests through the elimination of competitive currency depreciation. Cooperative efforts along this line came to an end with the outbreak of war in Europe, but the United States continued to make stabilization agreements with the American Republics.[2]

In the course of the preparations for the Conference of Ministers of Foreign Affairs of the American Republics, consideration was given by the State and Treasury Departments to the possibility of broadening these bilateral arrangements through the creation of an international stabilization fund. At this conference, which met in January, 1942, the United States delegation introduced a resolution to the effect that: "the Govern-

[2] See, for example, "Joint Statement by the Secretaries of the Treasuries of the United States and Mexico," Nov. 19, 1941, *Annual Report of the Secretary of the Treasury, 1942,* p. 291.

ments of the American Republics participate in a Special Conference of Ministers of Finance, or their representatives to be called for the purpose of considering the establishment of an international stabilization fund." [3] The purpose of this action was both to foster the Good Neighbor policy and to promote American policy in the field of foreign exchange. Meanwhile, work had been progressing in the Treasury Department under the direction of Dr. Harry D. White,[4] on a plan for a United Nations stabilization fund. In the months that followed, a series of discussions on Dr. White's proposals were carried on within the United States government, and the idea of an inter-American conference was abandoned in favor of preparations for a United Nations stabilization fund.

The Development of the Monetary Fund Agreement. The early Treasury Department drafts of a stabilization-fund proposal not only placed major emphasis on exchange-rate stabilization but were exceedingly restrictive with respect to changes in currency parities. Members could change their rates only when a change was essential to correct a *fundamental disequilibrium* and then only with the approval of *four-fifths* of the member votes, a provision which would have assured the United States of a veto over all changes in the par values of the currencies of other members. Although the minutes of these early interdepartmental discussions reveal that some of the participants believed that consideration ought to be given to greater flexibility of exchange rates, especially for smaller countries, the prevailing sentiment favored the provisions of the Treasury draft on this point. These provisions regarding rate changes, which were carried over into the first published draft of the proposal of April, 1943,[5] were not modified in the American drafts until after preliminary discussions had been carried on with representatives of the British government and with those of other countries.[6]

[3] Final Act and Resolutions, Art. XV, Jan. 28, 1942, in *Documents on American Foreign Relations,* World Peace Foundation, Boston, Vol. IV, p. 317.

[4] Dr. White's original memorandum entitled, "Proposal for a Stabilization Fund of the United and Associated Nations," was prepared in December, 1941. See J. P. Young, "Developing Plans for an International Monetary Fund and a World Bank," *Department of State Bulletin,* Nov. 13, 1950.

[5] Preliminary Draft Outline of Proposal for a United and Associated Nations Stabilization Fund, in *Proceedings and Documents of the United Nations Monetary and Financial Conference,* Department of State, 1948, Vol. II, Appendix IV, p. 1538.

[6] Exploratory discussions with the British representatives on a postwar monetary organization, which began in the fall of 1942, centered around a comparison of the "Proposals for an International Clearing Union" prepared by Lord Keynes ("the Keynes Plan") and the Treasury proposals for an international stabilization fund (the "White Plan"). The Keynes Plan was transmitted to the United States State and Treasury Departments in August, 1942, while the White Plan had been given to the British

In the discussions which followed throughout the spring and summer of 1943,[7] it became clear that the United Kingdom as well as a number of other countries could not agree to the American provisions with respect to exchange-rate changes.[8] The British also found unacceptable the requirement of an 85 per cent majority vote for changing the gold value of the new currency unit to which all currencies were to be tied.[9] At a meeting with American technicians in Washington in September, 1943, Lord Keynes proposed an agreement on exchange rates along the following lines:

1. Members would agree not to propose a change in exchange rates unless the change was essential to correct a "fundamental disequilibrium." (This provision was already in the White Plan.)

2. The Fund should not withhold its approval of a proposed change if the change, inclusive of previous changes, did not exceed 10 per cent within any 10-year period.

3. Special consideration should be given to members which had exceeded their quota rights.

4. In the event that it was not possible to obtain the Fund's prior approval to a change in its rate, a member could make the change, and if the Fund disapproved, the member could then either reverse its action or withdraw from the Fund.

5. The Fund should not disapprove a change in a rate necessitated by social or political policies of the member.

The American experts finally accepted with certain modifications points 1, 2, and 5 of Lord Keynes's proposals on exchange-rate changes but, in

---

sometime earlier on an informal basis. Text of the Keynes Plan was published in *Proceedings and Documents of the United Nations Monetary and Financial Conference,* Vol. II, pp. 1548–1573.

[7] Both the White and Keynes plans were published in April, 1943, and informal discussions with a number of countries were conducted in Washington in the course of that year, including a 15-nation informal conference in June, 1943.

[8] The Canadian proposal entitled, "Tentative Draft Proposals of Canadian Experts for an International Exchange Union," while similar in many respects to the American draft, was nearly identical with the Keynes Plan on the subject of exchange-rate alterations. See *Proceedings and Documents of the United Nations Monetary and Financial Conference,* Vol. II, pp. 1575–1596.

[9] The international currency unit in the White Plan was called "unitas," while a similar unit in the Keynes Plan was called "bancor." Later on the idea of an international currency unit was dropped, but that of a simultaneous change in the gold value of all currencies was retained in the Articles of Agreement on the International Monetary Fund. In the final version of the Bretton Woods Agreements, the gold value of all currencies could be changed by a majority vote provided that all members having 10 per cent or more of the total of the quotas in the Fund concurred and provided further that any member could elect not to go along in the proposed change.

addition, asked Britain to agree that it would not depreciate the value of the pound (which at that time was $4.03), prior to the establishment of the Fund. (This condition is interesting in the light of the unofficial view on the part of a large number of American officials that the pound was overvalued prior to its devaluation in September, 1949.) Final agreement with the British on the Fund's provisions on changes in exchange rates was reached in the spring of 1944 and published in the Joint Statement by Experts on the Establishment of an International Monetary Fund of the United and Associated Nations in April, 1944.[10] The Joint Statement set forth the main outlines of the Fund Agreements, which were expanded but not significantly altered in principle at the Bretton Woods Conference in July, 1944.[11]

The exact meaning of the term "fundamental disequilibrium" was not defined in the Fund Agreement, nor do the published documents of the

[10] *Proceedings and Documents of the United Nations Monetary and Financial Conference*, Vol. II, pp. 1629–1636.

[11] The provisions on changes in par values as adopted by the Bretton Woods Conference were as follows:

"(a) A member shall not propose a change in the par value of its currency except to correct a fundamental disequilibrium.

"(b) A change in the par value of a member's currency may be made only on the proposal of the member and only after consultation with the Fund.

"(c) When a change is proposed, the Fund shall first take into account the changes, if any, which have already taken place in the initial par value of the member's currency as determined under Article XX, Section 4. If the proposed change, together with all previous changes, whether increases or decreases,

"(i) does not exceed ten per cent of the initial par value, the Fund shall raise no objection;

"(ii) does not exceed a further ten per cent of the initial par value, the Fund may either concur or object, but shall declare its attitude within seventy-two hours if the member so requests;

"(iii) is not within (i) or (ii) above, the Fund may either concur or object, but shall be entitled to a longer period in which to declare its attitude.

"(d) Uniform changes in par values made under Section 7 of this Article shall not be taken into account in determining whether a proposed change falls within (i), (ii), or (iii) of (c) above.

"(e) A member may change the par value of its currency without the concurrence of the Fund if the change does not affect the international transactions of members of the Fund.

"(f) The Fund shall concur in a proposed change which is within the terms of (c) (ii) or (c) (iii) above if it is satisfied that the change is necessary to correct a fundamental disequilibrium. In particular, provided it is so satisfied, it shall not object to a proposed change because of the domestic social or political policies of the member proposing the change.

See Art. IV, Sec. 5, Articles of Agreement, International Monetary Fund, Washington, D.C.

Bretton Woods Conference throw much light on this question. The central problem, which has been the subject of considerable debate among economists in recent years, is whether or not a country can be in a condition of fundamental disequilibrium (and hence entitled to change its rate) when it does not have a deficit in its balance of payments. Professor Alvin Hansen [12] and Dr. Robert Triffin [13] have argued that it is possible for a country to be in fundamental disequilibrium without having a balance-of-payments deficit, since if it has an overvalued currency there may be a deflationary effect on prices, income, and employment. Professor G. Haberler, on the other hand, has taken the position that "a country which thinks that it is entitled under the 'fundamental disequilibrium clause' of the Articles of Agreement, to a depreciation should at first attempt to protect itself through compensatory domestic policies and should be allowed to depreciate only after a deficit in its balance of payments has actually occurred." [14]

The author's view on this question is in agreement with Haberler's position. Although a country's exchange rate may not be compatible with both satisfactory levels of income and employment and with equilibrium in its balance of payments,[15] it is impossible to determine the degree of exchange-rate alteration which is required until the country has actually taken all the appropriate internal measures for securing a level of monetary demand consistent with reasonable levels of employment. Under conditions in which a large number of countries are depressed, each one of them might decide that it was in a condition of disequilibrium and engage in competitive exchange depreciation; whereas if all of them were to take appropriate measures for expanding internal demand first, the resulting balance-of-payments pattern might indicate that no rate changes were called for or that only certain countries were properly entitled to them.

[12] A. Hansen, "Fundamental Disequilibrium," *Foreign Economic Policy for the United States,* edited by Seymour E. Harris, Harvard University Press, Cambridge, Mass., 1948, pp. 379–383.

[13] See R. Triffin, "National Central Banking and the International Economy," and a comment by G. Haberler in *International Monetary Policies,* Postwar Economic Studies 7, Federal Reserve Board, Washington, D.C., September, 1947.

[14] Haberler, *op. cit.,* p. 98.

[15] By balance-of-payments equilibrium is meant a condition in which receipts from exports of goods and services plus long-term capital imports are equal to payments for imports plus long-term capital exports, at satisfactory levels of employment and income, without a change in direct trade and exchange controls, and after allowing for seasonal and short-term cyclical movements. This is essentially the definition given by R. Nurkse in his *Conditions of International Monetary Equilibrium,* International Finance Section, Princeton University, Princeton, N.J., 1945.

This question must be decided by the executive directors of the Monetary Fund in the course of their operations, since the Fund's Articles of Agreement provide no direct answer. As we shall shortly see, however, the criteria for setting the initial parities in the Fund Agreement did refer to the balance of payments. Also, for what it is worth, the author is in possession of an unpublished memorandum, circulated informally among the technical experts of other governments just prior to the Bretton Woods Conference, which discusses the concept of "fundamental disequilibrium" in terms of a condition in which "other satisfactory measures cannot be taken to restore equilibrium in a country's balance of payments position."

The following interpretation of the executive board of the Fund on Art. IV, Sec. 5 (f), at the request of the United Kingdom provides an indication of the official view of the Fund with respect to the concept of fundamental disequilibrium:

> The Executive Directors interpret the Articles of Agreement to mean that steps which are necessary to protect a member from unemployment of a chronic or persistent character, *arising from pressure on its balance of payments,* are among the measures necessary to correct a fundamental disequilibrium; and that in each instance in which a member proposes a change in the par value of its currency to correct a fundamental disequilibrium the Fund will be required to determine, in the light of all relevant circumstances, whether in its opinion the proposed change is necessary to correct the fundamental disequilibrium.[16]

It should be observed that the Fund has no power to require a country to change its exchange rate once the initial parity has been accepted by the Fund. Alteration in a country's exchange rate has such an important effect upon the economic life of that country that it was believed that almost no country would find it politically possible to submit to dictation in this field. However, the Fund might withhold its resources from a country which maintained what the Fund believed to be an improper rate. The Fund was given the power in Art. XX, Sec. 4, of the Articles of Agreement to reject the initial parity of a country which is to be "based on the rates of exchange prevailing on the sixtieth day before the entry into force of this Agreement," if "in its opinion the par value cannot be maintained without causing recourse to the Fund on the part of that member or others on a scale prejudicial to the Fund and to members."

The Fund's Exchange-rate Policy in Operation. On December 18, 1946, the managing director of the Fund announced the schedule of par values

[16] Italics inserted. *Report of the Executive Directors and Summary Proceedings,* First Annual Meeting of the Board of Governors, Sept. 27–Oct. 3, 1946, International Monetary Fund, November, 1946, pp. 105–106.

which had been accepted by the Fund.[17] Except in the case of those members which had requested in accordance with Art. XX, Sec. 4, more time for the determination of their initial parities, the Fund accepted all the parities proposed by members, which were based on existing rates of exchange. The Fund's Report justified this action as follows: [18]

> The Fund realizes that at the present exchange rates there are substantial disparities in price and wage levels among a number of countries. In present circumstances, however, such disparities do not have the same significance as in normal times. For practically all countries, exports are being limited mainly by difficulties of production or transport, and the wide gaps which exist in some countries between the cost of needed imports and the proceeds of exports would not be appreciably narrowed by changes in their currency parities. In addition, many countries have just begun to recover from the disruption of war, and efforts to restore the productivity of their economies may be expected to bring their cost structures into line with those of other countries. Furthermore, for many countries now concerned with combatting inflation there is a danger that a change in the exchange rate would aggravate the internal tendencies toward inflation.

The United States National Advisory Council (NAC) in its report of June 24, 1947,[19] stated that it had "expressed views substantially in accord with those contained in the statement issued by the Fund," and quoted with approval excerpts from the Fund's statement. There were many people who were disappointed that the Fund did not attempt to establish a more appropriate pattern of exchange rates at the outset, since it was admitted in the Fund's statement that some of the rates involved "substantial disparities" in price and wage levels among members. The decision not to challenge existing rates was made partly on economic grounds, as given in the Fund's statement quoted above, and partly on political grounds. The decision was in effect based in large measure upon the philosophy that the Fund should not initiate or seek to force changes in the exchange rates of members. Basically, the job of the Fund was to see that, when rate changes were made, they were made in an orderly manner which did not give rise to competitive exchange depreciation.

In the period from December, 1946, when the initial parities were accepted, to September, 1949, only two countries, Colombia and Mexico, established new parities with the Fund. During this period, the Fund

---

[17] *Annual Report of the Executive Directors for Year Ending June 30, 1947,* International Monetary Fund, Appendix X.

[18] *Ibid.*

[19] *Report of the Activities of the National Advisory Council on International Monetary and Financial Problems to March 31, 1947,* House Document 365, 80th Congress, 1st Session.

took the position that "so long as an exchange rate does not hamper a country's exports, there is little to be said in present world conditions for altering it." Since most countries' exports were limited by their ability to produce rather than their ability to sell in a world characterized by sellers' markets for nearly everything that moved in international trade, it was difficult to show that exports were being limited by overvalued rates. However, the level of rates undoubtedly influenced the allocation of resources in investment programs in favor of production for home consumption or of production for export to other high-cost areas rather than to the dollar area. In addition, the existence of overvalued rates in Latin-American countries tended to stimulate a volume of imports which could not be paid for out of current foreign-exchange earnings.[20]

That the NAC concurred in the general position of the Fund on exchange rates is indicated by the following statement in its report for the period October 1, 1948, to March 31, 1949:

> The Council has given continual attention to the problem of the exchange rates of participating countries. It concluded that in 1948 a general revaluation of the European exchange rates was inadvisable in view of the possible international repercussions of devaluation on the participating countries in a period when their economies still exhibited serious inflationary tendencies, while their levels of production were not adequate to maintain an expanded volume of international trade. (p. 15.)

By the spring of 1949, however, it was evident that both the Fund and the NAC were becoming convinced that the time for exchange-rate revision had arrived. The Council's report for the period ended March 31, 1949, went on to state that it

> recognizes that if viability of the European economies is to be attained by 1952, greater progress must be made by the European countries in redressing their balance of payments position with the Western Hemisphere, and in attracting private foreign investment. It is the Council's opinion that in some cases the revaluation of currencies may constitute an important means of bringing about the desired expansion of exports to the dollar area. . . . While fully aware of the difficulties involved in exchange rate adjustments, the Council believes that the problem should be explored with some of the European countries. Where adjustments of exchange rates are indicated, it is expected that member countries will make appropriate proposals to the International Monetary Fund. (p. 15.)

[20] The author has criticized the postwar rate structure in an article entitled, "The International Monetary Fund, 1944–1949," *International Conciliation*, November, 1949; and in "The International Monetary Fund," *Journal of Political Economy*, October, 1949.

Informal discussions on the exchange-rate issue were held with a number of European Recovery Program countries by representatives of the ECA, the Treasury Department, and other governmental agencies during 1949.[21] As will be seen in our discussion of the ERP, the United States has taken the initiative in discussing with the appropriate officials in these countries and with the officials of the Organization for European Economic Cooperation (OEEC) all questions concerning the economic welfare of the recipients of ERP assistance, and indeed the ECA has a duty to do so under the ECA Act. However, no country has been forced to change its rate under threat of the withdrawal of ECA aid, nor has any country been told what its rate ought to be. The position of the United States government has been that in the last analysis the Monetary Fund has the responsibility for the supervision of exchange-rate adjustments.

In its *Annual Report of the Executive Directors for the Year Ending April 30, 1949,* the Fund also indicated the need for action on the part of deficit countries to improve their competitive position through exchange-rate adjustments and other measures designed to reduce export prices. Although discussions of the exchange rates of particular countries were carried on in the Fund, so far as is known to the author, direct pressure has not been applied to any member to change its rate except to the extent that the exchange rate may have been a factor in determining the member's eligibility for obtaining credits from the Fund.

We may conclude that it has been the basic position of both the Monetary Fund and the United States that countries ought not to be encouraged or subjected to pressure to alter their exchange rates until it could be shown that existing rates were hampering either total exports or a proper distribution of exports between dollar and nondollar markets. The essential reasoning behind this policy may be summed up as follows: (1) It was impossible for countries to achieve equilibrium in the transition period except at exchange rates which would have meant a drastic change in terms of trade, prohibitive prices for essential imports, and a drain into the export market of resources urgently needed for domestic reconstruction. (2) Until countries had achieved a reasonable amount of internal stability, any improvement in the trade balance achieved through devaluation would be quickly dissipated by a rise in prices.[22] (3) Devaluation would not appreciably increase exports in the short run, and the

---

[21] The tripartite discussions with the British and Canadian governments which were held in September, 1949, came after the British Government had decided on the devaluation of the pound sterling from $4.03 to $2.80 but before the actual devaluation announcement was made.

[22] For a discussion of the effect of exchange depreciation on inflation, see C. P. Kindleberger, *The Dollar Shortage,* Wiley, New York, 1950, pp. 202–204.

demand for imports in most countries was limited by direct controls. (4) To attempt to limit imports by means of exchange depreciation would work a severe hardship on low-income groups, increase luxury imports at the expense of essential commodities, and disrupt the recovery effort through inflation.

This position meant of course that in the transition period, at least, foreign trade and to some extent the volume and character of investment would be determined by direct controls rather than through the operation of the price mechanism. Nations would work toward equilibrium through planning the character of their production and trade rather than relying on the relative level of prices at home and abroad to secure a balance between imports and exports. Of course for the ERP countries, balance *at any exchange rate* could have been achieved only at standards of living which threatened political stability and at a level of investment which would not have permitted the rebuilding of war-ravaged economies and the making of fundamental readjustments to the changed conditions of world production and demand. American aid was necessary to bridge the gap between the amount of foreign exchange which these countries could earn (at any exchange rate) and what they needed to maintain tolerable living standards and a level of investment necessary for achieving viability within a reasonably short period of time. Hence so long as countries were receiving aid, the equilibrium rate would have been higher than a rate compatible with balance-of-payments equilibrium in the absence of such aid. Had the United States chosen to foster a policy of relatively free exchange transactions and equilibrium rates during the recovery period, it would have been necessary to have had a different kind of foreign-aid program. Instead of tying economic assistance to particular commodities and programs and of insisting upon a careful husbanding of dollar exchange on the part of all aid recipients, it should have simply given Western Europe the dollars in the form of a large dollar grant, without conditions as to where and how the funds should be spent.[23] In many ways, therefore, the manner in which American foreign assistance was provided was predicated on the maintenance of a system of internal and external controls in the recipient countries and the absence of an equilibrium exchange rate.

Fixed versus Fluctuating Rates. There have been many critics of the postwar foreign-exchange policy of the Fund and of the United States

[23] Aid recipients under such a program would have been required to adjust their exchange rates and adapt their fiscal and monetary policies in a manner which would have assured a balance in their international accounts after taking into account receipts of a given amount of United States aid, without the use of controls on current transactions.

government.[24] It has been argued that the Fund fosters exchange control by emphasizing rigid exchange rates. In a world in which the automatic correctives of the balance of payments fail to operate because of rigidities in the markets for commodities and productive factors, and compensatory fiscal and monetary policies,[25] balance-of-payments equilibrium without the extensive use of exchange and trade controls is only possible under a system of flexible exchange rates.[26] This criticism raises a number of questions with respect to exchange-rate policy for both the immediate postwar transition period and for the longer run. As regards the former, it is difficult to see how freedom of exchange transactions and equilibrium rates would have promoted the recovery of countries whose productive capacity was seriously impaired and whose exchange resources were barely sufficient to pay for imports essential for maintaining their economies as going concerns. In cases of extreme shortages of commodities essential to the health and welfare of a nation, the price mechanism must give way to some form of rationing. While we may question the appropriateness of the initial par values certified by the Fund from the standpoint of their long-run influence on the character of investment, production, and the pattern of trade, we must conclude that a system of fluctuating rates would have contributed more to the internal instability than to the viability of economies disrupted by the war.

Turning to the future, the problem of flexible vs. stable exchange rates is less clear. On the one hand, there are serious obstacles to the maintenance of balance-of-payments equilibrium with stable exchange rates under modern conditions of price rigidities and national economic planning. On the other hand, these very rigidities and controls render exchange-rate adjustments themselves a less effective instrument for restoring equilibrium once it is disturbed. It should be said, however, that there is nothing in the policies of the Monetary Fund or of the American government which would preclude frequent changes in exchange rates provided that the country in question is experiencing balance-of-payments difficulties and also provided that such changes are preceded by consulta-

[24] See, for example, Frank D. Graham, *The Cause and Cure of "Dollar Shortage,"* International Financial Section, Princeton University, Princeton, N.J., 1949.

[25] See Raymond F. Mikesell, "International Disequilibrium in the Post-war World," *American Economic Review*, June, 1949.

[26] Another view which was expressed by John H. Williams and others before the International Monetary Fund was established was that stabilization efforts should be confined to stabilizing the pound-dollar rate (the "key-currency" proposal) and that considerable flexibility be permitted for other currencies during the transition period. See John H. Williams, "Currency Stabilization: the Keynes and White Plans," *Foreign Affairs*, July, 1943; and "Currency Stabilization: American and British Attitudes," *Foreign Affairs*, January, 1944.

tion with or concurrence by the Fund. American exchange-rate policy is no longer motivated by a desire to protect America's competitive advantage by preventing necessary adjustments in the exchange rates of other countries through orderly means. Rather its primary concern is to reestablish world equilibrium and a system of international payments which would permit the restoration of world-wide multilateral trade.

Recent developments have shown an increasingly liberal attitude on the part of the Monetary Fund and the American government toward flexible exchange-rate systems involving fluctuating rates. Some Latin-American countries had, as a part of their multiple-rate systems, freely fluctuating rates for certain categories of transactions, when they became members of the Fund, and have been permitted to retain these arrangements under either Art. VIII, Sec. 3, or Art. XIV of the Fund Agreement. The Fund's policy with respect to free market rates as stated in its *Annual Report of the Executive Directors for the Fiscal Year Ending April 30, 1948,* p. 68, is as follows:

> When a multiple currency practice includes a free market with a fluctuating rate, the member should agree with the Fund on the scope of the transactions permitted to take place in that market. Any changes in the scope of these transactions should, of course, be subject to agreement with the Fund. The objective should be to eliminate the fluctuations in the free market as soon as such action is reasonably practicable. When it is not reasonably practicable to eliminate such fluctuations, the Fund will encourage members to exclude current transactions from the free market to the extent that this would be reasonable in the circumstances of each case.

Whatever the merits of fluctuating rates, the Fund has scarcely taken a rigid line on this matter. When Italy came into the Fund in 1947, her exchange system also involved a controlled free rate with respect to the dollar. In commenting upon the Italian system, the Fund made the following statement: [27]

> Arrangements which, in fact, result in fluctuating exchange rates are not in accord with the long-term objectives of the Fund. The Fund recognizes, however, that in some cases members may be required, for temporary periods, to institute extraordinary measures in an attempt to meet particular difficulties. The Fund will look on such measures for temporary periods with sympathy.

A somewhat different case was represented by the French action of January, 1948, in adopting a fluctuating rate system. France, unlike Italy, already had an agreed par value with the Fund and had had no history

[27] *Annual Report of the Executive Directors for the Fiscal Year Ending April 30, 1948,* International Monetary Fund, 1948.

of multiple rates. In addition, the new French system involved a discriminatory-rate arrangement. The Fund rejected the French proposal, for reasons which will be described later on, because of its discriminatory-rate feature, and not because it involved a devaluation and the substitution of a fluctuating for a fixed rate of exchange. This attitude is indicated in the following statement by the Fund: [28]

> The Fund gave careful consideration to the proposal to establish a market for convertible currencies along the lines indicated above. The Fund had no desire to be rigid or doctrinaire in its approach to the matter, particularly in view of the abnormalities of the present situation. Despite serious reservations regarding a system involving fluctuating rates, the Fund explored various alternatives designed to meet insofar as possible the objectives of the French authorities. . . .

Other examples of the Fund's willingness to agree to a system of fluctuating exchange rates for temporary periods are provided by the adoption, with the concurrence of the Fund, of a free market for the Mexican peso in July, 1948,[29] of a fluctuating rate for the Peruvian sol in November, 1949,[30] and of a free market rate for the Canadian dollar on September 30, 1950.[31]

The NAC has presumably been in complete agreement with the above actions and policies of the Fund. In addition, there has been a tendency in administrative circles to favor greater flexibility of exchange rates for Western European countries as a means of helping these countries eliminate trade barriers among themselves. The ECA has, for example, viewed with favor some of the proposals for economic integration of the ERP countries which involve the use of flexible rates. In discussing the problem of European integration, ECA Administrator Hoffman made the following statement in a speech before the OEEC on October 31, 1949: [32]

> Another essential of your plan, I believe, is that it should provide means for necessary exchange rate adjustments, subject, of course, to the general supervision of the International Monetary Fund, where these are the only feasible alternatives to imposing direct exchange controls within Europe.

In the opinion of the author there is little economic advantage, and serious disadvantages, in a system of day-to-day exchange-rate fluctuations

[28] *Ibid.*, pp. 76–77.

[29] A new par value and fixed exchange rate was established for the Mexican peso in June, 1949. See *Annual Report of the Executive Directors for the Fiscal Year Ending April 30, 1949*, International Monetary Fund, p. 25.

[30] *International Financial News Survey*, International Monetary Fund, Vol. II, No. 20, Nov. 18, 1949.

[31] *International Financial News Survey*, Vol. III, No. 14, Oct. 6, 1950.

[32] *The New York Times*, Nov. 1, 1949.

over one in which changes are made periodically subject to changes in fundamental balance-of-payments conditions. Day-to-day changes in demand-and-supply conditions reflect seasonal, speculative, and other temporary movements which could well be offset by means of stabilization operations, while at the same time a periodic review every six months or so would reveal any need for a change in the rate in response to more fundamental factors. Such a review could be made in consultation with the Fund, and rate adjustments could be effected without danger of competitive exchange depreciation and other retaliatory action on the part of other countries.

The objections to the system suggested above are largely psychological and political. Formal changes in established exchange rates or par values are frequently accompanied by adverse reactions against the government and a general loss of confidence. Governments find it easier to change exchange rates under a floating-rate system than to make periodic adjustments in the official par values of their currencies. In addition, if changes are made through the Monetary Fund, the country proposing the change is required to submit its case before an international body. It should also be said that, although there is nothing in the Fund Agreement or the rules and regulations of its executive board which limits the number of rate changes which can be approved in any period of time, a country which proposed exchange-rate changes for offsetting temporary movements in its trade balance could scarcely be meeting the test of fundamental disequilibrium in its payments position. Such movements are supposed to be handled by drawing on reserves or by borrowing from the Fund. Finally, it should be observed that most of the floating-rate systems in operation today do not involve true equilibrium rates. Rather, the exchange markets are hedged about by controls over the use of the foreign exchange which is purchased and the source of the exchange coming into the market. In addition, many of these rate systems involve discriminatory rates since arbitrage is frequently not permitted between the markets for different currencies. We shall now consider the policy with respect to multiple-currency and discriminatory-rate practices.

Multiple Currencies.[33] At the Bretton Woods Conference the Latin-American countries, most of which had multiple-rate systems, were concerned as to whether or not they would be permitted to continue these arrangements. Although American policy clearly favored the abolition of such practices, there was a desire to ensure the participation of these

[33] In this section, we shall deal with exchange-rate systems involving more than one rate with respect to a particular foreign currency. The problem of discriminatory rates, *i.e.*, those which violate official cross rates between the foreign currencies, will be considered in the following section.

countries in the Fund and to make every effort to reach a satisfactory compromise. In the final draft of the Bretton Woods Agreements, countries which had multiple-rate systems before joining the Fund were permitted to maintain them for a time either under Art. VIII, Sec. 3, which provided for their gradual removal in consultation with the Fund, or under Art. XIV, which deals with the transitional arrangements. In addition the Fund was given power to authorize their use by special permission.

Since the inauguration of the Fund, its policy with respect to multiple-currency practices has been an exceedingly tolerant one. This has been due in part to the fact that the transitional provisions of Art. XIV appear to sanction almost any type of exchange-control device [34] for countries with balance-of-payments difficulties, although the Fund does have the power to challenge any particular practice as being contrary to its purposes. It may also be said that the Fund's staff and executive board have been somewhat sympathetic to the use of multiple rates in certain circumstances which will be indicated below. The position of the United States government with respect to multiple rates is in general accord with the Fund's policies.[35] The continued existence of multiple-rate structures does, however, greatly complicate the Reciprocal Tariff Agreements program since a tariff concession on the part of a foreign government can be nullified by a change in the exchange rate applicable to the commodity in question. In addition, certain types of multiple rates may be regarded as export subsidies, and hence under American tariff laws commodities benefiting from them are liable to the imposition of countervailing duties. Thus the existence of multiple rates and their sanction by the Fund would appear to be inconsistent with certain aspects of American commercial policy. It may perhaps be said, on the other hand, that multiple exchange rates do not represent any greater violation of American commercial policy than quotas and exchange controls so long as both are employed for balance-of-payments reasons. When the need for restrictions for safeguarding the balance of payments disappears in most countries of the world, multiple exchange rates will appear solely as devices for the protection of domestic industry, for the subsidization of exports, or for raising revenue for the state. Except possibly for the latter purpose, the Fund would be clearly justified in insisting upon their removal.

The policy of the Fund with respect to multiple rates as stated in its *Annual Report for 1948* may be summarized as follows:

[34] Multiple-exchange rates inevitably involve exchange controls since in a completely free market there could be only one price for a foreign currency.

[35] See *Second Special Report to the President and to the Congress*, National Advisory Council on International Monetary and Financial Problems, May, 1950, p. 20.

1. Where multiple-currency practices are not needed for balance-of-payments reasons, early steps should be taken for their removal.

2. Where such practices are needed for balance-of-payments reasons, the Fund will encourage members to remove them by not later than the end of the transitional period.

3. Where complete removal by the end of the transitional period proves impossible, the Fund will assist the members concerned to eliminate the most dangerous aspects of their multiple-currency practices and to exercise reasonable control over those retained.

The Fund has maintained its right to review any proposed changes in existing multiple-rate structures of its members and has in general sought to promote changes which moved in the direction of a greater simplification of existing systems. Nevertheless, some Latin-American Fund members have quite complicated systems involving three or four buying rates and an equal number of selling rates for foreign currencies.[36]

Multiple-rate structures serve a variety of purposes which must be understood in dealing intelligently with their simplification or elimination. In some countries, a special buying rate for foreign exchange may serve as a means of taxation. For example, in Venezuela the petroleum companies are required to purchase the local currency which they require from the central bank at 3.09 bolivares to the dollar while the commercial rate for imports is 3.35 bolivares. Rates of 4.80 and 4.25 bolivares for the proceeds of coffee and cacao exports have the effect of subsidizing the exportation of these commodities.

Countries using multiple-rate systems to limit imports frequently have several categories of imports to which different rates apply. The most essential imports usually come in at the lowest rate for foreign exchange, while the higher rates apply to luxury commodities or commodities imported in competition with domestic production. In some cases, countries use multiple rates as an alternative to direct controls in limiting imports. This is accomplished by establishing one or more preferential rates for essential imports for which the foreign exchange can be obtained from the central bank and a free market or auction rate for all other imports. Some economists have argued with considerable cogency that a system whereby foreign exchange available for importing less essential imports is auctioned, after the more essential foreign-exchange payments have been met, involves less interference with trade and with market forces

36 For a description of exchange-rate systems, see *First Annual Report on Exchange Restrictions*, International Monetary Fund, March, 1950. For an excellent discussion of the economic effects of multiple rates, see E. M. Bernstein, "Some Economic Aspects of Multiple Exchange Rates," *International Monetary Fund Staff Papers*, Vol. 1, No. 2, pp. 224–237.

than one subjecting all imports to licensing or exchange control.[37] So long
as our international agreements and institutions sanction restrictions on
imports for balance-of-payments reasons, why not permit them to use the
multiple-rate device? The principal objection to this position is that,
where countries employing multiple-rate systems enter into reciprocal
tariff negotiations, changes in their rate structure may nullify any tariff
concessions which they may make. On the other hand, a change in the
par value of the currency of a country with a uniform rate, or the imposition of new quota or exchange-control practices, may also nullify tariff
concessions.

American foreign economic policy faces something of a dilemma on the
multiple-exchange-rate issue. On the one hand, there are a number of
countries whose fiscal and monetary systems make it difficult for them to
raise revenue through internal taxation and to maintain a balance in
their external accounts through fiscal and monetary controls. Multiple-
rate systems frequently provide a means of taxing foreign corporations or
of forcing them to turn over foreign exchange earned through exports.
Frequently, the administrative machinery for direct controls over imports
does not exist and would prove difficult to establish. It is doubtful whether
or not a number of Latin-American countries could be induced to give
up multiple-rate structures which have played such an important part in
their economic systems for many years, although they may be persuaded
to modify them. On the other hand, these practices make difficult or impossible the establishment of a set of rules of fair dealing in international
trade. The following principles are suggested as a way of dealing with
this problem:

1. The Fund should limit the use of multiple rates to two purposes, namely,
the protection of the balance of payments and the raising of revenue, where
feasible alternatives can be shown not to exist.

2. Rates which have as their purpose the protection of particular home industries or the subsidization of particular industries should be speedily abolished.

3. Where countries employ multiple rates as a means of protecting their balance of payments, rate structures should be simplified so that there would exist
only one export rate and no more than two import rates.

4. Any change in the classification of imports for exchange-rate purposes
should be subject to review by both the Monetary Fund and the General Agreement on Tariffs and Trade (GATT).[38]

[37] See R. Triffin, "National Central Banking and the International Economy," *International Monetary Policies,* Postwar Economic Studies 7, Federal Reserve Board,
Washington, D.C., September, 1947.

[38] Article XV, Sec. 9(a), of the GATT provides in effect that in the case of members
of the Fund, the Fund has sole jurisdiction over exchange practices. See the General
Agreement on Tariffs and Trade, Department of State, 1950, p. 36.

5. When a country has reached a position in which special arrangements are clearly not needed to protect its balance of payments, a uniform rate should be established except in cases where a particular arrangement serves a purely revenue function.

6. The application of countervailing duties by the United States to products from foreign countries employing multiple rates should be limited to those cases where the rate structure clearly involves a subsidy to the exportation of commodities produced in the United States and whereby substantial damage to the American industry can be shown.

7. Tariff concessions on the part of the United States to countries with multiple-rate systems should not be revoked unless the rate structure is altered in such a way as to involve the protection of domestic production of the commodity on which a concession has been negotiated.[39]

Discriminatory-rate Practices. Trade discrimination may be accomplished in one of two general ways: (1) There is the familiar device of direct controls in which the licensing or the exchange control system discriminates in favor of imports from or exports to a particular country or region. (2) There is the method of price discrimination in which imports are made cheaper or exports more profitable through the use of discriminatory tariffs, excise taxes, exchange taxes, or exchange rates. Before the war, discriminatory exchange rates were occasionally used for fostering trade between two countries even where no balance-of-payments problem was involved. For example, Argentina employed an exchange system whereby sterling exchange could be purchased 10 per cent cheaper than dollar exchange although the dollar and the pound were freely convertible. The same purpose can be served by a preferential tariff system which provides for lower rates for commodities coming from certain countries. American policy has been directed against the use of discriminatory rate practices for the same reason that it has opposed preferential tariffs and other discriminatory practices. Article VIII, Sec. 3, of the Articles of Agreement subjects discriminatory currency arrangements to the same conditions as it does multiple-currency practices, but, as we shall see, the Fund has treated these practices quite differently in the administration of this provision.

The use of discriminatory currency practices, *e.g.*, the employment of exchange rates which do not conform to official cross rates between two foreign currencies, has arisen in the postwar period, not for reasons of commercial policy, but for balance-of-payments reasons arising out of the complex of exchange control systems in world trade. A country which has

[39] Article II, Sec. 3, of the GATT provides that no contracting party shall alter its method of determining dutiable value or of converting currencies so as to impair a tariff concession.

an abundance of inconvertible sterling but which is short on dollars may seek to channel its trade in such a way as to import more from sterling sources and export more to the dollar area, either by the use of direct trade and exchange controls, or through price incentives. If it chooses the latter method, it will permit the price of dollar exchange in terms of its own currency to rise relative to the price of sterling exchange. But this device inevitably violates the cross rate between the dollar and sterling in terms of the official parity between these two currencies. Thus in the spring of 1948, France maintained a fixed rate of 862 francs to the pound sterling and a fluctuating rate for the dollar which hovered around 265. This meant a cross rate of $3.25 to the pound as against the official rate of $4.03.[40]

Italy, Greece, and certain Latin-American countries have also had discriminatory-rate systems in the postwar period. The reason these systems were instituted stemmed from the desire on the part of France and other countries employing them to loosen up on their direct controls somewhat or to establish a limited free market in dollars, while at the same time discriminating in favor of soft-currency imports and hard-currency exports. Since, with the dollar shortage, discrimination against American trade would take place in any case, the principal objection to these arrangements has come not from the United States but from Britain.[41] When the French government proposed a new official parity for the franc coupled with a discriminatory currency practice in January, 1948, the Fund rejected the proposal. The French government in its official statement announcing the new system [42] argued that the arrangement was necessary as a temporary measure for adjusting France's balance of payments and that it was fully in accord with the provisions of Art. XIV of the Fund Agreement on transitional arrangements. Without going into the legalities of the situation, it would appear that the Fund clearly had the power to approve or to reject the proposed arrangement.

The objections of the Fund and of the British to discriminatory-rate practices are worth reviewing because American officials may well find it necessary to deal with similar cases in the future. The Fund has objected

[40] France adopted this system in January, 1948, without the consent of the Fund, thereby rendering herself ineligible to use the resources of the Fund. (Article IV, Sec. 6, Articles of Agreement, International Monetary Fund.) In October, 1948, France revised her rate system in a manner which eliminated the discriminatory cross rate between the pound sterling and the dollar for most transactions.

[41] See "Anglo-French Statement on the Devaluation of the Franc," *The New York Times,* Jan. 26, 1948, p. 4; see also statement by the Fund on this issue, *Annual Report of the Executive Directors for the Fiscal Year Ending April 30, 1948,* International Monetary Fund, Appendix V.

[42] *The New York Times,* Jan. 26, 1948, p. 4.

to the use of discriminatory rates even in the transitional period on three grounds: (1) It is maintained that the practice tends to undermine the position of the currencies which are selling at a discount relative to the dollar and other hard currencies. Thus when the cross rate on the pound sterling in the French market was $3.30 rather than $4.03, doubts naturally arose as to the validity of the sterling parity. (2) A more direct disadvantage than the purely psychological effect of the sale of sterling at a discount arises when traders are able to buy sterling with dollars at a discount in France and purchase commodities in the sterling area with sterling rather than with dollars. (3) The Fund has also objected to the use of discriminatory-rate systems on the ground that they distort the pattern of world trade and add to the difficulties of eventually restoring currency convertibility.

The problem of eliminating discriminatory cross rates is by no means confined to the prevention of their use by members of the Fund under official government sanction. Before the September, 1949, devaluation, there was a growing traffic in free market transferable account sterling in countries which did not have official discriminatory-rate systems. By dealing in these markets, certain American wool importers were able to purchase Australian wool at a substantial discount over what they would have had to pay if they had bought the wool with dollars or American account sterling directly from Australia.

Discriminatory cross rates arise from the fact that currencies are not generally interconvertible. When Britain or a member of the sterling area buys goods with inconvertible sterling, such sterling may ordinarily be used only for making purchases within the sterling area (or within certain other countries designated as transferable-account countries if the recipient is itself a transferable-account country). This sterling is not supposed to be sold for dollars or other hard currencies except with the permission of the British Treasury. But unless the countries which acquire inconvertible sterling have tight exchange controls, some of this sterling may be sold for hard currencies. So long as dollars are generally more desirable than sterling, sterling sold in free markets will be at a discount compared with the official parity. Paradoxically, therefore, the only way that the Fund can eliminate discriminatory cross rates which result in a discount on inconvertible currencies from their official parities is to ask members dealing in these currencies to tighten up their exchange controls. Since a large part of the trading world outside the United States does business with the sterling area with inconvertible sterling, it becomes evident that the most essential key to the elimination of discriminatory trade and exchange controls is the restoration of sterling-dollar convertibility.

The devaluation of sterling in September, 1949, from $4.03 to $2.80 has not eliminated the problem of discriminatory cross rates, and the market for "cheap" sterling has continued.[43] So long as sterling remains inconvertible, illicit transactions will take place at less than the official rate since there will always be people in the sterling area or other sterling-using countries who would prefer to have dollars rather than sterling.

GOLD POLICY

Gold policy and exchange-rate policy are closely interrelated. The heart of the gold policy of the United States is the maintenance of the status of gold as an international standard of value and medium of settling international balances. Since gold is an international standard, it follows that exchange-rate stability cannot exist unless currencies have a fixed value in terms of gold and international transactions in gold are conducted at the official gold prices or gold parities of the countries involved. It also follows from this basic policy that, so long as gold is international money, it should not be traded in international markets as a commodity whose price in terms of national currencies is subject to the forces of demand and supply. In fact, with nearly all nations of the world off the gold standard, the only way to limit transactions in gold to the settlement of international balances at official gold prices or parities is to limit such transactions to those between central banks and treasuries or their agents.

Both America's domestic gold policy and the international policy which she has supported in the Monetary Fund are in line with the general policy outlined above. The Gold Reserve Act of 1934 vests title to all monetary gold in the United States Treasury, and no internal transactions in fine gold are permitted.[44] The Gold Reserve Act also authorizes the Treasury Department to license all exports of gold, and recently Treasury regulations were amended to the effect that licenses are no longer issued for the private export of fine bar gold and licenses for the export of gold refined from imported gold-bearing materials are issued only where the American refiner does not participate in the sale of the gold.[45] Licenses for export of refined gold are also subject to the requirement that gold-bearing material has been legally exported from the country of origin and that the refined gold is imported into the country of destination in accordance with the laws and regulations of the import-

---

[43] In November, 1949, transferable-account sterling sold in New York between $2.55 and $2.60. For a discussion of free market sterling sales, see "Sterling Since Devaluation," *The Economist*, Nov. 26, 1949.

[44] Transactions in gold ore are legal.

[45] *Annual Report of the Secretary of the Treasury, 1948*, p. 47.

ing country. Gold from domestic stocks is exported at $35 per ounce (plus one-fourth of 1 per cent) at the request of Treasuries and central banks holding dollar balances in this country. Imports of gold are subject to the Gold Declaration of February 22, 1944, which declared that the United States would not recognize transfers of title to looted gold and that the Treasury would not purchase gold located outside the United States from any country which had not broken relations with the Axis until it was satisfied that such gold was not acquired from the Axis and was not gold which was released as a result of the acquisition of Axis gold. Thus United States gold policy has been employed as an instrument of foreign political policy.[46]

In addition to the legal limitations on private transactions in gold within the territory of the United States, the Secretary of the Treasury and the Federal Reserve Board issued a joint statement on July 18, 1947, condemning gold transactions in foreign markets at premium prices and requested "American individuals, banks and business enterprises to refrain from encouraging and facilitating this traffic and in particular to refrain from extending the use of their facilities and funds for the carrying out of such transactions." [47]

The United States gold policy in the international field is expressed in the Monetary Fund. The early drafts of the American proposals provided for a special monetary unit called unitas (consisting of $137\frac{1}{7}$ grams of fine gold equivalent to $10 United States) in terms of which the accounts of the Fund were to be kept and the value of each member country's currency was to be stated. Although the special gold unit was dropped in the final agreement, all currencies are to be defined in terms of gold (or the United States gold dollar of 1944), and members may not buy gold at prices above or sell below the gold parities of their currencies, plus or minus a prescribed margin to be determined by the Fund (Art. IV, Sec. 2). The Fund did not of course require that its members adopt the international gold standard in the sense that their currencies would always be freely convertible into gold. This would have been quite unacceptable to other countries, and in fact Lord Keynes defended the Fund Agreement in Britain on the grounds that it was the "exact opposite" of the gold standard.[48] Since, however, all balances arising out of current

---

[46] *Annual Report of the Secretary of the Treasury, 1944,* p. 87. For a discussion of the relationship between United States gold policy and foreign policy objectives, see C. R. Whittlesey, "Political Aspects of the Gold Problem," *The Tasks of Economic History,* Economic History Association, 1949, Supplement IX, pp. 50–60.

[47] Text of statement printed in *Federal Reserve Bulletin,* August, 1947, p. 978.

[48] This statement was made by Lord Keynes in a speech in the House of Lords, May 23, 1944.

transactions were to be convertible into any currency, including the dollar which is a gold currency, the Fund agreement in effect embodied the essential elements of an international gold-exchange standard.

The fact that currencies have not been generally convertible since the war and that they have been generally overvalued in terms of gold at free market prices has presented serious difficulties for the Fund in implementing its gold policy. Gold is not only an international currency but a commodity whose production is quite important to the economies of countries such as Canada and South Africa.[49] The fact that its official price in terms of dollars has remained constant since 1934 while other prices have doubled or tripled has affected gold production throughout the world. (However, in 1949 the purchasing power of gold in terms of commodities was about the same as it was in the 1920's.) Gold is also in demand not only for industrial purposes but as a hoarding medium in many countries, especially in those with overvalued or weak currencies. Premium prices for gold have therefore developed in both illegal and legal markets the world over, and gold producers naturally desire to take advantage of those markets by selling gold at prices in excess of $35 per per ounce.

The Fund has opposed international transactions in monetary gold at premium prices on two general grounds. First, such purchases and sales directly or indirectly involve exchange transactions at exchange rates which differ from parity. Thus the seller of gold at a premium price is obtaining a larger number of currency units for the gold equivalent of his own currency than he would have obtained if he sold the gold at a price determined by the gold equivalents of the two currencies at parity.

The second objection advanced by the Fund is that premium transactions in gold result directly or indirectly in a loss of monetary reserves to the country buying the gold. When Frenchmen buy gold from abroad to be used for private hoarding, they must pay for the gold either in foreign currencies or in their own currency. When foreign currencies are used, it means that France has less foreign exchange for its imports, while when payment is made in French francs it means that the francs can be used in France to buy goods and services which otherwise might have been purchased with foreign exchange. When such transactions countervene French foreign-exchange regulations, it may mean that the country of the seller is failing to cooperate with France in the enforcing of French foreign-exchange regulations. This second objection has perhaps more practical significance than the first, although the extent of the loss of foreign

---

[49] The following discussion is an adaptation of the material presented by the author in an article entitled, "The International Monetary Fund, 1944–1949," *International Conciliation,* November, 1949, pp. 865–868.

exchange through illegal transactions in member countries is difficult to determine.

Closely related to international transactions at premium prices is the problem of government subsidies to gold producers. The Fund has taken the position that such subsidies may involve a price for gold in excess of the parity price plus the prescribed margin, even though the gold is sold to another country at the official price.[50] Of more practical significance, however, is the effect of gold subsidies on the principal buyer of the world's gold output, namely, the United States. The United States holds gold stocks far in excess of what it is likely to need for settling international deficits at any time in the foreseeable future. Although the United States government may be willing to buy unlimited amounts of gold at $35 per ounce to preserve the validity and stability of gold as an international standard, it is certainly not interested in acquiring monetary gold for its own sake. Hence it is not in the interest of the United States for countries to subsidize gold production as a means of solving their balance-of-payments problems.

In dealing with cases involving premium gold sales, the Fund has sought to make a distinction between gold intended for industrial or artistic uses and that which is intended for hoarding or speculative purposes. A full implementation of this policy would require the policing of premium gold transactions through the various stages to the end use to which the gold is put. The Fund's gold policy is the logical outcome of a condition in which currencies are defined in terms of a fixed weight of a commodity but which are not generally convertible into that commodity. It is doubtful just how long this fiction can be maintained. It seems likely that either countries must return to some form of gold or gold-exchange standard—which means the restoration of currency convertibility—or gold will cease to be an international standard of value.

[50] The Fund requires members to submit proposals for subsidizing gold production to the Fund for its approval. In general, the Fund will not approve a uniform payment per ounce for all or a part of a country's gold production. Subsidies to marginal mines determined in relation to producers' costs have been approved. (For statement of policy, see *Annual Report of the Executive Directors for the Fiscal Year Ending April 30, 1948,* International Monetary Fund, 1948, pp. 92–94 and Appendix VI.) The Fund has approved gold-subsidy programs employed by Southern Rhodesia, Australia, Canada, and South Africa.

CHAPTER 10

International Monetary Policy: Stabilization Credits and Exchange Controls

THIS CHAPTER will deal with America's postwar policies in the field of currency-stabilization credits and foreign-exchange controls except those involved in multiple-exchange-rate systems, which were discussed in Chap. 9. The special problems of America's relations with the sterling area and the European Recovery Program countries will be taken up in Chap. 11.

STABILIZATION CREDITS

American experience with stabilization credits dates from the activities of the Federal Reserve banks during the 1920's in lending support to European currencies. These activities came to an end with the depression and the breakdown of the international gold standard. In the early part of its history, the United States Exchange Stabilization Fund rendered technical assistance to other countries in stabilizing their currencies under the Tripartite Agreement, but as we have seen, these activities could scarcely be called stabilization operations. A true stabilization loan or line of credit is one which is made available to a country for use in stabilizing a currency for which there is a free market, and the rate to be stabilized is one which is considered to be an equilibrium rate capable of being held over a period of time without a net loss of foreign exchange. Thus a true stabilization loan supplements a country's foreign-exchange reserves not for the purpose of meeting a planned deficit, but rather to enable that country to meet deficits due to seasonal, speculative, or other short-term factors.

Operations of the United States Exchange-stabilization Fund. Few of the stabilization loans of the Exchange Stabilization Fund or of the Monetary Fund could meet the tests of a true stabilization loan. Either the loans were used to meet planned or expected balance-of-payments deficits, or they were made to countries without free exchange markets or freely convertible currencies, or both. Most of the early stabilization credits were backed by 100 per cent gold collateral and represented a means by which foreign countries could obtain dollar exchange without having to sell their gold reserves. The first loan for which no collateral was required was in reality a war loan to China in April, 1941.[1] Probably the closest approach to a true stabilization loan is represented by the stabilization agreements with Mexico of November 19, 1941, and of May 13, 1947.[2] Mexico has a free foreign-exchange market, and except for the period, July, 1948, to June, 1949, Mexico has maintained a stable rate for the peso. The 1947 Stabilization Fund credit was drawn down rapidly together with a credit of $22.5 million from the Monetary Fund, but with the improvement in Mexico's foreign-exchange position in 1950 the Stabilization Fund credits were repaid.[3]

The stabilization loans made by the Treasury Department from the Exchange Stabilization Fund were probably motivated more by a desire to give financial assistance to a foreign country, *e.g.*, China, Ecuador, and Liberia, in which the United States has a special political and economic interest, than by genuine currency-stabilization objectives. To some extent, the recent loans to Mexico have been motivated by a desire to help that country maintain a free foreign-exchange system, but in the case of most of the other loans the Stabilization Fund represented an accessible source of assistance for general balance-of-payments purposes. As of June 30, 1949, the assets of the Exchange Stabilization Fund totaled $305.8 million, of which $55.7 million represented foreign-exchange holdings.[4] The United States Fund will probably continue to be used to meet the need for short-term financial assistance to countries in which the United States

[1] *United States Relations with China,* Department of State, August, 1949, p. 31.

[2] Under the 1941 agreement Mexico was given the right to purchase up to $46 million worth of dollars with Mexican pesos and under the agreement of 1947 Mexico was given the right to purchase up to $50 million. *Report of Activities of the National Advisory Council on International Monetary and Financial Problems, April 1, 1947, to September 30, 1947.*

[3] As of Sept. 30, 1948, Mexico had drawn $37 million of the $50 million stabilization credit. See *National Advisory Council on International Monetary and Financial Problems, Semiannual Report to the President and to the Congress, for the Period April 1 to September 30, 1948,* p. 28. In June, 1949, Mexico was granted an additional $12 million credit by the United States Exchange Stabilization Fund, but the supplemental credit was not drawn upon. With the improvement in Mexico's dollar position in 1950, she was able to repay all the credits by the end of that year. See *Annual Report of the Secretary of the Treasury, 1950,* p. 49.

[4] *Annual Report of the Secretary of the Treasury, 1949,* p. 598. With the repayment of the Mexican credits, the Stabilization Fund's holdings of foreign currencies were reduced to $27.6 million as of June 30, 1950.

has a special political interest, when these needs cannot be met by the International Fund.

International Stabilization Credits: American and British Proposals. The technique for extending stabilization credits which was employed in the Treasury's stabilization agreements, *i.e.,* extending the right to a country to purchase dollars with its own currency under an agreement to repurchase, was carried over into the original drafts of the American proposals for an international stabilization fund. Like the United States Fund, the proposed international fund was not designed to support currencies directly in the foreign-exchange markets, but to sell foreign exchange to members when needed to meet a deficit on current account. Instead of the United States putting up all the funds, each member of the international fund would contribute gold and its own currency to the central fund. Each member would have normal drawing rights determined by its quota in the fund, and drawings in excess of this amount would require a four-fifths majority vote.[5]

In the preliminary negotiations with other countries prior to the Bretton Woods Conference, the fundamental issue was the size and character of the central reserve and the job which it was expected to do. According to the original American proposals, the total fund was to be about $5 billion, of which about $2 billion would be contributed by the United States and the remainder, consisting of about $750 million in gold and $2,250 million in the local currencies, contributed by other members. Such a fund could perhaps serve to iron out seasonal fluctuations and could provide emergency aid to individual countries provided that a large number of countries were not seeking assistance at the same time. It obviously could not deal with the balance-of-payments problems arising out of a serious international depression or even a minor depression which continued for more than a couple of years. Still less could it deal with the problem of general world-trade disequilibrium which almost inevitably would follow the war.[6]

In contrast to the Treasury, or White, plan, Keynes's Clearing Union proposal was along far more ambitious lines. The Clearing Union had no contributed gold and currencies, but rather each country would be given the right to run a deficit in a clearing account up to the amount

---

[5] Preliminary Draft Outline of Proposal for a United and Associated Nations Stabilization Fund, in *Proceedings and Documents of the United Nations Monetary and Financial Conference,* Department of State, 1948, Vol. II, Appendix IV.

[6] Although the capital of the Fund was increased to $8.8 billion and the American subscription to $2,750 million at the Bretton Woods Conference, by the time the Fund began operations the rise in world prices had nullified the increase in the monetary value of its assets.

of its quota with the privilege of settling a balance with any other member by drafts on the Clearing Union. Creditor countries would be given credits in the Union denominated in terms of *bancor*, but the credits which any member was obligated to accept in the clearing account were limited only by the sum total of the quotas (drawing rights) of the other members. The quotas themselves were to be quite generous, the amount suggested being 75 per cent of the sum of each country's exports and imports on the average of the three prewar years,[7] with the quotas to be adjusted from time to time on the basis of postwar trade. Under Keynes's scheme, the United States would have assumed a contingent obligation to grant credits of $25 billion up to possibly as high as $100 billion.

The function of the Clearing Union was not limited to currency stabilization in a more or less balanced world (as was the case with the United States scheme) but was to deal with the problem of world disequilibrium in the transition period,[8] as well as disequilibrium arising from depression in major countries like the United States. The Clearing Union was not expected to deal with a continuing disequilibrium but was designed to give members time to adjust their balance-of-payments position and to encourage members to take appropriate steps in this direction. Once a member had used up half its quota, the Clearing Union could impose conditions on further debits to its account, including (1) a reduction in its exchange rate, (2) the control of outward capital transactions, and (3) the surrender of a portion of its foreign exchange and gold reserves. In addition, the Union could make recommendations with respect to internal measures affecting the balance of payments of the country in question. Once a member had exceeded three-quarters of its quota, the Clearing Union could ask the country to take measures to improve its position, and if it failed to reduce its debit balance within 2 years it could be declared ineligible for further drawings.[9]

One final aspect of the Keynes Clearing Union proposal which ought to be noted is its treatment of the responsibilities of creditor nations. Not only were creditor nations given large contingent liabilities for providing credits to debtors, but charges were to be levied against both credit balances and debit balances which exceed 25 per cent of a coun-

---

[7] International Clearing Union, *Proceedings and Documents of the United Nations Monetary and Financial Conference*, Vol. II, pp. 1548–1573.

[8] Even the large drawing rights of the Clearing Union were not considered by the author of the plan to be sufficient to take care of relief and reconstruction needs of the war-torn countries. There would still need to be special financing for these and other purposes such as the stabilization of commodity prices. *Ibid.*, pp. 1569–1571.

[9] *Ibid.*, p. 1555.

try's quota. The underlying philosophy of the proposal is that both creditors and debtors may be responsible for balance-of-payments disequilibrium and that the burden of the readjustments should not rest on the debtor alone. The idea of a creditor paying interest on credits which he has extended involuntarily is utterly foreign to American thinking since few Americans accept the view of the average Englishman or Australian that the United States is largely responsible for this country's chronic export surplus since World War I. Just what America's responsibility is for her trade balance will be considered later on, but the truth probably lies somewhere between the view of the average American and that of the average Australian. The Fund Agreement puts the burden of making adjustments to balance-of-payments disequilibrium more heavily on the debtor countries. Moreover, the credits which the Fund can make available are insufficient to enable the world to weather more than a mild reduction in the world's supply of dollars, although a limited number of cases of disequilibrium on the part of individual countries could be handled. In this sense, therefore, the Fund has been correctly described as a "fair-weather" institution.

Thus the difference between the American and British proposals was not simply one of the amount of credits available for currency stabilization; they were not addressed to the same problem. In fact, the problem of currency stabilization which the proposed American Fund was designed to solve has scarcely even existed in the immediate postwar period, although once a measure of world equilibrium including the conditions for the convertibility of the major currencies has been restored, the Fund may be able to function in accordance with its original design. The desire of the American government to set up such an instrument to be available in the immediate postwar period can be explained only in terms of a gross underestimate of the magnitude of the problem of postwar disequilibrium.

The Monetary Fund's Stabilization-credit Policies. The differences between the American and European negotiators as to the function of the Fund's resources led to differences as to how the Fund should be managed. Because the American experts had in mind a somewhat narrower function for the Fund's resources than the European negotiators, the Americans wanted a Fund which would be actively managed by its executive board, which would keep a careful check to see that the Fund's resources were employed for current monetary stabilization purposes.[10] The European members, on the other hand, sought to establish

[10] The Bretton Woods Act of 1945 required the United States representatives in the Fund to seek an interpretation of the Fund Agreement to the effect that the resources of the Fund would be used for "current monetary stabilization operations to afford

the Fund on a more or less automatic basis in which each member would be permitted to draw on the resources of the Fund within the quota limitations established by its charter. An additional reason for this divergence of views was the desire of the American government to keep a close check on the use of its own contribution, while other governments wanted to avoid as much as possible any dictation over the conditions for using the Fund's resources.

This conflict, which was not fully resolved at the Bretton Woods Conference, was carried over to the inaugural meeting of the boards of governors at Savannah, Ga., in March, 1946. The issue here was whether or not the executive directors and their alternates should be full-time officials and be in more or less continuous session or whether they should meet only occasionally to decide major policy issues and leave the day-to-day operations of the Fund to the staff.[11] Although this question was decided in favor of the American position, and drawings on the Fund have in practice been carefully scrutinized by the board, the conflict between the American policy with respect to the use of the Fund's resources and the view of other countries that they should have a more or less automatic right to draw on the Fund to meet balance-of-payments deficits continues.

To some extent, this conflict stems from the fact that the Fund Agreement is not clear with respect to the question of drawings during the postwar transition period when countries would be in a condition of fundamental or long-term disequilibrium. Since it was expected by the authors of the Fund that the transition to world equilibrium would be of more or less short duration, and that the relief and long-term reconstruction financing would be adequately handled by other institutions, a clear policy for the Fund during the period was not provided in its charter. Obviously, world conditions have not been such as to permit the Fund to operate as an institution for currency stabilization by helping countries meet short-term fluctuations in their balance of payments. Many members, desperately in need of dollars and never fully convinced

---

temporary assistance to members in connection with seasonal, cyclical and emergency fluctuations in the balance of payments of any member for current transactions." (Public Law 171, 79th Congress, 1st Session.) This interpretation was approved by the executive board of the Fund. (See *Report of Executive Directors and Summary Proceedings,* First Annual Meeting of Board of Governors, Sept. 27 to Oct. 3, 1946, International Monetary Fund, Washington, D.C., November, 1946, p. 106.)

[11] The deliberations of the Savannah Conference on this point have been discussed in some detail by Raymond F. Mikesell, "The International Monetary Fund, 1944–1949," *International Conciliation,* November, 1949.

of the subtle distinction between short-term and long-term or transitional disequilibriums—a distinction which did not exist under the Clearing Union plan—have sought to supplement their dollar resources by drawing on the Fund without much regard to when they would be in a position to repay. In fact, there are no fixed maturities for credits extended by the Fund since repayment is a function of the improvement in the reserve position of the borrowing member, based on the assumption that a country not in fundamental disequilibrium would be subject to recurrent "swings" in its balance-of-payments position.

The United States has been presented with something of a dilemma in the determination of its policy with respect to drawing from the Fund. A strict adherence to its original conception of the Fund would probably require closing the vaults of the Fund until the world's major currencies are again convertible and a large measure of international equilibrium has been restored. Although the United States could probably force this position in the Fund, it would undoubtedly meet with a storm of opposition and possibly wholesale withdrawals. In addition, the United States has been willing to see the Fund's resources used in an emergency for general balance-of-payments purposes when other sources of financing have not been available and when the political and economic consequences of not meeting urgent dollar needs would have been extremely serious. Most of the Fund's credits to Western European countries before the ERP came into operation fall in this category.[12] On the other hand, the United States government hopes to preserve the bulk of the gold and dollar assets of the Fund for the posttransitional period when the Fund may be able to operate more in accordance with its original purposes.

Since the spring of 1948, the United States executive director on the Fund's board, with considerable support from the representatives of other countries, has sought to follow a middle course between closing down the Fund entirely and permitting its resources to be rapidly drained off as a modest contribution to the world dollar shortage. In April, 1948, the executive board adopted a resolution to the effect that further sales of dollars to ERP countries would be discontinued during the following year unless there developed "exceptional or unforeseen" circumstances.[13]

[12] By the end of 1950, the Fund had sold about $777 million in foreign exchange for their own currencies. Sales of dollars by the Fund totaled $760 million, about three-fourths of which was taken by the ERP countries.

[13] *Annual Report of the Executive Directors for the Fiscal Year Ending April 30, 1948*, International Monetary Fund, pp. 74–75. This rule was renewed for another year in 1949. See also *Second Special Report to the President and to the Congress*, National Advisory Council on International Monetary and Financial Problems, May, 1950, p. 21.

The Fund not only has adhered closely to the so-called ERP rule but has been largely successful in limiting drawings by all countries to no more than 25 per cent of their quotas, and in a number of cases there have been either no drawings or the amounts have been less than 25 per cent. Whether or not the bulk of the Fund's assets can be reserved for some future time when a large measure of international equilibrium may be restored depends upon the length of the transition period and the pressures which will be brought upon the Fund in the interim.[14] If, for example, there are emergency needs which cannot be met from other sources, the resources of the Fund may be considered to be expendable.

Apart from the difficulties of operation in the transitional period, there are certain other problems which arise in the operation of the Fund in a world of more or less planned economies and controlled balances of payments. We have already mentioned the fact that the provisions of repayment in the Fund Agreement are based upon the expectation that periods of balance-of-payments deficit will be followed by a restoration of a borrowing member's reserve position when its balance of payments improves [15] and that repayment is automatically called for when this improvement takes place.[16] There are several reasons why the Fund's resources may fail to become revolving in character under the repurchase provisions. First of all, the repurchase requirement does not apply to a member whose reserves are less than its quota, and there are a number of members whose gold and convertible foreign-exchange reserves are less than their quota. Secondly, members of the sterling area tend to hold their reserves in the form of inconvertible sterling and do not build up independent gold and dollar reserves. Third, many countries with large government-sponsored investment programs may be unable to build up their gold and dollar reserves to a point where they would be required to repurchase the Fund's holdings of their currency for many years to come. And finally, countries with planned balances of payments may choose not to increase their reserves or may be under continual pressure to employ any additional foreign-exchange earnings to increased imports.

The failure of the Fund's resources to revolve either because of a continuation of the present world disequilibrium or for one of the other

---

[14] As of Dec. 31, 1950, the Fund had about $2.8 billion in gold and dollars.

[15] Article VIII, Sec. 7, of the Articles of Agreement, International Monetary Fund.

[16] Some incentive to repay the Fund is provided by the charges levied on borrowing members (Art. V, Sec. 8, Articles of Agreement), but these charges are quite modest and below prevailing rates on long-term capital until the member has been in debt to the Fund for 8 or 10 years. After the charges, which increase with the amount and duration of the borrowed funds, have increased to 5 per cent, the Fund may impose such charges as it deems appropriate.

reasons listed above would soon strip the Fund of its ability to grant financial assistance to its members and, as a consequence, would deprive the Fund of most of its influence over the international monetary policies of its members.[17] Since the Fund is the principal instrument through which the United States expresses its international monetary policy and seeks to influence the policies of other nations, it is to the interest of this country to maintain the Fund as a going concern even though it may fall very far short of the objectives which motivated its inauguration. Thus the United States must either find a way to prevent the gold and dollar resources of the Fund from being drained away within the next three or four years, or be prepared to put up additional resources when the $2.8 billion in gold and dollars now remaining in the Fund is exhausted. (The Fund began operations with gold and dollar assets of about $3.4 billion.)

Although the details of the executive board's discussions on this question are confidential, the American executive director and the National Advisory Council are fully aware of the inadequacies of the repurchase provisions and various methods have been explored for preventing the Fund's assets from being frozen. It should be noted that the Fund Agreement and the executive board's interpretations of that Agreement are clear on the point that the Fund's resources are to be used for temporary or short-term assistance and that borrowing members have an obligation to repay the Fund within a reasonable period of time regardless of the repurchase provisions. The difficulty is that the obligation is indefinite as to time and criteria of ability to repay except for the repurchase provisions. One device, which has been explored and in some cases actually employed, is for the borrowing member to make an agreement with the Fund to repay within a specified period of time. Many members take the position, however, that to require compulsory repurchase agreements is a violation of the Fund Agreement. A full discussion of this problem, however, would involve a number of technical details of the Fund's operations and is beyond the scope of this book.[18]

Another problem which the Fund will have to face once the world's balance-of-payments position has improved sufficiently for the Fund to operate properly in the field of short-term currency stabilization is that

[17] As of Dec. 31, 1950, the following countries had repurchased with gold or dollars all or a portion of their own currencies previously held by the Fund: Belgium, Costa Rica, Egypt, Ethiopia, and Nicaragua. Total repurchases since the beginning of the Fund's operations were $33 million as against sales of foreign exchange of $777 million, of which $760 million was dollars.

[18] This question has been discussed in greater detail in Mikesell, *op. cit.*

of handling balance-of-payments disturbances due to cyclical forces originating in major countries such as the United States. It would be highly unfortunate if a recession in the United States forced a reinstitution of trade and currency restrictions all over the world before remedial measures for restoring production and incomes in this country could become effective. Although it is clearly a function of the Fund to provide financial assistance to members to tide them over short-term deficits due to cyclical causes, it is generally recognized that the present resources of the Fund are inadequate for the job or at least they would be exhausted even by a depression of modest depth and duration. This problem was recently the subject of a study by the Economic and Social Council of the United Nations.[19] One of the proposals of the group of experts appointed to study this problem was that the Monetary Fund should be amended along the following lines:

1. Whenever a country's imports fall as a result of a decline in employment in that country, and that decline is not offset by a fall in exports, that country should make a deposit of its own currency in the Monetary Fund equal to the fall in its imports less the decline in its exports.

2. The currencies deposited above would be available for purchase (with its own currency) by any other country whose exports have fallen as a result of a depression abroad by more than the decline in its imports.[20]

This proposal would require a country such as the United States to accept an automatic obligation to provide foreign credits whenever its imports declined as a result of a depression. Since the United States has not favored open-end obligations of this nature in the past, nor has it favored automatic drawing rights on the part of Fund members, it is highly unlikely that either the administration or Congress would agree to such a proposition.[21] The best solution to the problem of the counter-cyclical financing would seem to be one of providing sufficient resources to the Monetary Fund to enable it to handle a larger volume of deficits resulting from short-term cyclical causes.

[19] See *National and International Measures for Full Employment*, report by a group of experts appointed by the Secretary-General, United Nations, Lake Success, N.Y., December, 1949. This group consisted of J. M. Clark and Arthur Smithies of the United States, Nicholas Kaldor of the United Kingdom, Pierre Uri of France, and E. Ronald Walker of Australia.

[20] *Ibid.*, pp. 96–99. For a critical discussion of this report, see Jacob Viner, "Full Employment at Whatever Cost," *Quarterly Journal of Economics*, August, 1950; and Henry Wallich, "United Nations Report on Full Employment," *American Economic Review*, December, 1950.

[21] The United States delegation at the meeting of the Economic and Social Council in the summer of 1950 rejected the United Nations experts' proposal.

Exchange Controls

Although there are many examples of exchange controls going far back in the history of foreign-exchange transactions, their first employment on a considerable scale in peacetime occurred with the breakdown of the international payments system in the early 1930's. Although the United States government has always deplored their use in peacetime, it has recognized the necessity of at least some types of exchange controls under certain circumstances.

Exchange controls have been introduced in response to several different motives. First of all, the motive may be simply one of protecting home industry, or it may involve a discriminatory arrangement undertaken between two or more countries for their mutual commercial advantage. Exchange controls for such purposes have been opposed by the United States, and most of our commercial treaties during the 1930's provided for nondiscriminatory treatment of United States trade as well as for the right of the United States to denounce any tariff or other concessions which might be nullified by the imposition of quantitative import controls whether they be discriminatory or nondiscriminatory.

A second and perhaps more important purpose of exchange controls is to protect a country's balance of payments. Such controls may be nondiscriminatory in their application to different foreign currencies, or they may discriminate in favor of some currencies by providing foreign exchange for the purchase of a commodity in certain countries but not in others. During the 1930's, discriminatory controls were limited to bilateral clearing and payments arrangements [22] involving pairs of countries. Such arrangements were opposed by the United States since they involved discrimination against dollar exports. Although many countries had over-all balance-of-payments difficulties during the 1930's, there was no general dollar shortage since the key currencies, *i.e.*, those generally employed in financing international transactions, were all convertible into the dollar. Hence the bilateral-exchange arrangements employed by Germany and a number of other countries during the 1930's were largely for the purpose of securing a competitive advantage in world trade. The circumstances of the postwar world which gave rise to a general shortage of dollars and the inconvertibility of key currencies, such as the pound sterling, have resulted in a modification of the official position of the United States on discriminatory currency arrangements, at least as an interim measure. It should be recalled, however, that at the time of the

---

[22] For a discussion of bilateral clearing and payments arrangements during the 1930's, see M. S. Gordon, *Barriers to World Trade*, Macmillan, New York, 1941, Chaps. VI, VII.

Bretton Woods Conference restrictions on the convertibility of sterling were considered as a war measure, to be removed shortly following the close of hostilities.

A third purpose of exchange controls is to control undesirable capital movements. As a result of the experience of the 1930's, the United States has looked with favor upon capital controls for the purpose of preventing speculative and other undesirable capital flights which endanger the reserve position of other countries.

The early drafts of the American proposals for a stabilization fund had surprisingly little to say about exchange controls other than the fact that members were obligated to abolish controls on current transactions within a reasonable time after joining the Fund and were not to impose them without permission of the Fund.[23] It was recognized that countries might find themselves in emergency situations in which they would need to employ exchange controls on current transactions from time to time and also that there would be a short transitional period during which wartime controls would be removed. It was to be the job of the Fund to see that these exceptions to the general obligations of members were not abused. The American proposals, however, failed to provide any criteria for the supervision of exchange controls by the Fund, nor was there any differentiation between discriminatory and nondiscriminatory controls. The lack of emphasis on this important matter was undoubtedly a reflection of the predilections of the authors of the American proposals regarding the nature of the postwar world. By the time the American proposals for the International Trade Organization (ITO) Charter were developed (published December, 1945), the problems of the postwar era had become somewhat more clear and an attempt was made to develop some criteria with respect to the use of quantitative restrictions. We shall review these proposals later on.

In the international discussions which took place following the publication of the American proposals for a stabilization fund, some further elaboration of the exchange-control provisions was made, largely in the direction of safeguarding the interests of countries which might want to employ them but not in providing criteria for their supervision. One safeguard had to do with the right of members to retain wartime exchange controls, bilateral arrangements, and multiple-rate systems during the postwar transitional period. This right was stated in the Joint Statement of April, 1944, which represented an agreement between the Ameri-

[23] Preliminary Draft Outline of a Proposal for an International Stabilization Fund of the United and Associated Nations, in *Proceedings and Documents of the United Nations Monetary and Financial Conference*, Vol. II, p. 1615.

can and British experts on general principles for the establishment of the Monetary Fund prior to the Bretton Woods Conference. Although no definite time limit was set for the termination of the transitional period, the Joint Statement provided that "not later than 3 years after coming into force of the Fund any member still retaining any restriction inconsistent with IX, 3 shall consult with the Fund as to their further retention." [24] In the final agreement reached at Bretton Woods, the 3-year period for consultation was extended to 5 years, with the additional provision that members must report on restrictions on current transactions still in force 3 years after the Fund Agreement comes into force. [25] The Fund may make representations to a member that conditions are favorable for the abandonment of restrictions inconsistent with the Agreement, and failure to comply may mean expulsion. But the Fund and the American representative on its executive board are left with the problem of determining the criteria for judging the appropriateness of the exchange controls which members may choose to retain.

Another important question relating to exchange controls, which was the subject of considerable discussion prior to the Bretton Woods Conference, had to do with the scarce-currency problem. The early American drafts recognized that the Fund might run short of an important currency as well as the gold with which to buy it. This was a weakness of the American proposals not shared by the Keynes Clearing Union, since in the latter the sum of the drawing rights could never exceed the available credits even though they might all be concentrated on one country. The American proposals simply provided for the rationing of the scarce currency together with recommendations by the Fund as to how to deal with the situation. The representatives of other countries attending the pre-Bretton Woods discussions insisted that, in the event of a scarce-currency situation, other countries whose currencies were not in scarce supply should have the right to apply discriminatory exchange controls against the scarce-currency country. For example, the Canadian proposals which were circulated in June, 1943, [26] provided that discriminatory import restrictions against the scarce-currency country would be authorized for all members whose official gold and foreign-exchange reserves were less than 50 per cent of their quotas. Britain and other countries desired

---

[24] Joint Statement by Experts on the Establishment of an International Monetary Fund of the United and Associated Nations, in *Proceedings and Documents of the United Nations Monetary and Financial Conference,* Vol. II, pp. 1629–1636.

[25] Article XIV, Sec. 4, Articles of Agreement, International Monetary Fund.

[26] Tentative Draft Proposals of Canadian Experts for an International Exchange Union, *Proceedings and Documents of the United Nations Monetary and Financial Conference,* Vol. II, pp. 1575–1596.

to go much further. The resolution of this problem in the Joint Statement was as follows: [27]

> A decision by the Fund to apportion a scarce currency shall operate as
> an authorization to a member country, after consultation with the Fund,
> temporarily to restrain the freedom of exchange operations in the affected
> currency, and in determining the manner of restricting the demand and
> rationing the limited supply among its nationals, the member country shall
> have complete jurisdiction.

In Art. VII of the Bretton Woods Agreement, this clause was modified
somewhat by the statement that the arrangements "shall be no more restrictive than is necessary to limit the demand for the scarce currency to
the supply held by, or accruing to, the member in question; and they
shall be relaxed and removed as rapidly as conditions permit." The
American acceptance of the scarce-currency principle specifically authorizing a general discrimination against the dollar under conditions of
general dollar scarcity was an exceedingly important policy decision and
one which has been subject to a large amount of criticism and controversy. The same principle was carried over into our commercial policy
as represented by the original American proposals for the ITO Charter
and constitutes an important departure from the prewar principle of
nondiscrimination. Although the scarce-currency clause was not intended
to be invoked in the transition period, the applicability of the principle
during this period was obvious since the dollar resources of the Fund
were not large enough—they would have needed to be almost inexhaus-
tible—to prevent the dollar from being generally scarce. Once the principle was recognized, however, it became an important element in United
States foreign economic policy.

The scarce-currency principle is based on the theory that, if a large
number of countries are all seriously out of balance with an important
country or currency area so that a general shortage of that country's
currency develops, the maximization of trade requires discriminatory restrictions on imports from the surplus country and a limitation on the
convertibility or transferability of balances into the scarce currency.[28]
In support of this principle, it is said with considerable justification that,
if the deficit countries maintain convertibility of their currencies into the
scarce currency and do not enter into any discriminatory or bilateral
trading arrangements among themselves, each country will seek to main-

---

[27] *Proceedings and Documents of the United Nations Monetary and Financial Conference,* Vol. II, p. 1634.

[28] For a more complete discussion of the scarce-currency principle, see Raymond F.
Mikesell, "Discrimination and International Trade Policy," *Review of Economics and
Statistics,* August, 1950.

tain its imports from the scarce-currency country by reducing imports from the other countries. In this way, trade among the non-scarce-currency countries may fall to a very low level and total imports from the scarce-currency country will be unaffected. Thus it is argued that the only way to prevent a decline in trade among non-scarce-currency countries (or perhaps to permit an increase in such trade to compensate for the loss of trade with the scarce-currency country) is to limit convertibility into the scarce currency and to establish a system of payments among the remaining countries which will permit trade to take place on an inconvertible or limited-convertibility basis.

The validity of the above principle depends upon the assumption that exports to the scarce-currency country (and hence the supply of that currency arising from current transactions) are incapable of expansion and that the trade which is maintained or expanded among the soft-currency countries by means of discriminatory arrangements cannot be shifted to the scarce-currency country. Within limits, this assumption may be true for short periods such as one immediately following a war or other serious international dislocations such as a depression in a major country like the United States. But how long should discriminatory arrangements be employed, and what measures should be taken to eliminate the condition of fundamental imbalance? It is easy to see that the discriminatory arrangements which permit trade to go on among the non-scarce-currency countries may tend to interfere with the process of adjustment necessary to eliminate the scarce-currency condition. As we shall see later on, the acceptance of the scarce-currency principle and its actual implementation by the United States has presented this country with the danger of the establishment of a more or less permanent soft-currency trading bloc which may perpetuate the very condition which brought it into existence.

This is a major dilemma of American foreign economic policy, either horn of which is fraught with serious difficulties. On the one hand, we have a traditional policy of nondiscrimination and a major postwar goal of restoring world-wide multilateralism. On the other, we have had to recognize (from bitter experience with the Anglo-American loan agreement and elsewhere) that the world is not ready to trade on the basis of dollar-convertible currencies. Up to the present time, however, the United States has not followed a consistent policy in dealing with the problem. This fact has been demonstrated by our policy in connection with the British Loan Agreement. There is of course a third alternative, that of making sufficient dollars available in the form of untied [29] loans or grants so that the dollar would no longer be a scarce currency. Unless, however,

[29] Loans or grants in dollars which the recipient is free to use in any market and for any purpose that the recipient might choose.

this action were accompanied by appropriate policies on the part of other countries, it would require a tremendous amount of dollar assistance, so large in fact that inflation and lowered living standards in America would reduce her position to a level comparable with that of the rest of the world.

The Controversy over United States Acceptance of the Monetary Fund Agreement

The Bretton Woods Agreements had to be ratified by countries representing at least 60 per cent of the quotas established at Bretton Woods before the Fund and Bank could be established. Scarcely any country was willing to ratify before the United States had done so, and a large number were unwilling to do so until a decision had been made by Britain. From the time the American proposals were first made public, the Fund was the object of intense controversy in the United States. The proponents of the Fund were represented by administration supporters and liberal groups generally, together with people who were for anything which bore the label of international cooperation. The opponents consisted largely of conservatives who considered that the Fund represented too great a departure from traditional foreign-exchange policies and of economic isolationists who looked with disfavor on any proposals involving American financial assistance abroad.

While most Americans were unfamiliar with the technical issues involved in the Monetary Fund, mention should be made of a group of critics represented by internationally minded economists and bankers like Dr. John H. Williams and Winthrop Aldrich, who were opposed to the Fund on the grounds that it was not the way to tackle the postwar currency problem as they saw it. While a full discussion of the controversy over American participation in the Fund [30] would take us far afield, the intelligent conservative criticism of the Fund is worth noting since it provides an indication of an alternative approach to the problem of foreign-exchange policy which had the backing of a large section of enlightened opinion in the United States. The most significant criticism of the Fund made by this group was that any attempt at general currency stabilization immediately after the war was premature and that foreign assistance during the transition period should be largely confined to relief and to reconstruction loans. Thus it was argued that the functions of

[30] Most of the criticism of the Bretton Woods program was levied at the Fund rather than the Bank. Many of the critics including the American Bankers Association recommended joining the Bank but not the Fund. See *Practical International Organization,* published by the American Bankers Association, February, 1945.

the Fund should be combined with those of the International Bank into one institution, *i.e.*, the Bank, and that this institution should concentrate on reconstruction and development loans. The Bank would be empowered to extend stabilization credits to specific countries where their balance-of-payments position was such as to make possible a genuine stabilization operation.[31] It was also the view of Dr. Williams and certain members of the banking community that progress toward currency stabilization and the removal of exchange controls must begin with the restoration of the convertibility of sterling and a solution of Britain's sterling problem.[32] This approach to postwar monetary stabilization, known as the "key-currency" approach, was based on the fact that the bulk of the world's trade was conducted in dollars and sterling and that only a few "key" currencies were in fact used in the financing of international trade. Winthrop Aldrich of the Chase National Bank of New York suggested a large grant to Britain to establish stabilization and convertibility between the dollar and the pound as an alternative to the Fund.[33] Thus when the administration, more than a year after the Bretton Woods Conference, came around to the view that the Fund could not realize its objectives until sterling-dollar convertibility had been achieved, the banking community was generally favorable to the proposal for a loan of $3¾ billion to Britain, whereas they had opposed the $2¾ billion United States subscription to the Monetary Fund.

The international economic developments since 1944 have in considerable measure vindicated the critics of the Fund so far as its ability to realize its lofty objectives in the immediate postwar period is concerned. The Fund has nevertheless proved to be a useful instrument for international consultation and cooperation, and its success cannot be measured solely in terms of its ability to realize the objectives stated in its Charter. The Fund could not, as its proponents seemed to claim, alter the fundamental structure of the world economy, but has had to operate as best it could in the disturbed and unbalanced international environment of the postwar era. Despite the welter of economic arguments for and against the Fund, the Bretton Woods Agreements Act was passed by Congress not so much as an approval of any particular monetary mechanism—the mysteries of which few congressmen understood anyway—but as an expression of a desire to promote international coopera-

[31] See J. H. Williams, "International Monetary Plans," *Foreign Affairs,* October, 1944, pp. 3–21.

[32] *Ibid.,* p. 21.

[33] *The New York Times,* Sept. 16, 1944. A number of other prominent bankers and congressmen also advocated this approach. See Raymond F. Mikesell, "Key Currency Proposal," *Quarterly Journal of Economics,* August, 1945.

tion through an instrument which seemed to be in accord with the basic foreign economic policies of the United States. In its efforts to assure passage of the Act, the administration, as well as its friends outside the government, claimed too much for the Fund, and no doubt many people have been disillusioned by the fact that 6 years after its inauguration exchange barriers to trade are just as numerous as they were at the end of the war.[34] The administration's claim that the Fund was urgently needed to prevent competitive exchange depreciation in the immediate postwar period and that rapid progress could be made through the Fund for the removal of exchange controls was in part a reflection of a general underestimation of the problems of postwar international financial adjustment. There was also the fact that the presentation of such a complicated institution to the layman inevitably involved oversimplification of the obligations of its members and their relationship to the institution itself.

[34] See *First Annual Report on Exchange Restrictions,* International Monetary Fund, March, 1950.

CHAPTER 11

International Monetary Policy: The Sterling Area and the European Payments Union

IN THIS chapter we shall be concerned with the special problems of the sterling area and of intra-European trade. Since out of America's efforts to deal with the special problems of these areas there have developed certain modifications in her international monetary policies, we shall conclude this chapter with a summary of these policies as they appear to the author at the time of writing.

THE ANGLO-AMERICAN FINANCIAL AGREEMENT

By the fall of 1945, the administration became convinced that little or no progress toward the realization of America's fundamental foreign economic objectives could be made without a solution of Britain's postwar financial problems. Not only was there no prospect of Britain's being able to relax her wartime exchange controls following the war, but Britain lacked even the dollar exchange to keep her industries operating and her people fed and clothed without outside assistance. In addition, under the sterling exchange system, Britain was responsible for the balance of payments of the entire sterling area, which meant that she had to supply at least the minimum dollar requirements of India, Australia, Egypt,[1] and other members of the sterling area which had dollar deficits. Unless the pound were convertible, members of the sterling area as well as a number of other countries whose trade with nondollar countries was largely financed with sterling would be unable to abolish exchange and trade controls which discriminated against the dollar.[2] Since nearly 40

[1] Egypt is no longer a member of the sterling area. Currently, the sterling area includes all members of the British Commonwealth of Nations except Canada; the British Colonies, Protectorates, and Mandates; Burma; Ireland; Hashemite Kingdom of Jordan; Iraq; and Iceland.

[2] Transferable-account countries such as the Netherlands, Egypt, and Italy are permitted to use sterling for making current payments arising out of trade with the

per cent of the world's trade is financed in sterling (and perhaps another 40 per cent or more in dollars), it is clear that sterling-dollar convertibility was the most fundamental condition for realizing the objectives of United States financial policy.

The Anglo-American Financial Agreement which was negotiated in the fall of 1945 was designed to deal both with Britain's need for financial assistance for the postwar reconstruction of her economy and to provide Britain with sufficient reserves to enable her to restore the convertibility of sterling. Unlike the European Recovery Program and other foreign-assistance programs in the past two or three years, which have been developed primarily to realize political objectives, the British loan agreement was motivated to a very large degree by a desire to realize America's international monetary and commercial-policy objectives. It was feared that without special American assistance linked with a firm undertaking by Britain with respect to her exchange practices, Britain would retain her wartime sterling-area exchange controls and the sterling area would become the nucleus of a permanent soft-currency trading bloc based on multilateral trade within the area and discrimination against the dollar. There was widespread support in England from both leftist and conservative groups for such a policy, and British acceptance of what was almost universally termed in England as a "hard bargain" was largely a consequence of her desperate need for dollar assistance. This does not mean of course that there were not strong supporters of a liberal trading policy for England. Lord Keynes, for example, not only had grave doubts as to Britain's ability to hold together indefinitely the sterling area on an inconvertible basis, but also was critical of the policy of erecting a separate economic bloc on both economic and political grounds.

In defending the Anglo-American Financial Agreement before the House of Lords, Keynes stated [3] that

> separate economic blocs and all the friction and loss of friendship they must bring with them are expedients to which one may be driven in a hostile world, where trade has ceased over wide areas to be cooperative and peaceful and where are forgotten the healthy rules of mutual advantage and equal treatment. But it is surely crazy to prefer that. Above all, this determination to make trade truly international and to avoid the establishment of economic *blocs* which limit and restrict commercial intercourse outside them, is plainly an essential condition of the world's best hope, an Anglo-American

---

members of the sterling area and other transferable-account countries. Other so-called bilateral-account countries may use their sterling only within the sterling area. See *First Annual Report on Exchange Restrictions*, International Monetary Fund, Washington, D.C., 1950, pp. 47–51.

[3] Statement in House of Lords, Dec. 18, 1945.

understanding, which brings us and others together in international institutions which may be in the long run the first step towards something more comprehensive.

The Financial Agreement provided that Britain was to make sterling balances arising out of current transactions freely available for making current payments in any currency area within 1 year after the coming into force of the Agreement,[4] and that any discrimination arising from the operation of the so-called sterling-dollar pool would be eliminated.[5] Not all sterling balances were to become convertible, however. As a result of wartime expenditures overseas, there had been built up by June, 1945, about $13.5 billion in sterling balances and Treasury obligations owned by governments and individuals outside the United Kingdom. Since it would have been impossible to afford general convertibility privileges to all these balances, Britain undertook as a part of the Agreement to reach agreements with their owners for immobilizing a large part of them either by means of funding or of outright cancellation. Finally, Britain agreed not to impose restrictions on her own citizens with respect to payments in connection with current transaction with the United States. Since a nation may control the trade of its own residents either by means of rationing foreign exchange or through import licensing and other trade controls, the Financial Agreement also committed Britain to a policy of nondiscrimination with respect to the administration of import restrictions. As we shall see in our discussion of commercial policy, however, the term discrimination was not given a precise definition so that the provision has proved to be difficult to administer in practice.

It may be well at this point to distinguish between the convertibility of balances arising out of current transactions which are held by nonresidents and the elimination of trade and foreign-exchange restrictions by governments on their own residents. In the case of a currency such as sterling which is widely employed in international transactions, the former type of convertibility is of primary importance and may exist even though rigid controls are maintained on the foreign transactions of British residents. So long as countries make payments to residents of other countries in currencies which can be used only in the country making

[4] *Anglo-American Financial and Commercial Agreement*, Department of State, December, 1945. The Agreement became effective on July 15, 1946.

[5] The so-called sterling-dollar pool arises from the fact that sterling-area countries exchange all or a portion of their dollar earnings for sterling deposits in London and obtain their dollars for meeting current needs from London. Thus Britain holds the dollar reserves for the sterling area as a whole. It should be said, however, that certain sterling-area members, *e.g.*, South Africa, hold substantial independent gold and dollar reserves of their own.

the payment, or within a group of countries such as the sterling area, world-wide multilateral trade and the elimination of discriminatory trade and exchange controls become impossible. If, however, countries make payments to other countries only in the form of currencies which are convertible into the dollar and other currencies, it would be possible to have world-wide multilateralism even though a large number of countries restricted the total foreign purchases of their own citizens. It is for this reason that the convertibility of sterling, as distinct from the elimination of restrictions on residents of Britain, is of such great importance.

It is quite likely that many countries, particularly those which are undergoing rapid industrialization, may employ restrictions on imports for many years to come, largely because they may be unable to cope with the inflationary impact of new investments on imports in addition to the large foreign-exchange requirements of the capital projects themselves. If, however, convertibility of the world's international currencies can be achieved, foreign-exchange and trade restrictions need not be of a discriminatory character and their effects upon the multilateral pattern of world trade will not be so serious as they are at present.

In accordance with the terms of the Financial Agreement, the British government gradually relaxed restrictions on sterling transfers by nonresidents so that free convertibility was restored to a large portion of the currently acquired sterling well before the July 15, 1947, deadline fixed by the Agreement. But by the end of June, 1947, over $2 billion of the $3¾ billion credit was exhausted, and in July and August an additional $1,300 million was drawn. On August 20, 1947, with only $400 million of the credit remaining, the British government suspended automatic convertibility into dollars of sterling held by a large number of countries.[6] Although the suspension was a formal violation of the Anglo-American Agreement, it was in the nature of a *force majeur,* and the American government agreed on the necessity of the action. Just prior to the termination of convertibility, a British delegation headed by Sir Wilfred Eady arrived in Washington to consult with the National Advisory Council. The NAC came to the conclusion that "the fundamental purposes of the Anglo-American Agreement could not be fulfilled if this excessive drain of British dollar reserves were permitted to continue." It was therefore agreed between the representatives of the two governments that "the free convertibility of sterling should be temporarily suspended, and that the British government should be given an opportunity to revise its system of international payments with a view to carry-

[6] See "The British Crisis," *Federal Reserve Bulletin,* September, 1947, pp. 1071–1082.

ing out the basic objectives of the Anglo-American financial agreement." [7]
Access to the remaining $400 million of the credit was temporarily suspended, but withdrawals were again permitted in December, 1947, and by March 1, 1948, the total credit had been exhausted.[8]

In the course of the consultations with the British representatives in August and September, 1947, questions were raised regarding those portions of the Financial Agreement (Sec. 9) which provided that quantitative import restrictions should be administered "on a basis which does not discriminate against imports from the other country in respect of any product." When Britain suspended convertibility of sterling balances acquired by other nondollar countries,[9] it meant that the holders of such sterling would be forced to discriminate against the dollar and other hard-currency areas, since such sterling could not be used for making purchases outside the sterling area plus certain other so-called transferable-account countries. Britain herself, however, was obligated under Sec. 9 of the Financial Agreement not to discriminate in her own purchases against the United States. This section posed a difficult problem, since the British argued that in order to conserve dollars they ought to be permitted to discriminate in their purchases against dollar goods. Although the NAC refused at this time to agree to outright suspension of the British obligation under Sec. 9, it did agree that in its interpretation of the Agreement "it would take into consideration the unusual aspects of the financial position of the United Kingdom." [10] The interpretation of this section has proved to be difficult since a large part of British imports (about 60 per cent in 1947) have been under bulk-purchase contracts entered into by the British government, some of them involving agreements running for a number of years. In addition, purchases of manufactured goods involve differences in quality of products and terms of sale which make difficult the determination of whether or not discrimination has in fact taken place. The general rule adopted was that the British government should not acquire or issue licenses for the importation of goods from third countries if prices of comparable goods were substantially lower in the United States.

There has been a certain amount of dissatisfaction in both countries regarding the implementation of Sec. 9. On the one hand, the British

[7] *Report of Activities of the National Advisory Council on International Monetary and Financial Problems, April 1, 1947, to September 30, 1947,* p. 4.

[8] *Report of Activities of the National Advisory Council on International Monetary and Financial Problems, October 1, 1947, to March 31, 1948,* p. 12.

[9] Sterling legally acquired by residents of the dollar area, which is known as American account sterling, has remained freely convertible into dollars.

[10] *Report of Activities of the National Advisory Council on International Monetary and Financial Problems, April 1, 1947 to September 30, 1947,* p. 4.

have complained that they were unable to buy citrus fruits even though they had plenty of foreign exchange to buy it in Southern Europe and Africa because they would have been forced to buy Texas grapefruit and Florida oranges at the same time with dollars they could ill afford to spend. On the other hand, American traders have complained that the British have discriminated against their products. The problem of discrimination again came up for discussion in the course of the Anglo-American-Canadian financial discussions in September, 1949. Further deterioration of Britain's reserve position occurred in the spring and summer of 1949, and the British asked for permission to liberalize trade with areas with which it did not have a balance-of-payments problem, with a concomitant discrimination against the United States and the dollar area generally. This question also involved a conflict of United States policies, namely, that of a desire to liberalize intra-European trade on the one hand, and the adherence of Britain to Sec. 9, on the other. The text of the communiqué on the three-power talks stated the issue as follows: [11]

> There was agreement that one of the ways in which the competitive position of United Kingdom products might be improved was by a widening of the area in which such products competed freely with those of other countries. In this connection as an initial step toward a more general liberalization the United Kingdom delegation outlined its proposals for liberalizing trade with countries with which it did not have balance of payments difficulties, and raised the question whether the provisions of Section 9 of the Anglo-American Financial Agreement and Article 5 of the Anglo-Canadian Financial Agreement presented an obstacle of such plans. It was the view of the United States and Canadian delegations that such liberalization of United Kingdom import regulations should be considered since the United Kingdom shortage of dollars should not in itself force the United Kingdom to reduce its purchases from areas with which it does not have a shortage of means of payment. It was agreed that any United Kingdom import regulations as they affect United States and Canadian products would be the subject of continuing facilities for consultations.

Thus it is clear that with the inability of Britain to maintain sterling convertibility the United States has, reluctantly to be sure, been forced to give up, for the immediate future at least, its objective of establishing a system of world-wide multilateral payments. Britain was permitted to go ahead with a program of liberalizing her trade with other soft-currency countries and to impose a 25 per cent cut in dollar imports into Britain and into the sterling area generally. There have been continuing consultations, and the American government has objected to some aspects of the British program. An example of these objections is to be found in

[11] "Text of 3-Power Talks Communiqué," *The Washington Post*, Sept. 13, 1949, p. 9.

the controversy over the British action in reducing imports of petroleum from American oil companies and in taking over markets with sterling oil formerly supplied by American companies in third countries.[12] It is worth noting, however, that the solution to this problem which was put forth by the American government was not that American firms should be permitted to sell for dollars either in the sterling area or in third areas in which sterling oil was driving out dollar oil.[13] Rather it was that the American companies should be permitted to sell their oil for sterling which would then be available for making purchases in the sterling area, and to ask for conversion into dollars only that part of their costs which represent the irreducible dollar content.

The rapid rise in Britain's gold and dollar reserves since the September, 1949, devaluation [14] has raised new problems for Anglo-American financial relations. This rise in reserves has been accomplished largely by a combination of increased restrictions against dollar imports into the sterling area and an increase in the dollar earnings of certain members of the sterling area, notably Malaya, Ceylon, and Australia. During this same period, the United Kingdom continued to receive financial aid from the Economic Cooperation Administration, all of which she was able to add to her monetary reserves. While Britain's improved monetary position certainly indicated a reduction in her need for financial assistance from the United States,[15] the expansion of British reserves from the dangerously low levels of September, 1949, was highly desirable. In December, 1938, British gold and dollar reserves were $3.9 billion, equivalent in purchasing power to perhaps $9 or $10 billion in 1950 dollars. It is highly unlikely that Britain could safely embark upon convertibility unless her reserves increased to a level of say $6 billion, or unless she had access to dollar credits of this amount.

Another problem related to the rise in Britain's reserves has to do with the import policies of the sterling-area countries. As we shall see in a later chapter, the rules of the General Agreement on Tariffs and Trade provide that countries may employ import restrictions if they are needed to prevent a serious decline in their monetary reserves or if their monetary reserves are very low. In addition, the Monetary Fund could properly ask

---

[12] See Horst Mendershausen, *Dollar Shortage and Oil Surplus in 1949–50,* International Finance Section, Princeton University, Princeton, N.J., November, 1950.

[13] The reason why dollar oil cannot compete with sterling oil is that countries short of dollars but long on sterling would rather use their dollars to buy commodities which they can obtain only from the United States.

[14] British gold and dollar reserves rose from $1.4 billion in September, 1949, to $3.3 billion at the end of 1950.

[15] ECA aid to Great Britain was temporarily suspended in December, 1950.

members to relax their exchange controls if they were experiencing sub-stantial current-account surpluses. The question arises therefore whether or not the GATT or the Monetary Fund should ask certain members of the sterling area which may also be members of the GATT or the Fund to relax their exchange and trade restrictions. The question is complicated by the fact that most members of the sterling area pool their gold and dollar reserves in London and do not maintain substantial inde-pendent monetary reserves. On the other hand, individual sterling-area countries do have separate quotas in the Fund, and from a balance-of-payments standpoint they should be treated as separate countries. Thus if a sterling-area member of the Fund, say Australia, is experiencing a dollar surplus, should the Fund require that country to relax its import restrictions even though other members of the sterling area have dollar deficits which are being met by the earnings of the dollar-surplus coun-tries?

An affirmative answer to this question contravenes an important char-acteristic of the sterling-area system, namely, that of pooling and sharing the hard-currency earnings of all members. If each member's right to em-ploy exchange and trade restrictions is to be determined with reference to its own dollar earnings rather than with reference to the dollar posi-tion of the sterling area as a whole, then there may be no large contribu-tions to the dollar pool by individual sterling-area countries.[16] It is quite possible of course that Britain may be unable to induce independent sterling-area countries to continue to turn large amounts of gold and dollars over to the sterling pool in exchange for sterling, unless sterling itself becomes a strong, convertible currency. The restoration of the convertibility of sterling not only would enable a large part of the nondollar world to dispense with discriminatory exchange and trade con-trols, but it may also provide the only means of saving the sterling area itself.

[16] In the course of consultations between the Contracting Parties to the GATT and the International Monetary Fund during the Fifth Session of the Contracting Parties held at Torquay, England, the representatives of Belgium, Cuba, Canada, and the United States expressed the view that "the time had come when, with all due caution in the light of the uncertainties of the present situation, a progressive relaxation of the hard currency import restrictions of Australia, Ceylon, New Zealand, Southern Rhodesia and the United Kingdom might begin."

    .   .   .   .   .

"No suggestion was made during the consultations that it would be appropriate for Chile, India or Pakistan to engage in any further general relaxation of their restrictions on imports from the Dollar Area, and the International Monetary Fund was of the opinion that no further relaxations in the case of these countries were feasible in the present circumstances." (Press Release, International Monetary Fund, Dec. 13, 1950.)

The United States has an important political interest in the maintenance of the economic, financial, and political ties of the British Commonwealth of Nations. The unity of the British Commonwealth in time of war is essential to the defense program of the North Atlantic Pact and to America's security interests in the Far East. The sterling monetary area is an essential element in the economic and political relationships existing between Britain and the Commonwealth countries. The United States, therefore, would be reluctant to take measures to weaken or destroy the sterling area, even if it were disposed to do so on purely economic grounds. The United States, nevertheless, believes that it would be desirable to merge the sterling area into a system of world-wide multilateral settlements through restoring sterling convertibility.

A full discussion of the problem of sterling convertibility is beyond the scope of this book. We may, however, outline three essential conditions for its realization.[17] First, Britain must increase the competitive position of British exports to the point where Britain can make payments for her imports in convertible sterling without losing her export trade to the dollar area or other nonsterling countries. This must be achieved through appropriate economic policies undertaken by Britain herself. Second, a considerable portion of the foreign-held sterling balances must be funded or otherwise immobilized.[18] Such immobilization involves a serious political problem, since large sterling holders such as India have opposed any action which would affect the status of their holdings. The third condition is the accumulation by Britain of larger gold and dollar reserves. It is with respect to the last condition, namely, the acquisition of larger reserves, that the United States might be able to provide assistance to Britain for restoring sterling convertibility.

INTRA-EUROPEAN PAYMENTS ARRANGEMENTS

American foreign-exchange policy has been profoundly influenced by the developments in connection with the ERP. Although we shall deal in a later chapter with the broader aspects of American policy with respect to the ERP, we shall round out our development of American foreign-exchange policies with a brief discussion of the policy issues connected with intra-European payments arrangements under the ERP.

[17] By convertibility of sterling as an international currency we mean the right of nonresidents of Britain (or their governments) to use sterling currently received in international transactions for making payments in any currency area, including the dollar area.

[18] Sterling balances totaled £3,471 million as of June 30, 1950, of which less than £1,300 million was held in blocked accounts. (*The Economist,* Nov. 4, 1950.)

At the time of Secretary Marshall's speech of June 5, 1947,[19] inviting the countries of Europe to develop a program of cooperative self-help as a basis for American aid, intra-European trade was conducted almost entirely on the basis of bilateral trade and payments arrangements which existed between each of the pairs of countries. Except for a certain amount of sterling transferability among the European members of the transferable-account system and the members of the sterling area, these payments arrangements did not permit holders of balances in one country to transfer them to third countries in payment of deficits.[20] Moreover, one of the partners frequently exhausted its credits under the bilateral agreements so that trade was at times brought to a standstill.

The bilateral agreements usually required payment in gold after the credits were exhausted by one of the parties, but most European countries either had no gold to spare or were reluctant to use their gold and dollar resources in making purchases from soft-currency countries. In an attempt to make trade conform to a bilateral payments pattern, European countries entered into commodity trade agreements in which each country would agree to sell a certain volume of commodities of various kinds either through its state trading organizations or by issuing the requisite export licenses or production priorities and materials allocations. At the same time, each country would agree to purchase over a given period a certain quantity of goods from the other country, either through government purchase or by issuing the requisite import licenses. It became immediately obvious both to the American government experts and to the Europeans themselves that a fundamental step in Europe's recovery was the freeing of intra-European trade from this bilateral straitjacket. It is not surprising, therefore, that in its initial report the Committee of European Economic Cooperation recommended the setting up of an intra-European payments system which would permit the transferability of balances from one country to another so that countries could use surpluses with one country to pay deficits with others. It also recommended that a portion of the American assistance should be set aside to provide a fund for the conversion of excess credits arising out of the operation of the payments system.[21]

Meanwhile, American experts studied the problem of intra-European payments, but few government officials or congressmen had a clear idea

[19] *Department of State Bulletin,* June 15, 1947.

[20] See Judd Polk and Gardner Patterson, "The Emerging Pattern of Bilateralism," *Quarterly Journal of Economics,* November, 1947.

[21] *General Report,* Committee of European Economic Cooperation, Paris, Vol. I, September, 1947, pp. 133–134.

as to the exact nature of the problem or how it was to be solved.[22] In the Department of State's submission of draft legislation for the "Economic Cooperation Act of 1948," it recommended that the ECA be given the power of finance procurement for one participating country from another participating country as a means of promoting intra-European trade. It specifically rejected the proposal, however, that the United States make dollars available for the purpose of settling net debit balances accruing in a multilateral clearing union.[23]

In the initial efforts to deal with the problem of intra-European trade, action was taken along two lines. In the second and third quarters of 1948, ECA made available to the individual ERP countries a limited amount of dollars for purchases in other participating countries.[24] This so-called offshore purchase technique did not prove to be satisfactory, partly because of certain limitations of the ECA Act with respect to offshore procurement.[25] The method subsequently adopted was to make "conditional grants" to individual ERP countries, provided that they made grants in turn to other participating countries with whom they had bilateral surpluses. These conditional grants and their counterpart in "drawing rights" extended by the ERP countries to individual debtors were made on a bilateral basis, and the drawing rights were not transferable except by special agreement.

The other attack on the problem was in the efforts of the European countries themselves to establish a multilateral payments system in place of the existing network of bilateral arrangements. Serious differences developed among the ERP countries themselves with regard to the kind of payments arrangement to be established. On the one hand, Belgium and certain other Continental countries were anxious to develop a system whereby a surplus with one member could be used to discharge a deficit with any other member. At the same time, however, Belgium (which has tended to run a surplus with other ERP countries) wanted to be compensated in gold or dollars for surpluses beyond a certain amount. Britain, on the other hand, was fearful of any system which

[22] For example, the Harriman Report (*A Report of the President's Committee on Foreign Aid,* Nov. 7, 1947) scarcely mentions the problem of intra-European payments. It does mention the possible need for a $3 billion stabilization fund, but such a fund would scarcely be appropriate until such time as European currencies have a good prospect of becoming generally convertible into dollars.

[23] *Outline of European Recovery Program,* submitted by the Department of State for the use of the Senate Foreign Relations Committee, Dec. 19, 1947, p. 50.

[24] See *A Report on Recovery Progress and United States Aid,* Economic Cooperation Administration, Washington, D.C., February, 1949, pp. 204–218.

[25] For example, procurement with ECA funds outside the United States could not be made for surplus agricultural commodities.

would permit an accumulation of sterling in the hands of countries like Belgium with whom Britain had a bilateral payments agreement calling for the settlement of deficits beyond a certain limit with gold. Moreover, Britain and certain other countries were unwilling to give up the trade and payments controls required for the creation of a multilateral payments and nondiscriminatory trade system in Europe.

The first efforts to multilateralize intra-European trade were therefore exceedingly meager. The "First Agreement on Multilateral Monetary Compensation" was signed in November, 1947, by only five countries: Belgium, Luxemburg, the Netherlands, France, and Italy, with Denmark, Norway, Sweden, the United Kingdom, Switzerland, and Greece coming in as "occasional" members. The system which was managed by the Bank for International Settlements (BIS) as the administrative agency operated as follows: At the end of every month each member would report its bilateral position to the BIS, which in turn would suggest to the members possible compensations or multilateral offsets. Thus, for example, if Britain were $10 million in debt to Belgium and had a credit position of $5 million with Denmark, while Denmark in turn was a creditor to the extent of $5 million with Belgium, the BIS would suggest that Britain cancel its $5 million credit against Denmark in return for a cancellation of $5 million of its debt with Belgium; and Denmark in turn would cancel its $5 million credit with Belgium.

Only the five full-time members agreed to automatic compensation, the occasional members reserving the right to reject the recommendations of the BIS. It should be observed that no actual transfers of balances from one country to another were involved even in the automatic compensations, although the BIS might recommend such transfers.[26] A complete netting of surpluses and deficits would have involved the latter type of operation. But even the limited type of offsetting or first-category compensations were usually blocked by one of the occasional members. Thus in the example given above, Denmark may have refused to accept a cancellation of her credit with Belgium whose currency was relatively strong, for the elimination of a $5 million debt to Britain, whose currency was weaker. Thus at the end of December, 1947, bilateral debit balances of $762.1 million were reported to the BIS for the 11 participating countries. Had there existed a system for the complete netting of each country's position, $278.9 million of this amount could have been canceled, but a maximum of only $39.2 million in offsetting was possible under the system of first-category compensations. Because certain of the

---

[26] Operations involving only offsetting of balances were called "first-category compensations," while those involving actual transfers of balances were called "second-category compensations."

occasional members refused even these compensations, however, only $1.7 million was actually cleared.[27] Subsequently, somewhat larger compensations were realized but never more than a small fraction of the amounts which potentially could have been cleared under a more efficient arrangement.

In October, 1948, a new Agreement for Intra-European Payments and Compensation was signed by the participating countries.[28] This Agreement provided for mandatory first-category compensations in accordance with the recommendations of the BIS, but second-category compensations required the consent of the parties concerned.[29] Drawing rights established by countries in favor of other countries with which they had bilateral surpluses were made available to the clearing agent for use in carrying out first-category compensations, but again the drawing rights were bilateral in character and could not be transferred from one country to the other except with the consent of the parties concerned. Although the new system provided somewhat greater opportunities for multilateral settlements than did the original agreement, intra-European trade was still largely bilateral in character. Instead of freeing trade and permitting its course to be determined by competitive market forces, the bilateral-trade balances among European countries were programmed in advance on the basis of forecasts of imports and exports which were, in turn, planned through bilateral-trade agreements. In spite of a considerable degree of planning, the forecasts were subject to a substantial degree of error so that some countries found themselves with unused drawing rights on some countries and uncovered deficits on others. Since only first-category compensations involving no transfers of drawing rights or of credit

[27] See Robert W. Bean, "European Multilateral Clearing," *Journal of Political Economy,* October, 1948, pp. 403–415; see also Raymond F. Mikesell, "Regional Multilateral Payments Arrangements," *Quarterly Journal of Economics,* August, 1948, pp. 500–518.

[28] For text of this Agreement, see *Third Report to Congress of the Economic Cooperation Administration,* May, 1949, pp. 108–119.

[29] First-category compensations are defined in the Agreement as an operation which produces for any Contracting Party any of the following results:

"(i) a decrease in one or more debit balances against an equivalent decrease in one or more credit balances, or

"(ii) the offsetting, by the use of amounts in respect of drawing rights established in its favor, of the whole or part of its deficit for the month with the Contracting Party by which the drawing rights have been established, or, in the case of amounts which may be used under Article 14 (a) (ii), the offsetting of the whole or part of the deficit with that Contracting Party remaining uncovered from a previous month or months. . . ."

Second-category compensations are defined as any operation "which results in the increase of a balance or the formation of a new balance in comparison with the position before the operation." (*Ibid.,* p. 115.)

balances were ordinarily permitted, trade either had to proceed as planned or not go on. Finally, there was little incentive in this system for countries to achieve a balanced position either by competition for exports or by reducing imports. If debtor countries reduced their deficits from anticipated levels, they received no compensation for unused drawing rights. On the other hand, once the amount of conditional aid was agreed to and the counterpart in drawing rights determined, the creditor country was in little danger of losing its conditional aid (dollar assistance) if the drawing rights were not utilized. Moreover, in determining the amount of total dollar aid that a country received, conditional aid was not something which the creditor got as a supplement because of its performance in intra-European trade, but was simply counted as a part of the aid which it would have received anyway even if it did not have a surplus on intra-European account.

The ECA was well aware of these difficulties [30] and in the spring of 1949 sought to negotiate a system in which drawing rights would be transferable. Not only did the scheme described above prevent the maximum development of intra-European trade consistent with the best use of Europe's resources, but it stifled competition and interfered with a lowering of production costs which were necessary for the general improvement of Europe's competitive position. The ideal system for encouraging competition was one in which conditional aid would be completely transferable and in which drawing rights would be freely usable anywhere in the system. Thus, if country A used a portion of its drawing rights against country B, the latter would receive the conditional aid; or if country A were successful in reducing its intra-European deficit, it could claim the conditional dollar aid to the extent of its unused drawing rights. On the other hand, it was objected that this arrangement would tend to put intra-European trade virtually on a dollar basis and debtor countries would be led to use their drawing rights entirely for dollar purchases rather than for buying in Europe. Moreover, some countries such as Britain objected that this might mean a loss of dollar aid which they could ill afford and that they were not prepared to compete for conditional dollar aid on this basis. After considerable negotiation, a compromise was reached in July, 1949, the principal features of which were as follows: [31]

1. Twenty-five per cent of all drawing rights extended to each European debtor were to be freely usable anywhere in the ERP area, the actual use of which would

[30] See *A Report on Recovery Progress and United States Aid,* Economic Cooperation Administration, February, 1949, pp. 212–215.

[31] *Fifth Report to Congress of the Economic Cooperation Administration,* November, 1949, pp. 13–15.

determine the distribution of the corresponding conditional aid. The remaining 75 per cent of the drawing rights was to be granted on a bilateral basis as before.

2. Provision was made for the extension of $87.5 million in long-term credits by Belgium to the United Kingdom, France, and the Netherlands to meet part of the estimated deficits of these countries with Belgium. In addition, a ceiling was placed on the transfers of conditional aid to Belgium.

3. The Council of the Organization for European Economic Cooperation requested the abandonment of restrictive trade practices which did not correspond to the increasing degree of freedom to be achieved under the new payments system.

Although an improvement over the old system, ECA was still far from its goal of achieving a fully multilateral trading system for Europe, including complete transferability of drawing rights, and still further from the goal of establishing a system of intra-European payments which could stand on its own feet at the end of the ERP program scheduled for mid-1952. Beginning with the fall of 1949, ECA Administrator Hoffman became increasingly insistent that Western Europe take definite steps toward economic integration and the freeing of intra-European trade from trade and payments barriers considered to be fundamental to such a program.[32] In December, 1949, ECA backing was given to a proposal for a European Clearing Union, which had the following features: [33]

1. The establishment of a European Clearing Union in which each country would have drawing rights up to the amount of its quota.

2. At stated intervals each member would notify the Union of the amount of its holdings of the currencies of other members which it currently earned, and the Union would then determine the net position of each member vis-à-vis the Union, i.e., complete multilateral clearing or netting of credits and debits for each member.

3. Overdraft facilities of the Union would be limited in amount and duration, and anything more permanent than seasonal deficits and surpluses would have to be financed by long-term credits or ECA grants.

4. When debits or credits were converted into long-term credits, the creditor would receive a partial payment in gold or dollars and the debtor would pay part of his debt in gold or dollars, but the sums received by the creditors would not necessarily be equal to the payments of the debtors, since a creditor might reach the limit of its quota, which would entitle it to draw gold, before any debtor would reach the limit of its drawing right.

[32] See, for example, Hoffman's address before the Council of the OEEC, Paris, Oct. 31, 1949, *The New York Times,* Nov. 1, 1949.

[33] See "European Clearing Union," *The Economist,* Jan. 21, 1950; see also *Survey of United States International Finance, 1949,* International Finance Section, Princeton University, Princeton, N.J., 1950, pp. 147–151.

5. Additional gold and dollars for the European Payments Union (EPU) would be provided by ECA, or it might acquire dollars from other sources, *e.g.*, the Monetary Fund.

While the ECA was convinced of the desirability of the establishment of a EPU for the promotion of European recovery, certain other agencies of the executive branch of the government represented on the NAC (with which the ECA is required to consult on such matters) were fearful of its implications for United States international trade and financial policy.[34] After considerable debate, the NAC approved the EPU proposal with the reservation that:

> its operations should not conflict with the obligations undertaken by the United States and other member governments to the International Monetary Fund and that the establishment of the Union on the regional basis proposed should not prevent any one participating country or group of participating countries from moving as rapidly as possible toward currency convertibility and economic integration independently of the rate of progress of other members of the proposed Union.[35]

As a means of implementing the EPU, the ECA proposed that Congress give ECA the authority to allocate a portion of its funds for the fiscal year 1950–1951 to the EPU, and ERP creditor countries would have to compete for these dollars under the Clearing Union scheme. The ECA Act of 1950 authorized the use of $600 million of the total authorization of $2.7 billion "solely for the purpose of encouraging and facilitating the operation of a program of liberalized trade and payments, for supporting any central institution or other organization . . . and for furnishing of assistance to those participating countries taking part in such a program."

In July, 1950, the Council of the OEEC agreed upon the principles and procedures for the operation of the proposed EPU, and at the end of September the BIS, which was designated as the clearing agency, made the first periodic settlement under the new payments machinery, covering current payments for the first three months from July 1, 1950. Each participating country is assigned a quota equal to 15 per cent of its total visible and invisible trade with the other participating countries in 1949, and the terms of settlement for net deficits and surpluses are

[34] This problem is discussed in Chap. 17. While the NAC discussions have not been made public, their general nature has been revealed in the press. For a summary of these press reports, see *Survey of United States International Finance, 1949*, p. 150.

[35] *National Advisory Council on International Monetary and Financial Problems, Semiannual Report to the President and to the Congress, October 1, 1949 to March 31, 1950*, p. 13.

determined by the relationship between its net position and its quota. For net surpluses up to 20 per cent of its quota a country will make available credits to the EPU up to the full amount. Conversely, EPU will extend credits to deficit countries up to 20 per cent of their quotas. For the remaining 80 per cent of their quotas, creditors will receive gold payments from the EPU equal to one-half of their net surpluses and extend credits equal to the other half. Debtor countries whose deficits exceed 20 per cent of their quota will be required to cover progressively larger portions of additional deficits in gold, and the remainder will be covered by EPU credits. For the last 20 per cent of their quota, they will be required to pay 80 per cent in gold and 20 per cent in credits from the EPU, and deficits beyond their quota must be covered 100 per cent in gold. Total quotas amount to about $4 billion, and gold-free credit margins total around $800 million. Since in the initial stages of the operation of the system gold payments to the EPU by debtors will be less than the gold receipts of creditors from the EPU, the ECA has made available a free fund of $350 million as working capital for the Union.

Provision is also made in the plan for certain prospective debtors to receive a form of economic assistance corresponding to drawing rights under the old conditional-aid system for which they will assume neither a gold nor a credit liability. These free-deficit margins are called "initial credit balances." Conversely, prospective creditors are given "initial debit positions" which represent, in effect, grants to the EPU, in return for which they receive conditional aid in the form of ECA dollars.

The EPU agreement runs for a period of 2 years to June 30, 1952. Provision is made for the amortization (with interest) over a 2-year period of outstanding bilateral credits between ECA countries which existed at the time the EPU went into effect, and for the amortization (with interest) over a 3-year period of credits granted to and received from the EPU. A special arrangement for the treatment of sterling balances held by EPU members was included in the EPU agreement, whereby holders of sterling might under certain conditions use their sterling to meet deficits with the EPU. The special agreement also provides that Britain is to be protected against a gold loss from such transactions, by aid from the ECA.[36]

The European Payments Union described above represents a compromise between a closed system of multilateral payments for the ERP countries with no convertibility into gold or dollars, and a system of full dollar convertibility. Moreover, it is one which could be transformed into

[36] See *Tenth Report to Congress of the Economic Cooperation Administration for the Quarter Ended September 30, 1950*, pp. 27–32.

a system of full dollar convertibility after June 30, 1952, provided that the dollar positions of the ERP countries have improved sufficient to permit such transformation. This could be accomplished by reducing the gold-free credit margins and requiring 100 per cent gold settlements for creditors and debtors when these credit margins had been reached. It may be desirable at this point to provide the EPU with a sizable stabilization loan or grant as a means of giving greater liquidity to the system and greater confidence to its members to loosen up their trade and to compete fully on a dollar basis.

Summary and Conclusions on United States International Monetary Policies

In the following paragraphs, an attempt will be made to summarize what presently appear to be the policies of the United States with respect to the major international monetary issues which have been discussed in the last three chapters.

Exchange Rates. The United States position on foreign-exchange rates is one of encouraging other countries to change their rates after consultation with the Fund whenever such changes are necessary to restore international equilibrium for that country. The United States, however, has been in general agreement with the position of the Monetary Fund that equilibrium rates (in the sense of rates which could be maintained without the use of exchange and trade controls) are not necessarily desirable during a period of serious economic maladjustment such as that which characterized most countries in the immediate postwar period.

While at the end of World War II the United States favored rigid exchange rates and feared a possible outbreak of competitive exchange depreciation, the United States policy at the present time favors a temporary use of free or fluctuating rates if such a system will help a country to find an appropriate rate which it can maintain without balance-of-payments controls.

While opposing multiple-exchange-rate systems in principle, the United States has adopted a lenient attitude toward their use, particularly in Latin-American countries which lack the more efficient fiscal and other administrative machinery of Western European countries. It is generally recognized that progress toward the elimination of multiple-exchange rates will be slow but that the Monetary Fund should press for the removal of some of the more objectionable features of the systems now in operation.

Gold Policy. The United States government is opposed to a change in the gold parity of the dollar and to the establishment of a free market in gold in this country or to the existence of international free-gold markets abroad.[37] The United States has not favored the use of subsidies to foreign gold-mining industries, although the Monetary Fund permits its members to employ certain types of subsidy systems. Gold is looked upon as a means of settling international accounts and not as a commodity whose production may be stimulated by artificial measures as a means of earning more dollars.

International transactions in gold at premium prices are also frowned upon by the United States because they undermine official exchange parities and, in some cases, lead to a loss of foreign exchange by countries to which the United States is providing financial assistance. Except for its own gold transactions, the United States looks to the Monetary Fund as the chief instrument through which agreed international gold policies are implemented.

Stabilization Credits. While the Monetary Fund was designed to provide short-term stabilization credits to assist its members in dealing with deficits due to seasonal, short-term, cyclical, and emergency causes of a temporary nature, the bulk of the Fund's credits up to the present time have been used for meeting the deficits of members in long-term or fundamental disequilibrium. In other words, during the postwar period of world-wide disequilibrium it was impossible for the Fund, except in a few isolated cases, to extend its assistance for genuine stabilization purposes. In this situation the United States has favored a very restricted use of the Fund's resources.

Assuming that the world's dollar position were to improve, the adoption of liberal credit policies by the Fund with respect to members which remove their exchange controls on current transactions could be an important factor in encouraging countries to take such a step. Should a general liberalization of exchange transactions not take place, there appear to be just three courses of action open to it: (1) It could cease exchange operations entirely. Under this course it would have little influence over foreign-exchange practices and might as well close its doors. (2) It could finance continuing or long-term deficits. In this event its ability to extend credits would soon be exhausted since its limited gold and dollar resources would not revolve. (3) It could become a short-term credit institution and loan under definite repayment arrangements. There are, however, certain legal obstacles to such a procedure.[38]

[37] Neither the Monetary Fund nor the United States has objected to purely local gold markets in other countries. It is almost impossible, however, to prevent national gold markets from becoming international ones.

[38] The Fund's charter makes no provision for definite repayment agreements, and some members have held that the Fund would be acting *ultra vires* by insisting upon such contracts.

It is clear that the future of the Monetary Fund will depend upon the international environment in which it will have to operate. The Fund cannot create a world of liberal exchange and trading practices; it can only help to preserve such a system and to make it operate more efficiently. If America's postwar foreign-exchange and trade objectives are realized within the next few years, this country will need to support the Fund and perhaps subscribe additional dollars for its operations. If these objectives are incapable of realization, this country ought seriously to consider either withdrawing from the Fund or amending its charter so that it can operate as a short-term lending rather than as a currency-stabilization institution.

Exchange-control Policy. Developments in America's policy with respect to the exchange controls of foreign countries have been greatly influenced by a recognition of the world-wide dollar shortage and the special problems of the sterling area and of intra-European trade. Prewar opposition to controls which discriminate against the dollar gave way to a recognition in the Monetary Fund of the right of other countries to discriminate against the dollar in periods of general dollar scarcity. While the dollar has never been formally declared scarce by the Monetary Fund, the principle that countries which are short of dollars might liberalize their trade with one another while maintaining discriminatory restrictions against dollar goods has been widely recognized and encouraged. The best example of this has been America's sponsorship of the EPU. This does not mean, however, that the United States has given up its long-run objective of restoring a world-wide system of multilateral payments. On the contrary, a freeing of trade within a limited area of multilateral settlements is viewed as an essential step in the realization of the broader objective. It is believed that by freeing trade from the strictures imposed by bilateral balancing, a larger measure of competition will be introduced and costs will consequently be lowered.

The United States has considered the convertibility of the pound sterling to be the key to the restoration of a world-wide system of multilateral payments. With the failure of convertibility in 1947, however, the United States had to give up this objective for an indefinite period in the future. By agreeing in September, 1949, to a relaxation of the provisions of the Anglo-American Financial Agreement with respect to the use of discriminatory import controls against the United States, this country made it possible for Britain to become a member of the EPU. With Britain as a member of the EPU, the entire sterling area is linked with the ERP countries in a single system of multilateral settlements.

Whether the system of multilateral settlements represented by the EPU and the sterling area is eventually merged into a world-wide system including the dollar area, or whether it becomes a more or less permanent soft-currency bloc, will depend in part upon general international economic conditions and upon the policies adopted by the member countries themselves.[39] It will also depend upon the policies which the United States pursues. In the opinion of the author, two lines of action are indicated for the United States as a means of promoting a system of world-wide multilateral settlements: (1) We should provide encouragement and financial assistance to Britain for the restoration of sterling convertibility. (2) We should continue to support the EPU on condition that it be gradually transformed into a system whereby net debits and credits are settled fully in gold after modest amounts of credits have been exhausted.

[39] A possible third alternative is that the EPU and perhaps the sterling area itself will disintegrate and the world will return to a system of bilateral trade except for those countries which are or may become members of the dollar area, *i.e.*, make and receive payments in gold, dollars, or dollar-convertible currencies.

CHAPTER 12

International Investment Policy: I

IN CHAP. 8 we outlined the general postwar foreign investment policy of the United States as contrasted with that of the 1930's. In this chapter we shall discuss the implementation and subsequent development of that policy in the postwar period. As was the case in our discussion of America's international monetary policy, no attempt will be made to provide a systematic account of the structure and operation of international investment institutions as such. Rather our principal purpose is to discuss American policy and its implementation in this important international field.

During the war period, United States policy with respect to both private and governmental foreign investments was dominated by the requirements of national defense and the related objective of promoting cordial inter-American relations. Thus the Export-Import Bank made a number of developmental loans to Latin America, some of which contributed directly or indirectly to the ability of these countries to supply raw materials needed by the United States and its Allies. Materials and equipment for use in private direct investment projects were, of course, under allocation during the war, but certain private investments in Canada, for example, contributed directly to the war effort. Private investments in petroleum in Venezuela and in Saudi Arabia were also given special encouragement during the war.

At the close of the war, the United States government sought to promote a large flow of American capital abroad, a substantial part of which it was hoped would take the form of private investment, given some encouragement through guarantees by the International Bank for Reconstruction and Development (IBRD). There were in general three reasons for this objective: (1) There was the urgent need for the reconstruction of war-torn areas. (2) There was the strong desire of underdeveloped countries in Latin America, the Far East, and elsewhere for economic development. The United States had both an economic and a political interest in stimulating economic development in foreign countries. (3) The United States desired to promote foreign investment as a means of stimulating trade and of providing a productive outlet for surplus capital. While foreign investment has not been encouraged primarily as a means of promoting full employment in the United States, productive foreign investment has been advocated as a part of a well-rounded investment program by the Council of Economic Advisors.[1]

We shall discuss the means of implementing the above objectives under four headings: (1) the International Bank for Reconstruction and Development, (2) the Export-Import Bank, (3) efforts to promote private foreign investment, and (4) the Point Four technical-assistance program. While the latter is concerned in part with grants for technical assistance, it is so closely related to the general problem of foreign investment that it may properly be dealt with under this general heading. We shall not be concerned in this chapter with the British loan, the European Recovery Program loans, and other loans and credits which are more in the nature of emergency or general balance-of-payments loans rather than normal investment financing. The line between genuine foreign investments and loans of an emergency or general balance-of-payments character is difficult to draw since many of the International Bank and the Export-Import Bank credits were primarily of the latter type. There is perhaps no completely satisfactory definition of an investment-type loan, although we shall advance the proposition that it should be one which results in a permanent addition to the real capital of the borrowing country and that it contributes directly or indirectly to the improvement of the borrowing country's balance of payments in an amount sufficient to service the loan. General balance-of-payments loans which simply help to finance a deficit on current account would not seem to fulfill these conditions.

Origin of the International Bank

The idea of an intergovernmental bank is by no means new in the history of American foreign economic policy and has a strong tradition in the history of inter-American relations. The first International Conference of American States adopted a resolution on April 14, 1890, recommending the establishment of an International American Bank, and President Harrison recommended to Congress the incorporation of such a bank.[2] Subsequently on several occasions, the possibility of establishing an inter-American bank was discussed at conferences of the American Republics, and resolutions were adopted favoring the establishment of such an institution. The last effort in this direction was made in 1940

[1] See, for example, *The Economic Report of the President*, Jan. 8, 1947, p. 31.

[2] See "The Inter-American Bank," *Federal Reserve Bulletin*, June, 1940, pp. 517–525, for background and Charter of the Inter-American Bank, proposed by the Pan American Union in April, 1940.

when the Inter-American Financial and Economic Advisory Committee of the Pan American Union met in Washington to draft a charter and bylaws for an Inter-American Bank. The Committee was assisted in this work by a group of experts from the Departments of State and Treasury, the Federal Reserve Board, and the Federal Loan Agency. A draft of a convention on the establishment of the Bank was signed by a representative of the United States government on May 10, 1940, and President Roosevelt recommended that the convention be ratified by Congress.

Although the Inter-American Bank proposal, like the proposal for an inter-American stabilization fund which developed out of the Rio Conference a year and a half later, never came into being, it was similar in many respects to the original American proposal for an international bank, and some of the same American experts worked on both proposals.[3] It is also worth noting that both the International Monetary Fund and the International Bank developed out of proposals originally intended as inter-American institutions. To a considerable degree the Export-Import Bank confined its activities to Latin America and a few other areas in which the United States had special political and economic interests before the war, whereas after 1945 a large part of the Bank's loans were directed to Europe and other parts of the world. It is clear that American foreign economic interests have broadened with the extension of her political horizons.

From the earliest stages of the government's postwar planning, it was generally agreed that some kind of an international lending institution was desirable and necessary to American foreign economic policy. Not only was there a traditional policy of fostering sound economic development in Latin America, but it was also recognized that large amounts of reconstruction capital would be needed by the war-torn nations which either would not be supplied by private capital or would be supplied only at high rates of interest and on generally severe terms. There was a genuine desire to avoid the mistakes of post-World War I not only with respect to financing our allies during the war, but also to avoid unsound financing in the postwar period. It was believed, moreover, that, by making loans through, or guaranteed by, an international institution, the United States could avoid the stigma of the role of an international creditor and that the national interests of both lenders and debtors could be better served through an international lending organization.

---

[3] For example, Dr. Harry D. White, who together with his staff in the Division of Monetary Research in the Treasury Department were responsible for the original United States proposals for an International Bank for Reconstruction and Development, also played an active role in the development of the Inter-American Bank proposal.

During 1942, proposals for a United Nations lending institution were developed in both the Treasury and State Departments. The Treasury's original proposal for a Bank for Reconstruction and Development of the United and Associated Nations was circulated within the government in March, 1942. Although a separate institution was envisaged, the proposal was well integrated with that for the international stabilization fund, and membership in the latter was to be a condition for membership in the Bank. It is worth noting that the original Treasury draft provided for certain functions which were later omitted in the published version, such as the power to make gold loans to supplement the reserves of members, the issuance of notes in a new international currency, the organizing and financing of an international raw-materials development corporation, and the organizing and financing of an international commodity-stabilization corporation.[4]

The first announcement to other countries that an International Bank proposal was under consideration by the United States government was made at an informal meeting in the Treasury Department with the representatives of 15 other nations in June, 1943. Shortly thereafter, a draft of a proposal for an International Bank for Reconstruction and Development was circulated among the United Nations and this draft was made public on November 24, 1943.[5] Although the Bank proposal was put forward by the United States as a part of a general postwar program along with the Fund, there was relatively little negotiation on the details of the American draft up to the time of the Atlantic City Conference in June, 1944, which was called to prepare an agenda for the Bretton Woods Conference to be convened the following month.[6] Lord Keynes came to the Atlantic City Conference with a new draft of the Bank proposal, most of which was accepted by the American delegation. The major change in the original American proposal recommended by Lord Keynes had to do with the restrictions on the amount and use of the local-currency subscriptions of members. Keynes viewed the operations of the Bank to be almost entirely in the field of guarantees, with only a limited

[4] The suggestions for an international investment or development corporation and a commodity-control organization were also contained in Lord Keynes's International Clearing Union proposal.

[5] Preliminary Draft Outline of a Proposal for a Bank for Reconstruction and Development of the United and Associated Nations, *Proceedings and Documents of the United Nations Monetary and Financial Conference,* Department of State, 1948, Vol. II, pp. 1616–1636.

[6] There was some doubt up to the time of the Atlantic City Conference as to whether the Bretton Woods Conference would have time to draft a charter for the Bank. In the light of subsequent world developments, it is interesting to note the primary position given by the Treasury Department to the establishment of the Fund.

role for direct loans from paid-in subscriptions. Thus, paid-in subscriptions were to be limited to 20 per cent of total subscriptions, and the gold subscription was to be limited to 2 per cent of total subscriptions. Moreover, the local-currency subscriptions could not be used either for making loans or for conversion into other currencies without the consent of the member whose currency was involved, except when needed to meet the liabilities of the Bank arising out of contractual obligations which could not be met out of the Bank's assets. In addition, the requirement in the original American proposal that members repurchase from the Bank a part of their local-currency subscriptions with gold was dropped. Since most members of the Bank, including Britain, did not consider themselves to be in a position to permit their subscribed capital to be used for making loans, this recommendation meant that funds for the Bank's direct-loan operations in the immediate postwar period would be largely limited to the paid-in subscription of the United States plus what the Bank could borrow. The subscriptions of other countries would contribute to the financial strength of the Bank, however, as a surety against defaults on the Bank's obligations as a borrower or as a guaranteeing agency.

A number of other important issues in connection with the Bank proposal were debated at the Bretton Woods Conference, only a few of which can be mentioned here. Several issues were raised concerning the type of loans to be guaranteed or made by the Bank. For example, the Latin-American members were fearful lest the resources of the Bank be employed largely for reconstruction and that there would be little left over for development. Countries primarily interested in development advocated reserving a fixed proportion, say half, of the Bank's resources for each purpose. This proposal was defeated, but Art. III, Sec. 1 (a), places equal emphasis upon both purposes: "The resources and the facilities of the Bank shall be used . . . with equitable consideration to projects for development and projects for reconstruction alike." [7] The United States delegation was anxious to confine the activities of the Bank to financing specific projects which directly increase the productivity of the borrowing country. Although it was generally agreed that the Bank was not supposed to assist in financing rehabilitation and relief—since this type of assistance was to be rendered by United Nations Relief and Rehabilitation Administration—some delegations at the Conference pointed out that there would be a dire need of loans for restocking and

[7] Articles of Agreement, the International Bank for Reconstruction and Development. The Articles of Agreement have been published by the State and Treasury Departments and by the International Bank for Reconstruction and Development in Washington, D.C.

stabilization purposes and that such assistance might be just as productive as a specific project such as a steel plant or a hydroelectric dam. The principle as finally adopted was as follows: "Loans made or guaranteed by the Bank shall, except in special circumstances, be for the purpose of specific projects of reconstruction and development." (Art. III, Sec. 9.) It is worth noting that the American Congress in considering the Bretton Woods bill was convinced of the desirability of giving the Bank the power to make long-term monetary stabilization loans in the belief that such loans would make it easier for the Fund to confine its operations to short-term financing.[8] Thus far, no loans for this purpose have been made by the Bank, but the Bank has departed in certain cases from the specific project type of loan. We shall return to this question when we take up the experience of the Bank in its actual operations.

Two other conditions relating to the type of project financed by the Bank are worth noting. Although ordinarily local-currency expenditures in connection with any project are to be financed from capital raised within the borrowing country, the Bank may, in exceptional circumstances, provide the borrower with an appropriate amount of that currency as a part of the loan (Art. IV, Sec. 36). In addition, if the project gives rise indirectly to an increased need for foreign exchange by the borrowing member, the Bank may in exceptional circumstances provide as a part of the loan an amount of gold or foreign exchange not in excess of the local expenditure made in connection with the project (Art. IV, Sec. 3c).[9]

One of the conditions for the making or guaranteeing of loans by the Bank is that the balance-of-payments prospects of the country to which the loan is made are such as to provide reasonable assurance of repayment. This is not simply a matter of the productivity of the project or

[8] By long-term stabilization loans the Congress had in mind loans to reconstitute the gold and dollar reserves of foreign countries rather than for the purpose of meeting continuing deficits in a country's balance of payments. Congress was largely influenced in favoring this type of operation by the testimony of American bankers. See Report of the House Committee on Banking and Currency on H.R. 3314, 79th Congress, 1st Session, 1945, p. 71. In 1946, the Board of Executive Directors of the Bank adopted a resolution expressly stating that loans for monetary stabilization are within the authority of the Bank.

[9] The two conditions under which the Bank may make loans to cover local-currency expenditures will in most cases be the same. A country will usually need local-currency financing when it is unable to raise funds for investment from noninflationary sources. Since the International Bank is not likely to borrow funds in that country, the Bank will provide foreign exchange which can then be sold for local currency. The foreign exchange can be used to import goods as an offset to the inflationary impact of the local-currency investment expenditures. Looked at another way, the foreign exchange is required because of the additional demand created by the local-currency expenditures.

even of its contribution to the future balance-of-payments position of the borrowing country, but is one which concerns the over-all balance-of-payments prospects of that country. In a period in which most countries are in a condition of fundamental disequilibrium, this is a difficult criterion to apply. If applied narrowly, the Bank's activities might be restricted to loans to only a few countries. On the other hand, one of the duties of an institution such as the International Bank should be to help a country work out a broad financial, production, and investment program which would provide reasonable promise of servicing the loan. Little attention was paid to this problem in the 1920's when loans were made by competing private investors with little regard either to the use of the funds loaned or to the general financial position of the borrowing country. This may be regarded as an important argument for channeling a large part of foreign lending through public institutions.

A final issue at the Bretton Woods Conference concerns the financial resources of the Bank. Keynes's principle of limited paid-in subscriptions and severe limitations on their use (except for the 2 per cent gold subscription) won the day. The Bank, however, could borrow or make guarantees in an amount equal to its total subscribed capital, reserves, and surplus less the amount of its loans made out of its paid-in capital.[10] Some countries, including the United States, advocated giving the Bank the power to incur obligations up to 150 per cent of its paid-in capital and surplus, but the United Kingdom and certain other European countries took the position that the total amount of outstanding guarantees and loans should not exceed 100 per cent of the Bank's unimpaired subscribed capital, reserves, and surplus. Although at present this amounts to about $8,350 million, there are many who believe that the actual limit of the Bank's dollar loans and guarantees is set by the level of the United States subscription plus the 2 per cent gold subscription of the other members, *i.e.,* approximately $3.2 billion. Even this amount is limited by the Bank's ability to borrow in the American capital markets.[11]

In the discussions and Congressional deliberations leading up to the passage of the Bretton Woods Act of 1945, there was relatively little criticism of the Bank except by a few people who were opposed to the

[10] The Bank's lending power is also increased by those portions of 18 per cent paid-in subscriptions of other members, which are released by the members for making loans. Although borrowers are not restricted as to the country in which the proceeds of loans are to be spent, in practice nondollar currencies would be paid to borrowers who intended to use such currencies within the currency area of the member whose currency was employed.

[11] In the foregoing discussion, the author has drawn heavily upon Dr. Antonin Basch's article entitled, "International Bank for Reconstruction and Development, 1944–1949," *International Conciliation,* November, 1949.

principle of international lending by the United States government. In fact, the majority of the opponents of the Bretton Woods proposals favored the establishment of the Bank without the Fund. It should be noted in passing that the Bretton Woods Act of 1945 suspended the Johnson Act of 1934 with respect to those countries which were members of the Fund and Bank.

Policies of the International Bank in Operation

The policies of the Bretton Woods institutions have undergone a process of continuing development in the course of their operations. The charters of the two institutions were broadly drawn, and in many cases the provisions were based on preconceptions regarding conditions in the postwar world which have not been realized. Although the Bank is an international institution, its policies have been dominated by the United States, and particularly by the American presidents of the Bank, to an even greater extent than has been the case with the Fund. The necessity of raising funds in the American capital market has made it necessary for the management of the Bank to have not only the full support of the American government but also the confidence of the American financial community. In fact its present head, Eugene Black, and his immediate predecessor, John J. McCloy, were formerly associated with Wall Street.[12] This situation helps to account for the essentially conservative policies of the Bank, policies which have been more con-

[12] The first President of the Bank was Eugene Meyer, owner of *The Washington Post* and a former member of the Federal Reserve Board; the initial Vice President was Harold D. Smith, formerly United States Director of the Budget; and the United States member of the executive board was Emilio G. Collado, formerly of the State Department. Meyer resigned his position in December, 1946, and Smith died suddenly the following month. At this time the Bank was undergoing serious organizational difficulties, and the uncertainties regarding its future policies resulted in a lack of confidence on the part of the financial community in the institution. Such confidence was of course essential if the Bank was to market its securities successfully. The United States government therefore favored the appointment of a president and United States executive director who would have the complete confidence of the financial community and who would therefore provide an essentially conservative management for the Bank. On February 23, 1947, John J. McCloy, a Wall Street lawyer and former Assistant Secretary of War, was appointed President and Eugene Black, Vice President of the Chase National Bank of New York, United States Executive Director of the Bank. Robert L. Garner, Vice President of the Guaranty Trust Company of New York, was appointed Vice President of the Bank. Thus the complexion of the management was changed from one representing former government employees and administration supporters to one representing the United States financial community. Mr. Black became President of the Bank in 1949.

servative in fact than if the Bank had been an agency of the United States government.

Although the National Advisory Council indicates the general policy to be followed by the American member of the executive board of the Bank, it has not taken the initiative with respect to loan applications or sought to interfere in a positive way with the operations of the Bank.[13] It should also be said that the influence of the executive board in the Bank is far less than in the case of the executive board of the Fund since the policies of the Bank are to a large degree determined by the president and his staff. A serious controversy between the NAC and the president of the Bank would of course lead to the latter's resignation. But if the American financial community supported the Bank's president, as it is likely to do in a matter which involved, say, a substantial lowering of the Bank's lending criteria, the credit standing of the Bank would be endangered. In saying this we do not mean to imply that the NAC is in any fundamental disagreement with the policies of the Bank, since in its Reports the NAC has always stated its approval of the Bank's policies. We have simply sought to indicate the factors which have determined those policies.

During the first year after its formal establishment at the Savannah Conference in March, 1946, the Bank was engaged in organizational activities, and its first loan was not made until May, 1947. It is obvious therefore that the Bank's resources were not available to meet the immediate postwar needs for reconstruction financing. The Bank made four loans in 1947—France ($250 million), the Netherlands ($190 million), Denmark ($40 million), and Luxemburg ($10.8 million)—all of them to European countries for reconstruction purposes and all but the loan to Luxemburg were general-purpose loans, that is, they were not designed for financing a specific project or projects. The use of the loan proceeds was, however, tied to the purchase of a list of commodities approved by the Bank, and in accordance with its general practice, the Bank made sure by its end-use supervision that each loan was in fact used for the purposes stated in the loan agreement.

Well over half the Bank's total loan commitments on December 31, 1950 (about $1 billion), had been made to Europe, and the bulk of these loans were accounted for by the loans to France, the Netherlands, and Denmark. The loans to these three countries were of an emergency character and closely akin to balance-of-payments loans. In fact there was little to distinguish the assistance afforded these countries by the Inter-

[13] The NAC has given the Bank an unrestricted right to use the 18 per cent paid-in subscription of the United States. It does, however, retain the right of veto over the use of funds repaid to the Bank from loans made with the United States subscription.

national Bank and the Export-Import Bank in 1946 and 1947 from the ERP assistance given in 1948, except of course the conditions of repayment. The Bank recognized the emergency character of these loans in its Third Annual Report,[14] in which it stated that "these loans, by permitting the borrowing countries to sustain for a time the necessary volume of essential imports, helped to prevent a disastrous drop in production and possible economic collapse." Following the inauguration of the Marshall Plan in the spring of 1948, the Bank announced that for the time being it would not make further large loans to Europe. This action was in line with that taken by the Monetary Fund, which prior to the Marshall Plan had also permitted sizable drawings by its European members. The members of the Bank did not object to this curtailment of the Bank's operations in Europe since they would much rather have their imports financed by the Economic Cooperation Administration than incur a dollar obligation to the Bank. Since the beginning of ECA aid, modest loans have been made to the Netherlands, Turkey, Iceland, and Belgium for specific projects, and in addition loans were made to Finland and to Yugoslavia, which are not ECA members.

No loans have been made by the Bank to the Russian satellite countries of Czechoslovakia and Poland, although both countries have made loan applications and unsuccessful negotiations for specific project loans were carried on. In March, 1950, Poland withdrew from the Fund and Bank, charging that the institutions were being used to further American political objectives. Although the full details of the loan negotiations with Poland and Czechoslovakia have not been made public, there is no evidence that the United States has taken a position in the Bank against loans to these countries provided the Bank's general conditions were met. Czechoslovakia received assistance from the Fund ($6 million) in 1948 at about the same time negotiations with regard to loans from the Bank to Poland and Czechoslovakia were being carried on. On the other hand, it would be naïve to assume that political factors did not enter into the breakdown of the loan negotiations with these two countries. A serious question may be raised as to whether loans can properly be made to a member whose economic and political affairs are completely dominated by a country which is not a member of the Fund and Bank and which is carrying on economic and political warfare against the bulk of the members of these institutions. Can international economic cooperation between the satellite members and the other members of the Fund and Bank be anything but a sham under these conditions?

14 *Third Annual Report, 1947–1948,* International Bank for Reconstruction and Development, Washington, D.C., 1948, p. 8.

The experience of the Bank in making reconstruction loans to the ERP countries in 1947 raises the question as to whether proper loan criteria can be applied to countries in desperate economic straits and whose economies face imminent collapse without outside assistance. It seems obvious that what these countries needed was rehabilitation assistance in the form of grants and a measure of economic recovery before there could be any basis for determining their ability to service foreign loans. This is not to criticize the action of either the Fund or the Bank in providing urgently needed assistance at this time. What may be questioned is whether the Bank which by its very nature must make loans on a sound financial basis is the proper instrument to finance the reconstruction of war-devastated areas. Even after Europe has undergone complete reconstruction, many European countries will be in a precarious internal and external financial position for many years to come. To saddle such countries with a large external debt burden during the period of reconstruction does not augur well for their ability to maintain viability in the future.

Up to the end of 1948, the Bank had made only one development-type loan, a loan to Chile of $16 million. Although the Bank's lending operations were substantially expanded during 1950, by the end of that year less than $350 million had been loaned to the underdeveloped areas, of which only about $100 million had been actually disbursed.[15] This situation has been a source of great disappointment to the underdeveloped countries, and a great deal of criticism has been directed toward both the Bank and the United States. The reasons for the relatively large operations in Europe are clear. (1) There was the urgency for assistance to Europe to prevent imminent collapse, a condition which was not present in most of the underdeveloped countries. (2) The immediate productive use of railroad equipment, raw materials, and industrial and agricultural machinery in Europe was clear since it represented replacements for what had already existed. Moreover, there were on hand the technical skills and the supporting economic organizations to put these materials and equipment to immediate productive use in an integrated manner. (3) The countries of Europe, although temporarily disrupted by the war, had a reasonably respectable record of political and economic stability and a demonstrated capacity to finance foreign loans.

The situation as regards developmental loans was in most respects just the opposite. Developmental projects involved new industries and economic activities which had to be integrated with the rest of the economy.

[15] As of Dec. 31, 1950, the Bank's loan agreements totaled $1,006 million, of which $642 million had been disbursed. See *International Financial Statistics*, International Monetary Fund, Washington, D.C., January, 1951, p. 15.

Labor had to be trained in new skills, entrepreneurship and managerial talent found for new types of enterprises, and local capital raised in areas where markets for capital for local industry did not exist. Even the basic economic data with regard to markets, transportation, sources of raw materials, and labor supply are lacking in the underdeveloped countries. Finally, there was the factor of political and economic instability, the incompetence or outright dishonesty of public officials, and the absence of any historical record of ability to finance external debts or of the willingness of succeeding governments to honor the debts incurred by their predecessors. On the other hand, the longer run economic potentialities of many underdeveloped countries for servicing foreign loans may be better than that of many older industrial countries.

The Bank has insisted that it can make loans only on the basis of well-developed projects which involve not only detailed plans and specifications as to the end-use of the foreign purchases financed by the Bank but also a detailed picture of how the project will be integrated into the economy and contribute to its productivity. In addition, the Bank is concerned with the balance-of-payments prospects of the borrowing country and its relation to the country's general investment program. This does not mean that every project financed by a loan from the Bank must make a direct contribution to the foreign-exchange earnings of the borrowing country. The Bank recognizes that roads and irrigation projects may have an important effect upon both the productivity and the foreign-exchange position of a country. The Bank has also taken the position that foreign financing is only one element in economic development and that loans cannot properly be made until the other essential elements are dealt with. In listing the obstacles to the making of properly conceived developmental loans, the Bank has mentioned the following: [16]

1. A lack of capital to finance local-currency expenditures in connection with development projects.

2. The shortage of skilled and managerial personnel. Although some technicians can be hired from abroad, most of the skilled and semiskilled workers must be supplied from local sources. This often requires the institution of training programs.

3. The low level of education of the bulk of the people in the underdeveloped areas and the low physical productivity of workers with low standards of consumption and health services.

4. Economic instability due to unsound monetary and fiscal policies and unsettled political conditions, which tend to discourage foreign investment and domestic savings and investment.

[16] *Third Annual Report, 1947–1948,* International Bank for Reconstruction and Development, Washington, D.C., 1948, pp. 15–16.

5. A lack of any well-formulated development plan or any concept of the relative priority of possible types of projects and their relation to the available power, transportation, and other facilities and complementary industries necessary to support them.

The picture of the obstacles to economic development which the Bank paints would seem to indicate an exceedingly slow and painful process. According to the President of the International Bank, Eugene Black, the reason that the Bank has made so few loans "has not been the lack of money but the lack of well-prepared and well-planned projects ready for immediate execution." [17] (Much the same position has been taken by the officials of the Export-Import Bank.) On the other hand, we are faced with the aspirations of hundreds of millions of people in Asia, Africa, Latin America, and elsewhere, for achieving higher living standards through economic development. Are these people to be told that any substantial amount of economic development and a raising of their living standards will take generations because of the obstacles to the formulation of projects which the Bank will undertake to finance? What can be done to speed up the operations of the International Bank in this field?

In the study entitled *National and International Measures for Full Employment* prepared by a group of experts for the United Nations, it was recommended that the Bank be provided with additional resources from member governments for making loans for "general developmental purposes not only in special circumstances but generally." [18] In commenting on this recommendation before the Economic and Social Council, Eugene Black suggested that a loan for general developmental purposes "really means a loan for a purpose or purposes unknown" and that such a loan would represent "bad lending practice." The author is inclined to agree that loans without detailed planning as to what they are going to be used for and how the capital investments would function in relation to the rest of the economy either would represent a misdirection of resources or would simply amount to general balance-of-payments loans. Unless a loan contributes directly or indirectly to an increase in the productivity of the borrowing country including its capacity to service foreign loans, such assistance should not take the form of a loan but should be made in the form of a grant.

The answer to this problem seems to lie in two general directions: (1) Loans ought to be made not simply on a project by project basis, but on the basis of a well-formulated general developmental program

[17] Statement before the Economic and Social Council of the United Nations, Lake Success, N.Y., Feb. 16, 1950.

[18] *National and International Measures for Full Employment,* United Nations, Lake Success, N.Y., 1949, p. 92.

which would include a number of well-integrated projects. Some portion of the loan might also be available to finance the indirect foreign-exchange requirements engendered by the general program. This would be in accordance with the Bank's Articles of Agreement [Art. IV, Sec. 3(c)]. (2) Major emphasis should be given to helping countries formulate their investment projects and programs and in helping them to overcome as rapidly as possible some of the obstacles mentioned above. This means that the Bank cannot sit in Washington and wait for business to come to it in the form of well-formulated developmental projects. Rather it means that the Bank in cooperation with other national and international agencies must go out and assist countries in formulating the kind of developmental programs which meet the test of reasonably high international investment standards.

In its *Fifth Annual Report, 1949–1950,* the International Bank outlined a number of policies which gave indication that it had adopted a more liberal lending policy and a broader conception of its functions than was evident in the early period of its operations. The Bank has recently encouraged its members to formulate long-range development programs and is providing technical assistance for the purpose. Technical missions have recently been sent to Colombia, Turkey, Guatemala, and Cuba to make economic surveys in connection with long-range development programs. The objective of these missions "is to help the country formulate a program of investment which will indicate priorities among the important sectors of the economy and among types of undertakings within such sectors; to suggest methods and measures, other than investment, to improve productive efficiency in existing enterprises; and to recommend improvements in the government's economic and financial policies and organizations in order to facilitate and encourage further development." [19] Such surveys will make it easier for countries to submit loan applications covering a number of projects related to a broad development program.

Many projects which do not involve substantial direct foreign-exchange costs may nevertheless create large additional demands for foreign exchange as a result of the withdrawal of workers and resources from the production of consumption goods and of the higher incomes generated by the new investment. While borrowing countries should be encouraged to finance as much as possible of the local expenditures by domestic saving, some additional foreign-exchange drain may be unavoidable if economic hardship and inflation are to be prevented. In the past, the Bank has been

[19] *Fifth Annual Report, 1949–1950,* International Bank for Reconstruction and Development, pp. 17–18; see also, R. H. Demuth, "Technical Assistance Activities of the International Bank," in *Proceedings of the Fifth Annual Meeting of the Board of Governors,* International Bank for Reconstruction and Development, Nov. 30, 1950.

reluctant to make loans in amounts beyond what was needed to cover the direct foreign-exchange costs of the development projects. The Fifth Annual Report, however, provides a new statement of the Bank's policy on the financing of local-currency expenditures, which appears to be somewhat more liberal than has been indicated in the past. This policy is summarized as follows: [20]

> In general, the Bank's policy may be summarized by saying that local expenditures may be financed if the following conditions are satisfied: (a) if the project to be financed is of such economic urgency that the country's ability to undertake foreign borrowing—which is more or less limited in all cases—is better utilized in financing this project than in financing the direct foreign exchange costs of alternative projects; (b) if the local currency costs of the project cannot reasonably be met out of available domestic resources; and (c) if it is apparent that, unless foreign exchange is made available to the borrowing country to be employed for the import of either consumer goods or raw materials, the local currency expenditures involved in the project will lead to inflationary pressures.

The implementation of this policy on loans to finance the indirect foreign-exchange drain of local-currency expenditures should increase the scope of the lending activities of the Bank.

Contrary to the expectations of its founders, the Bank has not promoted the flow of international capital by guaranteeing loans made by private investors. The financial operations of the Bank have consisted largely of direct loans out of the paid-in subscription of the United States and from the $325 million (as of June, 1951) raised by the sale of the Bank's own obligations in the private capital market. Up to the end of 1950, only $70 million of the paid-in local-currency subscriptions of other members had been loaned by the Bank. Several countries including Belgium, Canada, Denmark, Mexico, Paraguay, and the United Kingdom have consented to a limited use by the Bank of their paid-in currency subscriptions, and the Bank expects to be able to make greater use of its nondollar currency holdings in the future.

Wartime Policies of the Export-Import Bank

Up until 1940, the operations of the Export-Import Bank were directed mainly to serving American commercial interests in the exporting business. There were a few exceptions such as the $25 million credit to the Chinese-owned Universal Trading Corporation, which was granted as a measure of support to China in her war with Japan, and developmental

[20] *Fifth Annual Report, 1949–1950,* International Bank for Reconstruction and Development, p. 11.

loans to Haiti (1938) and Chile (1939). But most of the loans were granted for the financing of exports of specific products such as heavy equipment and agricultural commodities. In 1940, the Bank's lending authority was increased from $200 million to $700 million and the original act creating the Bank amended in a manner which made it clear that Congress intended it to operate in the field of economic development. A portion of the Act as amended in September, 1940, read as follows: [21] "To assist in the development of the resources, the stabilization of the economies, and the orderly marketing of the products of the countries of the Western Hemisphere by supplying funds, not to exceed $500 million outstanding at any one time. . . ."

Thus it was clear that Congress intended the additional $500 million in the Bank's lending capital to be used for assisting in the development of the resources of the American Republics. The reasons advanced in support of the bill were (1) the importance of developing sources of strategic materials for the defense of the United States, and (2) economic support of Western Hemisphere countries as an aid to foreign policy.[22] Thus according to Mrs. Dulles, after 1940 the Bank became "a definite instrument of American foreign policy." Although the Bank has continued to make loans for financing the sale of American farm surpluses, e.g., cotton and tobacco, and has made loans from time to time to American exporters to finance specific transactions, since 1940 the main business of the Bank has been in the field of developmental and (after 1945) reconstruction loans.

The Export-Import Bank Act of 1945 [23]

By the time Congress began its consideration of the Bretton Woods bill, it had become obvious that the institutions which had been planned to handle the financial problems of the postwar world were not only inadequate from the standpoint of their financial resources, but they left the largest area of need more or less untouched. This area concerned the large gap between the dollars needed by the belligerent countries for maintaining consumption levels, restocking supplies of consumers' goods and raw materials, and rebuilding or replacing facilities damaged by the war or impaired for lack of maintenance, and the low level of current earnings immediately after the close of hostilities. There was in addition the problem, the magnitude of which was not yet known, of providing

[21] Public Law 792, 76th Congress.

[22] See Eleanor L. Dulles, "The Export-Import Bank of Washington," *Department of State Bulletin,* Dec. 3, 1944, p. 668.

[23] Public Law 173, 79th Congress, 1st Session, approved July 31, 1945.

assistance for the readjustment of the economies of other countries to the changed conditions of production, trade, and balance of payments after the war. These needs were over-all balance-of-payments require-ments which did not fall within the category of relief to be handled by UNRRA, or of credits for currency stabilization to be supplied by the Fund, or of bankable reconstruction projects to be financed after ade-quate investigation and deliberation by the World Bank. In the case of Europe the needs were large, and they were immediate if these highly complex industrial economies were to be restored and maintained as going concerns.

The administration had decided that, in the light of its legislative his-tory, lend-lease assistance could not be used in the reconstruction period except for a limited amount of "pipe-line" supplies which could be made available on credit. It was also evident that the gold and dollar reserves of the foreign countries themselves were inadequate for meeting their postwar deficits and that it would be undesirable for these reserves to be reduced below amounts which were regarded as minimum working levels. Although total gold and short-term dollar assets of foreign countries had increased from $15 billion on December 30, 1938, to $19.7 billion on June 30, 1945, the rise in world prices during the war had largely offset the monetary gain.[24] Moreover, these reserves were badly distributed from the standpoint of the urgency of need. For example, the gold and dollar reserves of Britain, France, and the Netherlands had declined substan-tially from prewar levels, while the reserves of Switzerland and most Latin-American countries had increased.

Since no long-range plans had been made to take care of Europe's immediate postwar financial requirements, the problem was dealt with largely on an *ad hoc* basis until the inauguration of the Marshall Plan in 1948. In July, 1945, the administration asked Congress to increase the lending authority of the Export-Import Bank to $3.5 billion to enable it to make emergency loans to foreign countries pending the beginning of operations by the International Bank. The Act which was approved on July 31, 1945, also removed the prohibitions of the Johnson Act on loans by the Bank and by private persons to governments in default on their obligation to the United States government and made the Bank an independent agency of the United States government.[25]

[24] See *First Semi-annual Report to Congress, for the Period July–December, 1945,* Export-Import Bank of Washington, pp. 13–14, for a statement of United States policy with respect to the level of gold and dollar assets.

[25] The Act of 1945 vested the management of the Bank in a board of directors, con-sisting of the Secretary of State ex officio and four full-time members appointed by the President with the advice and consent of the Senate. An Act of June 9, 1947, reincor-porated the Bank under a Federal charter and extended its life to June 30, 1953.

In addition to the emergency reconstruction loans, the Bank was expected to continue its activities in the field of foreign economic development, its financing of surplus agricultural exports, and its credits to American firms to help them finance specific exports and imports. This represented a somewhat strange mixing of functions in one institution which was originally created as an instrument of American commercial policy and was now entrusted with the job of making large emergency-type loans to implement the foreign policy of the United States. This latter task was assigned to the Export-Import Bank in part because it had a favorable reputation both in Congress and in financial circles generally. Up to June 30, 1945, the Bank had disbursed $504 million in loans, of which $290 million had been repaid. Its losses had been negligible, and its net earnings had amounted to $42 million since it began operations in 1934. During the course of the hearings on the 1945 bill, Randolph Burgess, President of the American Bankers Association, testified in favor of the bill in the name of the association,[26] whereas the association had been opposed to the Bretton Woods bill upon which hearings were also being held at the same time. Moreover, it was implied during the hearings that in its new role of emergency reconstruction financing the Bank could maintain the same standards of sound bankable loans which had characterized its operations in the past.

In the course of the testimony on the bill, administration officials continually stressed the importance to the American economy of maintaining exports. It was pointed out that the Export-Import Bank would directly promote United States exports since its practice was to make loans only for the purchase of American commodities whereas the loans of the International Bank were not tied.[27] The State Department was also desirous of having an American institution equipped to make sizable foreign loans in order to deal with special situations in which this country had an important national interest, and which for one reason or another could not be made through the International Bank. It is worth noting that in the course of the hearings the administration stated that it had in mind a $1 billion loan from the Export-Import Bank to Russia. This loan, however, failed to materialize, owing largely to subsequent political developments. In April, 1946, the Bank earmarked $500 million to China, but no loan was to be made until the termination of the civil conflict in China. The reservation expired on June 30, 1947, and was never renewed.

[26] Hearings, House Committee on Banking and Currency, on H.R. 3771, 79th Congress, 1st Session, July 11 and 12, 1945, pp. 78–80.

[27] See Hearings, Senate Committee on Banking and Currency on H.R. 3771, 79th Congress, 1st Session, July 17 and 18, p. 11.

Postwar Operations of the Export-Import Bank

During the period following V-J Day to the end of 1947, the Export-Import Bank authorized about $2 billion in loans to Europe, largely of the emergency balance-of-payments type. The largest loans were made to France ($1,200 million), the Netherlands ($210 million), Belgium ($150 million), and Italy ($151 million).[28] About $655 million of the credits extended during this period represented lend-lease credits to finance the purchase of products and services for which requisitions had been approved before September 2, 1945. The terms called for repayment of principal over a 30-year period beginning on July 1, 1946, with interest at $2\frac{3}{8}$ per cent. Loans for reconstruction purposes with a maturity of 20 to 30 years bore a rate of interest of 3 per cent, whereas other long-term loans were made at $3\frac{1}{2}$ per cent provided that they were made to governments or were guaranteed by governments.[29] Higher rates from 4 up to 6 per cent were charged on loans to private borrowers without effective governmental guarantees, and lower rates were charged for short-term loans.

While the large reconstruction loans made during 1946 and 1947 were tied to the financing of lists of particular commodity exports—largely raw materials, transportation equipment, and agricultural and industrial machinery—they were not in general tied to specific projects. In a sense they were general balance-of-payments loans related to a rather broad shopping list. Although made in the form of loans, such aid can scarcely be differentiated from the extraordinary assistance largely provided in the form of grants under the Marshall Plan. While, according to the Bank's statement of its criteria for making loans,[30] capacity to repay is given as one of the important considerations in any loan negotiation, it is difficult to see how a significant judgment of the ability of most European countries to repay large emergency loans could have been made in the light of the deep-rooted structural maladjustments in their balance of payments at that time. The fact that a grant program several times the magnitude of these emergency reconstruction loans was found to be

[28] *Fifth Semi-annual Report to Congress, for the Period July–December, 1947*, Export-Import Bank of Washington.

[29] See *Third Semi-annual Report to Congress, for the Period July–December, 1946*, Export-Import Bank of Washington, p. 28. The general level of interest rates to be charged by the Bank was recommended by the NAC. The $3\frac{1}{2}$ per cent rate was calculated to cover the cost of borrowing the Bank's funds to the United States government plus an allowance for risk and administrative expenses necessary to keep the Bank on a self-sustaining basis.

[30] *First Semi-annual Report to Congress for the Period July–December, 1945*, Export-Import Bank of Washington, p. 10.

necessary shortly after the loans were made bears out this point. The explanation for the large emergency-type loans by both the Export-Import Bank and the International Bank lies in the gross underestimation of the problems of rehabilitating and readjusting the economies of Europe and elsewhere after the war.

Table 8 shows the net credits authorized by the Export-Import Bank from July 1, 1945, to September 30, 1950, by category of loan. Out of the total of $3,209 million in credit authorizations for the period, $1,220

*Table 8. Net Credits Authorized by the Export-Import Bank,**
July 1, 1945, to Sept. 31, 1950

(In millions of dollars)

Area and country	Total	Recon- struction	Develop- ment	Lend- lease requisi- tions	Cotton purchases	Other
Total, all areas.....	$3,208.6	$1,008.0	$1,220.1	$655.0	$177.8	$147.7
Europe...........	2,064.5	971.8	315.5	655.0	104.6	17.6
Latin America......	623.2	....	498.0	......	......	125.2
Asia and Africa.....	371.0	36.2	261.6	......	73.2	
Canada...........	145.0	....	145.0			
Miscellaneous......	4.9	....	....	......	......	4.9

* Cancellations and expirations deducted.
SOURCE: *National Advisory Council on International Monetary and Financial Problems, Semiannual Report to the President and to the Congress for the Period April 1, 1950, to September 30, 1950.*

million is listed as developmental credits, and of this amount $315 million was made available to European countries. The distinction between the reconstruction credits and the developmental credits so far as Europe was concerned lies in the fact that the latter were in connection with specific projects, whereas the emergency reconstruction credits tended to be more general in nature. Developmental loans to Latin America totaled $498 million for the period. Of the $262 million in developmental loans to Asia and Africa, $100 million was loaned to Israel, $100 million to Indonesia, and the remainder to Afghanistan, Saudi Arabia, Egypt, Liberia, and the Philippines. All but $5 million of the $145 million in credits to Canada was made, not for specific projects, but to improve her reserve position in late 1947 at a time when this country was subject to a serious dollar drain.[31] The bulk of the remainder of the credits was for the purpose of financing cotton and tobacco purchases of foreign countries. These credits are generally repayable in 15 months at 2½ per cent interest.

Although the bulk of the Export-Import Bank loans are made directly to foreign governments or their agencies, some of the credits are made to American exporters to finance shipments abroad on terms, and a few are made to private foreign concerns and to subsidiaries of American concerns operating abroad. The Bank has recently made a number of loans to American firms for raw-materials production abroad.

As was the case with the International Bank, the Export-Import Bank made few loans to the ERP countries after the inauguration of the Marshall Plan, except as a lending agency for the ECA.[32] Loans were made to Finland and Yugoslavia however. Three loans totaling $55 million to Yugoslavia [33] are of particular interest from the standpoint of their relation to America's foreign economic policy. After Yugoslavia's break with the Soviet Union in 1948, it became necessary for this country to reorient her trade from Eastern Europe to the West, since planned deliveries from the Eastern European countries were suspended. Since it was the policy of the United States to encourage Yugoslavia's isolation from Russia, efforts were made to assist Yugoslavia in rebuilding her economy and maintaining her economic and political independence. During 1949, Yugoslavia received financial assistance from the International Bank, the Monetary Fund, and the Export-Import Bank. The $55 million in Export-Import Bank funds authorized for Yugoslavia was made available to cover a broad range of raw material and equipment imports and was not tied to a few specific projects.

Two other loans which have political overtones are worth mentioning, the $100 million loan to Israel made in January, 1949, and the $100 million credit to the Republic of Indonesia announced in February, 1950. Both of these loans cover a wide range of commodities to finance a general development program and are not related to a few specific projects as in the case of most of the other development loans. Without reflecting upon its soundness, the large loan to Israel obviously reflects the strong

[31] The original credit authorization to Canada was for $300 million, only $145 million of which was drawn upon. The Canadian government borrowed $150 million in the private American capital market to repay the loan. *Seventh Semi-annual Report, for the Period of July–December, 1948,* Export-Import Bank of Washington, p. 9.

[32] That part of the ECA funds which Congress directed to be made available in the form of loans was administered by the Export-Import Bank under the direction of the ECA.

[33] These loans were authorized in September, 1949, February, 1950, and August, 1950, respectively.

sympathies of the administration and of the majority of the American people for the welfare of the new state. The loan to Indonesia reflected America's political interest in the development of southeast Asia as a means of combatting communism in the area. Neither one of these loans could have been made by the International Bank because the borrowers are not members.

In general the Export-Import Bank's development credits to Latin America have been for the financing of individual projects or a few related projects and have been more modest in size. The largest credits since July, 1945 (to September 30, 1950), have gone to Brazil ($103.8 million), Mexico ($206.8 million), and Chile ($93.1 million), the aggregate amounts covering a number of separate loan authorizations.[34] In the case of Colombia and Ecuador, loans were made to assist these countries in recovering from sudden disasters. In making developmental loans in Latin America and elsewhere, the Export-Import Bank has encountered the same obstacles which have been cited by the International Bank: lack of local capital, skilled labor, and entrepreneurial ability; the failure to develop well-formulated projects; and general political and economic instability. There are, however, certain differences in the lending policies of the two banks which must be kept in mind in any comparison of the lending experience of the two institutions.

The Respective Roles of the Export-Import and International Banks

At the time that the International Bank was established in March, 1946, the NAC announced that the International Bank was to be the principal medium for foreign investment from public funds or funds raised under a guarantee by the United States government.[35] Nevertheless, as is shown by Table 9, the Export-Import Bank has been disbursing loan funds at a faster rate than the International Bank. Recently, the International Bank has been making loan commitments at a somewhat faster rate, and this will be reflected in larger disbursements in the fiscal year 1951. As of December 31, 1950, the International Bank had made loan commitments aggregating about a billion dollars, but actual disbursements were only $642 million.

[34] In May, 1950, the Export-Import Bank authorized a credit of $125 million to a group of Argentine banks to assist Argentina in liquidating past-due dollar obligations to United States commercial creditors. *National Advisory Council on International Monetary and Financial Problems, Semiannual Report to the President and to the Congress for the Period April 1, 1950, to September 30, 1950.*

[35] See *Report of the National Advisory Council on International Monetary and Financial Problems to March 31, 1946,* p. 17.

Table 9. Loan Disbursements by the International and Export-Import Banks

(In millions of dollars)

Loans	Fiscal 1948		Fiscal 1949		Fiscal 1950	
	Export-Import Bank	International Bank	Export-Import Bank	International Bank	Export-Import Bank	International Bank
To "developed" areas...........	$509.2	$378	$135.4	$37	$ 82.6	$18
To "undeveloped" areas.........	89.4	....	79.0	19	113.7	70
Total......................	$598.6	$378	$214.4	$56	$196.3	$88

SOURCE: *Report to the President on Foreign Economic Policies* (Gray Report), Washington, D.C., November, 1950, pp. 122–123.

Several factors must be kept in mind in any comparisons of the operations of the two institutions. First of all, the Export-Import Bank is an agency of the United States government and a direct instrument of American foreign policy. The International Bank, on the other hand, is an international institution whose operations are normally only indirectly related to American foreign policy. While in the ordinary course of its operations the Export-Import Bank seeks to apply much the same lending criteria as does the International Bank, the paramount consideration in many cases is the relation of the loan to some important foreign-policy objective of the United States. The Export-Import Bank is frequently called upon to meet certain emergency requirements for funds in situations where the bankability of the loans may be somewhat doubtful. In addition, the International Bank has a larger staff for surveying projects and supervising the use of its funds. By reason of the fact that the IBRD is an international institution, it can enquire more extensively into the operations of foreign economies and can impose more rigid conditions with respect to the use of the loans and the general economic policies of the borrowers than can an agency of the United States government.

Many of the Export-Import Bank loans have been made to countries which are not members of the IBRD such as, for example, Argentina, Israel, and Indonesia. Also the Export-Import Bank can make loans to private concerns, not guaranteed by governments, whereas the IBRD can make loans only to member governments or to private organizations where the loan is guaranteed by a member government. In addition, the Articles of Agreement of the IBRD require that loans must be for specific projects of reconstruction and development,[36] while the Export-Import Bank has frequently made general-purpose loans when they were urgently needed to implement American foreign policy.

In one important respect the lending policy of the IBRD is more liberal than that of the Export-Import Bank. The Export-Import Bank, unlike the International Bank, will not ordinarily permit its funds to be used for making purchases in third countries. Although there is nothing in the Export-Import Bank Act which specifically requires loans to be tied to the purchase of United States exports, the principle is firmly embodied in the legislative history of the Bank.

[36] As was noted above, certain of the IBRD's reconstruction loans to Western Europe in 1947 were of the general-purpose type.

CHAPTER 13

International Investment Policy: II

IN THIS chapter we shall be concerned with the President's Point Four program and the implications of present United States investment policies for the long-run foreign-investment position of the United States. We shall begin the discussion with a brief statistical analysis of the pattern of United States foreign investment since the war.

United States Government Foreign Investment, 1946 to 1950

Table 10 shows the foreign credits of United States government agencies during the period from V-J Day to the end of 1950. The vast bulk of the United States governmental capital outflow during this period represented emergency-type reconstruction and balance-of-payments loans such as the large loans to Western Europe by the Export-Import Bank, the lend-lease pipe-line credits, the $3¾ billion loan to Britain, and the loans made to European Recovery Program countries by the Economic Cooperation Administration. If, in the future, United States governmental and International Bank loans are confined to developmental-type loans, we may expect, if present policies continue, a much smaller volume of capital outflow than took place in the 1946 to 1948 period.[1] This is indicated by the experience in 1950 during which Export-Import Bank loan disbursements amounted to $200 million (offset by repayments of $160 million) and disbursements of the International Bank amounted to only $75 million. Unless there occurs a substantial increase in the volume of lending by public investment institutions, net capital outflow from the United States is likely to remain at a relatively low level in the future.

The expansion of lending by public international lending institutions will depend both on the lending policies of these institutions and on the willingness of the United States to supplement their existing resources. Assuming that the power of the International Bank to make dollar loans

[1] Table 10 does not include International Bank loans since the Bank is not an agency of the United States government. Dollar-loan disbursements by the International Bank were $299.9 million in 1947, $193.2 million in 1948, $61.8 million in 1949, and $67.4 million in 1950, making a total of $622.3 million since the Bank began lending operations. The United States government's paid-in subscription to the Bank is $635 million.

is limited by the United States subscription plus the gold subscriptions of the other members, the Bank has potentially available less than $2.5 billion for additional dollar loans. As of December 31, 1950, the Export-Import Bank had an authorized capacity for making additional loans of about $500 million.[2] In order to maintain a net outflow of capital through public lending institutions equal to the average annual net outflow of United States governmental and International Bank capital in the period from 1946 to 1948 (exclusive of the United States subscription to the Monetary Fund), the International Bank and the Export-Import Bank would have to make (net) loans at a rate of about $2.7 billion per year. This rate would exhaust the dollar lending capacity of both institutions in less than two and a half years. But, as we have seen, nothing like this rate of capital outflow is likely to take place under present lending policies.

The rapid expansion of United States government loans since the war has created a substantial debt burden on foreign countries which must be serviced in dollars. As of June 30, 1949, the outstanding foreign indebtedness to the United States government totaled $9,846 million, and there was $1,692 million in additional authorized credits which had not been utilized. (These amounts do not include dollar indebtedness to the International Monetary Fund and Bank.) Interest payments on the outstanding indebtedness (as of June 30, 1949) will amount to $4,230 billion over the next half century.[3] Aggregate principal and interest payments on the June 30, 1949, indebtedness to the United States government will reach a maximum of $518 million in 1952. Thereafter, the annual payments on this indebtedness will decline, but in 1969 the payments will be at the level of $326 million. Payments on principal alone reach a high of $329 million in 1952 and decline to $226 million by 1969. These amounts will of course be larger by reason of the additional loans made after June 30, 1949. It is evident that if there is to be no net disinvestment by the United States government in the foreign field, government lending would need to continue at a rate of better than $300 million annually. If government lending is to be equal to total service payments, the rate will need to be in excess of $500 million annually.

If public lending institutions are to play a significant role in foreign investment in the future, these considerations must be kept in mind. Just as the world's balance of payments could not adjust itself to a sudden cessation of private dollar investment in the 1930's, so also might a sharp fall in public investment in the postwar period create serious difficulties.

[2] In his budget message of January, 1951, President Truman recommended an increase of $1 billion in the lending authority of the Export-Import Bank.

[3] F. W. Ryan, "Servicing Foreign Credits of the United States Government," *Survey of Current Business*, March, 1950, p. 14.

Table 10. United States Government Foreign Grants and Credits, by Program: July 1, 1945, through Dec. 31, 1950

(In millions of dollars)

Program	Total postwar period	Before European Recovery Program period	During European Recovery Program period			
			Total	1948 April–December	1949	1950
Gross foreign aid........	$ 30,194	$ 15,495	$ 14,699	$ 4,138	$ 6,052	$ 4,509
Grants utilized........	20,802	8,061	12,740	3,320	5,360	4,060
Less: Credit-agreement offsets to grants.....	1,256	1,253	3	1	*	2
Credits utilized........	10,648	8,687	1,962	819	692	451
Less: Returns...........	$ 2,400	$ 1,022	$ 1,378	$ 420	$ 483	$ 475
Reverse grants and returns on grants......	946	499	447	51	243	153
Principal collected on credits.............	1,454	523	931	369	240	322
Equals: Net foreign aid..	$+27,793	$+14,473	$+13,321	$+3,718	$+5,569	$+4,034
Net grants...........	+18,600	+6,309	+12,290	+3,268	+5,118	+3,905
Net credits...........	+9,194	+8,163	+1,030	+450	+451	+129
Grants utilized..........	$ 20,802	$ 8,061	$ 12,740	$ 3,320	$ 5,360	$ 4,060
European recovery....	7,884	....	7,884	1,397	3,279	2,758
Civilian supplies.......	4,710	2,360	2,351	1,012	985	353
UNRRA, post-UNRRA, and interim aid.........	3,443	3,172	271	270	1	†
Philippine rehabilitation...............	619	130	488	119	203	166
Korea and Far East (general area of China) aid..........	264	....	264	96	92	75
Lend-lease............	1,968	1,968	*	*		
Mutual-defense assistance	516	....	516	....	....	516
Greek-Turkish aid.....	656	165	491	258	172	61
Chinese stabilization and military aid.....	240	120	120	72	44	5
Technical assistance and inter-American aid...............	137	66	71	14	30	27
Other...............	365	80	285	83	104	99

Program	Total postwar period	Before European Recovery Program period	During European Recovery Program period			
			Total	1948 April–December	1949	1950
Reverse grants and returns on grants......	$ 946	$ 499	$ 447	$ 51	$ 243	$ 153
Counterpart funds.....	396	....	396	22	230	144
Reverse lend-lease.....	133	133	1	1		
Return of lend-lease ships..............	297	250	48	26	13	9
War-account cash settlements	120	117	3	3		
Credits utilized..........	$ 10,648	$ 8,687	$ 1,962	$ 819	$ 692	$ 451
Special British loan....	3,750	3,750				
Export-Import Bank...	2,733	2,087	645	261	185	200
Direct loans........	2,582	1,942	640	284	163	193
Loans through agent banks...........	150	145	5	Cr. 23‡	21	7
European recovery....	1,068	....	1,068	476	428	163
Surplus property (including merchant ships)..............	1,339	1,234	106	77	28	*
Credit-agreement offsets to grants.......	1,256	1,253	3	1	*	2
Lend-lease (excluding settlement credits)...	69	63	6	1	4	1
Other...............	433	299	134	3	47	84
Principal collected on credits.............	$ 1,454	$ 523	$ 931	$ 369	$ 240	$ 322
Export-Import Bank...	720	196	523	220	144	160
Direct loans........	556	149	408	189	100	118
Loans through agent banks...........	163	48	116	31	43	41
Surplus property (including merchant ships)	144	29	115	29	44	42
Credit-agreement offsets to grants.......	25	10	15	6	2	7
Lend-lease (excluding settlement credits)...	26	9	17	5	6	6
Other...............	540	279	261	108	46	107

* Less than $500,000.

† Negative entry of less than $500,000 results from refunds of cash aid.

‡ Negative entry results from excess of Export-Import Bank repurchases from agent banks over agent bank disbursements.

SOURCE: *Survey of Current Business*, March, 1951, p. 16.

If public investment is to continue year after year to make a net contribution to the world's dollar supply, gross investment must exceed amortization and interest payments. Even then there may be no net contribution to the supply of "free" dollars unless a substantial proportion of the gross investment is in the form of untied loans. Unfortunately, most United States government lending is in the form of tied loans, although the commodities supplied by the loans may free other dollars for other purposes, including debt service.[4]

United States Private Foreign Investment

Turning to United States private foreign investment, we find that while private capital outflow was far higher than in the 1930's, net exports of private capital in the period from 1946 to 1948 were less than in the 1926 to 1928 period.[5] While during the 1920's 66 per cent of American foreign investments consisted of publicly offered dollar bonds, during the period from 1946 to 1948 there was practically no net movement in foreign dollar bonds since purchases of new issues were about equal to amortization and retirement of old issues.[6] Except for the refunding of old issues, new American purchases of foreign securities during the period were largely confined to the $250 million worth of securities issued by the International Bank and a $150 million loan to the Canadian government by American insurance companies. Although the market for foreign dollar bonds has improved considerably in 1949 and 1950, in 1948 yields were substantially higher, even for the government issues of countries such as Australia and the Netherlands whose credit standing is relatively high, than the rates charged by the International Bank for similar maturities. For example, at the end of 1948, the Australian 3⅜ per cent issue due in 1962 was quoted at 84, the Netherlands 3¾ per cent issue due in 1957 was at 95, and the Norway 4¼ per cent issue due in 1965 was at 86.5. As long as these countries can borrow from the International Bank or the Export-Import Bank at 3½ to 4½ per cent with maturities of 20 years,

[4] For a discussion of the tied-loan question, see C. P. Kindleberger, *The Dollar Shortage*, Wiley, New York, 1950, pp. 87–89.

[5] The data for the following discussion of private investments were derived from *The Balance of International Payments of the United States, 1946–1948*, Department of Commerce, 1950, and the *Survey of Current Business*, November, 1949; March, 1950; and January, 1951. During the period from 1926 to 1928, net United States private capital outflow, *i.e.*, net flow through change in United States assets abroad, amounted to $2,933 million. During the period from 1946 to 1948, net United States private capital outflow totaled $1,680 million.

[6] Net additional portfolio investments abroad including the purchase of International Bank bonds amounted to only $12 million in the period from 1946 to 1948.

they are not likely to seek loan capital in the private markets. In fact it is doubtful whether or not dollar bonds with maturities of 15 or 20 years could be successfully floated in United States markets except perhaps at interest rates higher than the borrowers would be willing to pay.

The bulk of the private capital which flowed abroad during the period from 1946 to 1949 took the form of direct investments, principally in enterprises engaged in the development of natural resources for export for dollars rather than for the establishment of plants in foreign countries which produced for local consumption. From the end of 1945 to the end of 1949, the value of United States direct investments abroad increased by $4,103 million, of which $2,362 million represented new capital outflow and the remainder reinvested earnings and revaluation of assets. Of the $2,362 million in net new capital outflow in this form, $1,762 million was invested in the petroleum industry.[7] The return on direct foreign investments to American investors was quite favorable over the 1946 to 1948 period. The ratio of earnings to equity (adjusted to eliminate investments in countries to which American investors no longer had access) was 12.2 per cent in 1946, 15.2 per cent in 1947, and 17.1 per cent in 1948. This return averaged 2 to 3 per cent higher than on comparable investments in the United States. The return on direct foreign investments, however, varied widely from industry to industry. For example, in 1948 the return on public-utility investments abroad was only 4.0 per cent; on manufacturing investment, 20.1 per cent; and on petroleum, 27.6 per cent.[8] In spite of the favorable returns on foreign investments abroad, there is considerable doubt as to whether the margin over earnings on capital invested in the United States is sufficiently wide to induce American enterprises to incur the additional risks which characterize foreign investments. For example, in 1948 the net income of the leading manufacturing corporations in the United States amounted to 18.9 per cent as compared with a ratio of earnings to equity for United States direct investments abroad of 20.1 per cent.[9] This is not to suggest that American firms should be permitted to make higher profits on investments abroad. Unless the bulk of American earnings are reinvested abroad, the drain on foreign countries' exchange resources for making transfers of earnings may be so great that they could not afford to have the investment made. This situation presents a serious barrier to the flow of American capital

[7] See "Private United States Direct Investments Abroad," *Survey of Current Business,* January, 1951, p. 22.

[8] *The Balance of International Payments of the United States, 1946–1948,* pp. 92–93.

[9] *Monthly Letter on Economic Conditions,* National City Bank of New York, April, 1949, p. 40.

abroad and must be given careful consideration in any discussion of the future of American direct foreign investment.

Closely related to the problem of earnings on direct foreign investments is the question of the relationship of direct-investment dollars to the world's supply of dollars. The substantial flow of American direct investment abroad since the war has made only a small initial contribution to the world's supply of free dollars available to foreign countries.[10] In the first place, nearly all the equipment and technical and managerial services relating to the new investments have come from the United States. As materials and equipment from sources outside the United States become more plentiful, it is hoped that larger expenditures will be made abroad. Even so, American engineers are more familiar with American products, and their construction plans usually call for types and specifications of equipment supplied by American firms. Expenses for local labor and materials, rents and royalties paid in dollars improve the dollar position of the country in which the investment is made. The effects on the dollar position of the country in which the investment is made depend a great deal on whether the investment is made for the production of something which is to be exported for dollars, or whether the product is sold locally. If the product is exported for dollars, the country gets back a part of the dollars in the form of local payments, but the effect upon the world's supply of dollars depends upon where the commodity is sold. If as in the case of banana growing in Costa Rica or the production of paper and pulp in Canada the product goes to the United States, the world's supply of free dollars is increased. On the other hand, in the case of Middle East petroleum, the product of the American firms goes largely to Europe and payment is made in dollars. If the Middle East petroleum sales by American companies merely replace exports which would otherwise have come from the United States, the world's supply of dollars is increased by the amount of the dollar expenditures of the companies in the Middle East. But if such sales should displace petroleum which would otherwise be sold by British companies, the world's supply of dollars may actually be reduced by the American investment. With the development of a world surplus of petroleum in 1949, this became a real problem both for the American producers and for their foreign competitors. The answer to this problem, both for petroleum as well as for other American foreign enterprises competing in the world markets for dollars, would seem to lie in inducing American firms to acquire as much of their equipment, materials, and services as possible outside the United States. As was pointed out in Chap. 11, the United States government has

[10] *The Balance of International Payments of the United States, 1946–1948,* p. 140.

officially recognized this principle as a means of dealing with the problem of the marketing of foreign-produced petroleum by American firms in nondollar areas.

If the American direct investments are made for the purpose of producing goods for consumption in the country in which the investment is made, the effect on the dollar position of that country will depend upon the proportion of the initial investment expenditures made in that country, the extent to which the products take the place of those which would otherwise be imported from dollar sources by that country, and the amounts of earnings and other payments transferred to the United States. An American investment in a night club or a Coca-Cola factory might well result in a net dollar drain on the country, while an investment in a steel mill might improve its dollar position. These are factors which must be taken account of in evaluating the contribution of American direct investments to the world's dollar problem.

The President's Point Four Program [11]

Fourth, we must embark on a bold new program for making the benefits of our scientific advances and industrial progress available for the improvement and growth of underdeveloped areas. . . . We should make available to peace-loving peoples the benefits of our store of technical knowledge in order to help them realize their aspirations for a better life. And, in cooperation with other nations, we should foster capital investment in areas needing development. Our aim should be to help the free peoples of the world, through their own efforts, to produce more food, more clothing, more materials for housing, and more mechanical power to lighten their burdens.

The Point Four program was America's response to the aspirations of the nations embodying two-thirds of the world's population for economic development as a means of achieving a better life. It was boldly conceived, but it has not as yet been boldly planned. A beginning has been made, however, and the ultimate dimensions of the program cannot as yet be foreseen. Someone recently said that the term "economic development" has become the shibboleth of our time. It has become since the war the byword of the peoples of the underdeveloped areas of Latin America, Africa, and the Middle and Far East. It is closely associated with nationalism and the desire for independence on the part of colonial areas or countries whose internal economic affairs have been largely dominated by foreign economic interests. It is associated with the growing unrest on the part of hundreds of millions of people who after countless generations

[11] President Truman's Inaugural Address, Jan. 20, 1949, *Department of State Bulletin,* Jan. 30, 1949, p. 125.

of unquestioning acceptance of their traditional manner of living have suddenly yearned for and demanded a social and economic revolution. This new social ferment was in part the product of the political and economic upheavals of the war, and in part the consequence of the contacts of many millions of people with representatives of the industrial nations of the world. The sight of a jeep or an army truck passing long lines of Chinese coolies climbing hills with sacks on their backs, the American bulldozers doing the work of hundreds of natives working with crude picks, the luxuries available to the lowest ranking American soldiers at the PX made a lasting impression on millions of Chinese, Indians, and Egyptians.

The awakening aspirations of the peoples of the underdeveloped areas have been echoed by their leaders at home and abroad and have been frequently used as an argument for greater economic and political independence on the grounds that foreign domination is a barrier to the realization of economic development. These aspirations have been repeated time and again in councils of the United Nations and other international bodies. There are frequent references to economic development in the charters of our international institutions such as the Food and Agricultural Organization, the International Bank, the proposed International Trade Organization, and other organizations. The Communists have been quick to capitalize upon this desire of the underprivileged masses for a better life. They have declared—and with considerable justification—that the pashas, the rajas, the foreign companies, and the reactionary politicians are barriers to a more abundant life for the masses and that the way to begin is to destroy the existing social and political fabric. The Communists have pointed to the success of Russia's 5-year plans in industrializing the Soviet Union without the help of Western capital. They have had an alarming degree of success among people who have had nothing to lose but their chains, even though it meant simply exchanging old chains for new ones.

The Point Four program represents an effort to meet the aspirations of the underdevelopment peoples and at the same time an effort to meet the challenge of the Communists. In a recent address, Secretary of State Acheson said:

> The Communists talk of organizing great masses of people in five-year plans to carry out elaborate economic programs. They say this is the way for people to get more of the necessities of life. They promise hungry, distressed people food and material comforts if only they will accept slavery to the state in return. And to people who have always been miserable, who have never known the protection of a Bill of Rights, these spurious promises sound real.

The alternative that is offered these people through the President's idea is a way to improve their material welfare and at the same time live as free men, retain their personal dignity and independence, and develop to the full extent of their individual capacities. They are offered a way of life that leads not only to freedom from want but also the most priceless freedom—the right to be let alone.

We shall not attempt to present more than a broad outline of the Point Four program as it has been developed to the time of writing.[12] The basic elements of the program are as follows:

1. An expanded program of technical assistance to be conducted by the State Department and other existing agencies of the United States government in cooperation with intergovernmental and private organizations.

2. The promotion of private foreign investments by means of a program of guaranteeing private investments against certain risks peculiar to foreign investment, e.g., inability to transfer earnings and expropriation.

3. The negotiation of treaties with foreign countries which would improve the climate for foreign investment.

4. Loans for economic development in underdeveloped areas by the Export-Import Bank and the International Bank.

In the development of this program, primary emphasis has been given thus far to technical assistance to foreign countries. It is believed that a great deal of progress can be made toward higher productivity and better living conditions at a relatively small cost. The fields that are covered by such technical assistance include agriculture and forestry, reclamation, hydroelectric power and flood control, mineral resources, industry, transportation, labor, health, education, social services, statistics, public administration and finance, housing and communications.[13] The program inaugurated by the Economic and Social Council and by the United States government is being administered in large part by existing United Nations organizations, including the Food and Agricultural Organization (FAO), the World Health Organization (WHO), the United Nations Educational Scientific and Cultural Organization (UNESCO), and the International Labor Organization. In addition, certain programs are being administered by agencies of the United States government such as the Institute of Inter-American Affairs and the Departments of Interior, Commerce, and Agriculture, under the direction of the Technical Cooperation Administration in the State Department. The cost of the program, originally

---

[12] See *Point Four*, Department of State, January, 1950, for a comprehensive description of the program.

[13] These fields are among those covered in the proposed $85.6 million program for the first year technical cooperation program which was adopted by the Economic and Social Council in the summer of 1949. *Point Four*, Department of State, 1950, p. 81.

estimated at $85.6 million, is borne in part by the recipient countries, in part from the budgets of the international agencies and other members of the United Nations, and the remainder by the United States.

The President in his message of June 24, 1949, asked Congress for $45 million for the first year of the technical-assistance program, including $10 million already in the Federal budget for the Institute of Inter-American Affairs and for other programs already in operation. The Foreign Economic Assistance Act of 1950 authorized $35 million for technical assistance, but Public Law 759 (approved September 6, 1950) appropriated only $26.9 billion for the new program, of which about $12 million has been allocated for the use of the UN agencies. A much larger amount of funds is being spent upon technical assistance under other appropriations for foreign aid, however. For example, a considerable portion of the funds appropriated for the use of the ECA in the Far East are devoted to various types of technical assistance. Altogether it is estimated that about $150 million in United States funds has been made available for technical assistance during the fiscal year 1951.[14]

Although a great deal of good can undoubtedly be accomplished through even a modest amount of technical assistance, substantial progress in increasing productivity and living standards must be accompanied by an increase in real capital in the underdeveloped countries. The President has said that we should make available the benefits of our store of technical knowledge to all peace-loving peoples. But this store of technical knowledge which the United States and other industrial countries possess cannot be dissociated from the capital which is embodied in the industrial facilities, agricultural equipment, and economic organizations of these countries. Moreover, even where technical knowledge and a small amount of capital would substantially increase the productivity of existing resources in the underdeveloped countries, the limiting factor is frequently not a lack of such technical knowledge on the part of local governmental officials. Rather the problem may lie in the existing economic and social organizations and in the absence of an adequate governmental machinery, including large numbers of trained personnel for disseminating such knowledge. For example, there are in India perhaps several hundred graduates of first-class agricultural schools with adequate knowledge of what is needed to reform Indian agricultural methods. What is required, however, is perhaps 10,000 or more trained workers who would be willing to work directly with the many millions of peasants in the country. This is essentially a local governmental problem which cannot be solved simply by sending a few dozen more agricultural experts to India. The same is

[14] *Report to the President on Foreign Economic Policies* (Gray Report), Washington, D.C., November, 1950, p. 69.

true regarding health and sanitation services. Most countries have doctors and sanitation experts who know what ought to be done, perhaps even better than any foreign experts who might be sent in to advise them. But to do the job for the country as a whole might mean a vast undertaking involving substantial governmental outlays for equipment and supplies and large numbers of trained medical personnel which the country does not now possess.

The purpose of these remarks is to show the limitations of a technical-assistance program based on the idea of spending a few million dollars for acquainting the rest of the world with America's vast store of technical knowledge. A really effective program may need to include financial aid to local governments, as well as substantial numbers of trained personnel, to help them create the large organizations needed to educate the masses in new techniques, supply them with simple tools where needed to carry out the recommendations and to bring about the changes in economic organization, *e.g.,* land reform, necessary for the adoption of the more productive methods. In addition, technical assistance in the industrial and communications fields and in the field of reclamation, hydroelectric power, and flood control can be of little value without capital in the form of local funds and foreign exchange. Whether capital funds for these purposes should be provided on a loan or a grant basis will depend upon the financial ability of the underdeveloped country to service foreign loans.

Capital for Development

The problem of capital funds for developmental purposes may be divided into two parts: domestic capital and foreign capital. In most underdeveloped countries, only a small amount of savings is available for domestic investment.[15] Such saving as there is frequently finds its way into sterile hoards of precious metals or is invested abroad. Government saving for capital projects is rendered difficult because of the absence of efficient tax-administration systems so that frequently the only way government-sponsored development can be financed with local funds is through an expansion of the money supply. In the short run at least, this expansion will be inflationary even though there is in most underdeveloped countries a large amount of disguised unemployment, *e.g.,* too many family workers on small plots of land. Even though the employment of the additional workers has not caused a reduction in the current output of consumers' goods, effective demand for both domestic and imported commodities may expand rapidly and prices will inevitably rise.

15 See *Methods of Financing Economic Development in Under Developed Countries,* United Nations, Lake Success, N.Y., 1949, for a discussion of this problem.

It may be impossible to have development programs in some countries without inflation and without restrictions on imports to prevent balance-of-payments deficits. The shift of a considerable portion of the labor supply from overpopulated agricultural areas to the status of wage earners will inevitably be accompanied by an increase in the general level of money incomes, long before there is a corresponding increase in physical product. Many underdeveloped countries lack the monetary and fiscal machinery to avoid inflation while carrying on extensive investment programs. If this conclusion is correct—and it has been generally true in the past—we have to accept a certain amount of inflation as an inevitable cost of economic development. To a degree at least, it would be desirable to minimize this inflationary impact by providing a certain amount of free foreign exchange in connection with developmental loans. This is, as we have seen, specifically provided for in the case of International Bank loans, and should also be considered in developmental loans by the Export-Import Bank. It is unlikely, however, that the amount of free foreign exchange which these institutions would be willing to advance would be sufficient to enable countries undergoing rapid economic development to dispense with some form of import restrictions.

Turning to the question of foreign capital funds for developmental purposes, we find that the administration has placed major emphases on increasing the flow of private foreign investment in connection with the Point Four program.[16] Without questioning the desirability of encouraging a large participation of private capital in the Point Four program, it should be pointed out that there are very large areas of investment which are either not suitable to foreign private enterprise or not likely to be attractive to American private enterprise. Considering the low return on invested capital and the extent of governmental control, American private enterprise is not likely to be interested in investments in public utilities, transportation, and communications. Nor are the fields of agriculture, irrigation, reclamation, and housing generally suitable for private foreign investment. Except for the field of merchandising (which does not ordinarily make a significant contribution to development) this leaves only the fields of industry and the exploitation of natural resources available for private foreign investment. Of these two fields the latter has accounted for the bulk of the American private foreign investment since the war, and such investment has been concentrated in fields such as petroleum where the product is exported on the world markets rather than used locally. Many underdeveloped countries are not blessed with abundant

[16] See, for example, the testimony of Under Secretary of State Webb before the House Committee on Foreign Affairs, *Department of State Bulletin,* Oct. 10, 1949, p. 551.

mineral resources of this type. While there are undoubtedly abundant opportunities for private foreign investment in the field of manufacturing, we must keep in mind that the industrialization of underdeveloped areas must be accompanied by large expenditures in other fields which are generally not suitable for or attractive to foreign private enterprise. Moreover, in many underdeveloped countries industrial development should be, for the time being at least, secondary to the development of agriculture, transportation, and general social services. It may be desirable in many cases to confine industrialization for a time to small industry serving local markets and employing local materials with relatively simple capital instruments—a type of industry which is not likely to be appropriate for foreign investment.

The purpose of the foregoing remarks is to indicate why we believe that the bulk of the foreign capital for the development of backward areas must come from public institutions such as the International Bank and the Export-Import Bank. Therefore, to carry out this vital part of the Point Four program these institutions must have both the lending capacity and the lending policies appropriate for the job. The President in his Economic Report to Congress in January, 1950, stated, "It is unlikely that private funds, including those invested through the International Bank, and the present resources of the Export-Import Bank will be sufficient to meet the need for investment abroad. It will probably become necessary at a later time to increase the lending authority of the Export-Import Bank."

It is in the field of lending policies and operations that the technical-assistance program can make one of its most important, if not the most important, contributions. Much can be done through technical missions operating in underdeveloped areas in overcoming the obstacles to loans by the two public lending institutions and in assisting foreign governments in preparing the kind of projects which are suitable for international financing. In addition, the International Bank and the Export-Import Bank ought to give consideration to loans which would cover a number of well-integrated projects plus a certain amount of foreign exchange which would cover the indirect needs for foreign goods and services arising out of the developmental program. Countries could be assisted in the formulation of developmental programs which would require, say, as long as 15 or 20 years to complete. If countries could look forward to a steady inflow of capital over the next generation or so, the question of capacity to service loans could be viewed in a much broader perspective. Thus a country might be able to count on future capital inflows to help meet the service charges on past indebtedness, until such time as its total production and export capacity were developed to a point where it could maintain without difficulty an export surplus for financing its international obligations. Such a program would of course require that at least a portion of the loans be made in free foreign exchange and not tied to specific projects.

Thus far, we have confined our discussion of capital for economic development to foreign loans and direct investments. The ability of a country to absorb such funds is limited to its capacity to finance external indebtedness. In special circumstances, the foreign-policy interests of the United States may require a faster rate of development made possible through the provision of grants for working capital and even for longer term projects such as dams and irrigation systems. Even in the case of grants, however, there is a limit to the amount of productive capital that a country can absorb over a given period of time.[17] It is worth noting that the Gray Report on Foreign Economic Policies has suggested a grant program, including both technical assistance and capital, of up to $500 million per year for the underdeveloped areas.[18]

The Climate for Private Foreign Investment

Since the United States government has placed major emphasis on private investment as the principal source of capital for financing economic development abroad, measures for encouraging such investment naturally form an important part of the Point Four program. Inasmuch as the International Bank represents the principal medium for the encouragement of private loan capital—and it is generally believed that little private loan capital outflow will take place (except to Canada) other than through the International Bank—the proposed measures are concerned with the encouragement of direct investments abroad by American enterprise.[19] Although American direct investments since the war have been high when compared with the experience of the 1930's, they

[17] The lack of skilled labor and management, the absence of complementary industries and public-service facilities, and the time required to develop an effective economic organization set limits to the rate at which capital can be productively employed in the sense that it will result in an addition to the annual *net* product of the country (as contrasted with a subsidy to consumption).

[18] *Report to the President on Foreign Economic Policies* (Gray Report), November, 1950, p. 69.

[19] The ECA Act of 1948 provided for currency-transfer guarantees to American firms investing in the ERP countries, but the guarantee provisions of the Act have not proved to be attractive to American industry. As of June 30, 1950, the outstanding face value of the transfer guarantees issued by the Export-Import Bank (which is the administering agency for the guarantees, under the direction of the ECA) amounted to $22.3 million. *Ninth Report to Congress of the Economic Cooperation Administration*, November, 1950, p. 68.

have represented a relatively low percentage of private domestic investment in comparison with that of the late 1920's. In 1928 and 1929, net
additions to American direct investments abroad have been estimated at
$558 million and $602 million, respectively,[20] whereas during the period
from 1946 to 1949 such investments averaged $1,023 million.[21] Thus while
in the period from 1928 to 1929 net direct investments abroad amounted
to nearly 4 per cent of gross private domestic investment, the corresponding percentage for the period from 1946 to 1949 was less than three.

The problem of encouraging private foreign investment concerns not
only the special risks and obstacles to such investment, but also the attractiveness of foreign investment to American firms even in the absence
of these special risks. Although the expectation of a higher net return on
capital invested abroad is a primary factor in foreign investment, it is by
no means the only consideration. The fact that the average net return
on foreign direct investments abroad is little higher than for comparable
investments in the United States is by no means a complete deterrent to
foreign investment for several reasons. For example, many firms may prefer to expand production abroad rather than in this country because
additional domestic sales could be realized only at lower prices. This
assumes of course that it is either cheaper to produce the product abroad
for sale outside the country, or that exports of American products are
limited by foreign import controls. The desire for adequate supplies or
reserves of raw materials may also induce American companies to invest
abroad for the purpose of developing foreign natural resources. Such investments may take place without a strict comparison of present relative
returns on domestic and foreign investment.

It it difficult to say whether or not the general attractiveness of foreign
investment, apart from the existence of specific risks and obstacles, is relatively greater or less than in the 1920's or what it will be in the future,
given a favorable climate for such investment.[22] There are certain favorable factors to be considered, however. (1) There is the rapid exhaustion
of a number of minerals (or a growth of demand outrunning domestic
supplies) in the United States, e.g., petroleum, iron ore, and copper. This
condition is already expanding American foreign investments in the ex-
tractive industries. (2) Competition in the markets for certain commodi-

[20] The United States in the World Economy, Department of Commerce, 1943, p. 103.
[21] Survey of Current Business, January, 1951, p. 22. Both figures include reinvested
earnings.
[22] The National Association of Manufacturers in a report entitled Capital Export
Potentialities after 1952, March, 1949, has concluded that, under optimistic assumptions
as to the economic climate at home and abroad, private foreign investment will amount
to about $2 billion annually after 1952.

ties may force American producers to establish branch plants abroad as a means of holding markets.

Offsetting these possible favorable developments for private foreign investment are the obstacles to such investment, concerning which a good deal has been written.[23] Certain of these obstacles stem from the social and economic policies of the foreign countries, policies which are not likely to be altered in the near future. For example, there is the growing trend toward government ownership of industry and the increasing degree of governmental control over industry in general. Nationalization and comprehensive governmental controls over private industry tend to limit the area of foreign private investment. Frequently, special restrictions and controls are placed on foreign enterprise such as, for example, the requirement that foreign participation in the control of enterprises must be limited to 49 per cent of the shares of the enterprise. Public opinion in underdeveloped countries often urges the imposition of conditions on the entry of foreign enterprise such as limitations on management and control, the imposition of an obligation to reinvest within the country a certain percentage of the earnings, and limitations upon the number of foreign employees or the percentage of the total payroll which may be paid to foreign employees.[24]

Freedom of entry for foreign enterprise is also frequently limited on balance-of-payments grounds, since certain types of investments may result in a net drain on the foreign-exchange reserves of the country. To take an extreme case, an investment in a Coca-Cola plant or a night club by an American firm may not increase the foreign-exchange earnings or provide offsetting foreign-exchange savings sufficient to compensate for the transfer of earnings to the foreign owners. It would appear to be necessary for countries to reserve the right to screen foreign investments on balance-of-payments grounds, although admittedly this type of discrimination may be used to further nationalistic ends.

The obstacles mentioned above together with such factors as general monetary and fiscal instability, a high level of taxation on enterprise generally, and various factors making for economic and political instability in foreign countries are to a considerable degree incapable of being dealt with by specific measures such as investment guarantees or

[23] A good discussion of this problem may be found in *Survey of Policies Affecting Private Foreign Investment* (mimeographed), prepared by the United Nations Secretariat, Lake Success, N.Y., Feb. 15, 1950. See also *Foreign Investment Guarantees*, Hearings before the Senate Committee on Banking and Currency on S. 2197, Aug. 9 and 10, 1949; and *Export-Import Bank Loan Authority*, Hearings before the House Committee on Banking and Currency on H.R. 5594, Aug. 17 to 24, 1949; see also, *Methods of Financing Economic Development in Under Developed Countries*, Chap. 2.

[24] *Survey of Policies Affecting Private Foreign Investment*, p. 25.

special investment treaties. They are a part of the general climate for foreign investment which is deeply rooted in the social fabric of the foreign countries themselves. Within a given framework of national policies, however, it is possible to secure a more favorable climate for investment by investment treaties with foreign countries which define the conditions of treatment of foreign enterprise and by a program of investment guarantees which deals with some of the special risks attending foreign investment. The Point Four program encourages action along both of these lines.

Investment Treaties

In the negotiation of its Treaties of Friendship, Commerce, and Navigation (FCN), the United States government has for many years sought to protect the interests of its nationals doing business abroad. For the most part, however, the existing treaties, some of which date from the early part of the nineteenth century, are out of date or are otherwise inadequate for providing significant protection and encouragement to American private investments abroad. In the past two years both multilateral and bilateral treaties have been negotiated. Investment provisions were contained in both the Havana Charter for an International Trade Organization of April, 1948, and the Economic Agreement of Bogota at the Ninth International Conference of American States in May, 1948.[25] The United States has recently signed FCN treaties with Uruguay, Italy, Colombia, Ethiopia, Greece, Israel, and Ireland, all of which include provisions for the treatment of foreign investments, and is in the process of negotiating a number of other similar treaties. While a comprehensive analysis of the investment provisions of the recent FCN treaties is beyond the scope of this book, a few salient features of the November, 1949, treaty with Uruguay are worth noting.[26]

(1) U.S. nationals and companies are granted "national" treatment in Uruguay with respect to engaging in commercial, manufacturing, processing, financial, construction, publishing, educational, religious, philosophic and professional activities.

(2) Most favored-nation treatment is accorded to American nationals in certain other fields such as the exploitation of mineral products.

(3) Any expropriation of American property will be subject to procedures

[25] For an analysis of the Bogota Agreement, see Henry Chalmers, "The Economic Agreement of Bogota: An Inter-American Milestone," *Foreign Commerce Weekly,* June 12, 1948.

[26] Treaty of Friendship, Commerce and Economic Development with the Oriental Republic of Uruguay, 81st Congress, 2d Session, United States Senate, Jan. 13, 1950.

and conditions no less favorable than in the case of taking property of nationals. In case of expropriation Americans are assured of "just compensation in a prompt, adequate and effective manner."

(4) National treatment is accorded with respect to the acquisition of property for carrying on business enterprises, taxation, access to the courts, and a number of other matters.

(5) American nationals may freely obtain dollars for withdrawing capital funds and earnings and for transfers of compensation for property subject to expropriation. If more than one exchange rate is in force, the effective rate for such transfers shall be one which is "just and reasonable." Either party, however, "shall retain the right in periods of exchange stringency to apply exchange restrictions to assure the availability of foreign exchange for payments for goods and services essential to the health and welfare of its people. In the event that either Party applies such restrictions it shall within a period of three months make reasonable and specific provision for the withdrawals referred to, giving consideration to special needs for other transactions, and shall afford the other Party adequate opportunity for consultation at any time regarding such provisions and other matters affecting withdrawals. Such provisions shall be reviewed in consultation with the other Party at intervals of not more than twelve months."

Although the above provisions do not eliminate all the risks and obstacles to foreign investment, such treaties will go a long way toward creating a favorable climate for American investment, particularly if the transfer risk is dealt with by means of a program of investment guarantees. Not all investment treaties are likely to be as favorable to foreign investors as the one with Uruguay. For example, many countries are insisting on the right to screen foreign investments of all kinds.[27]

Investment Guarantees

In August, 1949, hearings were conducted by the Banking and Currency Committees of both houses of Congress on legislation authorizing the Export-Import Bank to guarantee United States private capital invested abroad in productive enterprises against the risks of inconvertibility and expropriation.[28] The exact nature of the program has not at this writing

[27] For example, the FCN Treaty between the United States and Ireland, signed in January, 1950, contains a reservation for regulating the establishment of manufacturing, processing, and insurance enterprises by Americans in Ireland. "If after the expiration of four years from the date the present Treaty enters into force the United States of America considers that the application of such measures departs in an unjustifiable manner from the treatment presented in such paragraphs, the Parties shall consult with a view to seeking an adjustment." (Article VI, Sec. 4.)

[28] See Hearings before the House Committee on Banking and Currency on H.R. 5594, 81st Congress, 1st Session, Aug. 17 to 24, 1929; see also Hearings before the Senate

been revealed by the Export-Import Bank.[29] The Bank would not guarantee ordinary business risks or even all the risks peculiar to foreign investment. Moreover, it is clear that the Bank need not extend guarantees to all foreign investments on application of the investors. The bill "would merely authorize the Bank to guarantee in appropriate instances that United States investors in foreign countries would, if they earned profits, be able within reasonable limits to convert those profits into dollars, and would, if their investments were expropriated, receive fair payment in dollars." [30] It may be noted that the guarantee provisions do not include the repatriation of invested capital, although profits might be defined to include an element of depreciation. It is expected that the investors would pay premiums for such guarantees, but there could be little actuarial basis for such guarantees.

It is expected that investment guarantees will be largely concerned with the problem of transferring earnings into dollars since most nations will probably agree to a reasonable compensation for expropriated property and, in accordance with the terms of our FCN treaties, make payment in a "prompt, adequate and effective manner." This is not to say that there will not be occasional transfer problems in connection with compensation for expropriation, but the problem of transferring earnings is likely to be a more general and continuing one. The risk of inability to transfer earnings from foreign investment is not simply the risk that the country in which the investment is made may find it necessary to impose exchange controls; nearly all countries already have exchange controls today. A number of countries that maintain exchange controls permit

---

Committee on Banking and Currency on S. 2197, Aug. 9 and 10, 1949. The two bills were virtually identical. As of the time of writing, this legislation had not yet been passed by Congress.

29 *Ninth Semiannual Report to Congress for the Period July–December, 1949*, Export-Import Bank of Washington.

30 *Ibid.* The text of the House and Senate bills (H.R. 5594 and S. 2197) is as follows: "Be it enacted by the Senate and House of Representatives of the United States of America in Congress assembled, That it is the policy of the United States, in the interest of its people as well as that of other peoples, to promote the development of economically underdeveloped areas of the world. It is the objective of this Act to further this policy by encouraging productive investment in such areas. To this end section 2 (a) of the Export-Import Bank Act of 1945, as amended (59 Stat. 526, 666; 61 Stat. 130), is hereby amended by inserting after the words 'to borrow and to lend money'; the words 'to guarantee United States private capital invested in productive enterprises abroad which contribute to economic development in foreign countries by assuring either or both (i) the conversion into United States dollars of foreign currency derived from an investment and (ii) compensation in United States dollars for loss resulting from expropriation, confiscation or seizure (by action of public authority).' " (House bill only.)

transfers of earnings by foreigners on invested capital without delay or burdensome red tape, although there is frequently a limit on the earnings as a percentage of capital invested that can be transferred in any one year.[31] In the case of a number of other countries, such as Argentina, Brazil, and Egypt, the transfer of earnings has been subject to restrictions and unreasonable delays.[32]

In some Latin-American countries, dollars are available for the transfer of earnings in legal free-exchange markets, but frequently the exchange rates prevailing in such markets are quite unfavorable as compared with the rates for other types of transactions. For example, in some countries the remittance rate is more than twice the basic selling rate for foreign exchange.[33] This fact poses a serious problem for the Export-Import Bank in the administration of a transfer guarantee program. Although an investor may be able to transfer his earnings, the rate at which such transfers are permitted may be an extremely unfavorable one. In no case is it expected that the Bank will guarantee an investor against exchange depreciation, but it may be desirable to provide guarantees against the imposition of a remittance rate which is so unfavorable as to be confiscatory.

We can only touch on a few of the problems involved in transfer guarantees.[34] A major problem in this field has to do with the treatment of investments subject to United States government transfer guarantees by the exchange-control authorities of the country in which the investment is made. Should such investments be treated differently from other investments which do not profit by the guarantees? It would appear to be unfair to the nonguaranteed investors to discriminate against them and unfair to the guaranteeing government to discriminate against the guaranteed investments. After investors have had to turn to the Export-Import Bank for compensation, the failure to provide facilities for transfers into dollars becomes a matter for negotiation between the two governments. This will immediately present a number of difficult diplomatic problems such as the criteria for judging the necessity of the restrictions on transfer pay-

---

[31] Profits on American-owned enterprises are freely transferable into dollars in Canada, the United Kingdom and most of the other sterling-area countries, and in many of the countries of Western Europe.

[32] See Laws, Regulations and Policies in Selected Less Developed Countries, in *Survey of Policies Affecting Private Foreign Investment*, Part II.

[33] See *International Financial Statistics* (published monthly by the International Monetary Fund) for current multiple-exchange rates.

[34] For an excellent discussion of the problem, see Yuan-li Wu, "Government Guarantees and Private Foreign Investment," *American Economic Review*, March, 1950, pp. 61–73; see also, *Survey of United States International Finance, 1949*, International Finance Section, Princeton University, Princeton, N.J., 1950, pp. 200–203.

ments, the terms and conditions for liquidation of the blocked balances to be asked for, and possible measures of retaliation. These are serious problems to which no general answer can be given, since they involve political as well as economic questions. The negotiation of investment treaties with countries in which guaranteed investments are made is certainly desirable, but their terms generally do not provide definite criteria for dealing with these problems. The interjection of the United States government into the foreign-exchange policies of other governments may possibly lead to considerable resentment in other countries. On the other hand, the existence of the government guarantees may lead to the adoption of a more satisfactory code of fair treatment for private investments generally.

In conclusion, it may be said that, while investment treaties and government-transfer guarantees will undoubtedly help to establish a code of fair treatment for foreign investments, there will remain many risks and barriers which cannot be covered. To a very large degree, the development of a favorable climate for foreign investment must depend upon a willingness on the part of foreign governments to adopt policies which will encourage such investment. This may be difficult in the face of popular prejudice against foreign enterprise. It may also be difficult or impossible if the foreign country has embarked upon a program of socialization or thoroughgoing economic controls.

How Much United States Foreign Investment?

We have seen that the contribution of the Point Four program to economic development of the underdeveloped areas will be quite limited unless there is a substantial flow of American foreign investment. We have also seen that private foreign investment is likely to be limited, both because much of the capital expenditure required in underdeveloped areas is not suitable for private enterprise, and because of the special risks and obstacles to such investment, which can be only partially removed through investment treaties and guarantees. We have concluded, therefore, that public investment must play a major role in the Point Four program. Several criteria have been suggested for the determination of foreign-investment targets,[35] only three of which will be presented here. One approach is to estimate the foreign capital required to finance the existing national developmental plans over the next few years. An FAO Re-

[35] See Seymour E. Harris, *Foreign Aid and Our Economy*, Public Affairs Institute, Washington, D.C., 1950, Part VI. This subject has also been dealt with by H. S. Pernburg in an unpublished manuscript entitled, "Limitations to Future Long-term Investment under the Point Four Program," and by Kindleberger, *op. cit.*

port of June, 1949,[36] estimates that about $8.5 billion of international financing per year over the next four years will be needed to finance economic development for both developed and underdeveloped countries outside the United States and Canada. On the basis of the FAO estimates based on existing developmental plans, Dr. Horst Mendershausen has suggested that the share of the United States and Canada should not be less than $6 billion per annum, with the remainder to be supplied by other countries.[37] This target of $6 billion per annum (90 per cent of which would have to be met by the United States) may be compared with an average net foreign financing by the United States of $8,455 million in the period from 1946 to 1948.

Another general line of approach is to determine the proper level of foreign investment as that level of capital exports which would be most desirable from the standpoint of the American economy. Thus the proper level of foreign investment might be regarded as one which is equal to the difference between the total investment needed to maintain full employment without inflation and the level of domestic investment which would take place under full-employment conditions.[38] Hence, if one is optimistic regarding the level of private domestic investment, the desired level of foreign investment would be smaller than if it is believed that there would exist a substantial shortfall in the volume of private domestic investment needed for full employment. If we took a depression period such as the period from 1931 to 1939 and calculated the shortfall of private domestic investment from that necessary for achieving full employment, we should of course arrive at a quite high target for foreign investment. Thus if our foreign investments were planned as a contracyclical device, they would be subject to rather wide fluctuations. Such a target would tend to stabilize the world's supply of dollars since foreign investment would rise as United States imports fell off.

Still another approach is to determine a target on the basis of the excess of United States exports over imports of goods and services (excluding interest and dividends) over some past period. This will give us a higher figure than net foreign investment, since the net financing of our export surplus will allow for gold imports, grants, interest, and dividends paid by foreigners, etc. For the period from 1914 to 1949 the net con-

---

[36] *Report on International Investment and Financing Facilities,* Food and Agriculture Organization of the United Nations, Paris, 1949 (mimeographed).

[37] Horst Mendershausen, "Future Foreign Financing," *Review of Economics and Statistics,* November, 1949, pp. 271–272.

[38] The level of domestic investment is likely to be higher, the higher the level of foreign investment.

tribution of the United States toward financing exports averaged $2½ billion annually. On the basis of our 1949 national income, Prof. Seymour Harris estimates that we would need to have net capital exports of $7 billion annually in order to finance an equivalent export surplus.[39] In other words, our foreign investment should be about 3 per cent of our national income, which was roughly the percentage of United States national income represented by net foreign financing during the period from 1914 to 1949.

An important problem which is closely related to the determination of the proper level of foreign lending has to do with the matter of repayments. In order to maintain a given export surplus through foreign investment, gross investment would have to increase every year in order to offset interest, dividend, and amortization payments. Thus it has been shown that in order to maintain an export surplus of $1 billion by means of 20-year loans at 4 per cent interest, gross lending at the end of 25 years would need to be at a level of nearly $6 billion annually.[40] Since such a rapid expansion of foreign lending is viewed as unlikely, it has been concluded that any export surplus achieved by foreign lending would soon turn into an import surplus, with consequent unfavorable repercussions on domestic income and employment.

This problem, however, is not so serious as it is frequently made out to be. By assuming no change in the general climate of foreign investment, there is little basis for the view that foreign lenders will not as a group reinvest their amortization payments and continue to make net foreign investments at least at the same level year after year. Foreign investment should present no greater problem in this regard than does domestic investment. But what about interest and dividend payments? Dr. Evsey Domar has shown that, if the gross outflow of capital increases at a percentage equal to the average interest and dividend rate, net foreign financing through investments will tend to remain constant.[41] Walter Salant has suggested that if net foreign investment increases at the same rate as the growth in our national product, let us say around 4 per cent per year, we could maintain an export surplus generated from

[39] Dr. Harris assumes that gold imports will be roughly equivalent to interest and dividend payments to this country. See Harris, *op. cit.,* pp. 38–39; see also Mendershausen, *op. cit.,* pp. 272–274.

[40] See Randall Hinshaw, "Foreign Investment and American Employment," *American Economic Review Supplement,* May, 1944, p. 667; see also discussion of Dr. Hinshaw's paper, by Raymond F. Mikesell, *American Economic Review Supplement,* May, 1944, pp. 710–713. See also, Kindleberger, *op. cit.,* pp. 73–76.

[41] E. D. Domar, "The Effect of Foreign Investment on the Balance of Payments," *American Economic Review,* December, 1950, pp. 805–820.

an initial expansion of foreign investment indefinitely.[42] Even if net foreign investment did not expand at a rate sufficient to offset the growing volume of interest and dividend payments, we would have a generation or two in which to adjust our trade balance to a lower export surplus or eventually to an import surplus. Surely a couple of generations of large outpourings of American capital will sufficiently change America's competitive position in world markets and the balance of the world's commodity production to enable the United States to make the transition to a mature creditor nation without serious difficulty.

In the opinion of the author, foreign-investment targets based on America's need for an outlet for capital or on foreign requirements based on the developmental plans of foreign countries are generally unsatisfactory. The experience of history provides an inadequate guide since it covers periods of prosperity and depression as well as periods of extraordinary foreign requirements. On the assumption that we need a certain amount of additional investment to achieve full employment, how do we determine whether that investment should take the form of domestic public works or government lending abroad? Also, if foreign investment were sufficiently attractive to American business, it might take the place of an equivalent amount of domestic investment. Unless there are compelling political reasons to the contrary, governmental investment abroad should not be so large as to endanger the stability of the American economy. If total private investment, both domestic and foreign, were too high, appropriate fiscal and monetary measures would serve to dampen both and no special restrictive measures need be applied to foreign private investment.

Likewise, fixed targets based upon the amounts of compensatory financing required to balance the United States current-account surplus over some period in the past have little real justification. America's export surplus over the decades since World War I has been the result of a variety of factors including wars, restrictive commercial policies, improper monetary and exchange policies, and structural maladjustments. The historical fact of this surplus provides no satisfactory guide as to the surplus which this country ought to finance by means of long-term capital exports in the future. From the standpoint of facilitating the transfer problem, however, some consideration ought to be given to the rate of growth of public investment and especially to the prevention of sharp fluctuations in the level of gross foreign investment. While fixed investment targets are not believed to be feasible for this purpose, pub-

---

[42] Walter S. Salant, "The Domestic Effects of Capital Export under the Point Four Program," *American Economic Review Supplement,* May, 1950, p. 506.

lic-investment institutions should keep this problem in mind in planning their investment programs.

We must also reject fixed targets based on existing developmental plans of other countries. In most cases these plans are only vaguely formulated, and adequate studies of the possible rate of capital absorption of the underdeveloped countries have not been made. Even apart from the capacity of a country to service foreign loans, there are a number of conditions which must be met before a country can employ additional capital in a manner which will make a permanent contribution to its productivity and not simply be dissipated in a temporary increase in consumption. Some of the difficulties in this field have already been mentioned.

While none of the targets for foreign investment discussed above appear to provide an adequate criterion for the foreign-investment policy of the United States, this country does have important economic, political, and security interests in the promotion of a high volume of foreign investment. At the time of writing, political and security interests are paramount, and the political benefits to be gained from foreign capital development must be weighed against alternative uses of our resources. In the long run, however, America's economic prosperity is tied to that of the rest of the world, and it is to our own interest to contribute to the fullest development of the world's resources. Moreover, foreign investments can become a net source of real income for the United States, whenever we achieve a balance of payments consistent with our creditor position. In place of fixed foreign-investment targets, the following long-run United States foreign-investment policy is suggested:

1. Promote private foreign investment to the maximum extent possible through investment treaties and guarantees.

2. Enlarge the technical-assistance program so as to formulate in cooperation with local governments comprehensive programs for capital development extending over the next twenty or thirty years and work out a schedule of projects with appropriate priorities based on the maximum absorptive capacity of the countries receiving the financial assistance.

3. Liberalize the lending policies of the Export-Import Bank and the International Bank in the direction of broadening the types of projects which they would finance and speed up consideration of loan applications.

4. In connection with the criterion of ability to repay, the two public lending institutions should take into consideration a long period of net capital imports based on long-range developmental plans. Some portion of the loans should be left untied to specific expenditures or projects so that the borrowing countries would have funds available for making payments on earlier loans.

5. The United States government should encourage these public lending institutions to make loans at the maximum rate possible within the limits of

their lending criteria, and additional funds should be sought from Congress as they are needed. Only by experience under actual operating conditions can we determine what the actual rate of lending will be and its relation to the American economy. Should the rate of foreign investment from both public and private sources prove to be running at a level which threatens to affect adversely the internal stability of the United States, we shall need to consider what measures should be taken in the light of both political and economic circumstances.

At the present time, the requirements of the defense program impose a serious limitation on America's capacity to make foreign investments. On the other hand, a certain amount of foreign lending is essential to the promotion of our foreign-policy objectives. The Gray Report has suggested a volume of public investment of $600 to $800 million annually, together with a grant program of about $500 million annually, as the amount of United States assistance for economic development consonant with our political and security interests in the underdeveloped areas.[43]

[43] *Report to the President on Foreign Economic Policies* (Gray Report), November, 1950, p. 13.

CHAPTER 14

The Truman Doctrine and
Foreign Economic Assistance

PRESIDENT TRUMAN'S message to Congress of March 12, 1947, re-questing aid for Greece and Turkey marks the beginning of what has come to be known as the Truman Doctrine. In the course of this message, the President said: [1]

> I believe that it must be the policy of the United States to support free peoples who are resisting attempted subjugation by armed minorities or by outside pressures.
>
> I believe we must assist free peoples to work out their own destinies in their own way.
>
> I believe that our help should be primarily through economic and financial aid which is essential to economic stability and orderly political processes.

The immediate occasion for the formal statement of the above policy was the internal crisis in Greece and the announcement by Britain that she could no longer assume the economic and other burdens of continued participation in Greek affairs. Fundamentally, however, this policy was based upon a recognition of the implications of certain far-reaching developments for the foreign policy of the United States. On the political side, the United States had come to realize that the United Nations machinery could not guarantee the peace of the world and that the U.S.S.R. was determined on a policy of political aggression which only the United States could arrest. On the economic side, the Truman Doctrine was a recognition that the postwar assistance and reconstruction plans which had been developed during the war were inadequate to rehabilitate the war-torn economies of the world and that something more was needed to establish a number of foreign countries on an economic basis which would assure political stability and enable them to resist Communist pressure from within and without. The Truman Doctrine implies a recognition that America's responsibility for the economic welfare of the rest of the world did not end with the immediate postwar period,

[1] For the text of this message and other early documents relating to the Greek-Turkish aid program, see "Aid to Greece and Turkey," *Department of State Bulletin, Supplement,* May 4, 1947.

but that foreign economic assistance and cooperation is a permanent obligation of this country if it is to survive in a hostile two-power world.[2]

Up until the time of writing the implementation of the Truman Doctrine has been largely oriented toward Western Europe. While communism was strong in the Far East, especially in China where as early as 1946 it appeared that the Nationalist Government of China was doomed to be overthrown by the Communists, the decision was made to make the major effort against communism in Europe. There were two basic reasons for this fundamental decision. First, the reports of the missions of General Marshall and General Wedemeyer together with those of the State Department's missions indicated that the Nationalist Government of China did not provide an adequate basis for large-scale economic and military support. Barring a major reform of the Chinese government or, alternatively, the assumption by the United States of full responsibility for the government and military defense of the Nationalist territory, the provision of economic assistance and military equipment to China would have been a waste of America's resources and would not have accomplished its purpose.[3] The second reason for the administration's decision against large-scale aid to China was the view that this country could not undertake a large-scale commitment both in Asia and in Europe, and that in the long run it was far more important from the standpoint of United States security to keep Western Europe out of Communist hands.

The administration's position on assistance to China has been bitterly opposed by certain members of Congress where there has been considerable sentiment in favor of a comprehensive aid program for the Far East similar to that undertaken for Western Europe. For example in March, 1949, some fifty Senators endorsed a proposal to provide up to $1.5 billion in aid to Nationalist China.[4] Partly as a consequence of this controversy, limited amounts of economic and military aid have been appropriated for China and for the Nationalist government in Formosa after the conquest of the mainland by the Chinese Communists.[5]

[2] A much stronger statement of the Truman Doctrine is contained in a statement by Secretary of State Acheson on Feb. 14, 1950, in which he said: "The only way to deal with the Soviet Union, we have found from hard experience, is to create situations of strength. Wherever the Soviet detects weakness or disunity—and it is quick to detect them—it exploits them to the full." (*Department of State Bulletin*, Mar. 20, 1950, p. 427.)

[3] For an official statement of American policy in China, see *United States Relations with China*, Department of State, August, 1949.

[4] For a discussion of United States aid to the Far East, see Dr. Gardner Patterson's excellent study, *Survey of United States International Finance, 1949*, International Finance Section, Princeton University, Princeton, N.J., 1950, pp. 43–54.

[5] From the end of the war through 1948, China had received $1.6 billion in assistance from the United States. See Patterson, *op. cit.*, p. 44.

While the administration did not support large-scale aid to China, it has favored strong support for the Republic of Korea which was inaugurated in August, 1948, as the government of South Korea. The American participation in the war between North and South Korea which began in the summer of 1950 is evidence of a determination of the administration to provide all-out aid in halting further Communist expansion in the Far East. American grant assistance now going to Indo-China, Indonesia, Burma, Thailand, and elsewhere in the general area of China adds up to a fairly sizable program. This area is likely to receive increasing attention by the United States in the future, and there is every indication that the United States is definitely committed to a major program of stopping further Communist aggression in the Far East as well as in Western Europe and the Near East. For example, Mr. Gray's *Report to the President on Foreign Economic Policies* (published in November, 1950) recommended a grant program of up to $500 million for the underdeveloped areas, most of which would be for South and East Asia. It is evident therefore that the Truman Doctrine and the principle of "building up situations of strength" is being extended to the entire world as the cold war grows in area and intensity.

THE FOREIGN-AID PROGRAMS

Limitations of space make it impossible to deal with all the foreign-assistance programs which are a direct outgrowth of the Truman Doctrine. Table 10 (page 218) shows total United States foreign assistance by major categories since the war to the end of 1950. Strictly speaking, only that part of the assistance represented by the European Recovery Program, Greek-Turkish aid, Interim Aid to Austria, France and Italy, the Mutual Defense Assistance Program, and Chinese and Korean aid are directly related to the Truman Doctrine. Assistance for Philippine rehabilitation was rendered in recognition of the responsibility of the United States for a country which until after the war was a part of the territory of the United States. The Army's civilian supply program in occupied territories is also related to a special obligation of this country growing out of the war. Grants to the International Children's Emergency Fund and for refugee assistance were made principally for humanitarian reasons. Some of the Export-Import Bank loans such as the $100 million loan to Indonesia and the loans to Yugoslavia might also be considered as an outcome of the Truman Doctrine.

The Greek-Turkish Aid Act (Public Law 75, 80th Congress, First Session, approved May 22, 1947) provided for $300 million in military and economic aid to Greece and $100 million in military aid to Turkey.[6] This was the first postwar foreign-assistance measure to be enacted almost solely in response to the political motive of arresting communism. During the same month that the Greek-Turkish Aid bill was passed Congress also passed the post-UNRRA relief bill (approved May 31, 1947)[7] authorizing $350 million for foreign relief to Austria, China, Greece, Italy, and Trieste. Although the other countries of Western Europe were not engaged in internal warfare as in the case of Greece, or were not subject to an imminent threat of attack by the U.S.S.R. as was Turkey, economic assistance was urgently needed if certain of them at least were to maintain internal stability and continued independence from communist domination. By the spring of 1947 it had become evident that further relief programs would be necessary if political and economic breakdown in Western Europe was to be avoided. In spite of the fact that by this time the United States had provided over $11 billion in loans and grants to Europe since V-J Day, Europe was far from being self-sufficient at politically tolerable living standards. France was running out of dollars to pay for food and other basic supplies, and soon this country would be added to those already "on relief" along with Austria, Greece, and Italy. It was this situation together with a realization of the political urgency of stemming the rising tide of communism which gave rise to the Marshall Plan, as put forward in Secretary Marshall's famous address of June 5, 1947. But before the ERP could be launched, the relief measures had to be carried on.

By the fall of 1947 another crisis was at hand, and the President called a special session of Congress to deal with emergency relief for France, Italy, and Austria, and to enact legislation to deal with domestic inflation.[8] The Foreign Aid Act of 1947 (approved December 17, 1947) authorized $597 million of relief aid for France ($328 million), Italy ($227 million), and Austria ($42 million). Only $540 million in funds was finally appropriated, however, $18 million of which was to be used for China.[9] This so-called Interim Aid program was essentially an extension of post-UNRRA relief, the aid being almost entirely in the form of food,

[6] In June, 1948, an additional $225 million was appropriated for military aid to Greece and Turkey, the economic aid to Greece being merged with the ERP. (Public Law 793, 80th Congress, 2d Session, approved June 28, 1948.)

[7] See Chap. 7.

[8] These two problems were to a degree related since domestic inflation was rapidly cutting down the purchasing power of the dwindling gold and dollar assets of foreign countries.

[9] Public Law 393, 80th Congress, 1st Session. Public Law 470, approved Mar. 31, 1948, appropriated an additional $55 million for France, Italy, and Austria, making a total appropriation for these three countries of $577 million.

fuel, and fertilizer. Many of the administrative provisions involved in the Interim Aid program such as the requirement for depositing local currency in special accounts equivalent to the amount of the dollar assistance, the provisions assuring the efficient use of the funds, full publicity in the recipient countries and supervision by United States officials were similar to the provisions of the Economic Cooperation Administration Act of 1948. The Interim Aid program, approved in December, 1947, was perhaps even more clearly identified as an instrument of American political policy than was the post-UNRRA relief Act of May, 1947.

The Development of the Marshall Plan

The Marshall Plan was the logical outcome of the Truman Doctrine of supporting the economies of friendly countries so that they could maintain their political independence and their democratic institutions. The countries which were to become members of the ERP program had a deficit on current account with the United States of $4.2 billion in 1946 and $5.4 billion in 1947, financed largely by United States grants, emergency-type loans, and the liquidation of gold and dollar assets. At the same time the living standards of these countries were well below prewar levels, and they were not making significant progress in adjusting their economies to a self-sustaining basis. Not only was the emergency relief assistance failing to promote permanent recovery in Europe, but several countries were faced with the immediate threat of communism, a threat which it was believed could be removed only by the assurance of adequate supplies of consumers' goods to sustain living standards and the inauguration of a long-range program to provide assurance of economic improvement.

In the light of this situation, the United States government came to two conclusions regarding further aid to Europe, which were revealed in Secretary Marshall's Harvard speech of June 5, 1947: [10] (1) Assistance to Europe should no longer be "on a piecemeal basis as various crises develop. Any assistance that this government may render in the future should provide a cure rather than a mere palliative." (2) Europe's economic problems must be dealt with as a whole and not country by country and that "before the United States can proceed much further in its efforts to alleviate the situation and help start the European world on its way to recovery, there must be some agreement among the countries of Europe as to the requirements of the situation and the part those countries themselves will take in order to give proper effect to whatever

[10] *Department of State Bulletin,* June 15, 1947, pp. 1159ff.

action might be undertaken by this government." [11] Thus the countries of Europe were invited to draw up a program for economic recovery which would be the basis for further United States assistance.

The principle of cooperative self-help and planning for Europe had both economic and political implications. The policy implied right from the beginning some form of economic integration for Europe, since Secretary Marshall certainly had more in mind than a European committee for dividing up the promised United States aid. We shall consider the nature of this cooperation later on, but for the immediate future the political implications of this policy were far more important. It became the signal for a sharpening of the political lines within Europe and a weakening of the movement in Europe for a neutral "third force" standing between the United States and Russia. It was obvious to Russia's representatives at the initial meeting of the European countries in Paris (July, 1947), called in response to Secretary Marshall's invitation, that if the countries of Eastern Europe were to join they would become the beneficiaries of the United States and that the democratic countries of Western Europe would dominate the Committee of European Economic Cooperation (CEEC). To permit the Eastern European countries which had not yet succumbed to complete domination by the U.S.S.R. to become members of the ERP would have provided an important political and propaganda weapon for the United States. On the other hand, the formation of an organization of Western European democracies alone, which would necessarily cooperate closely with the United States, paved the way for the North Atlantic Pact and its counterpart, the Military Assistance Program.

The basic organization in Europe for the working out of the ERP was the CEEC, consisting of representatives of the 16 participating countries: Austria, Belgium, Denmark, Ireland, France, Greece, Iceland, Italy, Luxemburg, the Netherlands, Norway, Portugal, Sweden, Switzerland, Turkey, and the United Kingdom. The basic program which was developed after 2 months of intensive effort was a 4-year program, 1948-1951, for the 16 participating countries and Western Germany. The objective to be achieved by the end of the program was the restoration of reasonable living standards (roughly at prewar levels) and the capacity to maintain such levels of living without further special assistance after 1951. The program which was embodied in the General Report of the Committee of European Economic Cooperation of September 21, 1947,[12] included certain production goals; a statement of import requirements

[11] *Ibid.*

[12] Published in two volumes by the Department of State, as *Publication* 2930, European series 28, September, 1947.

based on the production and consumption goals; estimates of the balance-of-payments deficits of the participating countries which resulted from the individual country programs; an agreement on measures of internal economic, financial, and monetary stability to be followed by the participating countries; and a general agreement with respect to measures of economic cooperation in the fields of trade, payments, electric-power facilities, standardization of equipment, and transportation and in other areas of economic activity. No specific request for United States assistance was made in the Report, although the aggregate Western Hemisphere or dollar deficit was estimated at $22,400 million.[13] The combined dollar deficit for the first year of the program (1948) was estimated to be $8 billion, with the annual deficits declining in subsequent years.

Studies relative to the ERP and its impact on the United States economy were carried on in the United States during the summer and fall of 1947 by several different groups. In addition to intensive work in the State Department in cooperation with other agencies of the government and by the National Advisory Council, the President announced on June 22 the formation of three special groups to undertake studies in specific fields. There was created the President's Committee on Foreign Aid, consisting of a group of distinguished citizens headed by Secretary of Commerce Harriman, which was requested to advise the President with respect to the limits within which the United States might safely and wisely extend economic assistance to foreign countries. An interdepartmental group under Secretary of the Interior Krug was directed to study the effects of foreign aid upon America's national resources, particularly raw materials, manpower, and production, while the Council of Economic Advisors under its chairman, Dr. Nourse, was called upon to review the general impact of foreign aid upon the domestic economy.[14]

In December, 1947, the Secretary of State submitted to Congress draft legislation on a proposed "Economic Cooperation Act of 1948" together with supporting documents.[15] This draft legislation called for the setting up of an Economic Cooperation Administration to administer a Euro-

[13] *General Report of the Committee of European Economic Cooperation*, Sept. 21, 1947, Vol. I, p. 59.

[14] The reports of these three committees concluded, in general, that the United States could and should undertake a foreign-aid program of the general magnitude suggested by the CEEC Report. See *Economic Recovery and Foreign Aid* (Harriman Committee Report), Washington, D.C., November, 1947; *The Impact of Foreign Aid upon the Domestic Economy*. A Report to the President by the Council of Economic Advisors, Washington, D.C., October, 1947; and *Natural Resources and Foreign Aid* (Krug Committee Report), Department of Interior, Washington, D.C., October, 1947.

[15] *Outline of European Recovery Program* (printed for the use of the Senate Committee on Foreign Relations, 80th Congress, 1st Session), Dec. 19, 1947.

pean aid program covering the period from the enactment of the bill through June 30, 1952. The cost of the entire program was set at not more than $17 billion, and the bill called for an appropriation of $6.8 billion to carry the program through June 30, 1949. The Foreign Assistance Act of 1948 (approved on April 3, 1948) authorized an appropriation of $4.3 billion for grants and $1 billion [16] for loans, for the first 12 months of the program. The Foreign Aid Appropriations Act of June 28, 1948, authorized only $4 billion in grants, the amounts to be spent over a 15-month period, until June 30, 1949, but with the provision that the funds could all be spent by April 2, 1949, "if the President, after recommendation by the administrator, deems such action necessary to carry out the purposes of said Act." [17] The salient features of Title I of the Foreign Assistance Act of 1948 (called the Economic Cooperation Act of 1948) [18] were as follows:

1. The European assistance program was to be administered by a new agency, the Economic Cooperation Administration, headed by an Administrator for Economic Cooperation. The Administrator is required to consult with the Department of State on matters of foreign policy but any dispute between them is to be decided by the President. The Administrator is made a member of the National Advisory Council and is required to consult with the NAC regarding certain matters of financial policy.

2. Specific provision is made for a special ECA representative in Europe to act as liaison with the European organization of the participating countries

[16] The ECA Administration was authorized to borrow $1 billion from the Treasury for funds to be made available to ERP countries on credit. (Foreign Assistance Act of 1948, Public Law 472, 80th Congress, 2d Session.)

[17] Public Law 793, 80th Congress, 2d Session. Public Law 47, 81st Congress, 1st Session, authorized the appropriation of an additional $1,150 million for the period Apr. 3, 1949, through June 30, 1949.

[18] Title II authorized the appropriation of $60 million for the International Children's Emergency Fund of the United Nations; Title III authorized $275 million for Greek-Turkish assistance; and Title IV, the "China Aid Act of 1948," authorized $463 million in aid to China. The Foreign Aid Appropriation Act of June 28, 1948, made the following appropriations:

(In millions of dollars)

European aid	4,000
International Children's Emergency Fund	35
Greek-Turkish aid	225
China aid	400
	4,660
International Refugees Organization	71
Army occupation program	1,300
Total	6,031

and there shall be in addition special missions in each of the participating countries.

3. Not less than $1 billion of the aid in the first year was to be made available in the form of loans, to be administered by the Export-Import Bank on terms specified by the Administrator in consultation with the NAC. Provision was also made for the guarantee of U.S. private investments in the participating countries up to the amount of $300 million.

4. Except for certain agricultural commodities to be procured from the Department of Agriculture, maximum use of private channels of trade was required. Although dollars were to be provided only for approved lists of commodities, accounts in favor of the participating countries were to be established against which withdrawals might be made under arrangements prescribed by the Administrator to assure the use of such withdrawals for approved purposes.

5. At least 50 per cent of the gross tonnage of commodities procured in the United States out of ECA funds were to be transported in United States flag vessels, to the extent that such vessels are available at market rates.

6. Procurement outside the United States was authorized but subject to certain limitations. With certain exceptions procurement of surplus agricultural commodities shall be made in the United States.

7. Bilateral agreements with each of the participating countries were to be entered into by the State Department in consultation with the Administrator. The content of these agreements is to include:

(a) An undertaking by the participating country to promote industry and agriculture in order to enable it to become independent of extraordinary outside assistance and to submit specific projects for such increased production.

(b) An undertaking to take financial and monetary measures necessary to stabilize its currency, to establish or maintain a valid rate of exchange, and to balance its budget as soon as practicable.

(c) An undertaking to cooperate in facilitating the interchange of goods with other participating countries.

(d) An agreement to facilitate the sale or barter to the United States of commodities in which the United States is deficient, for stock-piling or for other purposes.

(e) An agreement to place in a special account amounts of local currencies equivalent to the assistance made available on a grant basis. These local currency accounts were to be utilized only by mutual agreement with the Administration in consultation with the NAC, for purposes of internal financial stabilization, productive investment and the development of new resources, and for local currency expenses of the United States incident to the program.

(f) An agreement to provide upon the request of the United States any relevant information which would be of assistance to the United States in connection with the program.

8. The Administrator shall encourage the joint organization of the partici- pating countries to ensure the efficient use of the aid.

9. The Administrator was directed to refuse delivery to participating countries of commodities which go into the production of any commodity for delivery to any non-participating European country which commodity would be refused export licenses to those countries by the United States in the interest of national security.

We shall discuss the operation of the Marshall program in the next two chapters.

CHAPTER 15

The Marshall Program in Operation

THIS CHAPTER will be devoted to a brief discussion of the operation of the European Recovery Program with special emphasis upon the relationship of the Marshall program to certain American domestic economic and foreign political interests and objectives.[1] Chapter 16 will be devoted to an evaluation of the progress of the European Recovery Program in the realization of its objectives, together with a discussion of the outlook for aid to Western Europe in relation to the defense program. In order to set the stage for this discussion, we shall begin with a review of Europe's economic position at the end of 1947.

The Economic Position of Europe at the End of 1947

The explanation of the economic crisis in Europe in 1947, two years after hostilities had ceased and after large outpourings of American aid, must be found in a complex of internal and external factors, some short-run and some fundamental in nature. Statistics of production and income alone do not reveal the magnitude of Europe's problem. In fact, in a number of fields European recovery, particularly outside of Germany, was much more rapid during the two years following the end of World War II than it was for a similar period after World War I.[2] The adverse short-term factors in the European situation in 1947 were (1) the crop failures on the Continent and the severe winter which interfered with production and transportation in Britain and on the Continent, (2) the near breakdown of intra-European trade caused by payments difficulties, (3) the shortage of coal caused by the low level of German production, (4) the price inflation in Europe coupled with an administration of rationing and price controls which made farmers unwilling to sell their produce to the cities, and (5) the price inflation in the United States which greatly reduced the purchasing power of Europe's gold and dollar

[1] For an excellent and comprehensive account of the ERP, see Howard S. Ellis, *The Economics of Freedom,* Harper, New York, 1950.

[2] For example, European industrial production (excluding Germany) was 83 per cent of the 1913 level in 1920, and 95 per cent of the 1938 level in 1946–1947. *A Survey of the Economic Situation and Prospects of Europe,* Economic Commission for Europe, Geneva, March, 1948, p. 16.

reserves. The factors which required adjustments of a long-run or fundamental character include (1) the damage to Europe's capital equipment
(including the failure to maintain and modernize), resulting from nearly
6 years of warfare; (2) the deterioration of Europe's competitive position
in world markets; (3) the loss of invisible income resulting from disinvestment abroad and the large increase in external debt burden; and (4)
the increased dependence of Western Europe for food supplies from the
Western Hemisphere and elsewhere caused by the political barriers to
trade with Eastern Europe.

Although industrial production in Europe outside Germany and the
U.S.S.R. had exceeded the 1938 level by the last quarter of 1947, agricultural production was still about 20 per cent below the prewar level.[3] In
the production of certain basic commodities such as coal and steel, European output was substantially less than prewar, owing largely to the low
level of output in Germany. The production of grain in 1947–1948 was
only 84 million tons as compared with an average of 125 million tons in
the period from 1934 to 1938.[4] In spite of substantially increased imports
of bread grains over prewar imports, per capita consumption of bread
grains in 1946–1947 in Europe (excluding U.S.S.R. and Turkey) was 16
per cent less than the average per capita consumption in the period from
1934 to 1938.[5]

Comparative levels of real per capita income are exceedingly difficult
to estimate because of inadequate price and production statistics, but
there is little doubt but that in 1947 real per capita income in the participating countries was substantially lower than prewar. According to
the Economic Commission for Europe, per capita income in the five
countries of Western Continental Europe (Belgium, Luxemburg, France,
the Netherlands, and Switzerland) averaged $233 (in 1938 dollars) in
1947 as compared with $262 in 1938. In five countries in northwestern
Europe (United Kingdom, Denmark, Ireland, Norway, and Sweden) per
capita income in 1947 averaged $352 as compared with $362 in 1938;
while in Italy per capita income in 1947 was $100 as compared with $127
in 1938.[6] The reductions in per capita income from prewar were even
greater in the case of Austria and Greece. Per capita consumption was,
however, much lower than these figures would indicate because of the
larger percentage of national income devoted to capital investment and
governmental activities of all kinds.

[3] *Economic Survey of Europe in 1948,* Economic Commission for Europe, Geneva,
1949, pp. 4, 17.

[4] *Ibid.,* p. 17.

[5] *A Survey of the Economic Situation and Prospects of Europe,* p. 18.

[6] *Economic Survey of Europe in 1948,* p. 235.

The volume of intra-European trade in 1947 was only 55 per cent of the 1938 level,[7] and imports of participating countries from other participating countries and their overseas territories in 1947 were 65 per cent by volume of the 1938 level.[8] As was mentioned before in our discussion of the intra-European payments problem, only a part of this decline in intra-European trade can be ascribed to the decline in production from prewar levels. In fact, trade as a percentage of production declined substantially. The reluctance of European countries to settle their bilateral balances with one another with gold or dollars and their unwillingness to accept one another's currencies prevented the restoration of the prewar pattern of multilateral payments. Intra-European trade was not only restricted, but some of the trade which did take place was of an uneconomical and artificial character. This situation was due in part to the practice of tieing exports of essential commodities to the sale of unessentials both for bargaining purposes and as a means of creating a bilateral commodity balance, and also to the existence of wide price disparities in terms of official exchange rates among European countries.[9]

Turning to Europe's balance of payments with the outside world, we find that while Europe's imports were 114 per cent of the 1938 volume in 1947, exports were only 81 per cent of the 1938 volume.[10] Considering the ERP countries by themselves, we find that although imports in 1947 were 96 per cent of the 1938 volume, in 1947 these countries paid for less than 40 per cent of their imports through current earnings.[11] In 1938, the ERP countries were roughly in current balance with the rest of the world, their $1.8 billion merchandise deficit being offset by an equivalent net invisible balance. In 1947, however, the participating countries had a deficit on merchandise account of $7.5 billion with the outside world and in addition a small deficit on invisible account.[12] Of the total deficit, $5.7 billion represented the deficit of the participating countries with the United States. The total dollar deficit was somewhat larger since deficits with certain other Western Hemisphere countries had to be settled with dollars and since Britain had to meet the dollar deficits of other members of the sterling area.

[7] *Ibid.*, p. 87.

[8] *Interim Report on the European Economic Recovery Program,* Organization for European Economic Cooperation, Paris, Vol. I, Dec. 30, 1948, p. 82.

[9] For a discussion of intra-European trade patterns, see *Survey of the Economic Situation and Prospects of Europe,* pp. 102–114.

[10] *Economic Survey of Europe in 1948,* p. 57.

[11] *Interim Report on the European Recovery Program,* Vol. I, p. 51.

[12] *Economic Survey of Europe in 1948,* p. 117. Europe as a whole had an over-all current-account deficit with the outside world of $7.6 billion.

Table 11. Europe's Balance of Payments
(In billions of dollars in current prices)

Item	1938			1947		
	United States	Other non-European countries	Total	United States	Other non-European countries	Total
Europe's imports (f.o.b.)....	$ 1.3	$ 4.2	$ 5.5	$ 6.1	$ 7.8	$ 13.9
Europe's exports (f.o.b.)....	0.6	3.1	3.7	0.9	5.5	6.4
Balance-on-trade account.	$−0.7	$−1.1	$−1.8	$−5.2	$−2.3	$−7.5
Income from investment (net)................	+0.1	+1.1	+1.2	......	+0.6	+0.6
Transportation (net).......	+0.2	+0.4	+0.6	{ −0.7 { +0.2	+0.3 −0.5	−0.4 −0.3
Balance-on-invisibles account...............	$+0.3	$+1.5	$+1.8	$−0.5	$+0.4	$−0.1
Balance on goods and services...............	$−0.4	$+0.4	......	$−5.7	$−1.9	$−7.6

SOURCE: *Economic Survey of Europe in 1948*, Economic Commission for Europe, Geneva, 1949, p. 112.

Table 11 shows Europe's balance of payments with the United States and other non-European countries for 1938 and 1947. Although the decline in the real level of exports was in considerable measure responsible for the deficit, there were other significant factors. Of considerable importance was the reduction in net invisible earnings, which declined from $1.8 billion in 1938 to a deficit of $100 million in 1947. Another important factor in the 1947 deficit was the rise in world prices of imported commodities. Although the rise in the average dollar value of Europe's imports over 1938 levels was about equal to the rise in the average dollar value of her exports, *i.e.,* there was no deterioration in Europe's terms of trade in 1947 as compared with prewar,[13] the fact that world prices generally had approximately doubled meant an increase in the monetary value of the deficit. The rapid rise in United States prices immediately

[13] The index of the average dollar value of European exports was 208 (1938 = 100) and of European imports 213 in 1947.

after the war contributed substantially to Europe's deficit with the United States since Europe was selling relatively little to the United States, and even in 1938 Europe paid for less than half of her commodity imports from the United States with commodity exports to the United States.

Turning to the distribution of Europe's overseas deficit, we find that whereas Europe had a current-account deficit of $400 million with the United States in 1938, which she was able to settle with an equivalent surplus with other non-European countries, in 1947 Europe had a deficit with both of these areas. In fact the ERP countries made net dollar and gold payments amounting to $2.7 billion to countries other than the United States in 1947. Table 12 shows the gold and dollar financing of ERP countries in 1947.

Table 12. Gold and Dollar Financing of ERP Countries in 1947

(In millions of dollars)

Total financing requirements..........................	$8,103
Net United States exports of goods and services..........	5,363
Net gold and dollar payments to other countries..........	2,740
Sources of financing:	
United States government funds, net...................	5,248
United States private, net...........................	385
Total United States funds.........................	5,633
Liquidation of dollar assets and sale of gold to United States	2,470

SOURCE: *The Balance of International Payments of the United States, 1946–1948*, Department of Commerce, 1950, p. 174.

The problem before the Organization for European Economic Co-operation was to develop a program for dealing with these deficits with other areas, which would at the same time be consistent with an appropriate pattern of trade among the ERP countries themselves. Certain ERP countries normally had surpluses with other ERP countries which were settled in gold or currencies convertible into the currencies of non-European countries. For example, in the prewar period Germany tended to have an export surplus with the rest of Continental Europe, which the latter was able to settle by reason of an export surplus with the United Kingdom. The United Kingdom in turn had an import surplus with non-European countries as well as an import surplus with the Continent, but settlement was made by means of substantial net invisible earnings from non-European sources.[14] Moreover, sterling was freely con-

[14] Britain's average net invisible earnings in the period from 1936–1938 were £345 million. See *Statistical Material Presented during the Washington Negotiations*, British Information Services, Washington, D.C., December, 1945, p. 13.

vertible into dollars, which made it possible for both Britain and the Continent to run a trade and over-all current-account deficit with the United States. Britain's dollar income resulted largely from her ability to purchase gold from South Africa with sterling (and then sell the gold to the United States for dollars) and from invisible earnings from southeast Asia, *e.g.,* India, Malaya, and Ceylon, which in turn had export surpluses with the United States. Belgium and the Netherlands also earned dollars from their colonial possessions in Asia and Africa, but Belgium had an export surplus with the other Western European countries in 1938, while the Netherlands had an import surplus with Western Europe.

The changes in the external position of European countries brought about by the war greatly affected the pattern of intra-European trade. The loss of Britain's invisible income from non-European sources together with her great need for imports from the Western Hemisphere and other areas made it necessary for Britain to close the gap in her trade with the rest of Western Europe. While in 1938 Britain had merchandise imports from the rest of Western Europe valued at $1,020 million and exports valued at $663 million, in 1947 Britain's imports from this area were $1,075 million and her exports $1,295 million.[15] Belgium's prewar export surplus with the rest of Western Europe was substantially reduced in real terms in 1947, and Germany's trade was but a small fraction of its prewar volume. These changes in intra-European trade patterns contributed to Europe's economic maladjustment and to her need for outside assistance. One of the problems of the ERP was to restore an appropriate pattern of intra-European trade through a rearrangement of Economic Cooperation Administration aid. If some ERP countries are to have surpluses with other participating countries as they did before the war, there must be some means of settling their surpluses with non-European currencies. We shall consider this question in the following chapter, which deals with the development of the programs of ERP countries for reaching viability after 1952.

The Program for Western European Viability

In April, 1948, the nations participating in the Marshall Plan established a formal organization called the Organization for European Economic Cooperation.[16] The OEEC is responsible for taking the initiative in formulating plans for European recovery, including the submission of requirements for dollar assistance and its distribution among the mem-

[15] *Economic Survey of Europe in 1948,* p. 142.

[16] See *Convention for European Economic Co-operation, with Related Documents,* Paris, Apr. 16, 1948, Department of State Publication 3145.

bers, and for supervising the execution of the programs. The United States representative in Paris assists the OEEC in the formulation of the programs, and these programs are then screened by the ECA in Washington to see that they are consistent with the ECA Act and that they are in agreement with the foreign economic policies of the United States. Since the OEEC was unable to complete its program for the first year, July 1, 1948, to June 30, 1949, until October 16, 1948, the initial programs and allotments of ECA aid had to be determined on the basis of individual country submissions. The first annual program submitted by the OEEC for the year July 1, 1948, to June 30, 1949, set forth (1) an agreed distribution of $4,875 million in United States aid, (2) an intra-European payments system in which surpluses would be financed by an arrangement of the ECA aid, and (3) a set of commercial policy rules to guide the future financial economic and commercial relations of the member countries.[17] The supply program was screened by ECA, and certain adjustments were made in the total aid to be made available and in its distribution.

The ECA assistance to the participating countries for the period April, 1948 to June, 1949, consisted of direct grants ($4,209 million), conditional aid ($771 million), and loans ($972 million).[18] Since the ECA Act required that $1 billion of the aid may be made available in the form of loans and investment guarantees, it was necessary to distribute the loan portion of the aid in accordance with the principle of capacity to repay.[19] ECA grants were divided into direct grants and conditional grants, the amount of the latter being determined by the net drawing rights (total drawing rights granted minus drawing rights received) which the ERP countries agreed with the ECA to extend to one another in financing bilateral deficits in intra-European trade. The total amount of ECA aid was determined on the basis of the programed dollar deficit of the participating country and independently of the amount of drawing rights extended or received in the financing of intra-European trade. Thus a country received no additional aid from the United States as a result of the extension of drawing rights. The extension of drawing rights,

[17] *Report to the Economic Cooperation Administration on the First Annual Programme,* Organization for European Economic Cooperation, Paris, October, 1948.

[18] *Fifth Report to Congress of the Economic Cooperation Administration for the Period April 13–June 30, 1949,* p. 29.

[19] Of the $1 billion, $27.7 million was set aside for investment guarantees and $972.3 million allocated to the Export-Import Bank for loans negotiated by the ECA (with the advice of the National Advisory Council) with the participating countries. Loan disbursements out of $971.2 million authorized by the ECA amounted to $853.4 million at the end of December, 1949. *Ninth Semiannual Report to Congress for the Period July–December, 1949,* Export-Import Bank of Washington.

however, did affect the form of the ECA aid as between grants and loans. Thus had Belgium not received the bulk of its aid in the form of conditional grants, a much larger share of Belgium's aid would undoubtedly have been made available in the form of loans since Belgium's economic position is relatively strong.

We have discussed the relationship of the drawing rights to the system of intra-European trade and payments in Chap. 11. Although the European Payments Union system permits countries receiving drawing rights to use them against any country in the EPU, the principle of conditional aid has been carried over to the new system. Thus under the EPU, countries which are expected to be creditors on intra-European account are given initial debit positions in the EPU which are analogous to the extension of drawing rights under the old system.

During the first year of the ERP two participating countries, Portugal and Switzerland, received no aid of any kind, because their financial position did not warrant United States assistance. (ECA assistance was extended to Portugal in 1949–1950.) It was to the advantage of these countries to be members of the ERP, however, since they benefit from the more favorable allocation of those United States exports which are in short supply than would otherwise be the case.

The requirement of the ECA Act of 1948 that $1 billion of the aid appropriated be made available in the form of loans presented serious difficulties for the administration. The ERP countries had already accumulated a substantial dollar indebtedness in the postwar period. In 1948–1949, interest and amortization payments on United States and other dollar obligations of the participating countries absorbed about one-eighth of their total dollar earning, and in the period from 1949 to 1950 these payments were estimated to amount to about $230 million.[20] The addition of another billion dollars in indebtedness tended to defeat the objectives of the program by making more difficult the achievement of European viability after 1952 and by further impairing the borrowing capacity of the ERP at the end of the program when they may find it desirable to borrow for developmental purposes either from the International Bank or from private sources.[21]

---

[20] *A Report on Recovery Progress and United States Aid,* Economic Cooperation Administration, Washington, D.C., February, 1949, p. 113. By 1952, service payments on the indebtedness of ERP countries to the United States will be well over $400 million. See *Survey of Current Business,* November, 1949, p. 14.

[21] The terms and conditions for the ECA loans which were determined in consultation with the NAC were as follows:

1. Maturity of loan—up to 35 years.
2. Interest rate of 2.5 per cent.
3. No interest to be charged for the period through June 30, 1952; no amortization of

When Congress amended the ECA Act on April 19, 1949 (Public Law 47, Eighty-first Congress, First Session), no specific amount of the authorized aid for European recovery was specified for loans, the proportion of loans being left to the decision of the administrator. The appropriation bill for foreign aid of October 6, 1949 (Public Law 327, Eighty-first Congress, First Session), however, provided $150 million specifically for ECA loans during the fiscal year 1949–1950. The appropriation bill also reduced the total amount of ECA aid for the fiscal year 1949–1950 from the amount authorized by Congress under Public Law 47 of April, 1949 ($4,280 million), to $3,778 million plus the authority to borrow up to $146 million from the Treasury for investment guarantees provided in Public Law 47. In September, 1950, Congress appropriated $2,250 million (Public Law 759, Eighty-first Congress) for ECA aid to the participating countries during the fiscal year 1950–1951 under the authority of the Foreign Economic Assistance Act of 1950. Of this amount, $500 million could be used to stimulate intra-European trade, and $350 million of the latter amount has been set aside by the ECA for the EPU. Up to January, 1951, Congress had appropriated nearly $11 billion for the ERP.

Thus far our discussion of the operations of the Recovery Program has been concerned with the division of the ECA aid and the mechanism for financing bilateral deficits in intra-European trade. To a considerable degree, these operations have involved a resolution of individual country programs through a process of bargaining rather than an integrated economic program for Western European viability as a whole. Genuine cooperative economic planning must lie in that part of the program which has to do with the liberalization of trade through the elimination of restrictions on imports and exports, the creation of a multilateral payments system, the coordination of investment programs, the coordination of transportation and power facilities, joint programs for dealing with surpluses and shortages of manpower, and other measures looking toward a better integration of the economies of Western Europe. Although the Convention for European Economic Cooperation set for the certain general objectives in these fields, including an agreement to explore the possibility of organizing customs unions, progress along these lines has been exceedingly slow. We shall discuss this subject under the heading of European economic integration in the next section.

---

principle for a minimum period through June 30, 1952, and a maximum period through June 30, 1956.

4. The inclusion in the loan agreement of a clause permitting postponement of payment of interest or principal with the agreement of both parties. (*A Report on Recovery Progress and United States Aid,* p. 112.)

American Domestic and Foreign Policies and the ERP

It will not be possible to deal in a comprehensive way with the manifold operations of the ECA. Details on procurement procedure, the making of allotments, the control of counterpart funds, offshore procurement, and the screening of the OEEC programs are given in the quarterly reports and other publications of the ECA.[22] In this section we shall confine our discussion to those aspects of the ECA operations which are closely related to American domestic and foreign economic policies. American policies tend to be reflected in ECA operations in three general ways: (1) restrictions on the use of the dollars made available by ECA; (2) the efforts to influence internal policies of the participating countries through the bilateral agreements, the counterpart funds, and special ECA missions abroad; and (3) the efforts to promote trade liberalization, currency convertibility, and economic integration in the ERP countries as a whole. We shall consider each of these three categories under separate headings, although they are in many respects interrelated.

Restrictions on the Use of ECA Dollars. Although the allocation of ECA assistance has been made on the basis of estimates of the dollar deficits of the individual participating countries which would result from their import programs, the actual use of the funds is permitted only on the submission of applications to the ECA for procurement authorization covering lists of commodities and services to be financed. These applications must be reviewed and approved by ECA before the actual procurement authorizations are granted. Except in the case of certain agricultural commodities, actual contracts are made with private American exporters since the ECA Act specifies that maximum use shall be made of private trading facilities. The first purpose of such screening and programing of American aid is to see that the funds are used to the best advantage for accomplishing the objectives of the ERP. With the exception of the British loan of 1946 and of the United States Exchange Stabilization Fund loans, this has been a standard practice in American foreign financial-assistance programs. It might be objected that the foreign-aid recipients have free dollars from current earnings to buy what they please. The ability to spend free dollars for commodities which ECA has refused to finance and to concentrate applications for ECA financing on things which ECA will finance does represent a serious weakness in the pro-

[22] For a good review of ECA operations see *A Report on Recovery Progress and United States Aid;* see also, Ellis, *op. cit.*

cedure.[23] The ECA has to some extent, however, been able to influence the over-all import programs of the ERP countries.

In screening applications for procurement with ECA funds, ECA has declared as ineligible certain luxury commodities and has employed certain price criteria. In general, ECA will not permit procurement at prices in excess of competitive market prices, and the Foreign Assistance Act of 1948 provides that bulk purchases may not be made in excess of United States market prices. This condition made it difficult for ECA to promote intra-European trade by making offshore purchases within the participating countries for delivery to other participants and was one of the factors which contributed to the decision to use the conditional-aid approach. ECA has also refused to permit procurement of industrial equipment which would in its opinion involve undesirable duplication and surplus industrial capacity, e.g., iron and steel production and oil refining, in Western Europe.

In addition to the restrictions indicated above, there are certain restrictions on the use of ECA dollars which involve the protection of American interests, whether from the standpoint of the economy as a whole, or the interests of particular industries. During the early part of the program, limitations were placed on the export of certain commodities which were in short supply in the United States. Although by 1949 restrictions on United States exports for reasons of supply shortages had been almost entirely removed, restrictions for this purpose had to be restored after the outbreak of the war in Korea in 1950. ERP countries are also required as a condition of receiving aid to prohibit the export to Eastern European and other Russian-dominated countries of commodities produced from ECA financed materials, which for reasons of national security American citizens may not export to these areas.

Another type of limitation on the use of ECA dollars has to do with the restrictions on purchases outside the United States. In part, these limitations stem from a desire on the part of ECA to encourage ERP countries to obtain imports from third countries to the largest extent possible through credits or through payment of soft currencies. On the other hand, certain limitations on offshore procurement are clearly motivated by the desire to promote American exports. The ECA Act of 1948 required that all ECA financed purchases of agricultural commodities which have been declared to be in surplus by the Secretary of Agri-

23 It is frequently fortunate that this is the case since unless the ERP countries have free dollars they would be unable to make purchases of certain agricultural and other commodities in Canada and elsewhere because of the restrictions on the use of ECA dollars.

culture must be procured in the United States.[24] Moreover, if such commodities are held by the Commodity Credit Corporation they must be acquired from CCC stocks. In addition, American flour millers were given special protection by the requirement of the ECA Act of 1948 that 25 per cent of the total flour and wheat procured with ECA funds must take the form of flour. (This minimum percentage was cut in half in 1949 and completely eliminated in 1950.) [25]

Two other special American economic interests have received special protection in the administration of the European aid program. The ECA Act of 1948 provided that at least 50 per cent of the gross tonnage of commodities procured through ECA must be carried in American vessels. Although ECA requested Congress to relax this limitation, the 1949 amendment to the ECA Act was even more favorable to American shipping as a result of a redefinition of the calculation of gross tonnage. The ECA has also sought to restrict the procurement of equipment for the building of oil refineries by ERP countries on the grounds that total world productive capacity outside the United States, including that of American companies operating overseas, would be larger than world consumption.[26] Although this action has been taken in part to preserve a European outlet for American-produced petroleum outside the United States, there is a serious economic argument against duplication of facilities in the same area, simply because one group produces dollar oil and the other produces oil which is sold for soft currencies. Negotiations with regard to this problem have been conducted by representatives of the British and American governments, but the problem appears to have solved itself as a consequence of the rapid expansion in the world demand for petroleum products.[27] In this connection it should also be pointed out that ECA will finance the procurement of petroleum from overseas sources only from American concerns.

United States Influence over Internal Policies of ERP Countries. In the administration of its foreign-aid program, the United States govern-

[24] The administration of this policy was modified to permit larger United Kingdom purchases of agricultural commodities from Canada. See "Text of Anglo-American–Canadian Financial Talks," *The New York Times,* Sept. 13, 1949.

[25] An amendment to the ECA Act of 1950 which would have required that $1 billion of the authorized ECA aid be made available wholly in the form of United States surplus agricultural commodities was defeated in the House of Representatives by a narrow margin.

[26] See the testimony of Dr. Bransky, ECA Petroleum Branch, in the Hearings before House Special Subcommittee on Small Business, 81st Congress, 1st Session, pursuant to House Resolution 22, Part 2, Nov. 30, 1949, pp. 521*ff*.

[27] See Horst Mendershausen, *Dollar Shortage and Oil Surplus in 1949–50,* Princeton University Press, Princeton, N.J., 1950.

ment has not as a general principle sought to dictate the form of social and economic organization of the recipient country. For example, in spite of the desires of some congressmen, it has not attempted to interfere with the nationalization of British industry or to restrain independent countries from embarking on programs of socialization. It has of course taken a definite stand against political communism and interferences with civil liberties and democratic processes and has in the case of Greece and Korea taken strong measures to require governments to hold free elections and adopt representative governments. Nevertheless, the ECA and other agencies responsible for the administration of United States foreign-assistance programs have certain legislative responsibilities to see that United States funds are wisely employed toward the achievement of the economic goals which the programs were intended to serve. These responsibilities involve a degree of interference with the internal policies of other countries and inevitably reflect the economic and social philosophy of this country.

Mention has already been made of the legislative requirement to the effect that all countries receiving ECA aid must conclude bilateral agreements with the United States, which deal in part with the internal policies of the recipient countries. These bilateral agreements, although somewhat general in character, provide for such matters as the establishment of a valid rate of exchange, balancing the governmental budget, the maintenance of monetary and financial stability, the removal of barriers to private trade with other countries, the elimination of restraints on competition and of monopolistic practices, and consultation with American officials with respect to the details of their economic programs.[28] ECA representatives abroad frequently consult the representatives of the ERP countries and of the OEEC with respect to these matters. Although caution had to be observed in discussing questions of national interest with foreign officials, American officials have been able to exert considerable influence in certain fields.

The legislative requirements that ERP countries must deposit in special accounts an equivalent value of their own local currency upon the receipt of United States grants provides a more direct means of influencing the internal policies of ERP countries. These local-currency counterpart funds may be used only for certain specific purposes and upon agreement with the ECA. Except for the 5 per cent set aside for use by the United States for administrative expenses and the purchase of strategic materials, these local-currency funds are, to the extent consistent with

[28] See, for example, the "Economic Cooperation Agreement between the United States of America and Italy," *First Report to Congress of the Economic Cooperation Administration*, October, 1948, Appendix I.

the internal financial stability of the country, available for productive investment, the exploration and development of new resources, and for other purposes approved by ECA. Another important use of the local-currency counterpart funds relates to the financing of intra-European trade under the conditional-aid system already described.

One of the most important functions to be served by the counterpart funds is to immobilize, at least for a time, the proceeds from the sale of ECA commodities supplied on a grant basis. Unless offset by an expansion of purchasing power somewhere else in the country, the placing of the sale proceeds in the counterpart fund will have the same effect as the normal financing of an import surplus through the sale of foreign exchange to the public by the banking system in exchange for a reduction in deposit liabilities. The policy of the NAC [29] in advising ECA on the handling of requests by ERP countries for the use of the counterpart funds is that such funds should

> be released for debt retirement and for investment purposes only where the governments concerned have recommended such releases in conjunction with a financial program aimed at the achievement of monetary and financial stability. In several instances it has been necessary for the Council to recommend approval of these releases at the outset of a program of reforms. But it has recommended that subsequent releases be made contingent upon a demonstration of effective implementation of the reform measures.

Since the deflationary effects of the counterpart funds can be offset by other means such as credit expansion and budgetary deficits, policies with respect to their use must take into consideration the general monetary and financial program of the country concerned. Thus it would do little good to insist on the noninflationary use of counterpart funds if the ERP country simply expanded purchasing power by some other means. In practice, the counterpart-funds arrangement has given ECA an opportunity to comment on the general fiscal and monetary policies of the aid recipients. Because of the political importance of balanced budgets and of preventing further increases in the quantity of money, participating countries have been eager to obtain approval for the release of these funds from ECA. This situation has provided an opportunity for the ECA and the NAC to influence internal financial policies of the participating countries and frequently to strengthen the hands of governments in inducing legislatures to adopt financial reforms. Of the $8.2 billion paid into local-currency accounts as of March 31, 1951, about $5.8 billion had been

[29] *National Advisory Council on International Monetary and Financial Problems, Semiannual Report to the President and to the Congress, for the Period April 1 to September 30, 1948,* pp. 19–20.

approved for use by the participating countries. Of this amount, about $2 billion was approved for debt retirement, another $3 billion for the promotion of production, and the remainder for a variety of purposes including public works and relief projects.[30]

In addition to working for internal financial reforms and seeking to bring about a more rational employment of European resources through screening industrial projects financed by ECA funds, ECA has endeavored to change the external trading practices of the participating countries by pressing for the elimination of quantitative import restrictions, dual pricing for internal and external trade, and currency barriers to intra-European trade. ECA missions have also encouraged some participating countries to devalue their exchange rates and to expand their dollar earnings through dollar export drives and programs for increasing the productivity of their export industries. These efforts, to the extent that they are successful, undoubtedly influence the basic character of the European economies since they are inconsistent with systems of rigid internal economic controls and autarchic policies which have characterized most European countries since the war.

On the other hand, the Recovery Program has to a considerable extent been a factor in promoting government planning and economic controls. The necessity for governmental control over the use of ECA funds and of the local-currency counterpart funds, the development of long-range recovery programs involving the major industries of the participating countries, and the programing of external trade to be financed directly or indirectly by ECA have tended to enlarge the scope of governments in economic affairs. It might well be argued that, had the United States wanted to promote a maximum of free trade and private enterprise and a minimum of government interference, it should have provided its assistance by channeling American dollars into free foreign-exchange markets in ERP countries and frowned on all government planning and controls.[31] But the time was too short and the funds too limited for a recovery program of this kind. The American government and Congress have favored a program which would assure that United States aid would accomplish certain specific objectives within a relatively short period of time. To this extent therefore, we have fostered government planning and controls abroad while at the same time professing adherence to the prin-

30 For data on use of counterpart funds, see *Twelfth Report to Congress of the Economic Cooperation Administration for Quarter Ended March 31, 1951*, p. 138.

31 Much the same thing can be said regarding United States government foreign lending which has taken the form of tied loans to governments for carefully controlled purposes.

ciples of free enterprise and a minimum of governmental planning and interference both for ourselves and for the world at large.

European Economic Integration. One of the most important American policy objectives with respect to Western Europe during the postwar period has been that of fostering European integration—political, military and economic.[32] All three types of integration are closely interrelated, and the motives behind United States promotion of economic integration are in part related to the desire for political and military integration, while the desire for political integration is in part prompted by its necessity as a counterpart to the realization of the economic benefits of economic integration. We may summarize the motives for America's promotion of European integration as follows:

1. It is generally believed that a sound recovery in Western Europe will be impossible without a substantial degree of economic integration. The political divisions of Europe represent highly uneconomic units for modern states which tend toward economic controls and planning from a national point of view. Western Europe cannot maintain high living standards and restore its competitive position in the world without an economical allocation of its resources from the standpoint of the area as a whole, which implies the development of a single market for commodities, joint planning of investment, coordination of transportation and power, etc.

2. The political stability and external security of Western Europe depends upon a high degree of political integration and the coordination of military defense. Economic integration is essential to military coordination and strength and to political stability and cooperation.

3. Western Germany must be made strong economically as a condition for the economic recovery and the military strength of Western Europe. On the other hand, Germany must not again be in a position of political and economic domination of this area. A powerful independent Germany could play one country off against the other and quickly achieve political domination. The best solution to this problem is a politically and economically integrated Western Europe in which the German economy can be merged with that of Western Europe as a whole.

4. It is believed that the development of a single market for Western Europe's 250 million people will restore competition in the area, reduce costs, and thereby

[32] See, for example, ECA Administrator Paul G. Hoffman's address to the Council of the OEEC in Paris on Oct. 31, 1949, printed in *The New York Times,* Nov. 1, 1949. This policy objective was also expressed in the Fulbright Resolution adopted by Congress in March, 1949, which declared that "Congress favors the creation of a United States of Europe within the framework of the United Nations," and the 1949 ECA Act, which declares it to be "the policy of the people of the United States to encourage the unification of Europe." For a discussion of American and European objectives for European integration, see *Major Problems of United States Foreign Policy, 1949–1950,* The Brookings Institution, Washington, D.C., 1949, pp. 403–472.

help to improve the competitive position of the area vis-à-vis the rest of the world and generally promote free competitive enterprise and the eventual restoration of world-wide multilateral trade.

The term "economic integration" has been used rather loosely in expressions of policy in the United States and abroad, to cover a variety of meanings.[33] Without attempting to canvas what various spokesmen have meant by the term, we shall define economic integration as *an arrangement between sovereign states aimed at securing the same distribution of resources in the light of the total consumer and investment demand as might take place if the several states were combined into one political and economic unit.* There are in general two roads toward this goal. First, there can be an elimination of all barriers to the free movement of trade, capital, and manpower among the nations to be integrated. Thus the formation of customs unions coupled with freedom of movement of labor, capital, and business enterprise would secure effective economic integration among countries characterized by a maximum of free enterprise and a minimum of governmental ownership and control. The second path to economic integration lies in the coordination or centralization of governmental controls and planning among countries largely characterized by governmental intervention and state ownership.[34]

One of the obstacles to the economic integration of Western Europe is the fact that not only are the economies neither wholly controlled nor wholly free, but they are characterized by varying degrees of freedom and control. Thus Belgium's economy is relatively free from governmental intervention, while the British economy is characterized by a substantial amount of state trading, government ownership and controls over production, investment, and consumption exercised by both the government and powerful trade associations.

Except for cooperation in the OEEC in connection with the programing of imports, the United States has largely stressed those aspects of European economic integration which relate to the elimination of barriers to the free flow of intra-European trade. Thus ECA Administrator Hoffman's speech before the Council of the OEEC on October 31, 1949, stressed the elimination of trade and currency restrictions and the coordination of monetary and fiscal policies necessary to permit balance-

[33] The following discussion is based on an article by Raymond F. Mikesell, "Economic Integration of Sovereign States," in *Money, Trade and Economic Growth*, Macmillan, New York, 1951.

[34] Frequently, controls are exercised by trade associations operating with or without government participation. Under these conditions, integration could be achieved by the elimination of private cartels and the establishment of intergovernmental arrangements.

of-payments equilibrium among the participating nations. This approach, which proposes that Western Europe become a great free trading area similar to that encompassed by the 48 American states, fails to take into account the fundamental economic and political structure of the countries of Western Europe. The ERP countries can move along this road only a short distance unless they also make progress in the coordination of the controlled sectors of their economies, including the fiscal operations of the national governments. Although the trade-liberalization program has been a significant factor in expanding intra-European trade, it has not taken Western Europe very far in the direction of a single trading area. Even with a considerable reduction in import quotas with respect to private trade, the trade of the state-trading monopolies would not be affected.[35]

It is significant that one of the most spectacular proposals in the direction of European economic integration is the French plan for pooling the coal and steel industries of the ERP countries.[36] This scheme, which has had the support of the United States government, proposes to place Western Europe's coal and steel industries under a joint authority which will determine common production, investment, price, and marketing policies. The political implications of such a proposal are obvious since the mobilization of these basic industries is the *sine qua non* of preparing for modern warfare. But the implications for economic integration are also of fundamental significance since the French proposal may provide a pattern for integration in the controlled sectors of the Western European economies. It was useless to attempt to bring about free trade and a single market in coal and steel as long as these industries were operated in response to decisions based on national political and economic policies. But if these industries, whether nationalized or controlled by private associations under close governmental direction, are brought under a joint Western European authority, trade barriers, dual pricing, and restrictive measures of all kinds imposed by individual governments could be quickly swept away. Although there are dangers in unified economic authorities in any field, the results are likely to be a more rational allocation of resources than would be achieved by national economic authorities operating independently and at cross-purposes with one another.

[35] Government trading accounts for 27 per cent of all British and 23 per cent of all French imports from other participating countries. *Seventh Report to Congress of the Economic Cooperation Administration,* May, 1950, p. 11.

[36] For text of the French announcement, see *The New York Times,* May 11, 1950; see also *Ninth Report to Congress of the Economic Cooperation Administration,* November, 1950, pp. 34–35.

The establishment of joint or centralized authorities for the controlled sectors of the economies of the ERP countries will, in the absence of a large measure of political unification, be a slow and painful process. Not only do the national governments maintain a large number of direct controls over production, investment, and internal and external trade, but the national budgets represent a substantial percentage of the national income of the participating countries.[37] The level and pattern of government revenues and expenditures have an exceedingly important influence on the internal and external trade, production, and allocation of resources of the individual countries. In addition, monetary, banking, and foreign-exchange policies are powerful instruments for the determination of the patterns of activity in the countries. Effective integration of the economies of the participating countries must involve close coordination of all these instruments of national control.

A full discussion of the problems involved in Western European economic integration is beyond the scope of this book, and we can do little more than point up the complexities and difficulties for the realization of a goal which is not only a fundamental objective of the United States but an aspiration of a large proportion of the Western European peoples themselves.[38] In dealing with measures for economic integration of sovereign states, account must be taken of the following fundamental national policies and interests:

1. Freedom to undertake governmental expenditures without limit in time of national emergency natural or man-made.

2. The universal policy of preventing widespread unemployment and low levels of business activity.

3. The policy of promoting economic development and a steady rise in living standards. For example, no government is likely to agree to becoming an essentially agrarian area or to arrest its industrial development in favor of a

---

[37] Government expenditures as a percentage of national income in 1948:

Belgium	32.4	Norway	28.1
France	31.7	Sweden	21.7
Italy	26.7	United Kingdom	34.6
Netherlands	36.4		

SOURCE: *Economic Survey of Europe in 1948*, Economic Commission for Europe, Geneva, 1949, p. 40.

[38] According to the results of a public-opinion poll announced by Major General William J. Donovan, Chairman of the American Committee on United Europe, and by Paul-Henri Spaak, President of the Consultative Assembly of the Council of Europe, a majority of the people of Norway, the Netherlands, France, Italy, and Western Germany favored the creation of a European political and economic union. This announcement was made to the press on May 4, 1950.

more rapid industrialization of some other area perhaps better suited to such development.

4. The unwillingness of governments to tolerate a sudden impoverishment of any major industry. A government might, however, agree to a gradual adjustment of the relative position of an industry in return for the opportunity to build up some other industry.

5. The unwillingness of governments to agree to a fundamental change in their social welfare and income and wealth-distribution programs or to their programs for the ownership and control of the means of production. Such policies have their roots in the political and social fabric of the nation and cannot be changed without a social and political revolution.

6. The opposition of governments to economic programs which would impair their political security or their political ties with other nations. Thus, for example, it is unlikely that Britain would enter into any arrangement which seriously affected her political relations with other members of the British Commonwealth.

Unless the sovereignties of the individual participating countries are merged under a single government for Western Europe, existing national governments are not likely to relinquish any of their fundamental responsibilities to their own people and to other countries with which they have close political and economic ties. Within these limitations, however, gradual progress can be made along the following lines:

1. The EPU should be retained after 1952, but it should be gradually modified so as to permit the financing of continuing surpluses and deficits of individual members with the other EPU members as a group, along the lines suggested in Chap. 11. True economic integration is not achieved by forcing a balance between each member of the integrated region and the rest of the region.[39]

2. There should be a gradual reduction of restrictions on private trade and the establishment of joint authorities for controlling production and trade in commodities subject to state trading or in which governments have an important national interest. Trade regulation cannot be separated from the control of production and investment in commodities now subject to control for reasons other than the protection of the balance of payments. Where trade restrictions are imposed for balance-of-payments reasons, the character of the restrictions should be subjected to review by joint boards.

3. Each of the major industries should be brought under the control of a joint authority for the purpose of coordinating governmental policies with respect to investment, production, pricing and trade, in so far as the governments themselves determine the policies of these industries or they are determined by associations of private firms.

4. There should be established a Western European monetary and financial

[39] For example, such a balance does not exist among the various regions of the United States. See P. C. Hartland, "Inter-regional Payments Compared with International Payments," *Quarterly Journal of Economics*, August, 1949, pp. 392–407.

commission to review and make recommendations with respect to the fiscal, monetary, credit, and foreign-exchange policies of the participating governments.

5. Governments should agree to permit the maximum mobility of labor, capital, and business enterprise among the participating countries.

6. Joint authorities in the fields of transportation, electric power, and other utilities should be established.

The above suggestions would not achieve complete integration for Western Europe, but they would go as far in that direction as is possible for sovereign states. The United States could encourage this process in several important ways: (1) This country should provide support through the Monetary Fund and perhaps directly in the form of a stabilization loan or otherwise for the continued functioning of an adequate system of intra-European payments. (2) The United States could promote industrial coordination in Western Europe through a mutual-defense program which would include the coordination of the vital defense industries for supplying the common defense needs of the Atlantic Treaty forces. (3) The United States could make loans and grants for the development of European industries as a part of the Mutual Defense Assistance Program. Thus the ERP might be followed by a program of industrial mobilization for defense in which American assistance would be channeled through and screened by an organization of the participating countries established for carrying out a program of economic integration.

CHAPTER 16

The Realization of United States Objectives for Western Europe

THE DETERMINATION of economic goals and of the conditions for realizing them through the provision of financial assistance and other measures is far from being an exact science. In spite of the elaborate estimates of requirements and projections of performance which have been carried on by the Organization for European Economic Cooperation and the Economic Cooperation Administration, results have frequently been wide of expectations. It will not be the author's purpose to provide a comprehensive analysis of these goals and projections nor to develop detailed projections of his own for the future under present circumstances of rapidly moving events. Some discussion of the determination of the economic goals of the OEEC and of the ECA will, however, reveal important policy decisions.

The OEEC Interim Report

In the summer of 1948, the OEEC asked each of the participating countries to submit a plan of action by means of which it intended to maintain its economy in 1952–1953 without extraordinary assistance, assuming a continuation of ECA until the middle of 1952. The individual country submissions were analyzed by the OEEC, and the results, together with the individual country submissions, were published in December, 1948.[1] The Interim Report set forth the commodity production and the trade and balance-of-payments goals for the participating countries for 1948–1949, 1949–1950, and 1952–1953. The long-term production programs called for an increase in industrial production by 1952–1953 to approximately 30 per cent above the prewar level or at an annual rate of increase of about 6 per cent for the 4-year period.[2] In the case of agricultural production, which was still well below prewar levels at the beginning of the Recovery Program, the participating country programs

[1] *Interim Report on the European Recovery Programme,* Organization for European Economic Cooperation, Paris, Vols. I and II, Dec. 30, 1948.
[2] *Ibid.,* Vol. I, pp. 24–25.

called for a level about 15 per cent above prewar and a level of 25 to 40 per cent higher than the 1948–1949 season, a year of good harvests, or 40 to 80 per cent above the 1947–1948 season, a year of poor harvests.[3] In terms of gross national product, the programs envisaged for Western Europe as a whole a 20 per cent increase over the 1938 level by 1952–1953 and 35 per cent over the 1947 level.[4] The realization of these production goals would mean a level of consumption in 1952–1953 slightly below the 1938 level but well above the level of 1948.[5] In evaluating the individual country programs, however, the OEEC Council considered them to be somewhat overoptimistic and concluded that the production and consumption goals are not likely to be fully realized by 1952–1953.[6]

Table 13 shows the projected balances of trade by areas of the OEEC countries as derived from their long-range national programs for viability in 1952–1953. Although this projection has little more than historical significance today, it does reveal certain policy decisions which went into the planning. Imports from North and Central America were to be reduced from $7.3 billion in 1947 to $3.8 billion in 1952–1953, or $0.3 billion less than imports from this area in 1938. Exports to North and Central America, on the other hand, were to be increased from $1.05 billion in 1947 to $2.1 billion in 1952–1953, or by about a third larger than the level of exports to this area in 1938. Yet by 1952–1953 real national income in the United States is likely to be nearly double that of 1938,[7] and in addition, United States tariffs are lower than they were in 1938. It is evident, therefore, that the OEEC countries planned a major shift in their imports from the United States to other areas and to home production. It will also be noted that the volume of imports from all areas projected for 1952–1953 was actually less than in 1938.

The national programs of the participating countries provided for imports of $12.8 billion in 1952–1953 and for exports of $10.6 billion and net invisible earnings of $1.4 billion, leaving an uncovered deficit of

[3] *Ibid.,* p. 32.

[4] *Ibid.,* p. 93.

[5] *Ibid.,* pp. 103–105. Population in Western Europe in 1952–1953 will be 9 per cent above that of 1938.

[6] The OEEC Council concluded that consumption levels in 1952–1953 will be 5 to 10 per cent above the 1948 level, but somewhat less than the 1938 level, assuming the continuation of ECA assistance until mid-1952. *Ibid.,* pp. 103–104.

[7] Dr. Howard Ellis has pointed out that if the United States were to import an amount of goods from Western Europe equal to the same percentage of our 1948 gross national product which United States imports from Western Europe in 1928 bore to the 1928 GNP, United States imports from this area would have been $3 billion in 1948. Howard S. Ellis, *The Economics of Freedom,* Harper, New York, 1950, p. 73.

Table 13. OEEC Countries Trade with the Outside World
(Other Than Dependent Overseas Territories)

(In billions of dollars, 1948–1949 prices)

Countries	1938		1947		1952–1953 production	
	Exports	Imports	Exports	Imports	Exports	Imports
North and Central America......	$1.45	$ 4.1	$1.05	$ 7.3	$ 2.1	$ 3.8
South America................	1.0	1.7	0.75	1.7	2.0	2.1
Nonparticipating sterling area....	1.9	2.9	2.0	2.0	3.1	3.3
Eastern Europe................	2.5	3.0	0.75	0.9	2.0	2.2
Other countries................	1.1	1.3	0.85	0.6	1.4	1.4
Total......................	$7.95	$13.0	$5.4	$12.5	$10.6	$12.8

SOURCE: *Interim Report on the European Recovery Programme,* Organization for European Economic Cooperation, Vol. I, Paris, Dec. 30, 1948, p. 61.

$0.8 billion.[8] The realization of this projected balance of payments would mean substantial external balance for the European Recovery Program countries in the sense of their being able to achieve the goals of the programs since they could certainly count on some United States foreign investment and loans from the International Bank and some drawings from the International Monetary Fund (IMF) if the funds are needed for short-term purposes. In addition, the United States was expected to continue to provide a certain amount of extraordinary assistance to individual ERP countries which may not have attained a condition of viability by 1952, e.g., Germany, Austria, and Greece. The OEEC Council in its Interim Report was, however, quite skeptical of the likelihood of achieving these balance-of-payments goals. In fact, the Interim Report stated that "it is doubtful whether exports can exceed say $8.5 billion or net invisible earnings $1.3 billion. Western Europe would then be able to afford only $9.8 billion worth of imports—little more than three-quarters of the imports proposed in the national programs." [9]

The conclusion of the Interim Report was that on the most favorable assumptions Western Europe would be able to buy only 85 to 90 per cent of the volume of imports programed for 1952–1953, or a reduction of

[8] *Interim Report on the European Recovery Programme,* Vol. I, p. 72.
[9] *Ibid.,* p. 73.

about $1½ billion. Further reductions might occur in the event that supplies are not available in the sterling area, Eastern Europe, and the Far East. The Interim Report concluded therefore that the long-range programs submitted by the participating countries did not appear to provide a reasonable basis for Western European viability after 1952 at consumption standards comparable to prewar levels. The Interim Report recommended the following actions on the part of the participating countries as essential to the realization of the recovery goals: (1) The acceleration of export drives, increasing the competitive position of European exports; (2) the encouragement of tourism; (3) the expansion of shipping earnings; (4) the encouragement of primary production at home and in other areas, including an expansion of European agriculture; and (5) an increase in intra-European trade and other forms of cooperation.[10]

The Outlook at the End of 1950

In certain respects, the somewhat gloomy predictions of the Interim Report have proved to be unfounded. By the middle of 1950, it appeared that many of the ERP goals were going to be realized perhaps, in some cases, well ahead of mid-1952. By June, 1950, industrial production in the ERP countries had reached 128 per cent of prewar, and exports to the rest of the world were 28 per cent above 1938. Western Europe's over-all current-account deficit had declined from $7.4 billion in 1947 to less than $3 billion in the period 1949–1950. By 1949–1950 the gold and dollar deficit on current account had also been reduced to well under $3 billion.[11] Since ERP countries had received $4 billion in American aid during 1949–1950, they were able to increase their gold and dollar reserves by $2.1 billion between September, 1949, and September, 1950, of which about two-thirds was accounted for by the United Kingdom. Merchandise imports of the ERP countries from the United States declined from $5.7 billion in 1947 to about $3.4 billion in 1950. There was, however, only a modest increase in merchandise exports to the United States from $843 million in 1947 to $1.3 billion in 1950.

These over-all figures conceal many important differences in the positions of individual ERP countries. While in the second quarter of 1950 industrial production in Sweden was 169 per cent of prewar and in Britain 149 per cent, production in Western Germany was less than pre-

[10] *Ibid.,* pp. 79–80.

[11] In the second half of 1950, the current-account deficit of the ERP countries and their dependencies with the United States had fallen to an annual rate of less than $1.2 billion as compared with $5.8 billion in 1947. *Survey of Current Business,* March, 1951.

war and in Italy and Greece 109 per cent and 119 per cent of 1938,[12] respectively. Similar differences existed in the recovery of exports in the second quarter of 1950, with Britain leading with exports at 165 per cent of the 1938 volume, and France, 160 per cent, while Western Germany (78 per cent) and Italy (99 per cent) were exporting less than prewar.[13] It should be said in the case of Germany that the 1950 levels of production and exports represent a remarkable improvement over the levels of 1947 when they were only 34 and 8 per cent, respectively, of the 1938 volume.

The difference in the degree of progress toward independence of dollar aid between the ERP countries is even more striking. In 1950 the United Kingdom's current account with the United States was nearly balanced, while the sterling area as a whole had a surplus on current account with the United States of over $300 million. Since Britain has been able greatly to reduce her gold and dollar payments to other nonsterling-area countries, Britain's gold and dollar reserves increased by more than her ERP aid during 1950.[14] The vast bulk of the current-account deficit of the ERP countries with the United States during 1950 was accounted for by the Continental countries of Western Europe. Unlike Britain, many of these countries do not have dependent territories or countries in associated monetary areas through which they may earn dollars.

Since Britain is by far the largest gold and dollar earner among the ERP countries, it was considered desirable for the sterling area to have a deficit with the other ERP countries and permit the latter to earn some gold and dollars multilaterally. This possibility will depend in part upon the extent to which the sterling area liberalizes its imports from Western Europe and upon the competitive position of Western Europe's exports. The results of the operations of the European Payments Union during 1950, however, indicated a substantial surplus position for the United Kingdom, thereby enabling her to receive gold payments from the other ERP countries.[15]

While it is too early at the time of writing to discern the impact of the Korean war on the position of the ERP countries, certain trends may

[12] *Ninth Report to Congress of the Economic Cooperation Administration,* November, 1950, p. 109.

[13] *Ibid.,* p. 98.

[14] Dollar earnings of Malaya and Ceylon and the gold output of South Africa have contributed heavily to the British gold and dollar reserves. After the devaluation of September, 1949, British reserves rose from $1.4 billion to $3.3 billion at the end of December, 1950.

[15] *International Finance News Survey,* Jan. 12, 1951, p. 205. In the second quarter of 1951, Britain developed a deficit with the European Payments Union, and the gold and dollar surplus of the sterling area decreased sharply.

be noted. First of all, there has been a rapid rise in United States prices which, unless offset by an increase in United States imports from Western Europe, will mean an increase in the latter's current-account deficit with the United States. This would occur even if the prices of European exports to the United States rose by the same percentage as our own; but the increase in the deficit is likely to be further enhanced by the fact that a considerable portion of Europe's imports from the United States are agricultural commodities, the prices of which are likely to experience the greatest rise. On the other hand, the rise in United States imports has been largely concentrated in food products and raw materials. The increased United States demand for raw materials plus the rapid rise in raw-material prices has substantially improved the dollar position of the non-European sterling area, thereby offsetting the deterioration of Britain's own current-account position with the United States and Canada resulting from the rise in prices in the dollar area.[16] To a lesser extent, certain other ERP countries, mainly the Netherlands, and to a minor degree France, Belgium, and Portugal, have gained additional dollars through territories or countries associated with them in the same monetary area, as a result of the increase in the value of United States raw-material imports. On the other hand, Germany, Italy, Switzerland, Austria, and the Scandinavian countries stand to lose as a result of the rise in United States prices. The only way that this loss could be offset would be for these countries to be able to take advantage of the large demand for United States manufactures, which America's own industries may not be able to fill because of defense orders, by marketing industrial products in the United States and in Latin America and other countries where they may be able to earn dollars. As was pointed out above, however, all the countries of Western Europe will find it more difficult to achieve a surplus with the raw-material-producing countries because of the rise in raw-material prices. By the summer of 1951, the economic position of the ERP countries showed signs of deteriorating under the double impact of higher defense expenditures and higher import prices.

The Realization of the Pre-Korean Objectives

Prior to the outbreak of the war in Korea in the summer of 1950 and of the decision to promote a rapid expansion of the military forces of the members of the Atlantic Pact, it appeared that the economic objectives

[16] One effect of the rise in world raw-material prices has been to increase the value of Britain's imports from the rest of the sterling area, with a consequent increase in the external holdings of sterling balances. Hence, while Britain's dollar reserves increased substantially during 1950, her sterling indebtedness also rose.

of the Marshall program would be largely realized. Except in the case of a few countries, *e.g.,* Austria and Greece, most ERP countries were rapidly expanding their productive capacities to the point where they would not require additional net resources to maintain living standards at politically tolerable levels. There were of course some factors which remained in doubt. Viability required not only the ability to produce but the ability to find markets and to earn sufficient dollars or dollar-convertible currencies with which to pay for essential imports from the dollar area. Whether or not most ERP countries would need additional United States assistance after 1952 appeared to depend upon (1) their ability to convert surpluses with nondollar countries into dollars, (2) their ability to switch from dollar to nondollar sources of supply, (3) their ability to expand exports to the dollar area, and (4) the degree of deterioration in their terms of trade. Given the continued high level of United States demand for imports, however, the outlook for the realization of these basic considerations appeared, in the light of conditions in June, 1950, to be a favorable one.[17]

While the economic results of the Marshall program are tangible and far easier to measure than the realization of its political objectives, there has undoubtedly been a shift in the political balance in the Marshall Plan countries since the start of the program. American observers in Europe find morale far higher than in 1947, and Western European governments have shown a willingness to cooperate in a program of mutual defense. While communism is still strong in Italy and France, there has been a notable weakening of Communist strength in Western European parliaments generally.[18] Without the ERP program, there would have been neither the economic nor the political and psychological basis for the rearming of Western Europe under the Mutual Defense Assistance Program.

The decision to promote a rapid expansion of the military forces of the Western European members of the Atlantic Pact following the outbreak of war in Korea has added a new and perhaps overriding objective to America's program for Western Europe. The pre-Korean objective of

[17] ECA aid to Britain was suspended in December, 1950.

[18] Paul Hoffman has pointed out that, in the Netherlands, Communist seats in the provincial assemblies have declined from 10 per cent in 1946 to 5 per cent in 1950; in Denmark, the Communists won 12 per cent of the popular vote in 1945 and only 4 per cent in the 1950 elections; in Belgium, Communist strength in parliament dropped from 17 per cent to 10 between 1947 and 1950; and in Norway, Communist seats in parliament have fallen to zero. Paul Hoffman, "Most Courageous," *Life,* Feb. 5, 1951. See also, Calvin B. Hoover, "Foreign Economic Aid and Communism," *Journal of Political Economy,* February, 1951, pp. 1–13.

viability for the ERP countries by mid-1952 no longer has significance in the context of the new goals and the economic requirements for realizing them. Since military and economic strength and political stability are all closely interrelated and interdependent, it will be necessary to combine these objectives into a single comprehensive program in the future. We shall now turn to a discussion of the Mutual Defense Assistance Program.

The Mutual Defense Assistance Program

We have seen that, in the development of the Truman Doctrine, foreign economic assistance and military aid have been closely allied. The Greek-Turkish aid program, the several programs for aid to China,[19] and United States assistance to Korea [20] have involved a combination of economic and military assistance. These countries have been subject to or under the immediate threat of Russian or Communist-inspired aggression, and the United States' assistance has been of an emergency character. The North Atlantic Treaty of April 14, 1949, opened the way for a military program based on a long-range plan for the common defense of the 12 North Atlantic Treaty nations.[21] Since all these countries except Canada were already receiving grant assistance under the ERP, they were obviously not in a position to meet the dollar cost of a substantially expanded defense program. The Mutual Defense Assistance Act of 1949, therefore, authorized the extension of a billion dollars in grant aid to be supplied

[19] The Foreign Economic Assistance Act of 1948 provided for both military and economic assistance to China; and provision was made for the continuation of such assistance in the Foreign Assistance Act of 1949. Economic assistance in the general area of China (including Formosa) was authorized in the Foreign Economic Assistance Act of 1950 (Public Law 535, 81st Congress, 2d Session, approved June 5, 1950) out of the $94 million of unobligated funds originally appropriated by Public Law 793, 80th Congress, 2d Session. The Mutual Defense Assistance Act of 1949 (Public Law 329, 81st Congress, 1st Session, approved Oct. 6, 1949) authorized the expenditure of $75 million for military assistance to the general area of China.

[20] Since 1945 when United States troops occupied South Korea, the United States has extended various types of military and civilian economic assistance to the area. In February, 1950, Congress approved $120 million for economic assistance to Korea (Far Eastern Economic Assistance Act of 1950) and the Foreign Economic Assistance Act of 1950 authorized an additional $100 million of assistance for Korea for the fiscal year ending June 30, 1951. Military assistance to Korea was provided under the Mutual Defense Assistance Act of 1949.

[21] The North Atlantic Treaty signatory nations are Belgium, Canada, Denmark, France, Great Britain, Ireland, Italy, Luxemburg, the Netherlands, Norway, Portugal, and the United States. For background discussion of the Atlantic Pact, see Halford L. Hoskins, *The Atlantic Pact*, Public Affairs Press, Washington, D.C., 1949.

in connection with a program of integrated defense for the North Atlantic area.[22]

On June 1, 1950, the President asked Congress for an additional $1,223 million to carry out the Military Defense Assistance Program during the fiscal year ending June 30, 1951.[23] Following the outbreak of war in Korea, the President asked Congress for an additional $4 billion or $5,223 million in all for foreign-defense aid for the fiscal year ending 1951. Congress quickly appropriated these additional amounts, of which $4.5 billion was allocated for the North Atlantic Treaty countries and the remainder to other areas.[24]

Three types of assistance were authorized under the 1949 Act: (1) military equipment and materials from existing military stocks or new production; (2) technical training and assistance in connection with the use of military supplies; (3) machine tools, materials and components, and technical assistance which would enable the recipients to increase their production of military supplies. No provision was made for the indirect foreign-exchange or local-currency costs of the expanded defense program of these countries. Depending upon the size of the country programs, these costs could become so significant as to endanger the recovery of certain of the ERP countries. Local production and man power devoted to defense will, in the absence of unemployed resources, divert production from export markets and home consumption. Large military programs will also add to the difficulties of maintaining balanced national budgets and reducing inflationary pressure.

At the time of writing it had not been determined whether or not economic assistance for additional military production in Western Europe (apart from military end-use items supplied directly by the United States) will be administered separately from economic assistance for the last year of the Marshall program or by the same organization. Regardless of the type of administrative machinery in operation, the two types of assistance are closely interrelated. This applies particularly to the $475 million of

[22] For a discussion of the Mutual Defense Assistance Program, see *First Semi-annual Report on the Mutual Assistance Program*, House Document 613, 81st Congress, 2d Session; see also *The Military Assistance Program*, Department of State, July, 1949. In addition to authorizing a billion dollars in grants for arms and the equipment for producing them to the North Atlantic Treaty powers, the Mutual Defense Assistance Act of 1949 authorized an additional $211,370,990 for Greek-Turkish aid; $27,690,000 for military assistance to Iran, Korea, and the Philippines; and $75,000,000 as an emergency fund for the President, to be used in the general area of China. These funds were appropriated under Public Law 430 (81st Congress, 1st Session), Oct. 28, 1949.

[23] *First Semi-annual Report on the Mutual Defense Assistance Program*, pp. 50–52.

[24] Public Law 759, 81st Congress, 2d Session, Sept. 6, 1950, and H.R. 9526, as amended, Sept. 23, 1950.

the Mutual Defense Assistance allocated for financing raw materials and industrial equipment for additional military production in Western Europe. A country needs steel not only to produce tanks and guns but also for a whole range of commodities needed for civilian use and for export. No calculation of how much a country requires in the way of materials can be made apart from an evaluation of its entire economic situation, including its balance of payments. Such an evaluation inevitably involves a consideration of living standards and their relationship to political stability.

It may also be noted that, whereas the Mutual Defense Assistance Act does not permit the direct payment of dollars to countries to offset the indirect exchange costs of the expanded defense program, purchases with dollars may be made for materials in one Atlantic Pact country for delivery to another. Since dollar-financed transfers of materials destined for military production will be only a part of the total of such transfers, it is necessary to decide which countries are going to receive these off-shore purchase dollars. Such decisions could be made in accordance with the dollar needs of the exporting countries.

A common defense program has certain important implications for the future foreign economic policies of the United States and other nations, particularly if the danger of external aggression continues to grow. Modern defense, like modern warfare, involves the organization of the entire economy, and the integrated defense of a region compromising a number of states can only mean the mobilization of the common resources of the entire region. During World War II, resources for military and civilian use were allocated on the basis of requirements derived from a joint program, and lend-lease was substituted for distribution under the price system. The decision that England should produce more bombers and less Austin cars for export meant that she received her wheat and cotton on a grant basis from the United States. Under a joint defense program, decisions as to whether France should build up a larger military establishment than she can now afford with her own resources, or that Britain should produce more planes at the expense of her exports, must be made from the standpoint of optimum resource allocation for the region as a whole for the realization of the common objective. From a budgetary standpoint, it may be cheaper for the United States to provide grant assistance to other countries to enable them to make larger outlays for defense than for this country to expand its own military budget to accomplish the same purpose. Such calculations will inevitably raise questions regarding the distribution of sacrifice among the countries involved in the common defense program. As was pointed out in Chap. 7, this question was raised during World War II, but the principle of "parity" of sacrifice was never actually applied under lend-lease. Even if the United States were willing to apply the principle of parity, it would be exceedingly difficult to determine workable operating criteria for its application.

A related issue raised by a common defense program has to do with the development of certain industries which are vital to military preparedness. The Schuman plan for integration of Western Europe's coal and steel industries implies, in part, the substitution of international for national economic defense. Trade barriers and the subsidization of industries undertaken for reason of national security or protection, both in the United States and in other Atlantic Treaty nations, must give way to economic integration and long-range economic defense planning if an integrated program of defense is to be achieved. The Atlantic Treaty powers, upon whom the defense of the free world must ultimately depend, cannot face an economically integrated Soviet system if their own economic policies are based upon economic nationalization and isolationism. The economic resources of the entire North Atlantic community and the countries and territories closely associated with them must be mobilized for global defense if they are to survive a possible onslaught from an area comprising a third of the world's land and peoples organized under a single dictatorial power.

CHAPTER 17

Postwar Developments in United States Commercial Policy

THE FUNDAMENTAL principles of United States commercial policy had been developed prior to World War II in the trade-agreements program, the foreign agricultural program, the antitrust program, the maritime program, and in other governmental actions, agreements, and official statements of policy, which were reviewed in Chap. 6. Whereas before the war, the United States sought to implement its international financial and commercial policies largely through bilateral agreements with other countries, the distinguishing feature of postwar policy in these fields was the attempt to develop multilateral agreements and organizations.

Concurrently with the development of plans for an international monetary organization, work on an international trade organization was begun in the State Department and other governmental agencies well before the end of the war. In the autumn of 1943 while conversations were being carried on with the British in preparation for the Bretton Woods Conference in 1944, there were exploratory discussions with British representatives on the establishment of an international commercial-policy organization and an international commodity organization.[1] Interdepartmental committees formulated the outlines of proposals for an international commercial-policy organization and international organizations to deal with commodity and cartel problems.[2] This work culminated in the Anglo-American Financial and Trade Discussions held in the fall of 1945 during which the United States "Proposals for Consideration by an International Conference on Trade and Employment" were published, together with a statement by Secretary of State Byrnes recommending the calling of an international conference on trade and employment by the United Nations in 1946.[3] These Proposals

[1] *Postwar Foreign Policy Preparation 1939–1945,* Department of State, 1949, pp. 192–193.

[2] *Ibid.,* pp. 622–625.

[3] *Proposals for Expansion of World Trade and Employment,* Department of State, November, 1945.

were discussed with the British representatives before they were published and agreed to in principle by them as a part of the Anglo-American Financial and Commercial Agreement of December, 1945.

The British delegation was at that time anxious to move forward on
an international agreement regarding the use of quantitative import restrictions since they were obligating themselves to a policy of nondiscrimination in trade under Sec. 9 of the Anglo-American Financial Agreement. Consequently, the British were just as anxious as the United
States to obtain a commitment on trade practices from other countries.
At the same time, the British favored less restrictive obligations in the
International Trade Organization Charter since the Anglo-American Financial Agreement implied that the obligations of Sec. 9 could be super-
seded by a multilateral agreement. Moreover, the obligations of Sec. 9
of the Financial Agreement were to terminate December 31, 1951.

During the spring of 1946, these Proposals were elaborated by an interdepartmental committee in a document called a Suggested Charter for
an International Trade Organization, which in turn became the basis
for a series of international conferences which culminated in the Havana
Charter for an International Trade Organization.[4]

In addition to working for an international agreement on commercial
policy practices, the United States extended its Trade Agreements Act
in 1945 [5] and again in 1948 and 1949 and has sought to "multilateralize"
its tariff-bargaining procedure under the General Agreement on Tariffs
and Trade. While the actual negotiations are conducted on a bilateral
basis, negotiations are carried on simultaneously with other members of
the GATT. In this way it is possible to negotiate with several countries
who are suppliers of a particular commodity for concessions which would
be of interest to the United States rather than with one supplier alone.
Since all members of the GATT accord most-favored-nation (MFN)

[4] The first meeting of the Economic and Social Council of the United Nations, held
early in 1946, adopted a resolution (introduced by the United States) for the calling of
an International Conference on Trade and Employment and the appointment of a
Preparatory Committee to prepare its agenda. The first meeting of the Preparatory
Committee was held in London in October, 1946, and a second meeting was held in
Geneva in April, 1947. In addition to the preparation of another draft of the Charter
by the Preparatory Committee, the Geneva Conference also prepared the General
Agreement on Tariffs and Trade, and the 23 nations represented entered into tariff
bargaining which resulted in 123 negotiations. The results of these tariff negotiations
were embodied into the General Agreement on Tariffs and Trade (United Nations,
1947). The United Nations Conference on Trade and Employment was opened in
Havana in November, 1947, and in March, 1948, the Conference adopted as its Final
Act the Havana Charter for an International Trade Organization (Department of State,
September, 1948) to be submitted to the members of the United Nations for ratification.

[5] Under the 1945 Act, the President was given power to reduce tariff rates by not
more than one-half of the rate in effect on Jan. 1, 1945.

treatment to one another, the possibilities for granting and obtaining tariff concessions are substantially broadened.

Reciprocal tariff negotiations were carried on under the GATT at Geneva in 1947, at Annecy, France, in the summer of 1949 and in Tourquay, England, in the winter of 1950–1951. The General Agreement itself takes the place of the provisions of our earlier bilateral trade agreements which deal with general commercial policy. Most of the provisions of the GATT are also to be found in our bilateral agreements, but in the former these provisions are far more elaborate and represent a compromise of fundamental viewpoints of a number of major trading countries. The provisions of the GATT are similar but not in all cases identical with the relevant provisions of the Havana Charter, but the latter covers a range of subjects not dealt with in the GATT. Amendments to the GATT since its formulation in Geneva in 1947 have sought to bring its provisions into line with the Havana Charter of March, 1948.

Although the development of postwar United States commercial policy is in large measure concerned with the development of the ITO Charter and the GATT, we shall not attempt to deal in a comprehensive or systematic way with the numerous and complex provisions of these documents.[6] Rather we shall confine our discussion to an evaluation of America's efforts to obtain international agreement with respect to her fundamental commercial policies and to certain significant modifications in these policies which have occurred since the war and which have been brought about either as a result of a compromise with other powers in order to reach international accord, or because of changes in international economic conditions which have necessitated a rethinking of those fundamental policies set forth in Chap. 8. In most cases these modifications do not involve a clear-cut change in policy. Frequently, the modifications have taken the form of short-run exceptions to fundamental long-run policies or the recognition of special situations. But the long-run consists ultimately of a series of short-runs, and numerous exceptions change the character of the rule.*

[6] The most complete analysis of the ITO Charter and the GATT to be published to date is by William Adams Brown, Jr., *The United States and the Reconstruction of World Trade*, The Brookings Institution, Washington, D.C., 1950. In this chapter, the author has drawn heavily upon Dr. Brown's book. An earlier and shorter treatment to which the author is also indebted for material is Clair Wilcox's *A Charter for World Trade*, Macmillan, New York, 1949.

* Since this chapter was written, the administration has given up its efforts to secure Congressional authorization for American membership in the proposed ITO. However, most of the provisions of the ITO Charter dealing with tariffs, quotas, and other trade restrictions and regulations are identical with those contained in the GATT, of which the United States is a member. The GATT does not contain the Charter provisions dealing with cartels, subsidies, and intergovernmental commodity agreements.

AMERICAN ECONOMIC POLICY AND THE ITO CHARTER

The basic principles of the ITO and certain important exceptions to these principles are firmly rooted in traditional American economic policies which are, in turn, a reflection of fundamental American economic interests. The general rule against the use of quantitative restrictions is a reflection of the fact that, in general, the United States has not used quotas and exchange controls for purposes of protection,[7] nor has this country employed direct controls in industry and commerce (except in wartime) to any great extent as a measure of economic control. Moreover, the United States has never had occasion to use balance-of-payments restrictions of any kind. Tariffs are of course permissible under the Charter, but provision is made for the orderly reduction of tariffs through negotiation in a manner well established in American commercial policy. On the other hand, the use of quantitative controls for balance-of-payments reasons has been recognized as a legitimate exception, but only reluctantly has the United States recognized the use of quantitative restrictions for protectionist purposes. (Protection is recognized in the Charter principally under the name of economic development.)

Perhaps the most important single rule which the United States has championed in the negotiation on the Charter has been the rule of nondiscrimination. While nondiscriminatory restrictions have been countenanced in our commercial relations with other countries in the past, discrimination against American goods has usually been met with protest and lack of sympathy on the part of the American public and its governmental representatives. The strong competitive position of American products in world markets has frequently resulted in American exporters being the first and perhaps the only victims of discrimination as between sources of supply. Just as this country has in the past steered clear of exclusive political alliances with other countries, so also has it shied away from exclusive economic arrangements. Moreover, the absence of direct controls over industry and commerce and of state trading (except in agriculture since the 1930's) has made it impossible to administer a system of discrimination, except possibly tariff discrimination. Tariff preferences have been confined almost exclusively to Cuba and the Philippines, which were formerly United States dependencies, and these preferences developed largely out of a desire to ease the transition of these countries to an independent status. Americans have bitterly resented the British Imperial Preference system established in the early 1930's and have looked upon such devices as unfair competition and not on a par

---

[7] A notable exception is of course the use of quotas for agricultural imports.

with its own nondiscriminatory tariffs, however high. On the other hand, the formation of customs unions or even free-trade areas could scarcely be opposed since one of the most important economic consequences of the adoption of the Federal Constitution was the formation of a customs union among the states. We shall return to the economic justification of this position later on.

The principle of national treatment has also been fundamental in American commercial policy, but here the record is not especially favorable with respect to our willingness to accord such treatment to foreigners. Not being a colonial power, the United States has sought to afford its own businessmen freedom to operate in foreign countries and their dependencies under conditions at least as favorable as the residents of those countries or territories. Similarly, while recognizing the right of countries to impose tariffs, we have sought national treatment for American exports, in such matters as internal taxation and regulation. In matters of internal taxation,[8] freedom of entry for the operation of banks and insurance companies, and state and Federal purchases, i.e., "Buy American" laws, however, the United States has violated the principle of national treatment. In fact the provisions of the Charter on national treatment would require a change in certain American laws.

Among the most important exceptions to the general rules on the use of quantitative restrictions and export subsidies are the Charter's provisions with respect to agricultural commodities. Agriculture is one of the few American economic activities subject to direct marketing and production controls and to state trading operations. The emergence of governmental control in the field of American agriculture was the product of a serious structural maladjustment directly affecting the economic welfare of millions of people, and of the political strength of the farmers who hold something of a balance of power between labor and the middle-class city dwellers. The agricultural exceptions of the Charter can be squared with the general liberal commercial policy of the United States only if they are viewed as temporary arrangements looking toward an orderly transfer of resources necessary for the removal of structural maladjustments. As we shall see later on, however, the United States has not as yet developed a long-range farm program which gives promise of resolving the conflict between short-run price aims and a liberal commercial policy.

Before the war, the United States took a dim view of international commodity agreements since experience with them was largely confined to efforts of producing countries to push up or maintain the prices of

---

[8] The United States has processing taxes on certain imported vegetable oils.

certain commodities, *e.g.,* tin and rubber, through restrictive agreements which took little account of the interests of consumers or the long-run adjustment of the industries concerned. The acceptance of the principle of international commodity agreements may be regarded as an extension of the principle of domestic price and production controls in this field, although there has been considerable difference of viewpoint between the State and Agricultural Departments as to their ultimate desirability and as to their function. The inclusion of provision for such agreements in the original American Proposals may also be explained in part by the fact that, since there was strong pressure on the part of other countries for commodity agreements, the United States believed that such agreements ought to be under the supervision of an international organization and their operations rendered as harmless as possible.

The relationship of the provisions of the Charter on cartels and state trading to traditional American policy needs no explanation. That these provisions are weak from the point of view of American interests stems from the fact that they are a necessary compromise with countries whose institutions differ markedly from our own. To argue, as do some critics of the Charter, that these and other provisions of the Charter which depart from traditional American policy are a codification of malpractice is similar to the argument for unlicensed and unregulated prostitution on the grounds that regulation gives official recognition to its existence!

The Rule of Nondiscrimination

The development of American postwar policy on discrimination (as between countries or currency areas) in international trade has been regarded by some critics as a compromise with evil and by others as an attempt to cling to an outworn dogma based on classical economic theory which no longer has any relation to reality.[9] Less generous foreign critics see in America's policy of nondiscrimination an attempt to maintain America's dominant position in world markets by preventing other countries from creating areas of preference within whose protective shelter industrialization can be nurtured. The author believes that there is ample evidence to show that the American policy makers have earnestly sought to develop positions and policies which were in the best

[9] For a criticism of America's nondiscriminatory commercial policy, see T. Balogh, *The Dollar Crisis,* Blackwell, Oxford, 1949. The viewpoint that the United States has compromised with evil is expressed by Phillip Cortney in *The Economic Munich,* The Philosophical Library, New York, 1949; and by M. A. Heilperin, "How the United States Lost the ITO Conference," *Fortune,* September, 1949.

interests of all countries by adapting the general principle of nondiscrimination (which is derived from the principle of optimum use of resources) to the special requirements of other countries without sacrificing the general principle entirely. In the following paragraphs, we shall sketch the main elements in the development of these policies, which are still very much in the formative stage.

Since international monetary and commercial policy are closely interrelated, certain major decisions and agreements had already been reached in the formulation of the Articles of Agreement of the Monetary Fund (July, 1944) more than a year before the American Proposals for an ITO were prepared. Because it is possible to accomplish much the same results through the mechanism of quantitative trade controls as through the use of exchange controls, it follows that the general rules with respect to the use of import restrictions ought to be parallel with the rules on exchange controls. Both the American Proposals and the original American draft of the Charter [10] set forth the principle that members may employ nondiscriminatory quantitative import restrictions in the event of serious balance-of-payments difficulties.[11] Although the Havana Charter requires members to consult with the Organization regarding the causes of the maladjustment in their balances of payments in an effort to reach an agreement upon means of correction [Art. 21, 1 (c)], the fact remains that the Organization cannot require a member to remove restrictions for balance-of-payments purposes even though the maladjustment is due to the domestic fiscal, monetary, or other economic policies of that member. So long as independent countries have complete sovereignty over their internal economic policies, no other course is possible. Unlike the Fund, the ITO does not have the sanction of withholding financial resources from countries which are following improper policies.

Once the principle of the balance-of-payments exception to the use of nondiscriminatory quantitative import restrictions is admitted, a serious dilemma presents itself. Suppose the member has an inadequate supply of dollars to meet the demands of its residents for dollar goods, but it has plenty of sterling, and hence no balance-of-payments problem in trade with countries which accept sterling. The American Suggested Charter sought to deal with this problem by permitting a member to employ

[10] *Suggested Charter for an International Trade Organization,* Department of State, September, 1946.

[11] In the Havana Charter a member is given the right to employ quantitative restrictions "(i) to forestall the imminent threat of, or to stop, a serious decline in its monetary reserves, or (ii) in the case of a member with very low monetary reserves, achieve a reasonable rate of increase in its reserves." [Art. 21 (a).] The factual situation regarding a member's balance-of-payments position is to be determined by the Monetary Fund.

discriminatory import restrictions to the extent necessary to purchase needed imports with inconvertible currencies accumulated up to December 31, 1948.[12] At the time the Suggested Charter was prepared in the spring of 1947, the problem of accumulated inconvertible balances was not believed to be a serious one since, under the Anglo-American Financial Agreement, Britain agreed to undertake to secure agreements whereby a portion of the large accumulated sterling balances would be funded or written off and the remainder made freely convertible. This exception to the rule of nondiscrimination was not considered liberal enough by other participants at the London and Geneva meetings of the Preparatory Committee. The fact was that a much broader exception to nondiscrimination was provided in Art. XIV of the Fund Agreement, the transitional provision, and it was argued with considerable justification that the ITO Charter obligations on trade restrictions should be at least as liberal as those contained in the Fund Agreement.[13]

Although the door to discrimination through exchange controls during the transition period had been opened by the Bretton Woods Agreements, the American delegation at the London Conference sought to close it at the London meetings of the Preparatory Committee, by outlawing trade discrimination except to the extent necessary to utilize inconvertible currencies accumulated before December 31, 1948.[14] Had the nondiscriminatory rule been adopted, members would presumably have been reluctant to accumulate inconvertible currencies after 1948 since they would be unable to adopt their import policies in a manner which would give preference to their use. Hence members would either limit their exports to countries making payment in inconvertible currencies to the amounts they could use by following nondiscriminatory import policies, or they would have exported only for convertible currencies or gold. Without going into the details of the protracted negotiations on this point, we may say that the position of most of the soft-currency countries was (1) that the ITO Charter should not provide rules which in effect preclude the use of the more liberal transitional exchange provisions of the Monetary Fund, and (2) that a country which has already fully utilized its earnings in hard currencies should not be precluded from acquiring additional imports from inconvertible-currency countries

[12] *Suggested Charter for an International Trade Organization,* Art. 22, 2.

[13] The original American Proposals recommended that the ITO Charter should provide for the determination of a transitional period during which quantitative trade restrictions, both discriminatory and nondiscriminatory, might be maintained under a procedure analagous to Art. XIV of the Fund Agreement. This provision was omitted in the American draft of the Suggested Charter.

[14] See Brown, *op. cit.,* pp. 85–89.

by special bilateral arrangements. The latter position went further than the one based on parallelism with the Fund Agreement, since what was proposed was that, so long as a country could obtain "additional" imports over and above what it could obtain by nondiscriminatory measures, it should always be permitted to employ discriminatory tactics. This is in substance the familiar scarce-currency argument which we have discussed at length in an earlier chapter. The crux of the issue lies not so much in the superficially reasonable argument that countries ought to be allowed to expand their trade by discriminatory devices once they have exhausted their hard-currency resources in imports from hard-currency countries, but whether they should be permitted to engage in practices which perpetuate the balance-of-payments maladjustment by diverting their exports to one another and away from the hard-currency area.

In reaching a position in this question of discrimination, the United States representatives were faced with a dilemma. On the one hand, a general requirement of nondiscrimination would have hampered the development of trade among soft-currency countries, which was necessary for their postwar recovery. On the other hand, discrimination tends to prevent the transfer of productive resources and the readjustment of trade patterns necessary for the elimination of international disequilibrium between the dollar area and the rest of the world, without which the maximum benefits from world trade cannot be achieved. Perhaps even more important is the fact that unless countries adjust their production and trade so as to expand their exports to the dollar area they will not be able to meet the requirements of their economies for commodities available in adequate supply only from the dollar area without continued American assistance. It should also be recalled that the United States had already accepted the scarce-currency principle in Art. VII of the Monetary Fund. Quantitative trade discrimination was specifically permitted in both the Proposals and in the Suggested Charter against a member whose currency was declared scarce by the Fund. Although this provision was not intended to be invoked during the transition period (since Art. XIV of the Monetary Fund already gave members permission to discriminate), a world dollar shortage obviously existed in the immediate postwar period. Thus it appeared to be inconsistent for the American delegation not to accept the application of the scarce-currency principle during the transition period. Perhaps the principal reason for the American position in the spring and summer of 1946—a position which was greatly modified at the Geneva Conference in the fall of 1947—was that the pound sterling was expected to become convertible by July, 1947, and the need for discrimination as a means of maintaining and expanding trade among soft-currency countries would have largely disappeared under a system of sterling convertibility.

The final position arrived at in the Havana Charter is not to be considered simply as a compromise with evil so far as the American delegation was concerned, but was rather an attempt to achieve two important American objectives, the realization of each of which was in large measure dependent upon the successful realization of the other. In the Havana Charter, members were given the choice between two sets of rules,[15] the Havana option which is embodied in the Charter itself, and the Geneva option, or Annex K of the Charter. Without going into the details of these alternative provisions, the Havana option provided in general that members were permitted to employ discriminatory trade restrictions consistent with those which they are permitted to employ under Art. XIV of the Fund Agreement and under the same conditions as to termination and consultation. The Geneva option, which was open to countries which became members of the contracting parties to the GATT before July 1, 1948 (and had therefore already accepted the principles of the Geneva option), permitted countries in balance-of-payments difficulties to employ discriminatory quantitative restrictions to increase their imports from certain countries, provided their hard currencies and gold reserves were not thereby depleted, *i.e.*, provided they did not use gold and dollars to increase imports from soft-currency countries at the expense of imports from hard-currency countries. In the case of both options, members must consult with the Organization regarding discriminatory practices maintained after March 1, 1952, and the Organization may request termination of any discriminatory restriction which it believes to be unjustifiable after that date.

It should not be thought that these provisions guarantee the elimination of discriminatory restrictions by 1952 or even shortly thereafter. Members are obligated in a general way to work toward a condition of equilibrium, but whether or not the Organization will be able to declare that discriminatory restrictions are no longer justifiable will depend upon the willingness and ability of all nations, creditors and debtors alike, to adopt policies which will eliminate the price and structural maladjustments in world trade. Again it will not be possible for the Organization to dictate specific internal policies of its members. It should be able to forestall or eliminate deliberate actions on the part of its members which have the effect of strengthening or of perpetuating economic trading blocs and which are unnecessary in the light of the balance-of-payments

---

[15] The Havana Charter permits members to employ discriminatory export controls for the purpose of expanding hard-currency exports by requiring that certain exports must be paid for in hard currencies. See Art. 24, 8 (b); see also Brown, *op. cit.*, p. 85.

situations of the members concerned. As economic recovery progresses, the Organization can through consultations with its members promote the restoration of multilateral trade. Contrary to what some of the countries participating in the conferences leading up to the formulation of the Havana Charter may have preferred, the idea of permanent discrimination and exclusive trading blocs was rejected and the use of discriminatory devices was permitted only as a temporary measure during which the fundamental balance-of-payments maladjustments brought about by the war were to be gradually eliminated.

The United States delegation's acceptance of the Charter's provisions on discriminatory restrictions involved a serious conflict with our traditional policy on nondiscrimination. This conflict was further demonstrated by the efforts of the Economic Cooperation Administration to promote a payments union for Western Europe and associated monetary areas involving discrimination against the United States. Equally important have been the efforts of the ECA in fostering the reduction of import quotas by the participating countries with respect to trade with one another and the substitution of global quotas, *i.e.*, quotas established without regard to source as among the participating countries, in place of bilateral quota arrangements generally included in bilateral trade agreements.[16] Obviously, trade liberalization and the multilateral payments scheme must go forward together if a multilateral trading system is to be established for Western Europe. Since restrictions will have to be continued on dollar imports so long as the demand for dollar goods in terms of local currencies is greater than dollar earnings, the establishment of a liberal multilateral trading area among the participating countries (together with a number of nonparticipating countries with close currency ties with European Recovery Program countries) might be regarded as an intensification of the degree of discrimination against the United States.

How has the ECA justified this policy? [17] First of all the establishment

[16] On Jan. 31, 1950, the Organization for European Economic Cooperation Council adopted a resolution calling for the removal of quantitative restrictions on at least 60 per cent of the imports of OEEC countries from other members as soon as the proposed European Payments Union comes into force, and a possible 75 per cent liberalization by the end of 1950. (*Second Report of the Organization for European Economic Cooperation,* February, 1950, pp. 221–223.)

[17] As was mentioned in Chap. 11, some officials of the United States government have had considerable misgivings regarding the establishment of a European Payments Union on the grounds that it might become a permanent soft-currency trading bloc. See, for example, Felix Belair, "Payments Union Held 'Pig in Poke,'" *The New York Times,* Mar. 23, 1950. The position of some critics of the plan is that the present bilateral trade and payments arrangements are unstable and that as individual countries become

of the European Payments Union is considered to be an essential step toward European economic integration, a policy which has strong support in both Congress and in the executive branch of the government. Secondly, the establishment of a regional trading system is viewed, not as a step away from world-wide multilateralism, but as an essential move in that direction. Before the ERP countries can make their currencies generally convertible and adopt nondiscriminatory policies, their industries must become competitive and their costs reduced. Governmental controls and barter trade must be eliminated through the creation of a liberal trading area within a group of soft-currency countries as a means of restoring competitive conditions. Once Western European industry and trade is freed from the shackles of bilateralism, it will be in a better position to compete on a nondiscriminatory basis with the rest of the world. Moreover, the EPU provides for partial gold settlements at the margin, and the payments system can eventually be merged with a system of world-wide multilateral settlements once the structural maladjustments in the world's balance of payments are removed.

Before leaving this subject we must deal briefly with customs unions,[18] the formation of which is permitted by the ITO Charter and is encouraged by the United States government. It has been said that the United States is inconsistent in favoring customs unions and free-trade areas on the one hand while opposing preferential arrangements which expand trade between countries in the same region on the other.[19] The author believes that there is an important distinction between the two situations which justifies the American position on this point. In the first place, the removal of border formalities in trade between two or more countries makes possible a highly significant reduction in costs and in institutional barriers to trade which cannot be claimed by a system of trade preferences. Secondly, a genuine customs union among modern states must inevitably necessitate a high degree of economic integration and coordination in monetary, fiscal, and other national economic policies which again is not present in a system of preferential arrangements. If

---

stronger financially they will withdraw from bilateral practices and make their currencies convertible. According to this view, the establishment of a clearing union would build up vested interests in a discriminatory system and postpone, perhaps indefinitely, the return to world-wide multilateralism by its members. The contrary position of the ECA, set forth above, appears to have been upheld by Congress in the 1950 ECA Act.

[18] The Havana Charter permits preferential arrangements by members which intend to enter into bona fide customs unions or free-trade areas, provided there is consultation with the Organization and provided certain conditions are complied with (Art. 44).

[19] See Sir Hubert Henderson, "The Havana Charter," *American Economic Review,* June, 1949, p. 609.

countries choose to establish a highly integrated economic area, that area must be treated as a single economic and political unit so far as international trade is concerned. The objection to a discriminatory system is not that trade will be increased within the preferential area, but that exports will be diverted from other areas or prevented from expanding to these areas so as to make impossible the optimum use of resources and the maximization of the gains from trade. Although the operation of a customs union may involve an element of discrimination against non-members and hence a loss of the advantages of international trade, there will also be a gain from the shift to lower cost production within the union and from trade which does not involve a diversion of trade with the outside world. Certainly the net results of the operation of a customs union are likely to be more economical than one could expect from a haphazard system of preferential arrangements which may be aimed more at protection from outside competition than an expansion of total trade within the preferential area.[20]

ECONOMIC DEVELOPMENT AND UNITED STATES COMMERCIAL POLICY

Perhaps the most vigorous challenge to the efforts of the United States to reach an international agreement on liberal commercial policies came from those who opposed such policies on the grounds that they interfered with the progress of economic development. Although the United States recognized the importance of economic development, its basic position was that industrial development is not primarily a question of protection and that quantitative restrictions or new preferences should not be authorized by the ITO for such purposes.[21] The American draft did permit direct subsidization under certain conditions and increases in tariffs for the promotion of economic development. But the delegations of the underdeveloped countries proposed a large number of amendments some of which would have permitted the use of almost any restrictive or discriminatory device for the promotion of economic development to be employed without prior approval of the Organization. The provisions of the Havana Charter dealing with exceptions for industrialization were frankly a compromise in which the American delegation in

---

[20] See Jacob Viner, *The Customs Union Issue*, Carnegie Endowment for International Peace, New York, 1950. According to Viner, a customs union moves in the direction of free trade to the extent that new trade takes place within the customs area, and moves in the direction of protection to the extent that trade is diverted from outside the area to within the customs area. It should be said that Dr. Viner is skeptical as regards the extent to which customs unions achieve a net increase in the degree of freedom of trade.

[21] Brown, *op. cit.*, p. 98; see also Wilcox, *op. cit.*, p. 141.

effect agreed that quantitative restrictions, increases in tariffs, and new preferences might be used to promote industrialization provided that in certain cases prior approval is obtained from the ITO or the consent of other members who would be affected or both, and provided that certain other conditions are complied with.[22] In all cases the ITO is authorized to place a time period on restrictions and new preferences. Moreover, the protective arrangements proposed are not supposed to involve an unwise use of resources or an impairment of the advantages of world trade.

Provided they are intelligently administered, the above provisions add up to a recognition of the infant-industry argument with respect to both individual countries and economic regions, together with the application of safeguards to assure that restrictions and preferences do not violate the infant-industry principle. Loosely administered, these provisions will mean international sanction of almost any kind of restrictive or discriminatory arrangement undertaken in the name of the industrialization of underdeveloped areas.

Administration of the escapes for industrialization in accordance with the infant-industry principle will undoubtedly run into serious difficulties and conflicts since it is frequently argued that industrialization is desirable for its own sake even though its promotion may involve a maldistribution of the world's productive resources and a reduction of the benefits of specialization and trade. It is maintained that the terms of trade have moved in favor of the industrialized countries, that agricultural countries are too much at the mercy of the vicissitudes of world demand, and that there are important internal social and economic advantages, *e.g.*, the breakdown of feudal economic structures, the encour-

---

[22] See Arts. 13, 14, and 15 of the Havana Charter. These provisions are quite involved and are summarized as follows:

1. An underdeveloped country desiring to promote a new industry may "in appropriate circumstances" employ trade restrictions or increased tariffs which are forbidden by a trade-agreement commitment previously entered into by that member, provided the consent of the other parties to the agreement who would be materially affected is obtained.

2. Release from commitments of the Charter on products not covered by trade agreements requires prior approval of the ITO. Such release must be granted by the ITO if the industry to be protected was first established between 1939 and 1948, or if the industry processes an indigenous primary commodity and if exports of that commodity have been seriously curtailed by increased restrictions abroad.

3. New preferences may be established with ITO approval provided that the territories of the members of the new preferential arrangement are contiguous or within the same economic area, that each preference is necessary to promote economic development, that the agreement is limited in time, and that certain other conditions are met safeguarding the interests of other members.

agement of capital accumulation, higher real incomes, and a more equitable distribution of income and wealth, to be gained through industrialization.[23] There is also a considerable amount of statistical support for the argument that industrialization expands world trade in industrial commodities as a result of the expansion of income in the newly industrialized areas. On the other hand, it can be shown that industrialization abroad has injured many of the established industries, e.g., the textile industry, of Western Europe and the losses have not been entirely replaced by other markets for European exports.[24] This may have been due to the fact that European export industries have been less adaptable to changing conditions of world markets than in the case of the United States which appears to have benefited more from the industrialization of less developed areas.

While a certain amount of protection for a limited time may be desirable for achieving the longer run benefits of industrialization, there is a real danger in carrying this argument too far. The world-wide benefits from industrialization of the "newer" economic regions in the past have been accompanied by conditions of relatively free trade. While tariffs played a role in the industrialization of some countries in the past, quantitative import restrictions were not employed on a large scale before the 1930's. In arriving at a compromise between the objectives of promoting industrialization on the one hand and securing the benefits of specialization and trade on the other, careful consideration should be given to the types of industries to be promoted. It seems reasonable to believe that in most countries or economic regions there are some industries, particularly those employing indigenous materials and perhaps a high proportion of labor to capital, which can be developed to a point where they can supply at least a portion of the local market without protection. But to create steel plants and other heavy industries in areas where they will always need protection in the name of fostering industrialization must surely be regarded as an unwise use of resources and, in addition, may contribute to world-wide maladjustments in the pattern of trade. We have already discussed the need for increased production of primary commodities in underdeveloped areas

[23] See A. J. Brown, *Industrialization and Trade*, Royal Institute of International Affairs, London, 1943; *Industrialization and Foreign Trade*, League of Nations, Geneva, 1945; and Eugene Staley, *World Economic Development*, International Labour Office, Montreal, 1944.

[24] World trade in manufactured goods has risen slower than world production or world trade in primary products. *Industrialization and Foreign Trade*, pp. 14ff.; see also *International Transactions of the United States during the War*, Department of Commerce, 1948, pp. 158–160.

as a source of supply for the older industrial countries of Western Europe. It is desirable that developmental capital should contribute to the technical improvement and expansion of primary production in the underdeveloped areas rather than be used to create facilities for the production of manufactured goods for the production of which Western Europe may have developed a surplus capacity.[25]

United States Postwar Agricultural Policy

United States agricultural policy represents the chief area of conflict with America's liberal international commercial policy. Our agricultural policy developed out of the emergency conditions of the 1930's, but certain structural maladjustments in American agriculture were present even during the prosperous period of the late 1920's. One of the well-known consequences of depression and low income is a disproportionate fall in the prices of primary commodities, particularly where they are produced under conditions of atomistic competition. The resulting price disparities further intensify the depression by drastically reducing the incomes of an important economic group; by causing farm mortgages to be foreclosed, bank credit to be restricted, and banks in rural areas to fail; and by reducing the demand for farm equipment and other industrial products. Thus an important element in the New Deal recovery program was that of raising the prices of farm commodities and the level of farm incomes. The Agricultural Adjustment Administration program took the form of farm-price supports through loans to farmers to enable them to hold commodities off the market, production controls and soil-conservation payments, an extension of credit facilities to farmers, measures to expand domestic consumption through food-stamp and school-lunch programs, and the dumping of surplus farm products abroad through export subsidies.

The criterion for the price-support programs was a concept of parity prices based on the relationship between the prices received by farmers and the prices paid by them in the period from 1910 to 1914, and the parity price has become in the minds of the farmers and their Congressional supporters something of a "just price" which the rest of the community is obligated to assure the farmers for their output. While granting that there may be justification for removing price disparities brought about by a depression, provided that a suitable criterion can be determined, this principle has no validity in dealing with problems of struc-

[25] For a discussion of the trend of economic development toward heavy industry, see J. H. Adler, *The Underdeveloped Areas: Their Industrialization,* Yale Institute of International Studies, New Haven, Conn., March, 1949.

tural maladjustment. The same thing must be said with regard to the principle of income parity, since it is largely through relative changes in incomes that an adjustment in resource utilization must be brought about.

During the war the United States government was faced with the necessity of greatly expanding farm output, and in order to increase farm production it was thought necessary to assure farmers that they would be protected against a sharp fall in prices immediately after the war. Under the Steagall Amendment of 1942, the prices of the major farm commodities were to be supported at 90 per cent of parity (cotton at 92½ per cent), by means of loans and direct purchases by the Commodity Credit Corporation for at least two years after the end of the war. For the most part, farm prices were well above parity during the war and immediate postwar period, although support had to be given to potatoes in 1947 and occasional support was given to wool, eggs, turkey, and a few other products.[26] With prosperous conditions in the United States and a high volume of agricultural exports, this country was presented with an excellent opportunity to initiate a program of long-term adjustment in its agriculture.

The Agricultural Act of 1948 extended the wartime price supports at the 90 per cent of parity level for the "basic" crops and certain other commodities until January 1, 1950. Section II of the Act, however, did provide for reducing price supports to as low as 60 per cent of parity, depending upon the volume of production. The flexible provisions of the 1948 Act carried with them the possibility of inducing long-run adjustments in agriculture along with minimum levels of protection against a sharp recession in farm prices. The Agricultural Act of 1949 (passed on October 31, 1949) postponed the application of the lower support prices in the 1948 Act due to become effective in 1950.[27] The operation of the 1949 Act has been overshadowed, however, by the announcement of the administration-supported Brannan Plan which involves a combination of direct payments to producers and support prices for basic commodities directed toward the stabilization of real farm income. Direct payments to the farmers in place of price supports would give consumers the benefit of lower prices, and some expansion in consumption would undoubtedly take place. The budgetary cost to the government of maintaining a given

[26] C. A. Hickman, *Our Farm Program and Foreign Trade,* Council on Foreign Relations, New York, 1949, p. 15.

[27] The 1949 Act provided for the support of basic commodities (except tobacco) at a level between 80 and 90 per cent of parity in 1951, and between 75 and 90 per cent of parity in 1952 and thereafter. Tobacco is to be supported at 90 per cent of parity thereafter.

level of farm income is likely to be higher, however, than if the prices of farm commodities for which there is an inelastic demand are supported at a high level.

The basic issue in America's future farm policy is whether it is to be directed toward an orderly adjustment of domestic production, consumption, and foreign trade, which is compatible with America's competitive position in agriculture under conditions of free trade, or whether it is to be directed solely toward the stabilization of the relative prices of agricultural commodities or real incomes of American farmers. It seems clear, from a comparison of the value added by manufacturing per employee with the value added by agriculture per man equivalent, that on the whole the marginal value productivity of labor in agriculture is less than in manufacturing.[28] It is also clear that a system which involves billions of dollars in governmental subsidies [29] at a time when the domestic economy is prosperous and foreign demand exceptionally high cannot be compatible with a program of long-range adjustment or consistent with a liberal commercial policy. During 1949, United States agricultural exports totaled about $3.6 billion, more than half of which went to Western Europe. In this same year, 39 per cent of America's wheat production, 26 per cent of her tobacco production, and 33 per cent of her raw cotton output were exported.[30] Unless the United States intends to pursue a policy of maintaining agricultural exports through grants of money or surplus commodities, or through dumping agricultural surpluses at low prices, a substantial reduction in agricultural exports will probably have to take place. Any attempt to maintain our large agricultural exports must inevitably discourage the production of these commodities in other parts of the world and hence inhibit an adjustment of the pattern of world production and trade necessary for the restoration of international equilibrium.

We shall now turn briefly to some of the specific measures which conflict with America's general liberal trading policies. Under present conditions of world shortages outside the United States, the specific measures involving a violation of liberal trading principles in the agricultural field are not especially serious and could perhaps be justified in terms of the requirements of the postwar adjustment of agriculture. The significant issues relate to the nature of our long-run adjustment program.

[28] See T. W. Schultz, "How Efficient Is American Agriculture," *Journal of Farm Economics,* August, 1947, Vol. 29.

[29] In April, 1950, the CCC held some $4 billion in surplus farm commodities. *The New York Times,* Apr. 2, 1950.

[30] *Foreign Commerce Weekly,* Apr. 24, 1950, p. 42.

Agriculture and United States Foreign-trade Policy

The American farm program conflicts with a liberal commercial trading policy by establishing a domestic support price for certain commodities at levels higher than world prices for like commodities; by subsidizing the exportation of agricultural commodities through sales by the CCC at prices lower than those paid to domestic producers; and by restricting the importation of agricultural commodities where such importation interferes with a domestic support program either by quotas, embargoes, or special import fees. In addition to these interferences with free trade in agricultural commodities, the United States imposes tariff duties on competitive commodities such as wheat, wool, beef, sugar, and butter; processing taxes on imported fats and oils; and a variety of administrative measures which effectively restrict imports of these commodities. In recent years, exports of a number of farm commodities such as cotton, tobacco, dried fruit, dried eggs, peanuts, and potatoes have been subsidized by the government either by means of direct payments to the exporters, or by sales from government stocks at prices below cost. Section 22 of the 1948 and 1949 Agricultural Acts authorizes the President to restrict imports of agricultural commodities if they interfere with any support program of the Department of Agriculture, by the imposition of import "fees" up to 50 per cent of the value of the commodities. Although such fees are not subject to reduction under the reciprocal-trade negotiations, they cannot be imposed in contravention of existing trade agreements. Under this provision, quotas limiting the volume of imports to which the 50 per cent import fees will not apply have been established for wheat, wheat flour, cotton, and potatoes. Absolute quotas have been established on sugar under the Sugar Act of 1948, and wartime legislation restricting imports of fats and oils and rice have been invoked to ban all imports of butter (an important Danish export to the United States), and import licenses have been required for imports of other fats and oils and rice.[31]

In April, 1945, the Department of Agriculture published a monograph entitled *A Postwar Foreign Trade Program for United States Agriculture* in which it recommended (1) reductions in barriers to world trade and the elimination of trade discrimination, "but in such a way as to permit the use of government income supports in connection with agricultural adjustment"; (2) the elimination of private barriers to trade arising from

[31] During the Geneva tariff negotiations in 1947, Congress passed a bill increasing the tariff on wool at a time when the United States delegation was negotiating a concession with Australia on wool. Had not the President vetoed this bill, the Geneva negotiations on the tariffs, the GATT, and the ITO might well have floundered.

monopoly controls; (3) the establishment of international commodity agreements covering the expansion of production and trade, the maintenance of buffer stocks, and the orderly disposal and eventual elimination of surpluses, and (4) the promotion of improved living standards of low-income groups in the United States and abroad through surplus-disposal programs. In essence, what this recommended program involved was essentially a continuation of the prewar United States agricultural policies and programs within the framework of international agreements. Instead of injuring other countries by dumping surpluses on world markets, the problem would be handled by international commodity agreements, including buffer stocks and perhaps international "food-stamp" plans. Governments would of course be free to maintain support programs and export subsidies, but the area of conflict with the commercial interests of other countries would be minimized by international commodity agreements. The essential elements of this program were written into the original American Proposals for an ITO, and these provisions were in large measure retained in the Havana Charter.

At the Geneva conference on the ITO Charter, the United States was in the position of having to plead for special exceptions for agriculture, a circumstance which undoubtedly weakened its bargaining power in dealing with exceptions for economic development and other demands for "escape" clauses. In the final draft of the Havana Charter, the agricultural exceptions were made sufficiently liberal so that no radical changes will be required in American farm policy should this country become a member of the ITO.[32] The Charter permits import restrictions on agricultural products "necessary to the enforcement of government measures which operate effectively: (i) to restrict the quantities of the like domestic products permitted to be marketed or produced . . . (ii) to remove a temporary surplus of the like domestic product . . . by making the surplus available to certain groups of consumers free of charge or at a price below the current market level. . . ." (Art. 20.) Prior approval by the ITO is not required—a principle which the United States insisted on in the case of restrictions for economic development—but opportunity for consultation is to be afforded to other members affected by the restrictions.

The other important agricultural exceptions in the Havana Charter have to do with subsidies. Article 27 permits

a system for the stabilization of the domestic prices or of the return to domestic producers of a primary commodity, independently of the movement of export prices, which results at times in the sale of the commodity for

[32] See Brown, *op. cit.,* p. 361. The same conclusion applies to the GATT.

export at a lower price than the comparable price charged for the like commodity to buyers in the domestic market . . . if the Organization determines that (a) the system has also resulted, or is so designed as to result, in the sale of the commodity for export at a price higher than the comparable price charged for the like commodity to buyers in the domestic market, and (b) the system is so operated, or is designed to so operate, either because of effective regulation of production or otherwise, as not to stimulate exports unduly or otherwise seriously prejudice the interests of other members.

Members may, however, under certain conditions grant subsidies for the stimulation of exports of primary commodities, provided that the subsidies do not have the effect of acquiring or maintaining for the member more than an equitable share of world trade in the subsidized commodity. In such cases, consultation with the Organization and with other affected members is required (Art. 28). Members are expected to deal with their surplus-commodity problems, so far as possible, through international commodity agreements.

The Havana Charter sets up machinery for dealing with surpluses in primary commodities through intergovernmental commodity-control agreements. The principles governing these agreements include (1) representation of consumer country as well as producing country interests; (2) provision for the satisfaction of national consumption and world-market requirements "from sources from which such requirements can be supplied in the most effective and economic manner, due regard being had to the need for preventing serious economic and social dislocation and to the position of producing areas suffering from abnormal disabilities"; [33] and (3) the adoption by the participating countries of programs of internal economic adjustment looking toward a solution of the commodity program involved (Art. 63).

If one accepts the fact that national governments, including the United States, are going to take steps to protect producers of primary products from the vicissitudes of market prices and to ease the burden of adjusting to long-run changes in demand and supply conditions, international, as opposed to unilateral, action is undoubtedly the best solution. If the principles of the Charter are followed, the postwar international commodity agreements will have little in common with the monopolistic arrangements of the past, and they will be perfectly compatible with an orderly adjustment of production and trade to fundamental demand and supply forces in world markets. The important question is whether or not the complex political forces which determine United States agricul-

[33] Art. 63 (c).

tural policy will permit the adoption of farm programs which involve adjustments that are compatible with America's competitive position. In the long run, the Havana Charter's admirable principles can be realized only when domestic farm prices are equivalent to world prices for like commodities. This does not necessarily mean low incomes for the American farmer. It may mean a shift of man power out of agriculture, the elimination of uneconomic farming units, a larger amount of capital per worker, shifts in the commodity distribution of farm output, and the retirement of marginal land.

What kind of a farm policy would be compatible both with an efficient distribution of American productive resources and with a liberal international trading policy? It is clear that except as mechanisms for mitigating the effects of short-term movements, price-support programs and parity income payments simply perpetuate fundamental maladjustments and violate the principles of free trade. Moreover, farm subsidies through price supports and income payments involve a highly unequal distribution of benefits among the farmers.[34] Agricultural subsidies therefore should be limited to (1) mitigating economic distress due to depression or rapid changes in demand conditions, (2) conservation and the improvement of agricultural efficiency, and (3) facilitating the transfer of resources from less productive to more productive employments.[35] Government support programs should be confined to short-term stabilization operations, and no effort should be made to combat long-term trends. Long-term adjustments could be encouraged through conservation measures, the transfer of workers, and by other direct means which do not interfere with market prices. Restrictions on international trade in farm products should be eliminated, although short-term price-stabilization programs involving the use of commodity reserves, but not production and marketing quotas, might be employed.

Sizable stocks of commodity reserves might also be accumulated to meet possible international as well as national emergencies. Emergency foreign requirements arise not only from normal fluctuations in world supply conditions, but also from war and civil disturbances. America's international responsibilities require therefore the maintenance of ample stocks of cotton, grains, and other staple commodities, and such stocks might well be built up in years of exceptionally large domestic output.

[34] Dr. D. Gale Johnson estimates that with an increase in farm income of $1 billion less than 25 per cent of the farmers receive 75 per cent of the increase and 45 per cent of the farmers receive less than 7 per cent of the increase. See D. G. Johnson, *Trade and Agriculture,* Wiley, New York, 1950, p. 90.

[35] For a suggested farm program which is compatible with a liberal commercial policy, see *ibid.,* Chap. 7.

Foreign Policy and Imports

In Chap. 6 we saw how American tariff policy had progressed from a unilateral high-tariff policy in 1930 to one in which the majority of the American people and most of the organizations representing them favored a program of reciprocal tariff negotiation after 1934.[36] During the war there was relatively little interest in protective tariffs, and the Reciprocal Tariff Act was renewed in 1943 with only minor opposition. Since the original authority permitting a 50 per cent reduction in the 1930 duties had been largely exhausted, the 1945 bill renewing the President's authority to enter into reciprocal tariff arrangements provided for a maximum reduction of rates of 50 per cent of the level existing on January 1, 1945. This bill, which was approved in July, 1945, was essential to the administration's policy of promoting trade liberalization through multilateral trade negotiations and to the establishment of the proposed international trade organization already on the drafting board in the State Department. The Act again came up for renewal in 1948 when there was a Republican majority in the House of Representatives. The 1948 Act altered the original 1934 Act in two important respects: [37]

1. The Reciprocal Tariff Act was renewed for only one year instead of providing authority for three as in the original Act.

2. The Tariff Commission was removed from the Interdepartmental Trade Agreements Committee and was set up as an independent judge of the decisions of the interdepartmental group. The 1948 Act required the Tariff Commission to determine the minimum tariff rate and other import restrictions ("peril points") which it believed necessary to avoid the threat of serious injury to domestic industry producing any article under consideration for trade-agreement concessions by the United States and to report such findings to the President.

In the words of Assistant Secretary of State Willard Thorp, "the 1948 Act returns to the old protectionist theory that only the prosperity of an individual industry is affected by a tariff or a quota and practically makes such narrow protectionism the sole criterion for determining the concessions which may be made by the United States." [38] In 1949, the Reciprocal Trade Agreements Act was renewed for two more years, and the original provisions of the 1934 Act were, with a few minor exceptions,

[36] The Republicans in Congress, a majority of whom consistently voted against the Reciprocal Trade Act each time it was renewed, generally based their opposition not upon the principle of reciprocity itself but upon the administration of the law and the lack of adequate safeguards in the law.

[37] Public Law 792, 80th Congress, 2d Session, approved June 26, 1948.

[38] Department of State Press Release 51, Jan. 24, 1949.

restored. During the hearings on the 1949 bill, support was given by such business organizations as the Chamber of Commerce of the United States, the Commerce and Industry Association of New York, and the National Foreign Trade Council. The principal national labor and farm organizations also supported the bill.[39] It should be remembered, however, that while national groups representing labor and business may support the general principle of tariff reduction, representatives of both labor and capital in particular industries are likely to fight tariff reductions which affect their own products.[40]

While the original motivation for reciprocal tariff negotiations was to expand exports by securing tariff reductions abroad on particular United States exports in return for an equivalent concession of our own, postwar negotiations under conditions of a world dollar shortage and widespread exchange and quota restrictions against American goods have involved a different type of motivation. To a large degree the concessions which the United States has received have not directly increased exports because of the quantitative restrictions abroad. The benefit to our exports must come largely through the increased dollar earnings of other countries as a result of American tariff concessions. But the motivation for tariff reduction goes beyond the interest of the administration in maintaining or expanding American exports. It concerns the problem of the so-called "dollar gap," which has both economic and political implications. It is argued that an expansion of United States imports is essential to the economic or political stability of friendly foreign countries since they have import requirements which can be obtained only from the dollar area. It is also argued that larger imports are an alternative to foreign-aid programs and hence save money for the American taxpayers.[41] Moreover, according to the Trade Agreements Extension Act of 1951, the benefits of tariff concessions are not to be made available to Soviet-dominated countries. Thus the tariff issue, which for centuries has been one of the most popular subjects for economic debate, has to a major degree succumbed to the logic of the cold war.

[39] Report of House Committee on Ways and Means on H.R. 1211, 81st Congress, 1st Session, Feb. 4, 1949.

[40] The Trade Agreements Extension Act, signed June 16, 1951, renewed the authority of the President to negotiate reciprocal tariff reductions until June, 1953. However, the 1951 Act differed from the 1949 Act in several respects, including (a) the restoration of the "peril-point" requirement, similar to that found in the 1948 Act; (b) a directive to withdraw trade-agreement concessions to imports from the Soviet Union and countries dominated by the U.S.S.R.; (c) a directive to insert "escape clauses" in both new and existing trade agreements as soon as practicable; and (d) the prohibition of the importation of certain furs from the Soviet Union and Communist China.

[41] Report of the ECA—Commerce Mission, Economic Cooperation Administration, Washington, D.C., October, 1949.

Progress toward the Reduction of Tariff Rates and Other Import Barriers

The difficulties in measuring the height of tariff rates and of changes in rates are well known, but there can be no doubt but that the Reciprocal Tariff Program has resulted in a substantial reduction in import duties. Before any trade agreements were concluded, the average ad valorem duty on dutiable imports (weighted by the value of imports in 1947) was 28.4 per cent. On the same basis the average of rates in effect on January 1, 1950, was 14.5 per cent, an aggregate reduction of 49 per cent from the preagreement rates.[42] Despite this improvement, many rates on important commodities remain quite high, so high as to be prohibitive in character.[43] Rates of 50 per cent or more are quite common, and increased authority for rate reductions will be necessary to bring these rates down to a point where foreign countries can actively compete with American producers.

In many cases, tariff-administration regulations and policies have presented more of a barrier to United States imports than have the duties themselves.[44] As was pointed out in Chap. 6 many of the regulations were written into our tariff laws with the full knowledge of Congress that they would operate to deter imports. In line with the administration's policy of fostering imports, a survey of the United States Customs Service was conducted by a private firm of management consultants financed by funds specifically authorized by Congress. As a result of this survey, a draft bill known as the "Customs Simplification Act of 1950" was proposed by the Treasury Department and introduced as H.R. 8304 in the spring of 1950. The principal reforms provided by this draft bill may be summarized as follows:

1. Countervailing duties against imports subject to a foreign subsidy will be assessable only if a United States industry is being caused or threatened with material injury or if the establishment of an industry is being prevented or materially retarded.

[42] *Operation of the Trade Agreements Program*, Report 172, U.S. Tariff Commission, 1951. Since many United States duties are specific or compound rates the rise in prices since 1930–1933 has been responsible for a considerable amount of the decline in the ratio of duties collected to the value of imports.

[43] See *Report of the ECA–Commerce Mission* for an analysis of United States tariff rates and case studies of their effects on imports. See also *Second Report of the Organization for European Economic Cooperation*, pp. 156–161.

[44] For postwar case studies on the restrictive effects of United States tariff administrative procedures, see *Report of the ECA–Commerce Mission*, Appendixes J, K, L, M, N, O, P, and Q.

2. The present method of valuation for customs purposes is changed as follows: The use of "foreign value" and "American selling price" are eliminated, and "export value" is made the preferred method of valuation. The Tariff Act of 1930 provides that "foreign value" or "export value" shall be used, whichever is higher, and if neither can be ascertained, then the "United States value." In a few special cases, the rate of duty is to be based on the "American selling price." The proposed amendments will make possible the elimination of considerable uncertainty, expense, and delay in determining the basis for valuation and will in general provide a lower and more fair basis for valuation.

3. Certain processing taxes on imported commodities are to be converted into import duties.

4. Discrimination against imports in certain internal-revenue taxes including those on butter, cheese, spirits, and wine would be removed.

5. Provision is made for changes in the procedure for dealing with cases of undervaluation of imports. These changes would increase the efficiency of the customs service and modify the application of penalty duties on importers arising out of undervaluation.

6. Other amendments to existing customs legislation contained in the bill include the repeal of certain special "marking" requirements, free-entry provisions for travelers, free entry for noncommercial exhibitions, and a change in the existing law dealing with the conversion of foreign currencies to bring it into line with existing foreign-exchange practices.

Certain of these changes in existing tariff laws such as the elimination of the use of "American selling price" as a basis for customs valuation and the elimination of discriminatory processing taxes on imported vegetable oils are necessary in order to comply with the provisions of the ITO Charter. Perhaps the most important reform from the standpoint of increasing American imports has to do with providing American importers with greater certainty as to the basis for valuation. In addition to the provisions for simplifying our customs administration, there is also a need for a change in the system of tariff classification.[45]

Other Commercial-policy Questions

There are a number of other important commercial-policy problems which are vitally important to the foreign relations of the United States. Foremost among these are stock-piling, conservation of domestic reserves, the maintenance of industries vital to defense, e.g., the production of synthetic rubber, and shipping subsidies. In addition, there are important international problems in the fields of international commodity agree-

[45] For a discussion of this recommendation, see *Report to the President on Foreign Economic Policies*, pp. 81–83.

ments,[46] state trading,[47] and international cartels,[48] which are dealt with in the Havana Charter. There are also a number of problems in the field of transportation and communications for the solution of which international organizations have been created. Limitations of space prevent a discussion of these issues in this book.

In the case of those issues which involve a conflict between the requirements of national defense and liberal commercial policies which affect the interests of other countries, it should be possible to resolve many of these conflicts within the framework of the common defense arrangements such as the North Atlantic Pact. For example, the development of plans for a common shipping pool in time of war might lessen the need for the subsidization of United States shipping.[49] Just as national military de-

[46] The Havana Charter provides for the establishment of intergovernmental commodity-control agreements under the supervision of the Organization. The principles governing such agreements include participation both by producing and importing countries in the agreement, that the agreements will afford opportunities for the expansion of production in areas where the controlled commodity can be produced most efficiently, that participating countries will adopt internal policies to ensure progress toward a solution of the commodity problem which necessitated the agreement, and that the agreement must include measures designed to expand world consumption of the commodity (Art. 63). Agreements may include the regulation of production, exports or imports and prices (see Havana Charter, Chap. 6).

[47] Article 29 of the Havana Charter provides that a state trading enterprise "shall, in its purchases and sales involving either imports or exports, act in a manner consistent with the general principles of nondiscriminatory treatment prescribed in the Charter for governmental measures affecting imports or exports by private traders."

[48] Articles 46 to 54 of the Havana Charter deal with restrictive business practices including international cartels (both private and governmental). Article 46 requires each member "to prevent, on the part of private or public commercial enterprises, business practices affecting international trade which restrain competition, limit access to markets, or foster monopolistic control, *whenever such practices have harmful effects on the expansion of production or trade and interfere with the achievement of any of the other objectives set forth in Article 1.*" (Italics inserted.) Although provision is made for dealing with complaints of members whose interests have been harmed by restrictive business practices of other members, the provisions regarding restrictive business practices are certainly among the least satisfactory in the ITO Charter from the standpoint of American policy objectives.

[49] Postwar protection of United States shipping has mainly taken the form of operating subsidies and cargo preferences such as those provided for in the ECA Act discussed above. It may be noted that Gordon Gray's *Report to the President on Foreign Economic Policies* (Washington, D.C., November, 1950) was severely critical of the use of cargo preferences and similar types of discrimination. The Report recommended that the government limit the use of subsidies to the amounts necessary to maintain the operation of shipping facilities required for national security. However, the Report called attention to the fact that plans are being developed for the pooling of the tonnage of all North Atlantic Treaty Organization members in time of war, and that this fact should be taken into account in determining United States requirements. (*Ibid.,* pp. 87–91.)

fense is giving way to international military programs so must national economic defense, which has become one of the greatest barriers to international economic cooperation, give way to a program of international economic defense.

The Future of United States Commercial Policy

During 1949 and 1950 there was evidence of a growing apathy on the part of Congress and of administration leaders with respect to the promotion of liberal commercial policies. The bill authorizing United States participation in the ITO, which was first submitted to Congress in 1948, had not been acted upon by the close of the Eighty-first Congress. In December, 1950, the President decided not to resubmit the Havana Charter to the new Congress which convened in January, 1951.[50] The ITO was expected to become the major instrument for the realization of America's commercial-policy objectives. Although the contracting parties of the GATT have been actively engaged in conducting tariff negotiations and in dealing with special problems arising out of the interpretation of the Agreement, the GATT itself lacks the funds, the administrative machinery, and the authority to provide an effective administration of fair-trading practices. The absence of an effective international organization in this field would endanger America's reciprocal-tariff program since the effectiveness of tariff concessions depends upon adherence to a set of commercial-policy rules covering the use of quantitative import and export restrictions and the operations of state-trading organizations. Moreover, unless there is an international organization which administers rules in the commercial-policy field which are parallel with the regulations of the Monetary Fund in the field of foreign-exchange practices, little progress can be made by the Fund in promoting liberal exchange practices.

In the absence of the ITO, the next best alternative is to strengthen the GATT by the creation of a permanent staff and the enactment by the United States and other countries of legislation to carry out its provisions more fully. The United States will need to enact the customs simplification bill and make certain other changes in its customs regulations and system of excise taxes.

Although the GATT contains most of the provisions of the Havana Charter dealing with tariffs and quantitative trade restrictions, important provisions of the Charter, such as those dealing with cartels and intergovernmental commodity agreements, are not covered in the GATT.

[50] Department of State Press Release, Dec. 6, 1950.

Machinery for certain intergovernmental commodity agreements has already been established, *e.g.*, the International Wheat Agreement. Perhaps other provisions of the Charter could be administered by special UN agencies provided that appropriate international conventions could be adapted.

The promotion of liberal trading policies has a special significance at the present time, in the context of the defense program. We shall discuss this subject in the concluding chapter.

CHAPTER 18

American Economic Policy and Global Defense

THE HISTORY of the decade since 1940 has been marked by a growing participation in and feeling of responsibility for world affairs on the part of the United States. Since the end of World War II, this assumption of responsibility has been intensified by the growing threat of communism, whose frankly avowed goal is world domination. The dream of a world order based on the prewar system of a large number of independent sovereign states whose mutual problems would be dealt with in democratic fashion through international economic and political institutions has been shattered. The United States as the leading power of the non-Communist world must take the lead in organizing the material and moral resources of the free world in a struggle for survival. This involves concerted action in the military, political, economic, and informational fields.

America must have an economic policy which is consistent with her objectives and responsibilities as a great power in a hostile two-power world. If total war is expected to break out in the near future, economic policy, both national and international, should be immediately subordinated to military requirements. Domestic allocation and export controls should be instituted on a comprehensive basis, and the principles of lend-lease and reverse lend-lease should replace dollar availabilities and competitive position as the prime movers of international trade. While it might well be argued that the United States and the free nations associated with her should prepare immediately for an all-out war, up to the time of writing at any rate this has not been the decision of the American government. Rather the decision has been to strengthen the defenses of the North Atlantic Treaty powers, including those of the United States, and to provide economic and military assistance to halt the spread of communism in the underdeveloped areas, without interfering to a major degree with peacetime production and trade. This general approach is obviously based on the assumption that the struggle against communism will be of long duration and that it will be carried on by every means short of all-out warfare. The remainder of this chapter will be concerned

314

with a discussion of the economic policies which are most suitable for the carrying out of America's fundamental international objectives and responsibilities under the assumption that the conflict with the U.S.S.R. will continue at the economic, political, and limited military level for the next five to ten years.

The Domestic Economy

While the United States has readily appropriated money for defense and foreign economic assistance when needed to carry out its objectives, the governmental machinery for making the appropriate adjustments in the domestic economy necessary to accommodate these expenditures without inflationary and other undesirable repercussions operates much more slowly and less effectively. This is due in part to the fact that taxation and credit controls involve more serious political issues than the appropriation of money, and partly because of the inability of indirect control measures to achieve the production objectives of the defense program while at the same time maintaining economic stability. The fundamental question thus arises as to whether the American economy could in fact remain relatively free from direct governmental controls in the kind of international political atmosphere which is likely to exist for an indefinite period in the future. We must face the fact that the present international tension is not likely to be a temporary phenomenon followed by a return to normalcy in two or three or even ten years. The necessity of organizing the resources of the free world for defense against a powerful totalitarian power with a third of the world's population and land area under its hegemony for an indefinite period in the future will inevitably have far-reaching implications for the American economy. Governmental budgets aggregating one-fourth to one-third of the national income may become a permanent feature.[1] At such levels of government spending, the problem of large-scale unemployment is likely to disappear, since private investment and governmental borrowing could absorb almost any conceivable level of savings at full employment. The problem becomes one of increasing tax receipts and of dampening private investment, sufficiently to prevent continual inflation, whether open or suppressed.

[1] The President's budget (January, 1951) called for Federal government expenditures of $71.6 billion for the fiscal year 1952, an amount which represented about 25 per cent of gross national product (annual rate) in the fourth quarter of 1950. Although GNP will undoubtedly be higher in fiscal 1952, if we add to the Federal budget the expenditures of state and local governments (which amounted to nearly $20 billion in 1950), total governmental expenditures in fiscal 1952 will run well over one-fourth of GNP.

Serious doubts may be raised as to whether reasonable price stability could be achieved without wage, price, and other direct controls under conditions of full employment maintained by a large volume of governmental expenditures.[2] While the decision of the government in January, 1951, to impose general price and wage controls[3] was in response to an emergency situation which obviously could not have been dealt with by indirect measures, it is by no means clear that stabilization without direct controls could be achieved even with a balanced budget and more effective credit controls. Private consumption and investment can be fed by the large accumulation of liquid assets. Moreover, higher taxes tend to reduce saving as well as consumption, and the high level of private and governmental demand makes for a high propensity to invest. It may very well be that monetary and fiscal measures sufficiently deflationary to produce price stability would be incompatible with the objective of achieving and maintaining maximum production for civilian and defense needs. We may therefore need to consider the implications of a complex system of direct controls over the American economy on a more or less permanent basis.

Stability of the American economy is essential not only to our economic welfare but to the discharging of America's international obligations as well. America produces and consumes half of the world's income and considerably more than half of the income of the non-Communist world. In the second quarter of 1950, America accounted for over 19 per cent of the world's exports and nearly 15 per cent of the world's imports.[4] Price and income stability in the United States are essential conditions of world stability. While the eleventh session of the Economic and Social Council of the United Nations meeting in the summer of 1950 was devoting most of its energies to a discussion of the harmful consequences of unemployment and deflation, the countries of Western Europe were experiencing a serious deterioration of their terms of trade as a consequence of rapidly rising raw-material prices. In the light of the rearmament programs of the non-Communist world, it would have been better for the Council to have devoted more of its attention to the study of the problems of inflation and world-wide commodity shortages.

The author does not want to minimize the importance of America's

[2] According to the Council of Economic Advisors, "Even the most rigorous tax program designed to keep disposable income in line with available production requires the assistance of price and wage controls." See *The Economic Report of the President*, Washington, D.C., January, 1951, p. 98.

[3] See *The New York Times*, Jan. 28, 1951, for text of price- and wage-control order.

[4] *Summary of World Trade Statistics*, United Nations Statistical Office, Lake Success, N.Y., January, 1951, pp. 12–13.

responsibility for preventing sharp fluctuations in the supply of dollars which it makes available to the rest of the world. The American depression of the early 1930's helped to produce a Nazi Germany which seriously threatened the security of the United States. Another serious depression could well be disastrous to the security and independence of the free world. Even minor recessions in the United States, which the author believes are more or less unavoidable in a competitive economy with relatively few direct controls, may have serious repercussions on other economies. While the United States delegation to the Economic and Social Council during the summer of 1950 rejected the suggestion of an automatic mechanism for dealing with balance-of-payments disequilibrium arising from fluctuation in business activity,[5] there could be little doubt that the United States recognized its responsibility in this field. In the opinion of the author, a more feasible approach would be to provide the International Monetary Fund with sufficient resources for contracyclical operations on an administrative rather than on an automatic basis. With all countries pursuing policies which will assure reasonably full employment and given a measure of stability of international investment through the International Bank, it should be possible for the Fund to perform this function with dollar resources of perhaps triple their present level.[6]

Meanwhile, a realistic appraisal of current trends would seem to indicate that the economic problems of the free world are more likely to be those arising from an economy of scarcity rather than one of abundance for the next few years. The greatest threat to world stability may be an American inflation rather than American depression. A competitive bidding up of raw-material prices with supplies going to the highest bidder will not provide the most efficient distribution of resources for the building up of the defense of the non-Communist world. While some countries will gain from higher raw-material prices, many will suffer a serious deterioration in their terms of trade. This is particularly true of the industrial countries of Europe which do not have territories or associated monetary areas that produce these materials. World-wide allocation arrangements are of course necessary in the present emergency period in the case of some commodities. But it would be unfortunate indeed if inflationary pressures in the United States and the rest of the free world made it necessary to conduct the bulk of the world's trade under conditions of direct controls. Such a development would put an end to all hope

[5] See *National and Fundamental Measures for Full Employment*, United Nations, Lake Success, N.Y., December, 1949. See Chap. 10 for a discussion of these proposals.

[6] The rise in world prices since the Fund was established in 1944 has reduced the real value of its gold and dollars by nearly half.

of reestablishing a free trading world just as the so-called "dollar short-age" is beginning to disappear. In fact, a world-wide commodity shortage would be even more damaging to the system of world-wide competitive trade than the dollar shortage has been in the past.

THE UNITED STATES BALANCE OF PAYMENTS AND FOREIGN ECONOMIC POLICY

The balance-of-payments problem of the United States is largely a re-flection of this country's concern with the economic problems of other countries. Having a strong currency which other countries are willing to hold and over half of the world's supply of monetary gold,[7] the United States could weather almost any conceivable current deficit. Even if gold were demonetized, the competitive strength of American exports is great enough to meet her peacetime demand for imports without marketing difficulties or a serious reduction in her terms of trade. On the other hand, America is not highly dependent upon foreign markets for her prosperity. Exports of goods and services in 1949 represented only about 6 per cent of America's gross national product and about 5 per cent in 1950. The export surplus, which amounted to $6.2 billion in 1949, was cut to $2.2 billion in 1950 while GNP and employment rose rapidly dur-ing this period. While it is true that a severe cutback in foreign trade would seriously affect certain industries and agricultural products,[8] the effects on the economy as a whole would be small, assuming appropriate monetary and fiscal policies and perhaps certain activities on the part

[7] The strength of the dollar is largely due to the ability to exchange it for American goods which the world needs. To a considerable degree the value of gold is dependent upon the fact that it is readily convertible into dollars at $35 per ounce. (The discount on the dollar in terms of gold has existed only in restricted markets, and the premium on gold could probably be eliminated by a sizable flow of gold into world markets.) Hence, it may be said that the value of America's gold stock as a means of meeting United States deficits depends upon the confidence of the rest of the world in being able ultimately to exchange the gold for American goods, *i.e.*, the economic strength of the American economy. If (as some students have predicted) the United States develops a substantial import surplus during the defense period, it will be the result of the imposition of export controls designed to conserve goods for other uses, and not be-cause of this country's inability to sell in world markets. Should foreign countries find it necessary to accumulate large amounts of gold and dollars because of their inability to import from the United States, they might appreciate their currencies or even re-strict exports except for payment in goods. In other words, a loss of confidence in both gold and dollars would be possible under these circumstances.

[8] For example, in 1949 the United States exported 39 per cent of her wheat produc-tion, 33 per cent of her raw cotton, 26 per cent of her tobacco, 32 per cent of her machine tools, and 11 per cent of her production of trucks.

of the government for easing the burden of adjustment on the section of the economy most affected. This is not to say, of course, that the nation would not benefit by higher levels of trade, both as a consumer and a producer, but unlike Britain or Australia or Belgium the economic welfare of the United States is not fundamentally dependent upon foreign trade.[9] While this situation exists today, it is entirely possible that, in future generations, America's dependence upon imports and foreign markets may be far greater than it is today. It is also true that, in time of war, America's need for raw-material imports tends to expand so that her national security may depend upon increased availabilities of certain strategic commodities produced in other countries, e.g., petroleum and nonferrous ores. But even in periods of emergency, America's dependence upon foreign sources of supply relates to a group of particular commodities, the total value of which is small relative to total domestic output, and does not present a balance-of-payments problem as such.[10]

It is clear that the balance-of-payments problem of the United States in the postwar period has been largely a problem of foreign rather than domestic economic policy. The statistical manifestation of this problem is the fact that United States exports have been larger than the *normal* means of financing them.[11] But this is not in itself the real problem. From the point of view of world equilibrium and the existence of international economic conditions which make possible the elimination of trade and currency restrictions, the significant problem lies in the fact that the rest of the world wants to buy more dollar goods than it is able to afford. But this situation in itself would not call for foreign-assistance programs—except possibly for stabilization credits to assist countries in restoring a balance in their international accounts. The world could conceivably be quite prosperous and still have a dollar-balance problem

[9] This generalization must be qualified to the extent of America's dependence upon a few critical raw-material imports for which adequate substitutes cannot be produced in commercial quantities.

[10] Although during World War II the United States had a cash deficit on current account, this deficit could easily have been turned into a surplus had this country released additional resources for cash exports or demanded cash for some of the exports financed under lend-lease.

[11] The usual definition of the "dollar gap" as the excess of exports of goods and services over imports is quite misleading since it gives the impression that an export or an import surplus is somehow abnormal or undesirable. Normal means of financing United States exports should include, in addition to imports, private long-term capital exports (including International Bank for Reconstruction and Development loans financed by United States capital), Export-Import Bank loans of a nonemergency character, regular private remittances, and the purchase by the United States of an appropriate portion of the world's current output of gold.

if appropriate domestic and foreign trade policies were not followed both in the United States and abroad.

Although the foreign economic policy of the United States is directed toward encouraging countries to adopt economic policies which will permit them to get along without trade and exchange restrictions, the most urgent problem in the postwar years has arisen from the fact that many foreign countries have been unable to earn an amount of dollars or other foreign exchange sufficient to maintain standards of living and rates of economic progress which the United States believes are necessary in the light of America's own foreign economic policy. Very often these standards have been somewhat arbitrary, and the calculation of the United States assistance required to meet them has been subject to wide margins of error. But the balance-of-payments problem which foreign aid has sought to deal with arises basically from the gap between what we think countries ought to have in the way of dollar imports and what they can afford to pay for. This is a matter of the *program* balance of payments rather than the *market* balance (resulting from what would occur if the world demand for dollar goods were uncontrolled) or the *accounting* balance,[12] *i.e.,* the actual current-account surplus or deficit.

In concluding this section we may say that the *accounting* balance of payments in itself provides very little guidance for American foreign economic policy. If United States exports are declining, it may indicate that other countries are becoming less dependent upon the United States for the goods which they need to keep their economies running, or it may mean that they lack the dollars necessary for essential imports which are unavailable elsewhere. If United States imports decline, it may mean that foreign export prices are too high relative to United States prices, that United States demand has shifted as a result of a fall in income or the development of domestic substitutes for imports, or that there has been a shift in foreign supplies of exports due to an impairment of productive facilities or a diversion of such facilities to other uses. Whether or not these shifts in the United States balance of payments requires special action on the part of this country and what kind of action depends upon a variety of conditions and upon how American foreign-policy objectives are affected. For example, the fact that United States exports exceed imports is not in itself a cause for concern, nor is the fact that our foreign trade is in balance a sign that our international economic relations are in good order. We must look behind the balance of pay-

---

[12] See Fritz Machlup, "Three Concepts of the Balance of Payments and the So-called Dollar Shortage," *Economic Journal*, March, 1950, pp. 46–48; see also Raymond F. Mikesell, "International Disequilibrium," *American Economic Review*, June, 1949, pp. 618–645.

ments in order to determine whether or not our foreign-policy objectives are being realized.

The Gray Report

While in most areas of the world satisfactory progress toward the recovery of production was being achieved, in 1949 a number of countries, including those of Western Europe, began to experience difficulty in marketing their exports for the currencies which they needed to meet their import requirements. Thus it appeared that while the European Recovery Program countries would be potentially viable by mid-1952, in the sense that they would be able to produce a physical volume of goods for home use and for export sufficient to maintain adequate consumption and investment standards, there were serious doubts as to whether these countries could find markets for their exports. Since a considerable portion of Western Europe's imports had to come from the dollar area, this meant that Western Europe had to earn dollars from third areas in order to meet her anticipated deficit in dollars. But so long as nearly every country in the world had a deficit with the dollar area it was difficult for any country to earn dollars multilaterally.

In 1949, the United States still had a surplus on current account with every major area in the world and a total surplus of $6.2 billion. United States government loans and grants plus disbursements of the Monetary Fund and International Bank were approximately equal to the United States export surplus (see Table 6, page 115). In these circumstances, the United States government and a large section of the informed public became seriously concerned about the domestic and international repercussions of the projected reduction of United States foreign aid. In recognition of this concern, in March, 1950, President Truman appointed Gordon Gray,[13] formerly Secretary of the Army, as his Special Assistant with the duty of studying the problem of the future adjustment of the United States balance of payments and of making recommendations for governmental action which would be consistent with the basic foreign-policy objective of the United States. While popular interest in this problem tended to be concerned with the accounting "dollar gap," Gray and his staff rightly approached the problem in terms of how best to deal with the import requirements of other countries in the light of the specific foreign economic and political objectives of the United States.

The artificial nature of an approach in terms of the dollar gap was demonstrated by the developments of the first six months of 1950, during

[13] For text of the President's letter of Mar. 31, 1950, to Mr. Gray, see *The New York Times*, Apr. 3, 1950.

which the United States surplus on current account fell from $6.2 billion in 1949 to an annual rate of only $2.9 billion, and foreign countries accumulated over a billion dollars in gold and dollar assets. In the third quarter of 1950, this current-account surplus almost disappeared.[14] Although a part of this shift in the United States balance of payments can be attributed to the increased military expenditures following the outbreak of war in Korea, a rapid trend toward international balance was clearly evident following the series of currency devaluations after September, 1949. The reasons for this shift in America's balance of payments lie in a combination of factors, including the expansion of United States business activity, the rise in prices of international raw materials such as rubber, coffee, and tin; increased restrictions on dollar imports into the sterling area; expanded production in Western Europe, and the increased competitive advantage of Western European exports resulting from the devaluations.

What was the significance of these international balance-of-payments developments from the standpoint of America's foreign-policy objectives? The fact that a number of countries in Latin America and Asia began to earn dollar surpluses made it possible for other countries having deficits with the dollar area to capture some of the surplus dollars. The marginal utility of other currencies began to increase relative to that of the dollar as the competitive position of nondollar exports improved. Moreover, some countries were able to earn more dollars, after taking account of United States aid, than they needed for the purchase of planned requirements of dollar and nondollar goods, and they were therefore able to build up their gold and dollar reserves. All this meant that, while many countries of the world had a balance-of-payments problem, their problem was not so much a dollar problem as it was a problem of obtaining additional resources. In other words, if countries had the capacity to export they could obtain the imports which they need to sustain their economies.[15]

The easing of the dollar shortage and the international political developments of the summer of 1950 changed the nature of America's foreign economic problems but by no means eliminated them. While some ERP countries have greatly benefited by the rise in world raw-material

[14] The United States current-account surplus in the third quarter of 1950 was only $91 million, and for 1950 as a whole it was $2.2 billion. *Survey of Current Business,* March, 1951.

[15] The world's dollar problem as such will not be entirely eliminated until all the currencies used in financing international transactions are convertible into dollars. Nevertheless, the possibilities for earning dollars multilaterally or of obtaining commodities produced in surplus only in the dollar area in trade with nondollar countries greatly increased during 1950.

prices, *e.g.*, Great Britain, the Netherlands, and Belgium, other countries which do not have territories or associated monetary areas producing raw materials have suffered a severe deterioration in their terms of trade, *e.g.*, Germany, Austria, and Italy, not compensated by a rise in invisible income. In addition, the projected increased defense budgets of the North Atlantic Pact countries will mean additional import requirements which these countries will not be able to finance with their own resources.

Another range of problems which will not be solved by the closing of the dollar gap has to do with the promotion of political stability in the underdeveloped areas. So long as two-thirds of the so-called free world, *i.e.*, the world outside the Soviet sphere, is ill-clothed, ill-housed, and ill-fed, and its peoples without hope of a better way of life, they are in danger of being turned to communism. Finally, America's objectives in the field of international trade and payments are a long way from being realized by a narrowing of the statistical dollar gap. Although the realization of these objectives will depend in part upon the policies of other countries, much depends upon what this country does to promote them.

It was to these problems that Gray and his staff addressed themselves in their *Report to the President on Foreign Economic Policies,* in an effort to provide an answer to the problem of what foreign economic policies America should adopt under conditions as they existed in the fall of 1950.[16] While this Report has not been officially recognized by the administration as representing United States government policy, it is on the whole consistent with administration policy, and must therefore be regarded as an important summary of America's foreign economic policy at the time it was written and an indication of future developments in this field. Although the following discussion is not to be regarded as a summary of the Gray Report, it is in general agreement with the Report, and the author has drawn heavily from the Report in its preparation.

The Role of Foreign Economic Assistance [17]

Three primary purposes which can be served by foreign economic assistance in a period in which the major objective of foreign policy is

[16] This Report was published Nov. 10, 1950. In addition to Gordon Gray, the staff consisted of Edward S. Mason, Deputy, Felix Belair, Jr., Theodore W. Braun, Kermit Gordon, G. Griffith Johnson, John H. Kaufmann, Raymond F. Mikesell, Walter S. Salant, Ralph N. Stohl, and Philip H. Trezise.

[17] We shall make a distinction between economic assistance and purely military assistance which takes the form of military end-use items such as tanks and military planes. Economic assistance in the form of coal, steel, or industrial machinery may of course be used to produce military end-use items by the recipient country.

the defense of the free world against threatened Communist aggression are (1) to enable friendly countries to build up their military strength for resisting external aggression, (2) to develop sources of raw materials needed for the defense and economic well-being of the United States and other friendly nations, and (3) to create economic conditions which will eliminate or weaken Communist forces operating within countries still outside the Soviet orbit. Where military action on a substantial scale has broken out, either in the form of a civil war as in the case of Indo-China, or in the form of external invasion as in the case of Korea, economic assistance becomes almost indistinguishable in its function from military assistance. Frequently, foreign economic assistance may serve more than one purpose. For example, Economic Cooperation Administration aid to France undoubtedly promotes political stability in France as well as assists in the French rearmament program. A loan to Bolivia for the development of her transportation system raises the living standards of the people, thereby promoting political stability, and at the same time helps to increase the supply of tin available to the United States and her allies.

Foreign economic assistance may be made available in the form of grants or loans, but in general loans should be confined to projects which meet certain standards of public investment. All too often the United States government has provided assistance in the form of loans simply on the grounds of feasibility or the availability of funds. We have seen, for example, that both the Export-Import Bank and the International Bank have made loans for emergency balance-of-payments purposes which could not be justified in terms of sound investment criteria. Such practices inevitably discredit public investment in the eyes of the public and weaken the respect for public-investment obligations in the minds of the borrowers since public investment becomes closely identified with grants. Public investment should be confined to loans for projects which make a contribution to the productive capital of the borrower and which directly or indirectly improve the foreign-exchange position of the borrower by an amount at least sufficient to pay interest on the borrowed funds.[18]

In general, economic assistance to provide countries with the additional resources for building up their defense establishments should be made in the form of grants. There may be cases, however, where loans for the creation of industrial facilities which contribute to both military output and to civilian production for home use and for export could properly be made to countries whose balance-of-payments prospects are

[18] Whether or not the project should be one which will result in an increase in the foreign-exchange earnings of the country sufficient to repay the principal depends upon the future borrowing pattern of the country in question.

favorable and where the projects to be financed will contribute to the balance-of-payments position of the country in question. Where countries are, however, in need of net resources for increased defense production which does not contribute to their civilian economy or to their foreign-exchange position, assistance should be made available in the form of grants.

Grants may also be employed in promoting better economic conditions in underdeveloped countries in the form of technical assistance, working capital, or the financing of large projects such as irrigation systems. Whether such assistance should be made available in the form of grants or loans depends upon the bankability of the project in terms of sound lending criteria and not upon the nature of the project to be financed. Under present conditions, highest priority in the provision of economic assistance to countries which are not expected to be able to defend them-selves against external aggression must be given to those areas which can contribute raw materials needed for building up the defenses of the free world and to those areas where internal Communist aggression pre-sents an immediate and serious threat to the independence of existing governments.

Assistance to Western Europe

Until 1949, the principal political motivation for Marshall Plan and other aid to Western Europe was the desire to prevent internal political breakdown and internal Communist revolution. After the formation of the North Atlantic Pact in 1949, and especially since the outbreak of war in Korea in 1950, America's principal objective has been the rapid rearmament of Western Europe and joint participation with the other North Atlantic Treaty Organization (NATO) countries in a common defense program. Under these conditions, economic requirements for recovery and well-being become inseparable from the economic require-ments for rearmament, since a country will devote to its military defense, in peacetime at least, only such resources as it can spare after its mini-mum civilian requirements have been met.

It would be exceedingly difficult to provide a country with the exact amounts and kinds of goods and services which it needs to offset the impact of a given defense program or of such part of that impact which the country was not expected to bear itself. Moreover, to provide economic aid on this basis would tend to disrupt normal trade channels by super-imposing a complex system of intergovernmental commodity transfers upon the system of international trade. Hence it would appear preferable to extend financial assistance to NATO countries after an over-all assessment of their economic needs including their contributions to the combined military program, in the form of dollar exchange rather than specific commodities tied to specific projects.[19] As a condition for receiving financial assistance in an untied form, however, the recipients should be held to certain performance standards based on agreed plans.

An important advantage in providing financial assistance in the form of free dollars as against specific commodities or dollars tied to the purchase of specific United States exports is that it enables the recipient nations to buy in the cheapest markets and increases the supply of dollars available for making multilateral settlements. Thus if dollars are made available to France, she may use them for making purchases in Germany or in Argentina. This assumes, however, that nondollar countries are in fact willing to use dollars in making settlements with other nondollar countries and that the exports of these other nondollar countries are sufficiently competitive with United States exports to induce France to use the dollars for purchases outside the dollar area. Under conditions of world-wide dollar scarcity, this assumption is not wholly valid. One way to assure the use of American dollar aid for purchases outside the United States is the familiar method of offshore purchases, employed by ECA in the first year of its operations. This system, however, has a number of administrative drawbacks and does not contribute to the restoration of competitive world markets and multilateral trade. The European Payments Union provides a mechanism through which a portion of United States aid can be channeled to Western Europe and the dollars employed for financing surpluses in intra-European trade. Thus a portion of the United States aid to France could be turned over to the EPU, which in turn would make France a grant in EPU credits.[20] France could use this EPU credit or drawing right for making additional purchases in other EPU countries including the entire sterling area and the French and Belgium monetary areas, without incurring any additional obligation. The dollars which were turned over to the EPU would be earned by those countries which had a surplus with the EPU countries as a whole. This procedure would stimulate competition in intra-European trade and increase the supply of dollars for making multilateral settlements.

19 An exception to this principle might be made in the case of United States transfers of military end-use items such as tanks and military planes, which do not enter into the normal course of foreign trade.

20 In the technical language of the EPU, France would receive an "initial credit position" in the EPU which would enable her to run a deficit with other EPU members equal to the amount of the grant, without being required to pay gold or assume any credit obligation to the EPU.

It is recognized, of course, that all United States financial assistance to Western European countries could not be made in the form of dollars channeled through EPU, since some countries will need dollars for purchases in the non-EPU area over and above what they can be expected to earn multilaterally. It would be preferable that even these dollars not be tied to the purchase of specific United States commodities. Financial aid should be determined in accordance with estimates of what a country will require to pay for needed imports to accomplish a particular set of objectives. While certain standards of performance must be insisted upon as a condition for continued aid, there should be as little interference as possible with the use of the dollars which are made available to the aid recipients. What is significant is how the foreign country employs its entire foreign exchange and internal resources, not how it disposes of that part of its total resources made available in the form of United States aid. Moreover, if the performance of the aid recipient turns out to be better than was anticipated, we should not be concerned by the fact that the country added a modest amount to its monetary reserves. In fact, some allowance ought to be made for moderate increases in the reserve positions of a number of countries whose gold and dollar reserves are quite low. Such an improvement is necessary if countries are going to be able to relax their trade controls and if substantial progress is going to be made toward the restoration of currency convertibility.

The Underdeveloped Areas: A World in Revolution

While the vast bulk of America's expenditures for defense must be concentrated upon building up the economic and military strength of the Atlantic Treaty nations, there are both immediate and longer range objectives to be realized in the underdeveloped areas which are equally vital to the independent existence of the free world. By the underdeveloped areas we mean the countries and dependencies with low per capita incomes—say less than $100 per year—relative to those of the countries of Western Europe, the United States, Canada, and Oceania. For the most part, these areas comprise the countries of South and Central America, Asia and Africa, the non-Communist areas of which contain over a billion people, or 70 per cent of the population outside the Soviet orbit. Despite the low level of incomes in these areas, they contain a large share of the world's resources of raw materials upon which the industrial nations depend for their economic well-being and for their defense.

Our immediate objectives for these areas are that they do not fall into Communist hands as a result of internal revolution and that they produce an expanding volume of raw materials available for the non-Communist world. Our longer range objective is for them to develop high living standards and independent democratic governments and to become bulwarks of strength for the preservation of a free and democratic world.

World War II has intensified a social revolution in these areas which has been going on for several decades. Millions of peoples are anxious to change the social and economic pattern which has characterized the lives of their ancestors for thousands of years. The vague yearnings of the masses in the underdeveloped areas for living standards comparable to those of the United States and Western Europe provided the power for the nationalist movements during the past four decades. But in many cases the formation of nationalist governments or the winning of greater autonomy on the part of Western dependencies has not changed the lot of the vast bulk of their populations. Western rule has been frequently replaced by inefficient and corrupt native governments whose principal interest has been maintaining a semifeudal economy operated for the benefit of the few. While in some cases the native leadership has been enlightened, and democratic institutions have been introduced, slow progress has been made in the field of agricultural reform, progressive taxation, and the introduction of social services financed by the state. Yet the United States and the other Western powers have had to deal with these governments and strengthen them against the revolutionary forces frequently led by the Communists.

The failure of the Western nations and of the local nationalist governments to satisfy the desires of the native populations for economic and social reform has been the basis for the strength of communism in the Far East and in the other underdeveloped areas. (This has also been true in certain Western European countries as well.) Where existing governments have failed to satisfy the longing of the masses for a better way of life, the Communists have been able to capture the imaginations of the people through their promises and have therefore been able to assume the leadership of the revolutionary movements.

The social revolution which is encompassing a large proportion of the peoples of the world cannot be denied or suppressed. Reactionary governments may be able to contain it for a time, but in the long run they will fail. The task of democracy and of the democratic governments of the world is to capture the leadership of this revolution and guide it toward constructive ends. We must show the peoples of the world that their desire for a better way of life can best be realized through the operation of democratic institutions and that communism can mean only continued privation and slavery. This cannot be accomplished by words alone. Nor are loans and grants a sufficient condition of success. In some cases, little can be achieved without a basic reform of local govern-ments. Governments must be established which will institute land re-form,[21] better conditions for the industrial worker, and an expansion of social services of all kinds and which will eliminate corruption and inef-ficiency among governmental officials. Any attempt on the part of the United States government to foment revolutions or to interfere in the political life of other countries is, however, likely to be resented by all groups within the country. This situation presents a real dilemma since we have to work through and cooperate with existing local governments which may not be responsive to the desires of the masses for social reform. Except by working through local governments we can do nothing; but in cooperating with them the United States has frequently been accused of supporting the forces of reaction.

The author believes that the answer to this problem is for the United States to work largely through the United Nations and its specialized agencies such as the International Bank and Monetary Fund and the Food and Agricultural Organization, in achieving these objectives in the underdeveloped areas. While the UN missions must work with the local governments, they are less likely to be charged with supporting reaction since the missions represent all countries. Moreover, UN missions can bring pressure on local governments and require standards of perform-ance which American representatives might be unable to do because of the danger of resentment against interference by a foreign power. This does not mean that America can shirk her own responsibility by letting the UN do the job. It means that we must transfer more of our dollars and above all more of our best technicians and administrative personnel into UN agencies and foreign missions. It is suggested, for example, that the United States government seek to train people in its own depart-ments for UN work and that it lend its own officials to the UN agencies for special missions from time to time.

While the United States may want to provide special financial assistance to achieve specific aims in certain underdeveloped areas, it follows from the analysis given above that the major effort ought to be made through

21 Most United States governmental officials working in the field of technical assistance to underdeveloped areas believe that the promotion of land reform, including reform of the systems of land tenure and tenancy, represents one of the most significant activi-ties for combating communism. One of the agencies which has had considerable success in this field is the Joint Commission on Rural Reconstruction (JCRR), which is com-posed of United States and Chinese members. The ECA has also promoted land reform in Korea and elsewhere in the Far East. The importance of reforming the system of land tenure was heavily stressed in the *Report of the Economic Survey Mission to the Philippines* (Bell Report), Department of State, Washington, D.C., October, 1950, pp. 55–56.

the agencies of the UN. The technical-assistance program of the UN Technical Assistance Board ought to be broadened to include grants for seeds, fertilizers, simple tools, health, sanitation, and other services, to be administered by UN officials perhaps jointly with local governmental personnel. There should also be close cooperation between the technical-assistance agencies and the International Bank in the development of projects and long-range developmental programs for these countries. Where special United States assistance is made available in the form of loans by the Export-Import Bank or grant assistance through the Point Four organization, there should be the closest cooperation between the UN and the American agencies. This would seem to require a greater coordination of programs of financial assistance of all kinds within the American government itself.

The amount of capital investment and grant assistance for the under-developed areas during the present period of high defense expenditures must necessarily be limited both by reason of the additional inflationary pressures which such expenditures would generate in the United States and the growing world shortage of commodities. The uncertain political situation and constant danger of local or generalized warfare will prob-ably have the effect of reducing private direct investment as well. On the other hand, the need for expanding foreign sources of raw materials will make it desirable for the United States and other Western nations to finance the development of strategic and critical materials throughout the free world. Since the expansion of the capacities of the underde-veloped areas for supplying materials in world-wide short supply will require a certain amount of general economic development, e.g., trans-portation, power, and housing, expenditures for this purpose can serve both the immediate needs of the defense effort and the longer run ob-jectives of economic development.

In spite of the competitive demands for resources, a measure of public investment and grant assistance for economic development is highly es-sential for the realization of even our defense objectives. We must not let the masses in the underdeveloped areas believe that they have been forgotten in the midst of a gigantic political struggle between the great powers. Our program for the underdeveloped areas must be carried on if these people are to be won over to the democratic way of life, and we must hold before them the promise of far greater assistance toward a better way of life once the menace of communism has been dispelled.

COMMERCIAL AND FINANCIAL POLICIES

Two world wars plus a steady growth of economic nationalism have wrought so much damage to the world's system of payments and trade that a large number of economists and government officials have all but abandoned hope for the restoration of liberal trading practices. For a time during and immediately following World War II a primary postwar objective of the United States was the freeing of world trade from direct controls of all kinds and the gradual reduction of tariff barriers. The high hopes for substantial progress in this direction were disappointed, and enthusiasm among government officials in Washington for vigorous action in pursuing these objectives has waned. Moreover, such efforts as are being made toward the restoration of a world-wide system of multilateral trade and payments have been greatly dampened by the outbreak of the Korean War and inauguration of the rearmament program.

What kind of commercial and financial policies should the United States adopt and seek to implement during the next few years? To be realistic we must admit that the defense of the free world, which must be our primary objective, seriously interferes with the promotion of liberal trading practices. The need for export controls over commodities in scarce supply and the necessity of rationing imports of scarce commodities must be regarded as inevitable consequences of the defense effort. In addition, many countries will be subject to new inflationary pressures which will require tighter import controls in order to achieve a balance in their international accounts. Finally, there are the trade restrictions which grow out of the need for preventing goods of military significance from reaching Soviet-dominated areas.

There are, however, a few favorable elements in the picture. For one thing, it should be easier for the United States to liberalize its own import restrictions which have been imposed for protective purposes. Also, the high level of demand in this country is likely to mean a continued rise in United States imports while exports are likely to be curtailed by export controls. During the summer of 1950, the United States reached approximate balance on current account for the first time since 1937. Of course this balance would not have occurred in the absence of continued severe import restrictions against dollar goods abroad, but with rising prices of raw-material imports coupled with a high and growing United States demand, the trend is toward a better balance between the demand for and supply of dollar exchange. This means that while for many countries the over-all demand for foreign goods will exceed the available supply, the excess of demand will not be concentrated to the same degree on the United States. In other words, the world-wide dollar shortage may tend to disappear.

One important consequence of a better balance in the world demand and supply for dollars is the possibility of restoring a system of multilateral settlements among the countries of the free world. In the absence of total war, a large part of the world's trade will be conducted and financed through normal channels, even though much of the trade may be subject to controls required by world-wide commodity shortages and the inability of a number of countries to balance their international accounts without import restrictions. These limitations on trade, however, are less serious than those imposed by the absence of a system of multilateral settlements. The inability of a country to use its surplus with another country or currency area to discharge deficits with other currency areas leads to trade discrimination. The widespread existence of trade discrimination makes for a less efficient use of the resources of the free world.

Even if most nations were to adopt permanent policies of controlling the foreign trade of their citizens or even in a world of socialist states in which foreign trade was entirely confined to state enterprises, a system of multilateral settlements would be necessary for the best use of the world's resources and for maximizing the gains from trade. Moreover, many nations which would otherwise prefer to adopt liberal trade policies are prevented from doing so by the lack of an international system of multilateral payments. We may conclude therefore that the United States ought to work for the restoration of a system of multilateral settlements among the nations of the non-Communist world during the rearmament period.

While a number of different types of multilateral settlement systems are possible, the essential element must be the ability of the central bank or monetary authority of each country to use a current balance with one monetary area for settling a deficit with another. At present, there are two lines of approach which appear to be the most feasible: (1) We should encourage and assist in the reestablishment of convertibility of sterling currently acquired by nonresidents of Britain or their central banks.[22] (2) The United States should continue to support the EPU but should require the system to move progressively toward full gold settlements and a narrowing of the credit swings. But the reestablishment of a system of multilateral settlements will not be effective in eliminating discrimination until nations agree to nondiscriminatory trade practices. The failure of the American Congress to authorize American participation in the International Trade Organization has undoubtedly hindered the promotion of liberal trading practices. As was suggested in Chap. 17, however, many of the objectives of the ITO could be realized by a strengthening of the General Agreements on Tariffs and Trade.

[22] Britain may prefer to make gold or dollar settlements only through central banks as a means of achieving better control over capital movements.

Although considerable progress in the field of tariff reduction has been achieved in recent years, America's own commercial and financial practices leave much to be desired. Tariff reduction is not only desirable as a means of promoting world economic welfare through larger trade, but it can be an important means of lessening inflationary pressures and promoting the defense effort in the United States. The present method of reducing tariffs through bargaining with other countries ought to be supplemented by a unilateral reduction in some duties. This should be left to administrative discretion, although Congress would probably want to put a time limit on the authority of the President in this field. Likewise, the present period of high demand for agricultural commodities would seem to provide an excellent opportunity to introduce major reforms in our agricultural support system and to eliminate import quotas and export subsidies on agricultural commodities. Finally, the United States could promote multilateral trade and reduce the pressure of demand in this country by permitting the proceeds of her loans and grants to be spent in markets outside the United States.

While recognizing the need for the removal of trade barriers as a means of achieving a better allocation of resources, there are important areas of production and trade which will need to be subjected to governmental control in the present period of rearmament. The rapid increase in demand for commodities with low short-run supply elasticities can only mean a rapid bidding up of prices with the supplies going to the highest bidder regardless of the priority of need. National priority and allocation controls should be supplemented by international control arrangements for commodities in international short supply. This policy was put forward by President Truman in *The Economic Report of the President* in January, 1951, and negotiations for the international control of essential commodities are being conducted at the time of writing.[23]

The Long Run

For the past two generations there have been two contradictory sociopolitical movements in the world. One has been a movement toward political and economic nationalism and higher barriers to the free move-

[23] See, for example, "Cooperation among Free World in Controlling Scarce Materials," *Department of State Bulletin,* Jan. 22, 1951, pp. 149–150; see also "Cooperation on Commodities," *The Economist,* Jan. 20, 1951, pp. 149–150. Since this chapter was written the International Materials Conference has been established, and in the summer of 1951 agreements were reached for the international allocation of a number of materials in short supply.

ment of commodities, capital, populations, and ideas. The other has been a movement toward closer physical contact and economic and political interdependence, as evidenced by new methods of transportation and communication, the growing dependence of modern economies upon imports and foreign markets, and the global nature of modern warfare which makes security depend upon strong and dependable allies. In the Soviet sphere, this conflict is being resolved by the political and economic integration of a large area of the world under a single totalitarian power. If the non-Soviet world is to remain a collection of independent states, these contradictory movements must also be resolved through a voluntary relinquishment of sovereignty over matters of common concern, to international agencies operated by and for a federation of democratic states. While some progress may be made in the direction of regional integration, the creation of a strong federation capable of meeting the needs of the free world for survival and progress will depend upon the determined leadership of the United States. American foreign policy has come a long way since the isolationism of the interwar period, but events are moving faster than our political and economic thinking. The problem of the coming generation is not whether we shall have one world; rather, it is on what principle the world is to be unified for the next millennium of human history.

Index

335